Economics 2Q03

TABLE OF CONTENTS
& ACKNOWLEDGEMENTS

PAGE

Unit 4 – Illegal Drugs and Prostitution

Unit 5 – (Crime and) Punishment

MODULE 3 – INDIVIDUAL LEGAL BUT RISKY BEHAVIOUR

Unit 6 – Obesity

Unit 7 – Risky Pastimes

Module 1- Economic Concepts and Models

Unit 2 – Economic Concepts and Models

REVIEW OF SELECTED MICROECONOMIC TOPICS[1]

1.　　Opportunity Cost

The opportunity cost of something is what you give up to get it (the next best alternative). The concept of opportunity cost can be seen in a production possibilities frontier (PPF) diagram.

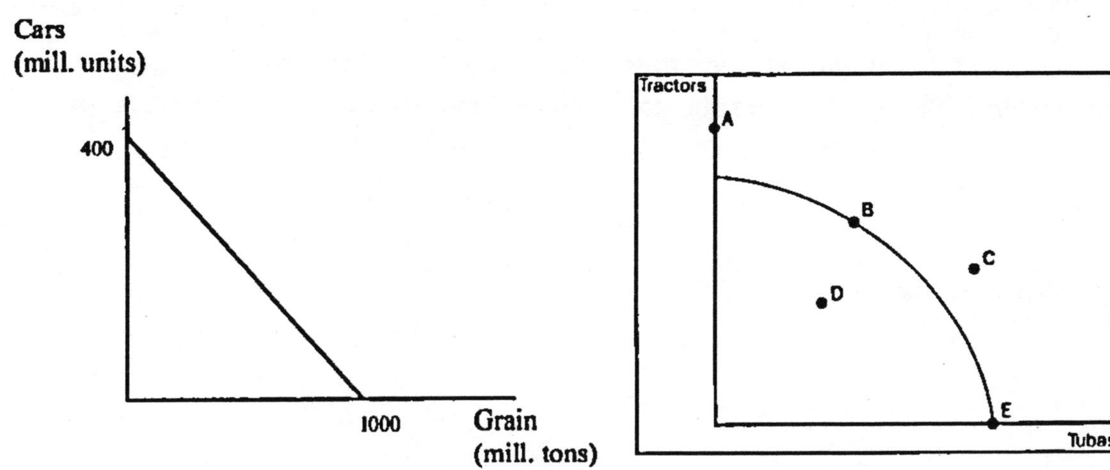

In the diagram on the left, the country can produce 400 million cars if it devotes all of its resources to the production of cars. If it devotes all of its resources to the production of grain, it can produce 1000 million tons. It can also produce any combination of cars and grain on or inside the PPF. In the diagram on the left, the opportunity cost is constant. In the diagram on the right, the opportunity cost depends on how much of each good is being produced. In the diagram on the right, we say that points on or inside the PPF are feasible (D, B, and E). Points outside the PPF are not attainable with current resources and technology (A and C). Points on the PPF are efficient – the only way to increase the production of one good is to decrease the production of the other good (B and E).

2.　　Thinking Like an Economist

Economists use "marginal analysis" – when deciding whether or not to take any action, a person should compare the marginal benefit of that action with the marginal cost.

---

[1] Guell, Robert C. _Issues in Economics Today_. (2010) and Mankiw, N. Gregory.

Economists focus on positive analysis (describing the world as it is) rather than normative analysis (describing the world as it ought to be). Normative analysis requires making a value judgment of some kind. Compare the following two statements:

(i)   When schools provide sex education classes teenage pregnancy rates drop.

(ii)   Schools should provide sex education classes.

The first statement, whether you agree or disagree, whether it is factually correct or not, is a positive statement. The second statement implies that a value judgment has been made and is therefore a normative statement.

Economists also devote a lot of attention to *incentives* and how people's behaviour can change in response to different incentives (such as receiving course credit for attendance) and disincentives (such as taxes).

3.   Supply and Demand

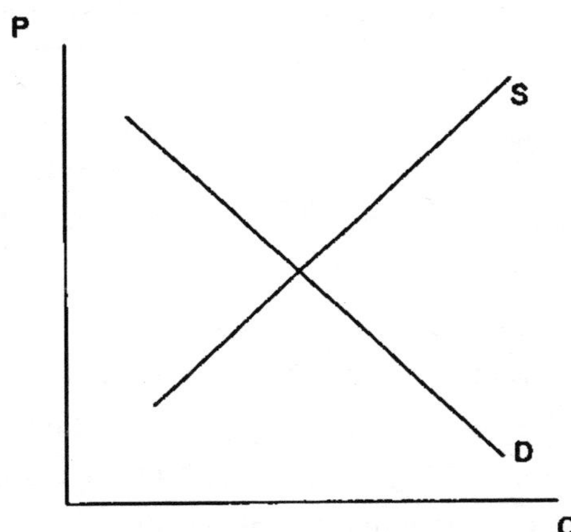

Law of demand – when price rises, quantity demanded falls.

Law of supply – when price rises, quantity supplied rises.

The equilibrium price is the price for which quantity demanded equals quantity supplied. If the price is above the equilibrium price, there is excess supply and there will be downward pressure on the price. If the price is below the equilibrium price, there is excess demand and there will be upward pressure on the price.

There is an important difference between the terms "change in demand" and "change in quantity demanded". The first refers to a shift in the demand curve, the second refers to a movement along a stationary demand curve. The same distinction applies to supply and quantity supplied.

Determinants of demand:
> tastes
> income – normal vs. inferior goods
> price of related goods – substitutes vs. complements
> number of buyers
> expectations

Determinants of supply:
> price of inputs
> technology
> number of sellers
> expectations

We use the demand and supply model to conduct "shock analysis" – to see what happens to price and quantity when something changes when we hold everything else equal. The steps to follow are:
1. Decide which curve is affected, demand, supply, or (very rarely) both.
2. Decide whether demand (or supply) increases or decreases.
3. Draw the new curve and see what happens to equilibrium price and quantity.

4. Elasticity and Surplus

Elasticity – percentage change in A brought about by a 1 percent change in B.

Usually, we look at the elasticity of demand or supply.
- Price elasticity of demand
- Income elasticity of demand
- Cross-price elasticity of demand

To calculate the elasticity, we use the following (and the mid-point method):

$$price\ elasticity\ of\ demand = \frac{\%\Delta Q^d}{\%\Delta P}$$

Example:

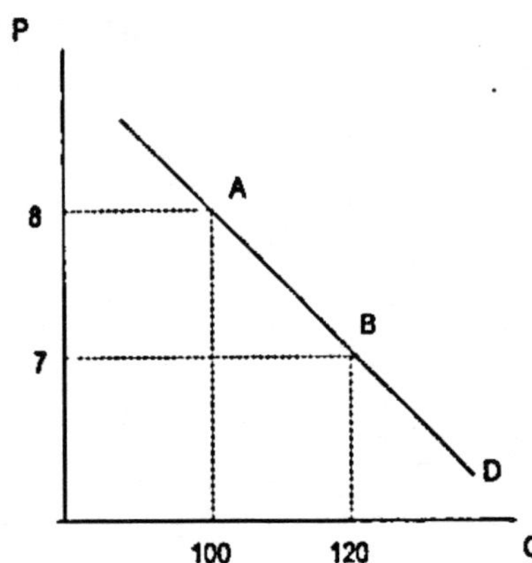

$$\varepsilon = \frac{(120 - 100)/110}{(7 - 8)/7.5} = -1.37$$

We use the mid-point method (i.e. 110 rather than 120 or 100) so that the elasticity is the same whether we go from point A to point B or from point B to point A.

What matters for price elasticity of demand is the size of ε relative to -1. If the absolute value of ε is greater than 1, the good is elastic, if it is equal to 1 it is unit elastic and if it is less than 1 it is inelastic. If the income elasticity of demand for a good is greater than zero, the good is normal, if it is less than zero the good is inferior. If the cross-price elasticity of demand is negative, the two goods are complements, if it is positive, the two goods are substitutes.

A flatter curve is more elastic, a steeper curve is more inelastic. A curve that has a constant slope will have different elasticities at different points. For an elastic demand curve, total revenue moves in the same direction as price, for an inelastic demand curve, total revenue moves in the opposite direction as price. (TR = P * Q)

Determinants of elasticity of demand:
- Number and closeness of substitutes
- Whether the good is a necessity or a luxury
- Time horizon – longer time periods = greater elasticity

Surplus

Consumer surplus = value you get in excess of what you pay (difference in demand curve and equilibrium price)

Producer surplus = money the firm gets in excess of its marginal cost (difference in equilibrium price and supply curve)

Total surplus = CS + PS

We say that a market is "efficient" when TS is maximized, which usually happens when $Q^d = Q^s$.

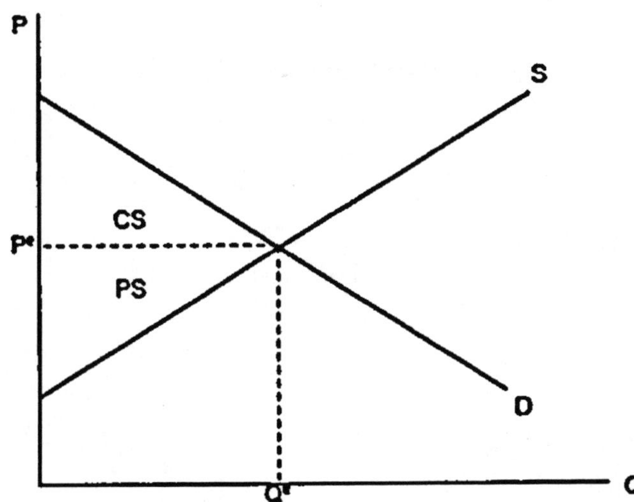

Deadweight loss occurs when TS is not maximized.

If $Q < Q^e$:

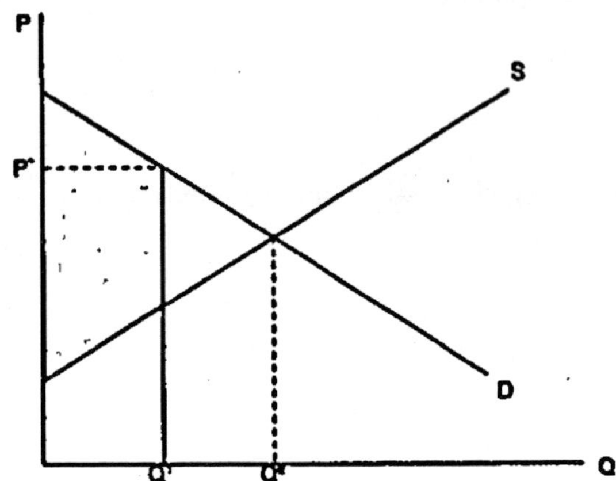

If people are paying P*, TS is the shaded area, the smaller triangle (between Q' and Q^e) is the deadweight loss.

If $Q > Q^e$:

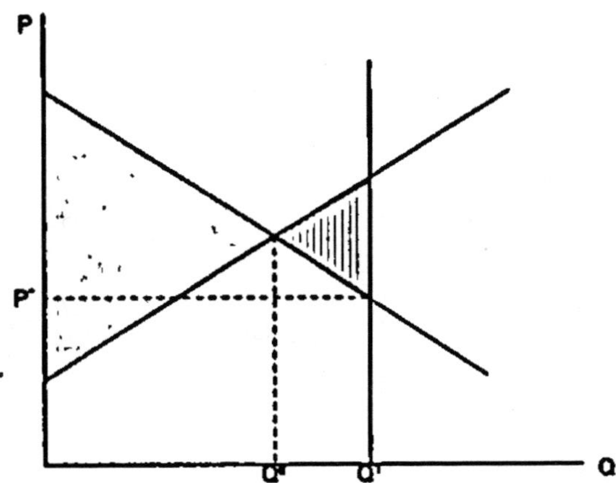

If people are paying P*, TS is the dark shaded area MINUS the striped shaded area.

TS is maximized at the intersection of supply and demand, or Q^e.

6

Example 1: International trade

Suppose Canada bans imports of tomatoes, then allows free trade.

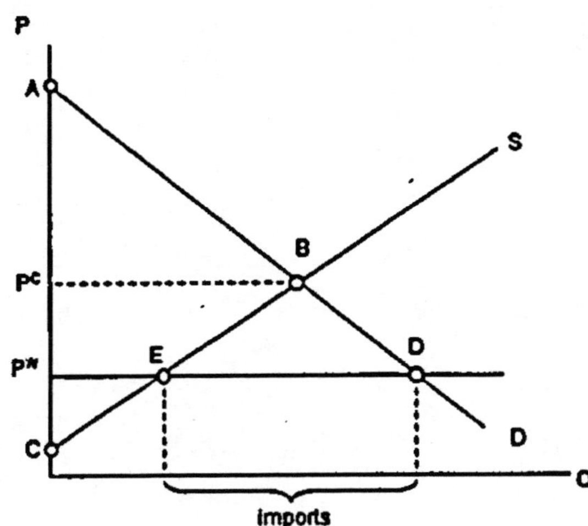

CS goes from ABP^C to ADP^W. PS goes from CBP^C to CEP^W. CS rises, PS falls, and TS rises by EBD.

Example 2: Introduction of a sales tax in a perfectly competitive market

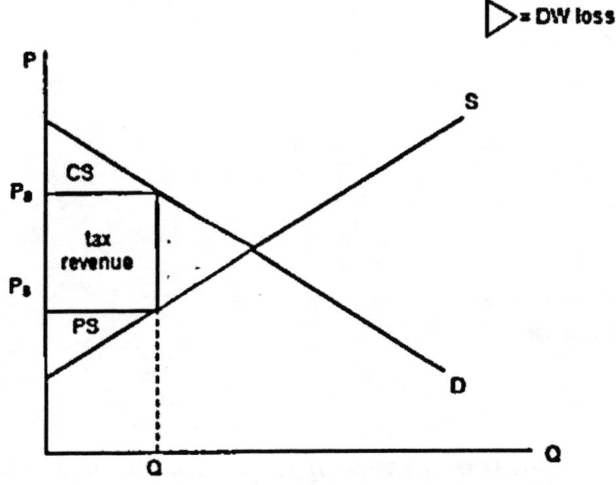

CS and PS both fall, tax revenue rises (from zero), TS falls by the shaded triangle. The sales tax puts a wedge between the price buyers pay and the price sellers receive.

7

Tax incidence refers to who bears the burden of a tax – this depends in large part on elasticity of demand and supply. Consider the following example, one market with an elastic demand curve, the other with an inelastic demand curve.

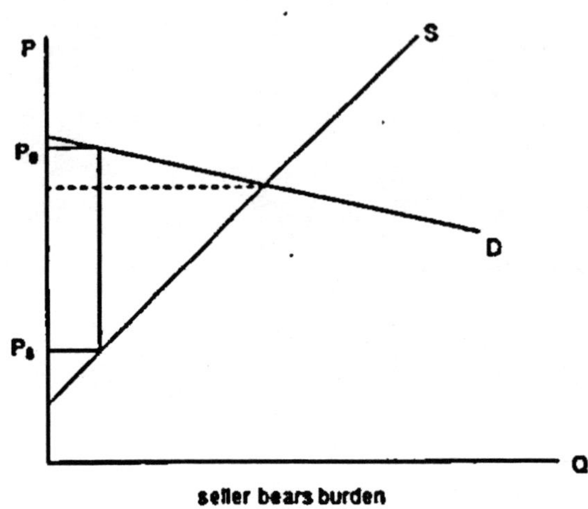

seller bears burden

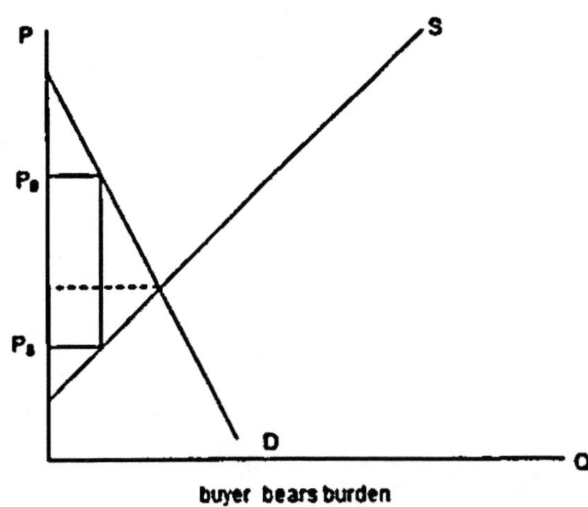

buyer bears burden

With an elastic demand curve, the price the seller receives drops by a lot – the price the buyer pays rises by a little bit. When the demand curve is inelastic, the price the buyer pays rises by a lot but the price the seller receives only declines by a small amount.

5.   Externalities

An externality occurs when a transaction between two parties has an impact on a bystander. Externalities can be either positive or negative and can occur on either the production or consumption side of the market. The existence of the impact on a bystander means that the usual demand and supply curves do not capture the total impact on society of the production or consumption of the good in question. In these cases the "social benefit" curve is different from the demand curve (which captures private benefits) and/or the "social cost" curve is different from the supply curve (which captures private costs). When the externality occurs because of the consumption of a good or service, there is a difference between the demand curve (private value curve) and the social value curve. When the externality occurs because of the production of a good or services the difference is between the supply curve (private cost curve) and the social cost curve. Total surplus is maximized at the intersection of the social cost curve and the social benefit curve. The private market equilibrium quantity occurs at the intersection of supply and demand. The market either produces too much of the good/service in the case of a negative externality or too little of the good/service in the case of a positive externality. In the diagrams below, the shaded triangle represents the deadweight loss that happens because of the externality.

Negative production externality:
(pollution)

Positive production externality:
(bee keeping)

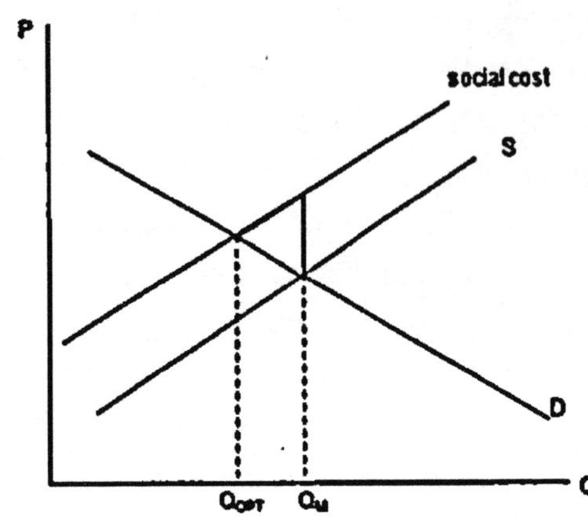

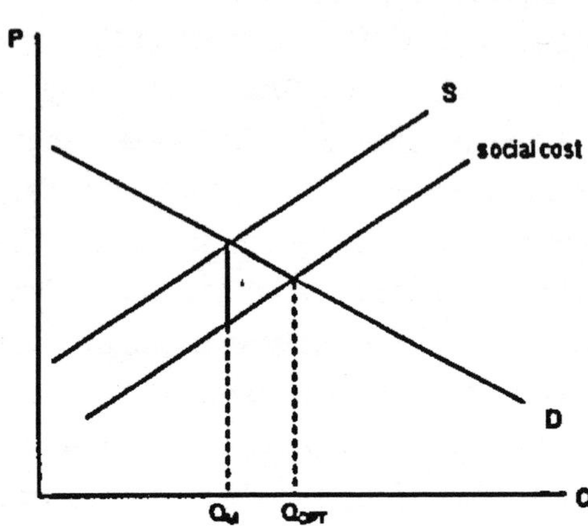

Negative consumption externality:
(cigarettes)

Positive consumption externality:
(vaccines)

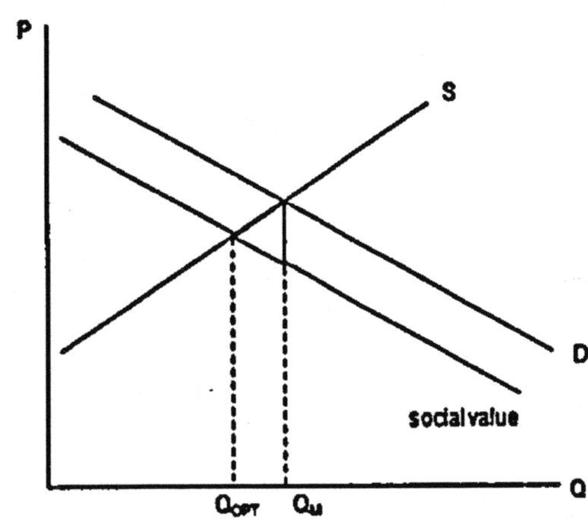

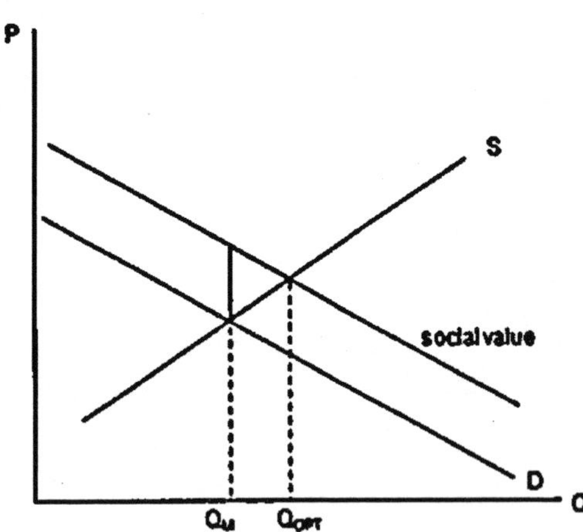

6.   Production, Cost, and Revenue

Economic cost = all costs of a business, including opportunity cost (next best alternative)

Accounting cost = only those costs that must be explicitly paid by the owner of the business

We can think of an example to illustrate the difference between the two concepts. In a perfectly competitive market, we assume that economic profit is equal to zero in long run equilibrium. This sounds unrealistic – why would anyone open a business in an industry where profits are zero? The answer lies in the difference between economic profit and accounting profit. Consider a lawyer who currently earns $200,000 and is considering opening a small business. A cook who works in McDonalds for $15,000 is also thinking of opening a business in the same field. In order for economic profit to be zero in both cases, the accounting profit needs to be $185,000 higher for the former lawyer than for the former McDonald's cook.

Production function – shows various combinations of inputs used to produce output. We usually assume that the production function is subject to diminishing marginal product – each additional unit of an input gives a smaller increase in output than the previous unit of the same input. For example, in a t-shirt factory, adding the 19th sewing machine (unit of capital) increases t-shirt production by less than adding the 18th sewing machine.

(1) Increasing then decreasing marginal product of labour:

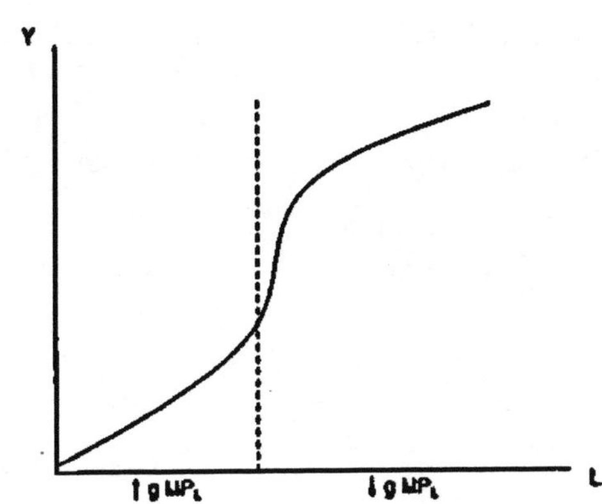

(2) Decreasing marginal product of labour:

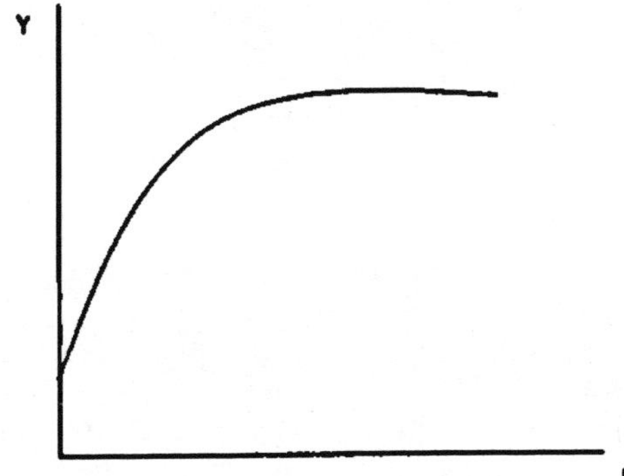

Cost

Since marginal cost and marginal product move in the opposite direction, the total cost curve is like a mirror image of the production function:

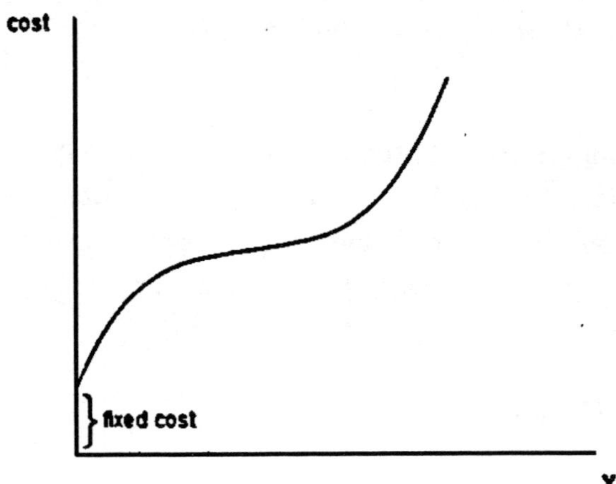

We can clearly see the fixed and variable costs in the above diagram – these are sometimes harder to distinguish in the real world.

Cost curves:

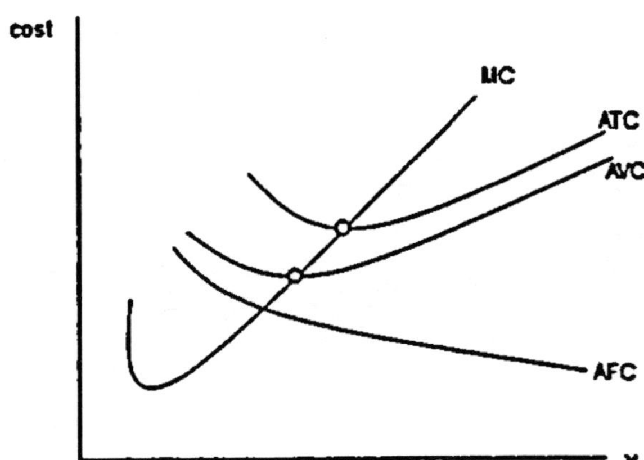

When drawing cost curves that the marginal cost curve should cut the ATC and AVC curves at the minimum point.

Revenue

Marginal revenue – the extra revenue a firm receives from selling an additional unit of product.

- Constant for perfectly competitive firms (price is set by the market – each firm receives the same price for their product)
- Decreasing for monopoly firms
- Firms want to maximize profit – in order to do so they produce a quantity that sets marginal revenue equal to marginal cost.
- A firm will shut down if P < AVC

Marginal revenue for a perfectly competitive firm:

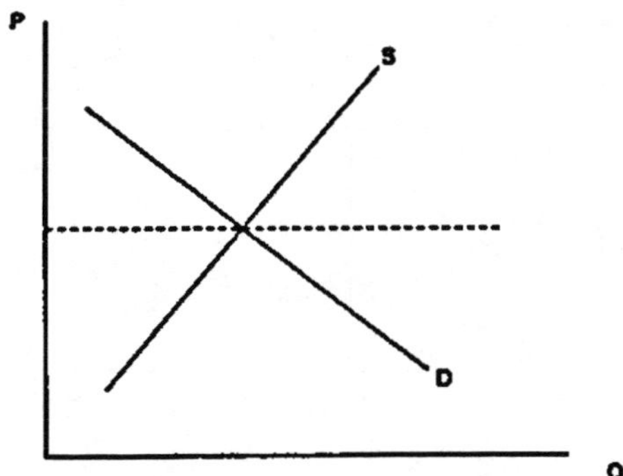

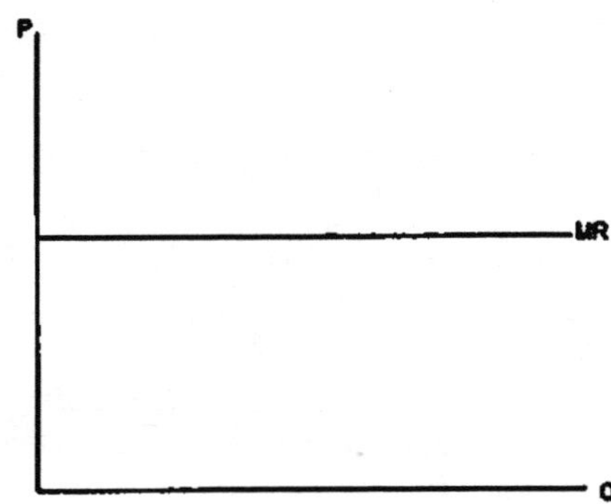

Marginal revenue curve for a monopoly

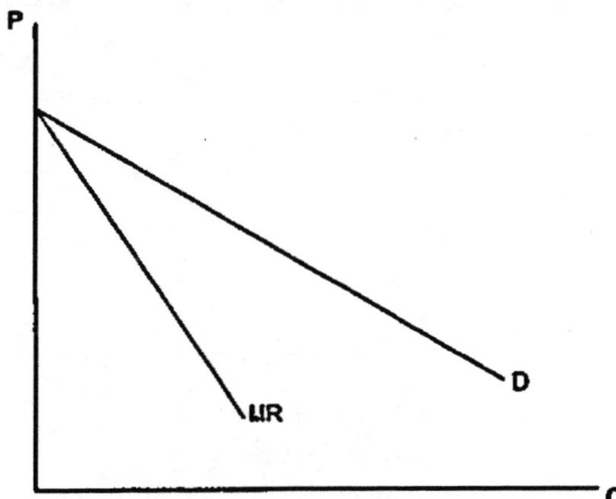

13

17

7.   Perfect competition and monopoly markets

The goal of a firm is to maximize profit:

Profit = (P – ATC) * Q

Profits are maximized by producing the quantity for which MR = MC. If profit is greater than zero, firms will enter the industry. If profit is less than zero, firms will exit the industry. In the long run, economic profit is zero.

· For a perfectly competitive firm, long run equilibrium looks like this:

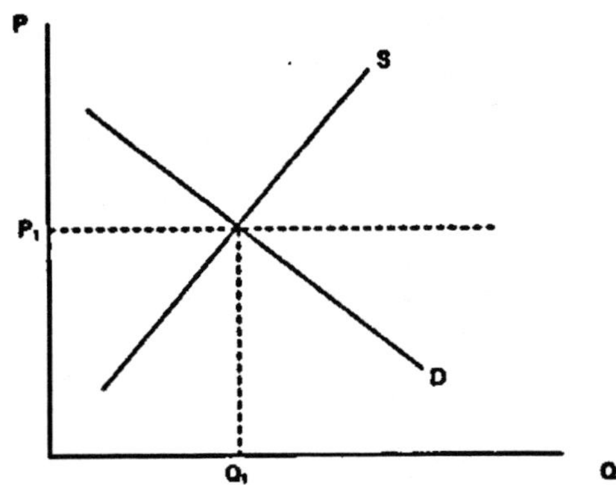

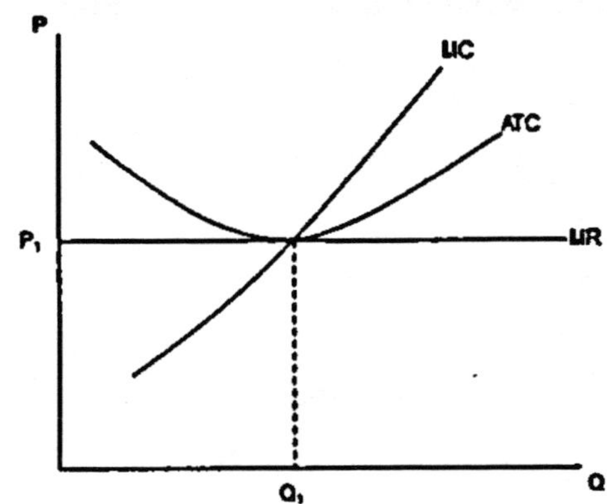

Industry diagram   Firm diagram

In the case of monopoly, the firm diagram IS the industry diagram since there is only one firm. The shaded area in the diagram below shows the firm's monopoly profit. Again, MC = MR, but now there are positive profits.

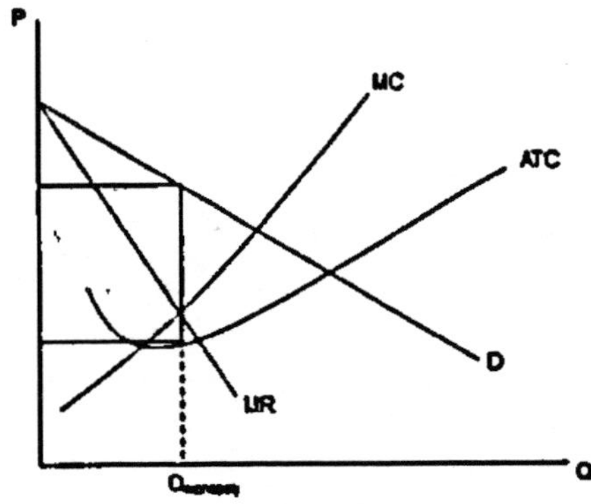

Module 2 - Individual Criminal Behaviour

Unit 3 – An Economist's Take on Crime

CHAPTER TWENTY-SIX

The Economics of Crime

Learning Objectives

After reading this chapter you should be able to

LO1 Describe how economics can contribute to the debate over crime and crime control.

LO2 Describe who generally commits crime and why.

LO3 Conclude that economists who study crime often assume that criminals are rational.

LO4 Analyze the cost of crime to society and whether we are currently spending the right amount, focusing on the right criminals, emphasizing the right crimes, and enforcing the right sentences.

LO5 Apply the principles of incentives, marginal cost and marginal benefit to crime control.

Chapter Outline

Who Commits Crimes and Why

The Rational Criminal Model

The Costs of Crime

Optimal Spending on Crime Control

Summary

Crime is a problem that does not naturally spring to mind as one for which economists would have much of value to contribute. Other than early work on crime by Nobel Prize–winning economist Gary Becker, we have not used much of our research time and money on this subject. Still, there are areas where economic analysis is uniquely suited to deal with the problems of crime. For instance, a potential criminal makes a decision to commit a crime based on the income potential of legal work, the booty to be gained from the crime, and the chance and consequence of getting caught. Couched in different words, this is not all that different from an investment decision in which small gains in safe assets are compared to large gains in risky assets. When looked at this way, economics and criminology have some important links.

The first thing we do in exploring the economics of crime is to look at who commits crime. We then see what a theoretical "investment-like" decision would tell us about who we should expect will commit crimes. Next, we use cost–benefit analysis to discuss how the non-criminal public should devote resources in the areas of crime prevention, detection, apprehension, and punishment. Last, we use economics to study whether the goals of life imprisonment and the death penalty have the desired effects of deterring or preventing future crime.

Who Commits Crimes and Why

Most crime is committed by young men who are socially and economically disadvantaged. The victims of their crimes are disproportionately from the same group. Young black men, for example, overwhelmingly commit crimes against other young black men. Moreover, when we examine the disadvantages attributed to racism and compound them with the economic disadvantage of poor job opportunities, the problem seems to magnify. For instance, in the latest data where we have the race of both the perpetrator and victims, white people are killed by other whites in about the number that would be predicted by the overall population (86 of 100), whereas 94 of every 100 murdered blacks are killed by other blacks. In this case the number predicted by the distribution of the population as a whole would be 12 out of 100, rather than 94 out of 100.

Crime statistics generally come to us from two sources: police reports and surveys of crime victims. Those who view the police to be racially biased may argue that statistics that come from police reports are racially biased, but it is hard to believe that crime victims would have an interest in biasing their reports. Falsely reporting an attacker to the police would diminish the likelihood that the perpetrator would be caught, and doing so in a survey would not serve any useful purpose. No matter whether you measure crime by looking at arrest reports sent to the FBI or by looking at victimization surveys, the data indicate conclusively that minorities commit far more crimes than their 28 percent proportion of the populace. The question is not whether poor blacks, Hispanics, and other needy members of minority communities commit more crimes, but why.

The Rational Criminal Model

In the late 1960s Gary Becker came up with a model of criminal behavior that explained crime in terms of a simple investment decision. According to Becker, the decision to commit a crime is one of risk versus return. The low-return investment, work at a legal job, has a low return, but the worker carries no risk of being arrested. On the other hand, the high-return investment, stealing or selling illegal goods, has a high return, but it puts the thief or drug dealer at risk of being caught and punished. In this context, a criminal is no different from an investment banker who is deciding whether to invest in tried-and-true U.S. Treasury bonds or a risky initial public offering of an Internet stock. Just as investors have a portfolio that contains a mix of risky and safe assets, you would expect to see that most criminals would have legitimate jobs as well. This is, in fact, the case.

We should take some time to explain what economists mean when they use the word "rational." To an economist, if people know what it is they want, know the constraints they face, know the costs of getting what they want, and choose to proceed with getting it, then they are rational. This does not mean that these rational people will do what society thinks is best for them. It means only that their actions are consistent with their goals, constraints, and costs. By this standard all but the insane are rational.

Crime Falls When Legal Income Rises

If a person has the potential for earning a higher income through legal means than illegal ones, then the person would be just plain stupid to pick the risky and lower-earning alternative of a life of crime. If you have the skills to be a doctor or lawyer and have a six-figure salary, the alternative of clearing $50,000 while selling cocaine is not all that attractive. Thus the rational criminal theory correctly predicts that people with high legal incomes are not likely to be prevalent in the criminal and prison population.

This conclusion may seem trivially easy to come to, but what is not trivial is how a person with a set of intermediate skills, earning $10 an hour, or about $20,000 a year, would treat the issue. To be at that level of income in today's society, most people have completed high school. It is therefore significant that less than half of those in the prison population graduated from high school, and 33 percent were not working at a legal job just prior to being arrested. Weighing a $20,000 a year job against a high-risk, high-income criminal life is hard, and the decision could go either way.

A full-time minimum-wage worker, earning approximately $14,500 (in 2009), would see the opportunity of earning a high criminal income as a significantly greater temptation than would a person making much more. We would expect that greater economic alternatives in the legal realm would translate into less crime, and fewer opportunities would lead to more crime. Why, then, did crime escalate during the sustained economic growth in the middle to late 1980s and fall during the sustained growth of the middle to late 1990s? The answer lies in the placing of economic opportunities.

If our rational criminal theory is accurate, raising a middle-, upper-middle-, or high-income person's economic prospects should have little to no effect on crime. Even without a growth in income, such a person would have virtually no incentive to turn to crime. An increase in income would simply lessen a trivially small temptation and would have no appreciable impact on crime. On the other hand, if the economic prospects changed at the low end of the economic scale, the effect on crime would likely be substantial.

In the decade and a half from the mid-1970s to the early 1990s, income inequality rose. Average income rose because the upper half of the income scale did very well, while people with little education and few job skills saw their real spending power remain stagnant or fall.[1]

---

[1] Of course, the material in Chapter 6 lays out the case that because the CPI overstates the effects of inflation, real incomes for the poor did not fall but rose slightly.

What you would expect to see from our rational criminal model did, in fact, happen. Crime increased substantially through the period, and it did so more in the lower-income groups than in the higher-income groups.

After the recession of 1990–1991, however, when crime was at a near-term high, the economic prospects of low-skill workers began to increase. The minimum wage was raised from $3.35 to $5.15 during the period, and both the overall unemployment rate and the unemployment rate for minorities and for low-skill workers fell. At the same time, either because of coincidence or because the model is right, crime fell, and it fell quickly.

The rational criminal model has a more difficult time explaining the general increase in crime during the 1960s, when incomes rose both in general and within the poor communities. This highlights an important thing to keep in mind when it comes to using economics to explain complex social phenomena. Sometimes a change in social norms, an area better left to sociologists, or a change in moral values, an area better left to the clergy, is at the heart of these social phenomena. Economics is then less capable of explaining them.

Crime Falls When the Likelihood and Consequences of Getting Caught Rise

The other variable that can change things in this rational criminal model is the probability and consequences of getting caught. We know that crime pays when you do not get caught. We also know that choosing to become a criminal becomes less attractive when the chances of getting away with crime diminish and when the potential punishment becomes more severe. It is usually true that if you knew you would get caught, you would choose a legal occupation. Sometimes, however, this is not true. For women who possess low levels of education and few marketable skills, for example, the occupation of prostitute entails getting caught regularly and going to jail for a few days as a part of the cost of doing business. The important thing here is that even given the lost time in jail, for such women, prostitution pays better than legal work.

To deter potential criminals from committing crimes, there are two things that we can do. We can make the chances of meeting punishment greater, and we can make the punishment more severe. In its simplest terms, the first implies that by having more police, judges, and jails we can increase the likelihood that criminals will be caught, be convicted quickly, and go to jail. The second suggests that we make the sentences longer or the fines greater.

Though these may seem like two aspects of the same approach, in part because we are talking about increasing spending on the same kinds of people, they are really distinct in their intent. The first is intended to make criminals less confident that they will get away with their activities. Depending on where in the judicial system the money is spent, this can provide additional funding for cops on the street, making detection and apprehension more likely, or it can provide funds for greater numbers of effective prosecutors, who may garner greater numbers of postarrest guilty verdicts. This differs from spending more money on prisons and allowing judges to sentence convicted criminals to longer terms.

Problems with the Rationality Assumption

Criminologists and sociologists have a hard time granting the assumption that the decision to become a criminal is a rational economic decision made by people capable of evaluating complex choices. In support of their view, you only have to look at the percentage of crime that is seemingly senseless. School shootings are not explainable using economic methods. One of the main criticisms of economic models is that they assume too much intellectual capacity on the part of humans. For instance, it might be argued that if criminals could evaluate the options as rationally as economists claim they can, they probably would be smart enough not to have to turn to crime. In any event, economists use the idea of the "rational criminal" when looking at criminality; and, as was seen above, the rational criminal model is often consistent with what we know about crime.

The Costs of Crime

We spend a total of $214 billion a year on the police, the judiciary, and prisons. Every year 14.4 million persons are arrested and some 770,000 of that number get jail time. Currently there are more than 2.4 million Americans in state or federal jails and prisons. This is all done in response to the 1.4 million violent and 13 million nonviolent crimes that are reported each year. When we see these numbers, we wonder whether the money we spend is worth it and whether the distribution of spending on police, justice, and prisons is a good one.

If we put any faith in the model we have been discussing, we are convinced that by spending money in this arena, we can change the probability of a criminal's being punished and the extent of the punishment. Of course, we could also talk about spending the money to raise the legal income potential of people. Some people argue, for example, that we should take money that is earmarked for building new prisons and put it into education and social programs like Head Start and employment training programs that might help people to get out of poverty legally. Others point to data that indicate that these programs do not work and suggest that building prisons is the best of a set of bad alternatives.

On the central questions of whether we are spending the right amount of money on crime control and whether we are spending on the right mix of control mechanisms, we need to examine how much crime there is and how much it costs us. Using a variety of criminological surveys, we know that, of the 14.7 million crimes reported annually, more than twice that number are actually committed. Though most murders get reported, robberies, rapes, and other crimes tend not to be universally reported. Some of this may be attributed to the rationality of crime victims. If the chances of catching the perpetrator of a crime are low and the psychological and monetary costs of testifying are high, then it is quite likely that some victims will not report crimes committed against them.

How Much Does an Average Crime Cost?

When a crime is committed there are several different kinds of costs to consider. If we could put a dollar value on the average crime, we could, at least theoretically, come to an estimate of the cost of crime in general. The first and most obvious cost of crime is the value of items taken or stolen. This is fairly easily measured but it is not always very important, especially if the crime is a form of assault rather than a form of theft. Even when the crime is a simple theft, if the stolen item is replaced with insurance, the cost of the crime to the victim doesn't account for the loss to society of the theft. Insurance rates, for instance, will rise when thefts are prevalent as will extraneous theft-prevention activities that add little to actual economic well-being.

As difficult as it is to estimate tangible costs of crime, it is much harder to estimate the costs of crimes like murder, rape, and assault, because so much of those costs are intangible. There are some aspects of the loss that are easier to estimate than others. For example, an assault victim who cannot work for a few days has a loss that is at least quantifiable. On the other hand, a sexual assault victim's loss in terms of quality of life is not so easily quantified. Moreover, there is no way of knowing whether having been a victim of a crime causes people to be less ambitious or productive than they would have been otherwise.

The monetary value of psychological trauma that comes with victimization is also difficult to estimate.

There are two general methods that are used to estimate these intangible losses. The first looks at how much money individuals pay to avoid crimes by looking at the relative price of homes in high- and low-crime neighborhoods. This allows economists to create a "willingness-to-pay" measure. If people have to pay $100,000 extra to reduce their likelihood of victimization by half, then crime "costs" $200,000. This method can be used to estimate the value of a human life. If someone is willing to pay $100 to reduce their likelihood of death from one in 5,000 to one in 10,000, then they are implicitly saying their life is worth $100/.0002 = $500,000.

Another method uses jury awards in wrongful death and personal injury cases to establish loss estimates. In this method, the average jury award to the widow of a drunken driving victim is used as a proxy for the value of the life lost. The average jury award to a nonfatal accident might stand in for the intangible loss from a nonfatal assault.

If we simply ignore all of the estimated costs of pain and suffering and lives lost, then the cost of the average crime has been estimated at a little more than $1,000. Adding the pain and suffering and other intangible costs, some economists have estimated the costs at up to $10,000 per average crime.

How Much Crime Does an Average Criminal Commit?

We can use these figures to estimate the cost of letting criminals go free and compare that to the cost of keeping them in jail. If we know how many crimes the average criminal commits, we can multiply the average cost per crime by the average number of crimes committed in a year to come up with the costs imposed on society by the early release of a still violent criminal. Looking at it another way, we can compute the average cost of not catching and imprisoning a criminal.

Even when we interpret sophisticated criminological surveys, we find that the average number of crimes committed by the average criminal ranges all the way from 180 down to 10. Most economists are comfortable with estimates in the range of 10 to 20 crimes. If we assume for a moment that crime would stay the same if we eliminated all expenditures on law enforcement, the average savings from keeping average criminals off the street would range from 10 crimes per criminal times $500 per crime, or $5,000, to 20 crimes per criminal times $10,000 per crime, or $200,000.

THINGS THAT MATTER IN CRIME

An interesting investigation of this issue was conducted by economist Steven Levitt. What he found was that "community policing," whereby police are in constant communication with the communities and subcommunities that they patrol, was less effective than simply increasing their numbers. What this implies is that visibility deters crime more than anything the police actually do.

Similarly, he found that stiffening the sentence for crime had little deterrent effect, but having more criminals locked up longer decreased crime. The reason for this is deceptively obvious. He argues that the patterns of drug dealers, for instance, fly in the face of the rational criminal model. These criminals are less apt to react to increases in potential punishment when they have already chosen an occupation where death at the hands of competitors is an occupational hazard. What he found was that longer and more certain sentences worked because they prevented the convicted criminal from offending again any time soon.

In terms of economics and crime, what Levitt found was that the significant decrease in crime in the 1990s was less associated with the growing economy of the time, than it was of a higher degree of "wantedness" of the children born 15 to 20 years before. In one of those conclusions that only an economist could come up with (see the discussion of how smokers help Social Security in Chapter 20), Levitt argues that the legalization of abortion in the 1970s increased the proportion of children born into homes where they were wanted. The argument, which some economists have taken issue with, is that children born into homes in which they are not wanted will grow up to commit more crime than children born into homes in which they are wanted.

Optimal Spending on Crime Control

What Is the Optimal Amount to Spend?

The average cost of holding a criminal in jail is $28,750 per year. Assuming that crime rates would rise if we eliminated all expenditures on law enforcement—either by the average criminal's committing more crimes or because otherwise law-abiding citizens turned to crime—it is quite clear that the money we spend on prisons is worth it. Even though more than 2.4 million people are in jail and prison at a cost of $69 billion a year, this may be a good expenditure.

The question of whether we spend the optimal amount on keeping people in prisons, however, remains to be answered. At this time, there are far more than double the number of felons on the street than in prison. These are people who have served their sentences, been released on parole, or were never imprisoned in the first place. If they are committing crimes at a rate similar to the 15 to 20 crimes a year that incarcerated criminals were committing, then we have too few people in prison.

Of key concern to economists is not necessarily whether the total amount spent on crime control exceeds the total amount saved from preventing crime, but whether we are spending the correct amount. At its heart, the problem is exactly the same as the profit-maximizing problem for a business firm. The mere fact that a firm's revenues exceed its costs does not mean that profit is as high as it could be. That means we are less interested in the costs and benefits of capturing, trying, and incarcerating the "average" criminal than we are in incarcerating the "marginal" criminal.

Think of it this way. Suppose we catch a prolific thief who costs society $100,000 a year, and it costs $28,750 a year to lock him up. Now suppose we catch a part-time thief who costs society only $10,000 a year, and it still costs $28,750 a year to lock him up. The intermediate or average thief costs society $55,000 each year, and we spend $28,750 per year keeping him locked up. This does not mean we should not have locked up the part-time thief. The marginal benefit to society of locking him up was less than the marginal cost.

Applying this information to the problem of optimal crime control means that we would need to look at who the people are who get arrested and put away when we increase spending on criminal justice. The practical problem is much harder to figure out than it is for a firm. In business we can see how much extra material and labor costs go into producing another unit of output and judge whether that is greater than the price, but we cannot easily determine which extra criminals are caught as a result of our spending more on police. Are these criminals more or less prolific than the average criminal caught before the spending increase? For this reason, much of the research on crime assumes that the "marginal" criminal is just like the "average" criminal.

Is the Money Spent in the Right Way?

Whether we spend the right amount of money is interesting but equally interesting is whether we spend the money in the right way. Again, marginal analysis is of use. If we spend $214 billon on the system, the allocation between police, justice, and incarceration should depend on how effective the marginal dollar is in combating crime in each category. If the optimal distribution is accomplished, the marginal benefit of a dollar should be equal in the three areas.

Are the Right People in Jail?

Of course there is the related issue of whether the right people are in jail. Of the more than 2 million people who are in prisons, just under half are there for violent crimes. The remainder are there for nonviolent crimes such as burglary, drug possession, and drug distribution. If these prison spaces are being used for drug offenders rather than violent criminals or thieves, perhaps the wrong people are in jail. If we release violent criminals in order to make room in prisons for drug users, we will have to either build more prisons or let the drug users go.

In recognition of this choice, state and local governments decided to go on a prison-building spree. In Texas, for example, prison capacity during the 1980s and 1990s was nearly doubling every four years. This phenomenon was certainly not confined to any one state, as state after state went to "truth in sentencing" laws that required criminals to serve at least 85 percent of their sentence. In Florida and Texas, felons had been serving less than a third of their sentences, a disparity these states and others found unacceptable.

What Laws Should We Rigorously Enforce?

In a formal way, economists look at crime control measures from a cost–benefit point of view. In Figure 26.1 the vertical axis represents the amount of marginal benefit and marginal cost associated with catching, adjudicating, and imprisoning an additional criminal. We will make three assumptions:

1. The marginal benefits are decreasing for each additional criminal.
2. We will deal with serious crimes first and petty crimes last.
3. The dollar benefits of preventing these crimes will fall.

Furthermore, we will assume that the marginal cost of dealing with criminals increases because the petty

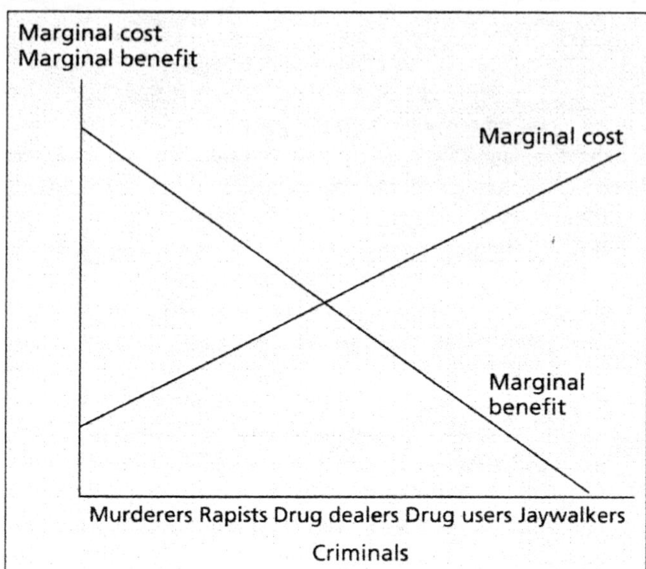

FIGURE 26.1 Marginal cost and marginal benefit analysis and crime.

criminals violating trivial laws are assumed to be more expensive to catch and convict than are criminals whose crimes are more serious. This assumption is predicated on the idea that we would have to have very many and, most important, less competent police[2] to catch such violators.

Figure 26.1 indicates that it makes sense to spend the money to catch, prosecute, and imprison all murderers, rapists, and high-end drug dealers. It also indicates that it makes no sense to do the same for jaywalkers, drug users, and low-end drug dealers. Though this picture is simplistic in its assumptions, you can see, roughly, how an economist reasons on the issue of crime control. Spend the money on the really bad guys and do not spend it on the not-so-bad guys.

That leaves one last issue to deal with in determining how we spend our law enforcement dollars: How do we divide the money among the various sectors? States, for example, have spent a growing part of their budgets to deal with crime and in doing so have changed the percentage that they allocate to the different sectors. The increase in resources has gone mainly to prisons and police, with a smaller percentage of money allocated to adjudication. Competent police are

---

[2]We assume they are likely to be less competent because cities hire the more competent of their applicant pool first and these are all gone when it comes time to hire more.

more effective in deterring criminals and apprehending criminals who have not yet been deterred. It also means that people sentenced stay in jail longer. The downside of this is that more cases are plea-bargained than ever before.

Since the increases in spending have not funded all sectors of the system evenly, criminals are more likely to be caught, plea to a crime that is less severe than the one they actually committed, and go to jail. The length of term they face has probably increased because 85 percent of a short sentence is often longer than 33 percent of a long one. Part of the reduction in crime since the early 1990s is also attributable to this policy of sending greater numbers of criminals to prison. A small minority of criminals commit a majority of the crime, and they now must stay in prison longer. Though estimates vary, an increase of 10 percent in the prison population has been shown to result in a 4 percent to 6 percent decrease in crime. Whereas some of this may be deterrence, it is likely that simply holding criminals prevents them from committing the crimes they would have committed had they been left on the streets.

What Is the Optimal Sentence?

One of the major debates of our time is whether criminals convicted of murder and other of the most heinous crimes should be put to death or be locked up with no opportunity for parole. While many religious leaders and lay persons alike approach this as a moral issue, economists again tend to look at it from the standpoint of the costs and benefits. If you sentence men and women to death, the sentences are carried out only after a long and drawn-out appeal process. Even then, many death row inmates die on their prison cots rather than face injection, asphyxiation, or electrocution. In economic terms we have to decide whether spending a lot of money over a 10-year period is worth the savings in imprisonment expenses. Life sentences, which are routinely given in murder cases, also have cost issues to face. If a 75-year-old is released from prison, is he or she likely to again become a menace to society?

To examine whether the death penalty saves money or costs money we need to recall the Chapter 7 concept of present value. Suppose it would take $1 million invested now to make the payments to house, adjudicate appeals, and put to death a condemned inmate. Suppose it would cost less than $1 million invested now to simply house the inmate from the time he or she is sentenced to the time that inmate would have died if given a life sentence. In such a circumstance the death penalty costs money. Otherwise it saves money. This of course assumes that the death penalty is not a deterrent. It may also be that it costs $1 million in present value to execute a person and $900,000 to imprison the same person for life but that we get $100,000 or more worth of satisfaction knowing that the worst of the bad guys got his or her due.

The cost–benefit trade-off is important also in establishing sentence length. Since nearly no crime is committed by 80-year-olds, does it make sense to sentence people to life in prison? Why not let them out when the chances of their committing a crime have gone away? It is not hard to figure that, as time goes on, a person violent enough to kill at age 18 is not as likely to commit murder at 50 and is even less likely to at 70. This point may not be worth considering since the life expectancy in prison is such that few inmates sentenced to life live long enough to outlive their own violent tendencies. Prison life is hard, and the food and medical care are not geared to keeping people healthy in their "golden years." Ironically, this makes the death penalty even less economically sensible since the "lifer's" life is not going to be that long.

Summary

You should now understand how economics, and in particular the use of marginal benefit–marginal cost analysis, can contribute to the debate over crime and crime control. Besides knowing who it is that generally commits crime and why, you have seen that economists often model criminals as rational human actors who are influenced by the risks and rewards of their decisions. You have seen how much crime costs society and how much we spend to control it. You have seen how an economist looks at issues of crime control to answer questions about whether we are spending the right amount on the right criminals and the right crimes and enforcing the right sentences.

Quiz Yourself

1. If judges had to be trained as economists before taking their position, they might use ____________ analysis when deciding on the right sentence.
   a. Marginal.
   b. Punitive.
   c. Religious.
   d. Average.

2. The optimal level of police protection would compare the ____________________________ with the ______________________.
   a. Marginal cost of hiring an additional officer; marginal benefit of crime reduction.
   b. Average cost of all officers; average benefit per officer of crime reduction.
   c. Total cost of all officers; average benefit of crime reduction.
   d. Length of the average sentence; history of sentences, per crime.

3. Economist Steven Levitt has drawn an unexpected connection between crime and ________________.
   a. Obesity.
   b. The political party in office.
   c. Abortion rights.
   d. Global warming.

4. The average cost per crime has been estimated at between
   a. $500 and $2,500.
   b. $1,000 and $10,000.
   c. $10,000 and $100,000.
   d. $100,000 and $1,000,000.

5. To an economist, the correct distribution of money among police, the justice system, and prisons is one that
   a. Sets an equal amount to each.
   b. Sets the amount each gets equal to its average benefit.
   c. Sets the amount each gets so that none is wasted.
   d. Sets the amount each gets so that no other element could get better use (in terms of crime reduction) of the marginal dollar.

6. The rational crime model explains crimes of
   a. Passion.
   b. Stupidity.
   c. Profit.
   d. Love.

7. The rational criminal model draws a parallel to the thought processes of
   a. Investors.
   b. Educators.
   c. Law enforcement officers.
   d. Politicians.

Think about This

The rational criminal model is often invoked to explain the behavior of drug dealers and their pushers. Economist Steven Levitt disputes this by suggesting that drug dealers engage in behaviors that are just as irrational as those who play the lottery. Is drug dealing rational?

Talk about This

Under what circumstances would you engage in a criminal activity? Would your actions be rational?

For More Insight See

Journal of Economic Perspectives 10, no. 1 (Winter 1996). See articles by John J. DiIulio; and Richard B. Freeman and Isaac Ehrlich, pp. 3–8.

Cohen, Mark, *The Costs of Crime and Justice* (New York: Routledge, 2005).

Levitt, Steven D., "Understanding Why Crime Fell in the 1990s: Four Factors That Explain the Decline and Six That Do Not," *Journal of Economic Perspectives* 18, no. 1 (Winter 2004).

Behind the Numbers

Federal justice system statistics on crime, Federal justice system expenditures—http://www.ojp.usdoj.gov/bjs/eande.htm.

Number of arrests and inmates, Bureau of Justice Statistics—http://www.ojp.usdoj.gov/bjs/prisons.htm.

Characteristics of victims, criminals, and types of crime committed, U.S. Department of Justice; Bureau of Justice Statistics; crime and victim statistics—http://www.ojp.usdoj.gov/bjs/cvict.htm; http://www.ojp.usdoj.gov/bjs/homicide/race.htm.

Crime in the United States, Federal Bureau of Investigation—http://www.fbi.gov/ucr/cius2006/index.html.

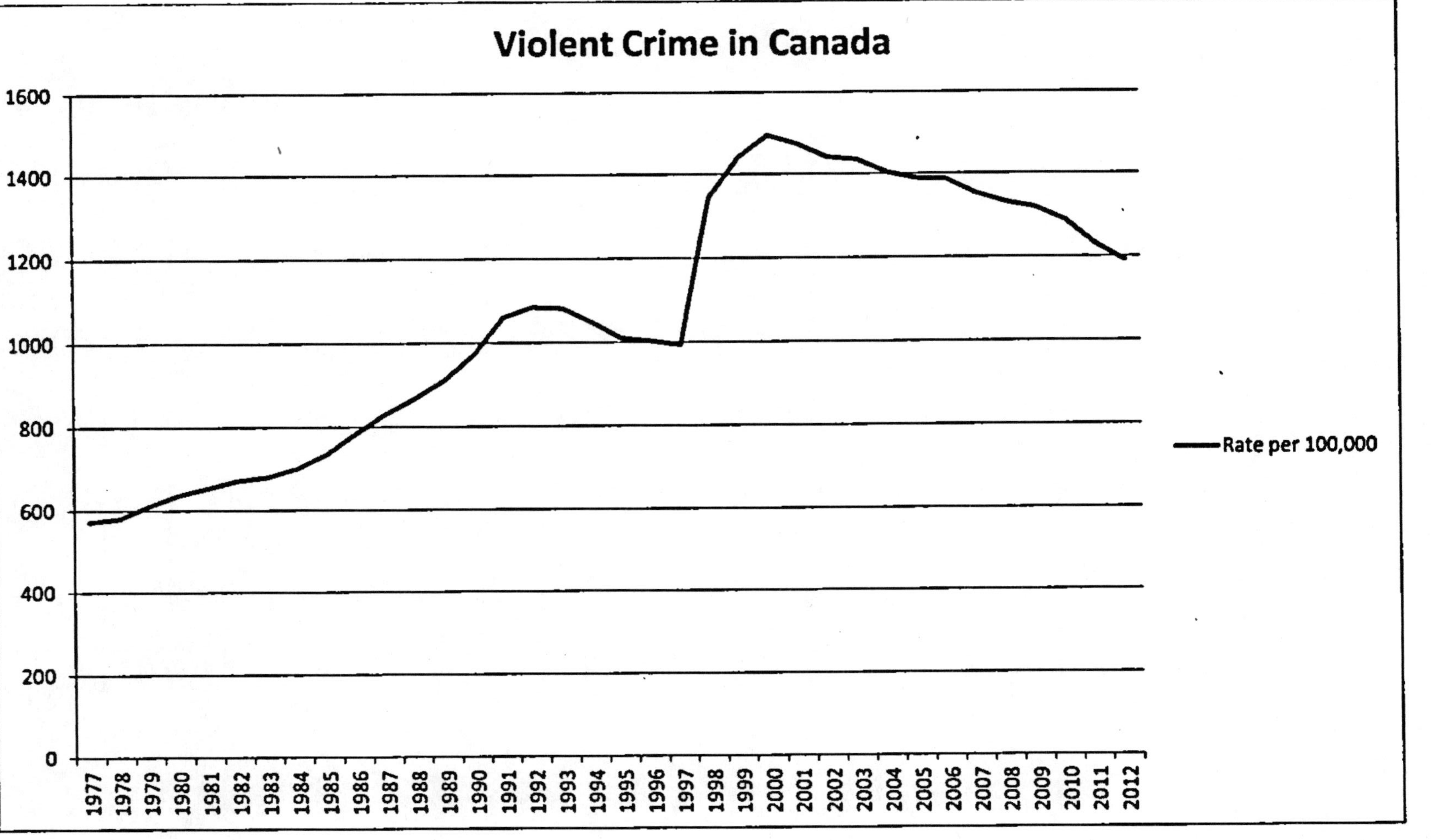

Statistics Canada. Table 252-0013 - Crime statistics, by detailed offences, annual (number unless otherwise noted) (1977-1997) (accessed: September 30, 2013)
Statistics Canada. Table 252-0051 - Incident-based crime statistics, by detailed violations, annual (number unless otherwise noted) (1998-2012) (accessed: September 30, 2013)

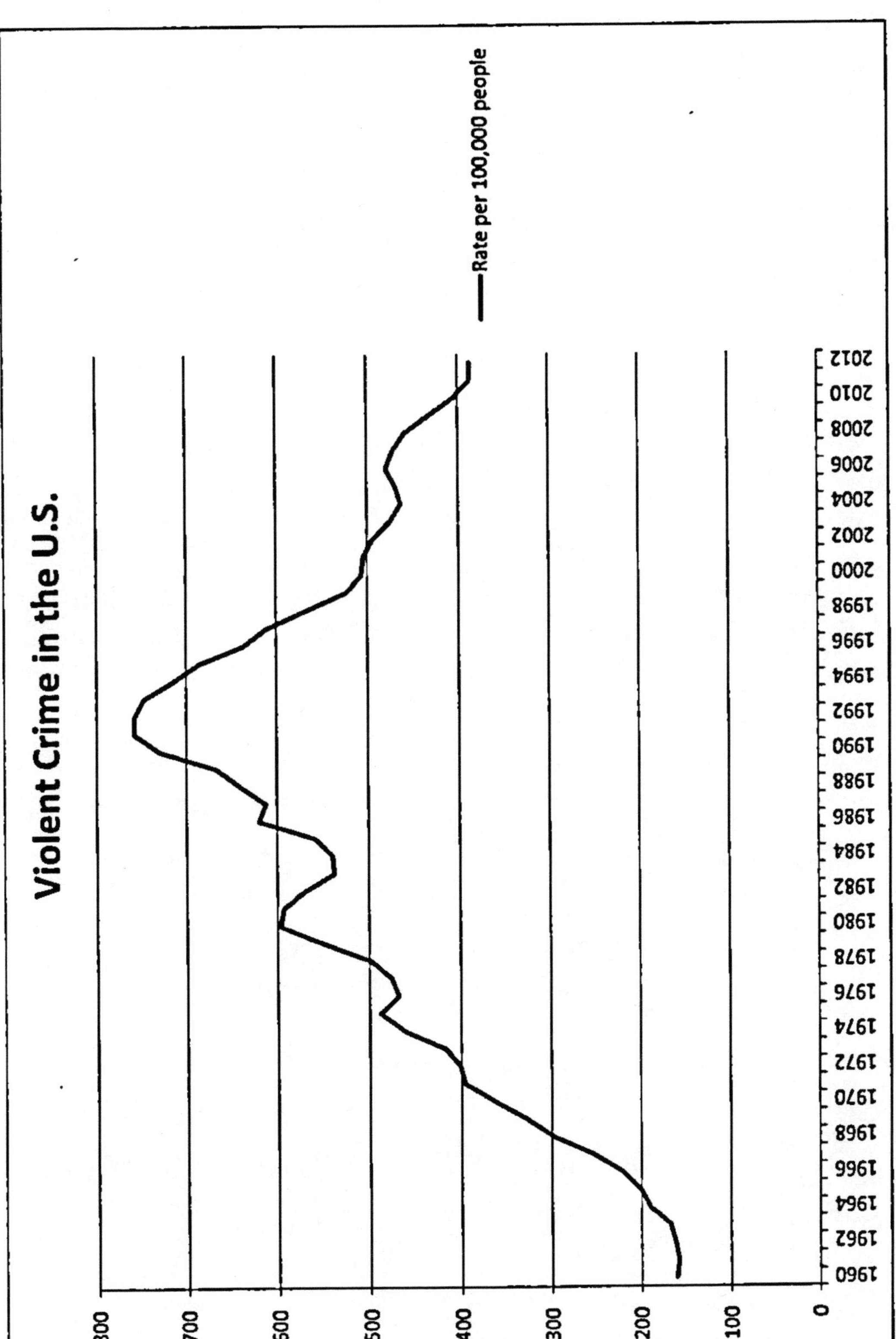

Sources: FBI, Uniform Crime Reports, prepared by the National Archive of Criminal Justice Data

Date of download: Sep 30 2013

4 Where Have All the Criminals Gone?

In 1966, one year after Nicolae Ceauşescu became the Communist dictator of Romania, he made abortion illegal. "The fetus is the property of the entire society," he proclaimed. "Anyone who avoids having children is a deserter who abandons the laws of national continuity."

Such grandiose declarations were commonplace during Ceauşescu's reign, for his master plan—to create a nation worthy of the New Socialist Man—was an exercise in grandiosity. He built palaces for himself while alternately brutalizing and neglecting his citizens. Abandoning agriculture in favor of manufacturing, he forced many of the nation's rural dwellers into unheated apartment buildings. He gave government positions to forty family members including his wife, Elena, who required forty homes and a commensurate supply of fur and jewels. Madame Ceauşescu, known officially as the Best Mother Romania Could Have, was not particularly maternal. "The worms never get satisfied, regardless of how much food you give them," she said when Romanians complained about the food shortages brought on by her husband's mismanagement. She had her own children bugged to ensure their loyalty.

Ceauşescu's ban on abortion was designed to achieve one of his major aims: to rapidly strengthen Romania by boosting its population. Until 1966, Romania had had one of the most liberal abortion policies in the world. Abortion was in fact the main form of birth control, with four abortions for every live birth. Now, virtually overnight, abortion was forbidden. The only exemptions were mothers who already had four children or women with significant standing in the Communist Party. At the same time, all contraception and sex education were banned. Government agents sardonically known as the Menstrual Police regularly rounded up women in their workplaces to administer pregnancy tests. If a woman repeatedly failed to conceive, she was forced to pay a steep "celibacy tax."

Ceauşescu's incentives produced the desired effect. Within one year of the abortion ban, the Romanian birth rate had doubled. These babies were born into a country where, unless you belonged to the Ceauşescu clan or the Communist elite, life was miserable. But these children would turn out to have particularly miserable lives. Compared to Romanian children born just a year earlier, the cohort of children born after the abortion ban would do worse in every measurable way: they would test lower in school, they would have less success in the labor market, and they would also prove much more likely to become criminals.

The abortion ban stayed in effect until Ceauşescu finally lost his grip on Romania. On December 16, 1989, thousands of people took to the streets of Timisoara to protest his corrosive regime. Many of the protestors were teenagers and college students. The police killed dozens of them. One of the opposition leaders, a forty-one-year-old professor, later said it was his thirteen-year-old daughter who insisted he attend the protest, despite his fear. "What is most interesting is that

we learned not to be afraid from our children," he said. "Most were aged thirteen to twenty." A few days after the massacre in Timisoara, Ceauşescu gave a speech in Bucharest before one hundred thousand people. Again the young people were out in force. They shouted down Ceauşescu with cries of "Timisoara!" and "Down with the murderers!" His time had come. He and Elena tried to escape the country with $1 billion, but they were captured, given a crude trial, and, on Christmas Day, executed by firing squad.

Of all the Communist leaders deposed in the years bracketing the collapse of the Soviet Union, only Nicolae Ceauşescu met a violent death. It should not be overlooked that his demise was precipitated in large measure by the youth of Romania—a great number of whom, were it not for his abortion ban, would never have been born at all.

The story of abortion in Romania might seem an odd way to begin telling the story of American crime in the 1990s. But it's not. In one important way, the Romanian abortion story is a reverse image of the American crime story. The point of overlap was on that Christmas Day of 1989, when Nicolae Ceauşescu learned the hard way—with a bullet to the head—that his abortion ban had much deeper implications than he knew.

On that day, crime was just about at its peak in the United States. In the previous fifteen years, violent crime had risen 80 percent. It was crime that led the nightly news and the national conversation.

When the crime rate began falling in the early 1990s, it did so with such speed and suddenness that it surprised everyone. It took some experts many years to even recognize that crime was falling, so confident had they been of its continuing rise. Long after crime had peaked, in fact, some of them continued to predict ever darker scenarios. But the evidence was irrefutable: the long and brutal spike in crime was moving in the opposite direction, and it wouldn't stop until the crime rate had fallen back to the levels of forty years earlier.

Now the experts hustled to explain their faulty forecasting. The criminologist James Alan Fox explained that his warning of a "bloodbath" was in fact an intentional overstatement. "I never said there would be blood flowing in the streets," he said, "but I used strong terms like 'bloodbath' to get people's attention. And it did. I don't apologize for using alarmist terms." (If Fox seems to be offering a distinction without a difference—"bloodbath" versus "blood flowing in the streets"—we should remember that even in retreat mode, experts can be self-serving.)

After the relief had settled in, after people remembered how to go about their lives without the pressing fear of crime, there arose a natural question: just where did all those criminals go?

At one level, the answer seemed puzzling. After all, if none of the criminologists, police officials, economists, politicians, or others who traffic in such matters had foreseen the crime decline, how could they suddenly identify its causes?

But this diverse army of experts now marched out a phalanx of hypotheses to explain the drop in crime. A great many newspaper articles would be written on the subject. Their conclusions often hinged on which expert had most recently spoken to which reporter. Here, ranked by frequency of mention, are the crime-drop explanations cited in articles published from 1991 to 2001 in the ten largest-circulation papers in the LexisNexis database:

CRIME-DROP EXPLANATION	NUMBER OF CITATIONS
1. Innovative policing strategies	52
2. Increased reliance on prisons	47
3. Changes in crack and other drug markets	33
4. Aging of the population	32

CRIME-DROP EXPLANATION	NUMBER OF CITATIONS
5. Tougher gun control laws	32
6. Strong economy	28
7. Increased number of police	26
8. All other explanations (increased use of capital punishment, concealed-weapons laws, gun buybacks, and others)	34

If you are the sort of person who likes guessing games, you may wish to spend the next few moments pondering which of the preceding explanations seem to have merit and which don't. Hint: of the seven major explanations on the list, only three can be shown to have contributed to the drop in crime. The others are, for the most part, figments of someone's imagination, self-interest, or wishful thinking. Further hint: one of the greatest measurable causes of the crime drop does not appear on the list at all, for it didn't receive a single newspaper mention.

Let's begin with a fairly uncontroversial one: *the strong economy*. The decline in crime that began in the early 1990s was accompanied by a blistering national economy and a significant drop in unemployment. It might seem to follow that the economy was a hammer that helped beat down crime. But a closer look at the data destroys this theory. It is true that a stronger job market may make certain crimes relatively less attractive. But that is only the case for crimes with a direct financial motivation—burglary, robbery, and auto theft—as opposed to violent crimes like homicide, assault, and rape. Moreover, studies have shown that an unemployment decline of 1 percentage point accounts for a 1 percent drop in nonviolent crime. During the 1990s, the unemployment rate fell by 2 percentage points; nonviolent crime, meanwhile, fell by roughly *40* percent. But an even bigger flaw in the strong-economy theory concerns violent crime. Homicide fell at a greater rate during the 1990s than any other sort of crime, and a number of reliable studies have shown virtually *no* link between the economy and violent crime. This weak link is made even weaker by glancing back to a recent decade, the 1960s, when the economy went on a wild growth spurt—as did violent crime. So while a strong 1990s economy might have seemed, on the surface, a likely explanation for the drop in crime, it almost certainly didn't affect criminal behavior in any significant way.

Unless, that is, "the economy" is construed in a broader sense—as a means to build and maintain hundreds of prisons. Let's now consider another crime-drop explanation: *increased reliance on prisons*. It might help to start by flipping the crime question around. Instead of wondering what made crime fall, think about this: why had it risen so dramatically in the first place?

During the first half of the twentieth century, the incidence of violent crime in the United States was, for the most part, fairly steady. But in the early 1960s, it began to climb. In retrospect, it is clear that one of the major factors pushing this trend was a more lenient justice system. Conviction rates declined during the 1960s, and criminals who were convicted served shorter sentences. This trend was driven in part by an expansion in the rights of people accused of crimes—a long overdue expansion, some would argue. (Others would argue that the expansion went too far.) At the same time, politicians were growing increasingly softer on crime—"for fear of sounding racist," as the economist Gary Becker has written, "since African-Americans and Hispanics commit a disproportionate share of felonies." So if you were the kind of person who might want to commit a crime, the incentives were lining up in your favor: a slimmer likelihood of being convicted and, if convicted, a shorter prison term. Because criminals

respond to incentives as readily as anyone, the result was a surge in crime.

It took some time, and a great deal of political turmoil, but these incentives were eventually curtailed. Criminals who would have previously been set free—for drug-related offenses and parole revocation in particular—were instead locked up. Between 1980 and 2000, there was a fifteenfold increase in the number of people sent to prison on drug charges. Many other sentences, especially for violent crime, were lengthened. The total effect was dramatic. By 2000, more than two million people were in prison, roughly four times the number as of 1972. Fully half of that increase took place during the 1990s.

The evidence linking increased punishment with lower crime rates is very strong. Harsh prison terms have been shown to act as both deterrent (for the would-be criminal on the street) and prophylactic (for the would-be criminal who is already locked up). Logical as this may sound, some criminologists have fought the logic. A 1977 academic study called "On Behalf of a Moratorium on Prison Construction" noted that crime rates tend to be high when imprisonment rates are high, and concluded that crime would fall if imprisonment rates could only be lowered. (Fortunately, jailers did not suddenly turn loose their wards and sit back waiting for crime to fall. As the political scientist John J. DiIulio Jr. later commented, "Apparently, it takes a Ph.D. in criminology to doubt that keeping dangerous criminals incarcerated cuts crime.") The "Moratorium" argument rests on a fundamental confusion of correlation and causality. Consider a parallel argument. The mayor of a city sees that his citizens celebrate wildly when their team wins the World Series. He is intrigued by this correlation but, like the "Moratorium" author, fails to see the direction in which the correlation runs. So the following year, the mayor decrees that his citizens start celebrating the World Series *before the first pitch is thrown*—an act that, in his confused mind, will ensure a victory.

There are certainly plenty of reasons to dislike the huge surge in the prison population. Not everyone is pleased that such a significant fraction of Americans, especially black Americans, live behind bars. Nor does prison even begin to address the root causes of crime, which are diverse and complex. Lastly, prison is hardly a cheap solution: it costs about $25,000 a year to keep someone incarcerated. But if the goal here is to explain the drop in crime in the 1990s, imprisonment is certainly one of the key answers. It accounts for roughly one-third of the drop in crime.

Another crime-drop explanation is often cited in tandem with imprisonment: *the increased use of capital punishment*. The number of executions in the United States quadrupled between the 1980s and the 1990s, leading many people to conclude—in the context of a debate that has been going on for decades—that capital punishment helped drive down crime. Lost in the debate, however, are two important facts.

First, given the rarity with which executions are carried out in this country and the long delays in doing so, no reasonable criminal should be deterred by the threat of execution. Even though capital punishment quadrupled within a decade, there were still only 478 executions in the entire United States during the 1990s. Any parent who has ever said to a recalcitrant child, "Okay, I'm going to count to ten and this time I'm *really* going to punish you," knows the difference between deterrent and empty threat. New York State, for instance, has not as of this writing executed a single criminal since reinstituting its death penalty in 1995. Even among prisoners on death row, the annual execution rate is only 2 percent—compared with the 7 percent annual chance of dying faced by a member of the Black Gangster Disciple Nation crack gang. If life on death row is safer than life on the streets, it's hard to believe that the fear of execution is a driving force in a criminal's calculus. Like the $3 fine for late-

arriving parents at the Israeli day-care centers, the negative incentive of capital punishment simply isn't serious enough for a criminal to change his behavior.

The second flaw in the capital punishment argument is even more obvious. Assume for a moment that the death penalty *is* a deterrent. How much crime does it actually deter? The economist Isaac Ehrlich, in an oft-cited 1975 paper, put forth an estimate that is generally considered optimistic: executing 1 criminal translates into 7 fewer homicides that the criminal might have committed. Now do the math. In 1991, there were 14 executions in the United States; in 2001, there were 66. According to Ehrlich's calculation, those 52 additional executions would have accounted for 364 fewer homicides in 2001—not a small drop, to be sure, but less than 4 percent of the actual decrease in homicides that year. So even in a death penalty advocate's best-case scenario, capital punishment could explain only one twenty-fifth of the drop in homicides in the 1990s. And because the death penalty is rarely given for crimes other than homicide, its deterrent effect cannot account for a speck of decline in other violent crimes.

It is extremely unlikely, therefore, that the death penalty, as currently practiced in the United States, exerts any real influence on crime rates. Even many of its onetime supporters have come to this conclusion. "I feel morally and intellectually obligated simply to concede that the death penalty experiment has failed," said U.S. Supreme Court Justice Harry A. Blackmun in 1994, nearly twenty years after he had voted for its reinstatement. "I no longer shall tinker with the machinery of death."

So it wasn't capital punishment that drove crime down, nor was it the booming economy. But higher rates of imprisonment did have a lot to do with it. All those criminals didn't march into jail by themselves, of course. Someone had to investigate the crime, catch the bad guy, and put together the case that would get him convicted. Which naturally leads to a related pair of crime-drop explanations:

Innovative policing strategies
Increased number of police

Let's address the second one first. The number of police officers per capita in the United States rose about 14 percent during the 1990s. Does merely increasing the number of police, however, reduce crime? The answer would seem obvious—yes—but proving that answer isn't so easy. That's because when crime is rising, people clamor for protection, and invariably more money is found for cops. So if you just look at raw correlations between police and crime, you will find that when there are more police, there tends to be more crime. That doesn't mean, of course, that the police are causing the crime, just as it doesn't mean, as some criminologists have argued, that crime will fall if criminals are released from prison.

To show causality, we need a scenario in which more police are hired for reasons completely unrelated to rising crime. If, for instance, police were randomly sprinkled in some cities and not in others, we could look to see whether crime declines in the cities where the police happen to land.

As it turns out, that exact scenario is often created by vote-hungry politicians. In the months leading up to Election Day, incumbent mayors routinely try to lock up the law-and-order vote by hiring more police—even when the crime rate is standing still. So by comparing the crime rate in one set of cities that have recently had an election (and which therefore hired extra police) with another set of cities that had no election (and therefore no extra police), it's possible to tease out the effect of the extra police on crime. The answer: yes indeed, additional police substantially lower the crime rate.

Again, it may help to look backward and see why crime had risen so much in the first place. From 1960 to 1985, the number of police officers *fell* more than 50 percent relative to the number of crimes. In some cases, hiring additional police was considered a violation of the era's liberal aesthetic; in others, it was simply considered too expensive. This 50 percent decline in police translated into a roughly equal decline in the probability that a given criminal would be caught. Coupled with the above-cited leniency in the other half of the criminal justice system, the courtrooms, this decrease in policing created a strong positive incentive for criminals.

By the 1990s, philosophies—and necessities—had changed. The policing trend was put in reverse, with wide-scale hiring in cities across the country. Not only did all those police act as a deterrent, but they also provided the manpower to imprison criminals who might have otherwise gone uncaught. The hiring of additional police accounted for roughly 10 percent of the 1990s crime drop.

But it wasn't only the number of police that changed in the 1990s; consider the most commonly cited crime-drop explanation of all: *innovative policing strategies*.

There was perhaps no more attractive theory than the belief that smart policing stops crime. It offered a set of bona fide heroes rather than simply a dearth of villains. This theory rapidly became an article of faith because it appealed to the factors that, according to John Kenneth Galbraith, most contribute to the formation of conventional wisdom: the ease with which an idea may be understood and the degree to which it affects our personal well-being.

The story played out most dramatically in New York City, where newly elected mayor Rudolph Giuliani and his handpicked police commissioner, William Bratton, vowed to fix the city's desperate crime situation. Bratton took a novel approach to policing. He ushered the NYPD into what one senior police official later called "our Athenian period," in which new ideas were given weight over calcified practices. Instead of coddling his precinct commanders, Bratton demanded accountability. Instead of relying solely on old-fashioned cop know-how, he introduced technological solutions like CompStat, a computerized method of addressing crime hot spots.

The most compelling new idea that Bratton brought to life stemmed from the broken window theory, which was conceived by the criminologists James Q. Wilson and George Kelling. The broken window theory argues that minor nuisances, if left unchecked, turn into major nuisances: that is, if someone breaks a window and sees it isn't fixed immediately, he gets the signal that it's all right to break the rest of the windows and maybe set the building afire too.

So with murder raging all around, Bill Bratton's cops began to police the sort of deeds that used to go unpoliced: jumping a subway turnstile, panhandling too aggressively, urinating in the streets, swabbing a filthy squeegee across a car's windshield unless the driver made an appropriate "donation."

Most New Yorkers loved this crackdown on its own merit. But they particularly loved the idea, as stoutly preached by Bratton and Giuliani, that choking off these small crimes was like choking off the criminal element's oxygen supply. Today's turnstile jumper might easily be wanted for yesterday's murder. That junkie peeing in an alley might have been on his way to a robbery.

As violent crime began to fall dramatically, New Yorkers were more than happy to heap laurels on their operatic, Brooklyn-bred mayor and his hatchet-faced police chief with the big Boston accent. But the two strong-willed men weren't very good at sharing the glory. Soon after the city's crime turnaround landed Bratton—and not Giuliani—on the cover of *Time*, Bratton was pushed to resign. He had been police commissioner for just twenty-seven months.

New York City was a clear innovator in police strategies during the 1990s crime drop, and it also enjoyed the greatest decline in crime of any large American city. Homicide rates fell from 30.7 per 100,000 people in 1990 to 8.4 per 100,000 people in 2000, a change of 73.6 percent. But a careful analysis of the facts shows that the innovative policing strategies probably had little effect on this huge decline.

First, the drop in crime in New York began in 1990. By the end of 1993, the rate of property crime and violent crime, including homicides, had already fallen nearly 20 percent. Rudolph Giuliani, however, did not become mayor—and install Bratton—until early 1994. Crime was well on its way down before either man arrived. And it would continue to fall long after Bratton was bumped from office.

Second, the new police strategies were accompanied by a much more significant change within the police force: a hiring binge. Between 1991 and 2001, the NYPD grew by 45 percent, more than three times the national average. As argued above, an increase in the number of police, regardless of new strategies, *has* been proven to reduce crime. By a conservative calculation, this huge expansion of New York's police force would be expected to reduce crime in New York by 18 percent relative to the national average. If you subtract that 18 percent from New York's homicide reduction, thereby discounting the effect of the police-hiring surge, New York no longer leads the nation with its 73.6 percent drop; it goes straight to the middle of the pack. Many of those new police were in fact hired by David Dinkins, the mayor whom Giuliani defeated. Dinkins had been desperate to secure the law-and-order vote, having known all along that his opponent would be Giuliani, a former federal prosecutor. (The two men had run against each other four years earlier as well.) So those who wish to credit Giuliani with the crime drop may still do so, for it was his own law-and-order reputation that made Dinkins hire all those police. In the end, of course, the police increase helped everyone—but it helped Giuliani a lot more than Dinkins.

Most damaging to the claim that New York's police innovations radically lowered crime is one simple and often overlooked fact: crime went down *everywhere* during the 1990s, not only in New York. Few other cities tried the kind of strategies that New York did, and certainly none with the same zeal. But even in Los Angeles, a city notorious for bad policing, crime fell at about the same rate as it did in New York once the growth in New York's police force is accounted for.

It would be churlish to argue that smart policing isn't a good thing. Bill Bratton certainly deserves credit for invigorating New York's police force. But there is frighteningly little evidence that his strategy was the crime panacea that he and the media deemed it. The next step will be to continue measuring the impact of police innovations—in Los Angeles, for instance, where Bratton himself became police chief in late 2002. While he duly instituted some of the innovations that were his hallmark in New York, Bratton announced that his highest priority was a more basic one: finding the money to hire thousands of new police officers.

Now to explore another pair of common crime-drop explanations:

Tougher gun laws
Changes in crack and other drug markets

First, the guns. Debates on this subject are rarely coolheaded. Gun advocates believe that gun laws are too strict; opponents believe exactly the opposite. How can intelligent people view the world so differently? Because a gun raises a complex set of issues that change according to one factor: whose hand happens to be holding the gun.

It might be worthwhile to take a step back and ask a rudimentary question: what *is* a gun? It's a tool that can be used to kill someone, of course, but more significantly, a gun is a great disrupter of the natural order.

A gun scrambles the outcome of any dispute. Let's say that a tough guy and a not-so-tough guy exchange words in a bar, which leads to a fight. It's pretty obvious to the not-so-tough guy that he'll be beaten, so why bother fighting? The pecking order remains intact. But if the not-so-tough guy happens to have a gun, he stands a good chance of winning. In this scenario, the introduction of a gun may well lead to more violence.

Now instead of the tough guy and the not-so-tough guy, picture a high-school girl out for a nighttime stroll when she is suddenly set upon by a mugger. What if only the mugger is armed? What if only the girl is armed? What if *both* are armed? A gun opponent might argue that the gun has to be kept out of the mugger's hands in the first place. A gun advocate might argue that the high-school girl needs to have a gun to disrupt what has become the natural order: it's the bad guys that have the guns. (If the girl scares off the mugger, then the introduction of a gun in this case may lead to *less* violence.) Any mugger with even a little initiative is bound to be armed, for in a country like the United States, with a thriving black market in guns, anyone can get hold of one.

There are enough guns in the United States that if you gave one to every adult, you would run out of adults before you ran out of guns. Nearly two-thirds of U.S. homicides involve a gun, a far greater fraction than in other industrialized countries. Our homicide rate is also much higher than in those countries. It would therefore seem likely that our homicide rate is so high in part because guns are so easily available. Research indeed shows this to be true.

But guns are not the whole story. In Switzerland, every adult male is issued an assault rifle for militia duty and is allowed to keep the gun at home. On a per capita basis, Switzerland has more firearms than just about any other country, and yet it is one of the safest places in the world. In other words, guns do not cause crime. That said, the established U.S. methods of keeping guns away from the people who *do* cause crime are, at best, feeble. And since a gun—unlike a bag of cocaine or a car or a pair of pants—lasts pretty much forever, even turning off the spigot of new guns still leaves an ocean of available ones.

So bearing all this in mind, let's consider a variety of recent gun initiatives to see the impact they may have had on crime in the 1990s.

The most famous gun-control law is the Brady Act, passed in 1993, which requires a criminal check and a waiting period before a person can purchase a handgun. This solution may have seemed appealing to politicians, but to an economist it doesn't make much sense. Why? Because regulation of a legal market is bound to fail when a healthy black market exists for the same product. With guns so cheap and so easy to get, the standard criminal has no incentive to fill out a firearms application at his local gun shop and then wait a week. The Brady Act, accordingly, has proven to be practically impotent in lowering crime. (A study of imprisoned felons showed that even before the Brady Act, only about one-fifth of the criminals had bought their guns through a licensed dealer.) Various local gun-control laws have also failed. Washington, D.C., and Chicago both instituted handgun bans well before crime began to fall across the country in the 1990s, and yet those two cities were laggards, not leaders, in the national reduction in crime. One deterrent that *has* proven moderately effective is a stiff increase in prison time for anyone caught in possession of an illegal gun. But there is plenty of room for improvement. Not that this is likely, but if the death penalty were assessed to anyone carrying an illegal gun, and if the penalty were actually enforced, gun crimes would surely plunge.

Another staple of 1990s crime fighting—and of the evening news—was the gun buyback. You remember the image: a menacing, glistening heap of firearms surrounded by the mayor, the police chief, the neighborhood activists. It made for a nice photo op, but that's about as meaningful as a gun buyback is. The guns that get turned in

are generally heirlooms or junk. The payoff to the gun seller—usually $50 or $100, but in one California buyback, three free hours of psychotherapy—isn't an adequate incentive for anyone who actually plans to use his gun. And the number of surrendered guns is no match for even the number of new guns simultaneously coming to market. Given the number of handguns in the United States and the number of homicides each year, the likelihood that a particular gun was used to kill someone that year is 1 in 10,000. The typical gun buyback program yields fewer than 1,000 guns—which translates into an expectation of less than one-tenth of one homicide per buyback. Not enough, that is, to make even a sliver of impact on the fall of crime.

Then there is an opposite argument—that we need *more* guns on the street, but in the hands of the right people (like the high-school girl above, instead of her mugger). The economist John R. Lott Jr. is the main champion of this idea. His calling card is the book *More Guns, Less Crime*, in which he argues that violent crime has decreased in areas where law-abiding citizens are allowed to carry concealed weapons. His theory might be surprising, but it is sensible. If a criminal thinks his potential victim may be armed, he may be deterred from committing the crime. Handgun opponents call Lott a pro-gun ideologue, and Lott let himself become a lightning rod for gun controversy. He exacerbated his trouble by creating a pseudonym, "Mary Rosh," to defend his theory in online debates. Rosh, identifying herself as a former student of Lott's, praised her teacher's intellect, his evenhandedness, his charisma. "I have to say that he was the best professor that I ever had," s/he wrote. "You wouldn't know that he was a 'right-wing' ideologue from the class. . . . There were a group of us students who would try to take any class that he taught. Lott finally had to tell us that it was best for us to try and take classes from other professors more to be exposed to other ways of teaching graduate material." Then there was the troubling allegation that Lott actually invented some of the survey data that support his more-guns/less-crime theory. Regardless of whether the data were faked, Lott's admittedly intriguing hypothesis doesn't seem to be true. When other scholars have tried to replicate his results, they found that right-to-carry laws simply don't bring down crime.

Consider the next crime-drop explanation: *the bursting of the crack bubble.* Crack cocaine was such a potent, addictive drug that a hugely profitable market had been created practically overnight. True, it was only the leaders of the crack gangs who were getting rich. But that only made the street-level dealers all the more desperate to advance. Many of them were willing to kill their rivals to do so, whether the rival belonged to the same gang or a different one. There were also gun battles over valuable drug-selling corners. The typical crack murder involved one crack dealer shooting another (or two of them, or three) and not, contrary to conventional wisdom, some bug-eyed crackhead shooting a shopkeeper over a few dollars. The result was a huge increase in violent crime. One study found that more than 25 percent of the homicides in New York City in 1988 were crack-related.

The violence associated with crack began to ebb in about 1991. This has led many people to think that crack itself went away. It didn't. Smoking crack remains much more popular today than most people realize. Nearly 5 percent of all arrests in the United States are still related to cocaine (as against 6 percent at crack's peak); nor have emergency room visits for crack users diminished all that much.

What *did* go away were the huge profits for selling crack. The price of cocaine had been falling for years, and it got only cheaper as crack grew more popular. Dealers began to underprice one another; profits vanished. The crack bubble burst as dramatically as the Nasdaq bubble would eventually burst. (Think of the first generation of crack

dealers as the Microsoft millionaires; think of the second generation as Pets.com.) As veteran crack dealers were killed or sent to prison, younger dealers decided that the smaller profits didn't justify the risk. The tournament had lost its allure. It was no longer worth killing someone to steal their crack turf, and certainly not worth being killed.

So the violence abated. From 1991 to 2001, the homicide rate among young black men—who were disproportionately represented among crack dealers—fell 48 percent, compared to 30 percent for older black men and older white men. (Another minor contributor to the falling homicide rate is the fact that some crack dealers took to shooting their enemies in the buttocks rather than murdering them; this method of violent insult was considered more degrading—and was obviously less severely punished—than murder.) All told, the crash of the crack market accounted for roughly 15 percent of the crime drop of the 1990s—a substantial factor, to be sure, though it should be noted that crack was responsible for far more than 15 percent of the crime *increase* of the 1980s. In other words, the net effect of crack is still being felt in the form of violent crime, to say nothing of the miseries the drug itself continues to cause.

The final pair of crime-drop explanations concern two demographic trends. The first one received many media citations: *aging of the population.*

Until crime fell so drastically, no one talked about this theory at all. In fact, the "bloodbath" school of criminology was touting exactly the opposite theory—that an increase in the teenage share of the population would produce a crop of superpredators who would lay the nation low. "Just beyond the horizon, there lurks a cloud that the winds will soon bring over us," James Q. Wilson wrote in 1995. "The population will start getting younger again. . . . Get ready."

But overall, the teenage share of the population *wasn't* getting much bigger. Criminologists like Wilson and James Alan Fox had badly misread the demographic data. The real population growth in the 1990s was in fact among the elderly. While this may have been scary news in terms of Medicare and Social Security, the average American had little to fear from the growing horde of oldsters. It shouldn't be surprising to learn that elderly people are not very criminally intent; the average sixty-five-year-old is about one-fiftieth as likely to be arrested as the average teenager. That is what makes this aging-of-the-population theory of crime reduction so appealingly tidy: since people mellow out as they get older, more older people must lead to less crime. But a thorough look at the data reveals that the graying of America did nothing to bring down crime in the 1990s. Demographic change is too slow and subtle a process—you don't graduate from teenage hoodlum to senior citizen in just a few years— to even begin to explain the suddenness of the crime decline.

There was another demographic change, however, unforeseen and long-gestating, that did drastically reduce crime in the 1990s.

Think back for a moment to Romania in 1966. Suddenly and without warning, Nicolae Ceauşescu declared abortion illegal. The children born in the wake of the abortion ban were much more likely to become criminals than children born earlier. Why was that? Studies in other parts of Eastern Europe and in Scandinavia from the 1930s through the 1960s reveal a similar trend. In most of these cases, abortion was not forbidden outright, but a woman had to receive permission from a judge in order to obtain one. Researchers found that in the instances where the woman was denied an abortion, she often resented her baby and failed to provide it with a good home. Even when controlling for the income, age, education, and health of the mother, the researchers found that these children too were more likely to become criminals.

The United States, meanwhile, has had a different abortion history than Europe. In the early days of the nation, it was permissible to have an abortion prior to "quickening"—that is, when the first movements of the fetus could be felt, usually around the sixteenth to eighteenth week of pregnancy. In 1828, New York became the first state to restrict abortion; by 1900 it had been made illegal throughout the country. Abortion in the twentieth century was often dangerous and usually expensive. Fewer poor women, therefore, had abortions. They also had less access to birth control. What they did have, accordingly, was a lot more babies.

In the late 1960s, several states began to allow abortion under extreme circumstances: rape, incest, or danger to the mother. By 1970 five states had made abortion entirely legal and broadly available: New York, California, Washington, Alaska, and Hawaii. On January 22, 1973, legalized abortion was suddenly extended to the entire country with the U.S. Supreme Court's ruling in *Roe v. Wade.* The majority opinion, written by Justice Harry Blackmun, spoke specifically to the would-be mother's predicament:

The detriment that the State would impose upon the pregnant woman by denying this choice altogether is apparent. . . . Maternity, or additional offspring, may force upon the woman a distressful life and future. Psychological harm may be imminent. Mental and physical health may be taxed by child care. There is also the distress, for all concerned, associated with the unwanted child, and there is the problem of bringing a child into a family already unable, psychologically and otherwise, to care for it.

The Supreme Court gave voice to what the mothers in Romania and Scandinavia—and elsewhere—had long known: when a woman does not want to have a child, she usually has good reason. She may be unmarried or in a bad marriage. She may consider herself too poor to raise a child. She may think her life is too unstable or unhappy, or she may think that her drinking or drug use will damage the baby's health. She may believe that she is too young or hasn't yet received enough education. She may want a child badly but in a few years, not now. For any of a hundred reasons, she may feel that she cannot provide a home environment that is conducive to raising a healthy and productive child.

In the first year after *Roe v. Wade*, some 750,000 women had abortions in the United States (representing one abortion for every 4 live births). By 1980 the number of abortions reached 1.6 million (one for every 2.25 live births), where it leveled off. In a country of 225 million people, 1.6 million abortions per year—one for every 140 Americans—may not have seemed so dramatic. In the first year after Nicolae Ceauşescu's death, when abortion was reinstated in Romania, there was one abortion for every *twenty-two* Romanians. But still: 1.6 million American women a year who got pregnant were suddenly not having those babies.

Before *Roe v. Wade*, it was predominantly the daughters of middle- or upper-class families who could arrange and afford a safe illegal abortion. Now, instead of an illegal procedure that might cost $500, any woman could easily obtain an abortion, often for less than $100.

What sort of woman was most likely to take advantage of *Roe v. Wade*? Very often she was unmarried or in her teens or poor, and sometimes all three. What sort of future might her child have had? One study has shown that the typical child who went unborn in the earliest years of legalized abortion would have been 50 percent more likely than average to live in poverty; he would have also been 60 percent more likely to grow up with just one parent. These two factors—childhood poverty and a single-parent household—are among the strongest predictors that a child will have a criminal future. Growing

up in a single-parent home roughly doubles a child's propensity to commit crime. So does having a teenage mother. Another study has shown that low maternal education is the single most powerful factor leading to criminality.

In other words, the very factors that drove millions of American women to have an abortion also seemed to predict that their children, had they been born, would have led unhappy and possibly criminal lives.

To be sure, the legalization of abortion in the United States had myriad consequences. Infanticide fell dramatically. So did shotgun marriages, as well as the number of babies put up for adoption (which has led to the boom in the adoption of foreign babies). Conceptions rose by nearly 30 percent, but births actually *fell* by 6 percent, indicating that many women were using abortion as a method of birth control, a crude and drastic sort of insurance policy.

Perhaps the most dramatic effect of legalized abortion, however, and one that would take years to reveal itself, was its impact on crime. In the early 1990s, just as the first cohort of children born after *Roe v. Wade* was hitting its late teen years—the years during which young men enter their criminal prime—the rate of crime began to fall. What this cohort was missing, of course, were the children who stood the greatest chance of becoming criminals. And the crime rate continued to fall as an entire generation came of age minus the children whose mothers had not wanted to bring a child into the world. Legalized abortion led to less unwantedness; unwantedness leads to high crime; legalized abortion, therefore, led to less crime.

This theory is bound to provoke a variety of reactions, ranging from disbelief to revulsion, and a variety of objections, ranging from the quotidian to the moral. The likeliest first objection is the most straightforward one: is the theory true? Perhaps abortion and crime are merely correlated and not causal.

It may be more comforting to believe what the newspapers say, that the drop in crime was due to brilliant policing and clever gun control and a surging economy. We have evolved with a tendency to link causality to things we can touch or feel, not to some distant or difficult phenomenon. We believe especially in near-term causes: a snake bites your friend, he screams with pain, and he dies. The snakebite, you conclude, must have killed him. Most of the time, such a reckoning is correct. But when it comes to cause and effect, there is often a trap in such open-and-shut thinking. We smirk now when we think of ancient cultures that embraced faulty causes—the warriors who believed, for instance, that it was their raping of a virgin that brought them victory on the battlefield. But we too embrace faulty causes, usually at the urging of an expert proclaiming a truth in which he has a vested interest.

How, then, can we tell if the abortion-crime link is a case of causality rather than simply correlation?

One way to test the effect of abortion on crime would be to measure crime data in the five states where abortion was made legal before the Supreme Court extended abortion rights to the rest of the country. In New York, California, Washington, Alaska, and Hawaii, a woman had been able to obtain a legal abortion for at least two years before *Roe v. Wade*. And indeed, those early-legalizing states saw crime begin to fall earlier than the other forty-five states and the District of Columbia. Between 1988 and 1994, violent crime in the early-legalizing states fell 13 percent compared to the other states; between 1994 and 1997, their murder rates fell 23 percent more than those of the other states.

But what if those early legalizers simply got lucky? What else might we look for in the data to establish an abortion-crime link?

One factor to look for would be a correlation between each state's abortion rate and its crime rate. Sure enough, the states with the highest abortion rates in the 1970s experienced the greatest crime drops in

the 1990s, while states with low abortion rates experienced smaller crime drops. (This correlation exists even when controlling for a variety of factors that influence crime: a state's level of incarceration, number of police, and its economic situation.) Since 1985, states with high abortion rates have experienced a roughly 30 percent drop in crime relative to low-abortion states. (New York City had high abortion rates *and* lay within an early-legalizing state, a pair of facts that further dampen the claim that innovative policing caused the crime drop.) Moreover, there was no link between a given state's abortion rate and its crime rate *before* the late 1980s—when the first cohort affected by legalized abortion was reaching its criminal prime—which is yet another indication that *Roe v. Wade* was indeed the event that tipped the crime scale.

There are even more correlations, positive and negative, that shore up the abortion-crime link. In states with high abortion rates, the entire decline in crime was among the post-*Roe* cohort as opposed to older criminals. Also, studies of Australia and Canada have since established a similar link between legalized abortion and crime. And the post-*Roe* cohort was not only missing thousands of young male criminals but also thousands of single, teenage mothers—for many of the aborted baby girls would have been the children most likely to replicate their *own* mothers' tendencies.

To discover that abortion was one of the greatest crime-lowering factors in American history is, needless to say, jarring. It feels less Darwinian than Swiftian; it calls to mind a long ago dart attributed to G. K. Chesterton: when there aren't enough hats to go around, the problem isn't solved by lopping off some heads. The crime drop was, in the language of economists, an "unintended benefit" of legalized abortion. But one need not oppose abortion on moral or religious grounds to feel shaken by the notion of a private sadness being converted into a public good.

Indeed, there are plenty of people who consider abortion itself to be a violent crime. One legal scholar called legalized abortion worse than either slavery (since it routinely involves death) or the Holocaust (since the number of post-*Roe* abortions in the United States, roughly thirty-seven million as of 2004, outnumber the six million Jews killed in Europe). Whether or not one feels so strongly about abortion, it remains a singularly charged issue. Anthony V. Bouza, a former top police official in both the Bronx and Minneapolis, discovered this when he ran for Minnesota governor in 1994. A few years earlier, Bouza had written a book in which he called abortion "arguably the only effective crime-prevention device adopted in this nation since the late 1960s." When Bouza's opinion was publicized just before the election, he fell sharply in the polls. And then he lost.

However a person feels about abortion, a question is likely to come to mind: what are we to make of the trade-off of more abortion for less crime? Is it even possible to put a number on such a complicated transaction?

As it happens, economists have a curious habit of affixing numbers to complicated transactions. Consider the effort to save the northern spotted owl from extinction. One economic study found that in order to protect roughly five thousand owls, the opportunity costs—that is, the income surrendered by the logging industry and others—would be $46 billion, or just over $9 million per owl. After the *Exxon Valdez* oil spill in 1989, another study estimated the amount that the typical American household would be willing to pay to avoid another such disaster: $31. An economist can affix a value even to a particular body part. Consider the schedule that the state of Connecticut uses to compensate for work-related injuries.

Lost or Damaged Body Part	Compensated Weeks of Pay
Finger (first)	36
Finger (second)	29
Finger (third)	21
Finger (fourth)	17
Thumb (master hand)	63
Thumb (other hand)	54
Hand (master)	168
Hand (other)	155
Arm (master)	208
Arm (other)	194
Toe (great)	28
Toe (any other)	9
Foot	125
Nose	35
Eye	157
Kidney	117
Liver	347
Pancreas	416
Heart	520
Mammary	35
Ovary	35
Testis	35
Penis	35–104
Vagina	35–104

Now, for the sake of argument, let's ask an outrageous question: what is the relative value between a fetus and a newborn? If faced with the Solomonic task of sacrificing the life of one newborn for an indeterminate number of fetuses, what number might you choose? This is nothing but a thought exercise—obviously there is no right answer—but it may help clarify the impact of abortion on crime.

For a person who is either resolutely pro-life or resolutely pro-choice, this is a simple calculation. The first, believing that life begins at conception, would likely consider the value of a newborn versus the value of a fetus to be 1:1. The second person, believing that a woman's right to an abortion trumps any other factor, would likely argue that no number of fetuses can equal even one newborn.

But let's consider a third person. (If you identify strongly with either person number one or person number two, the following exercise might strike you as offensive, and you may want to skip this paragraph and the next.) This third person does not believe that a fetus is the 1:1 equivalent of a newborn, yet neither does he believe that a fetus has no relative value. Let's say that he is forced, for the sake of argument, to affix a relative value, and he decides that 1 newborn is worth 100 fetuses.

There are roughly 1.5 million abortions in the United States every year. For a person who believes that 1 newborn is worth 100 fetuses, those 1.5 million abortions would translate—dividing 1.5 million by 100—into the equivalent of a loss of 15,000 human lives. Fifteen thousand lives: that happens to be about the same number of people who die in homicides in the United States every year. And it is far more than the number of homicides eliminated each year due to legalized abortion. So even for someone who considers a fetus to be worth only one one-hundredth of a human being, the trade-off between higher abortion and lower crime is, by an economist's reckoning, terribly inefficient.

What the link between abortion and crime does say is this: when the government gives a woman the opportunity to make her own decision about abortion, she generally does a good job of figuring out if she is in a position to raise the baby well. If she decides she can't, she often chooses the abortion.

But once a woman decides she *will* have her baby, a pressing question arises: what are parents supposed to do once a child is born?

America's Real Criminal Element: Lead

New research finds Pb is the hidden villain behind violent crime, lower IQs, and even the ADHD epidemic. And fixing the problem is a lot cheaper than doing nothing.

—By Kevin Drum | January/February 2013 Issue Illustration: Gérard DuBois

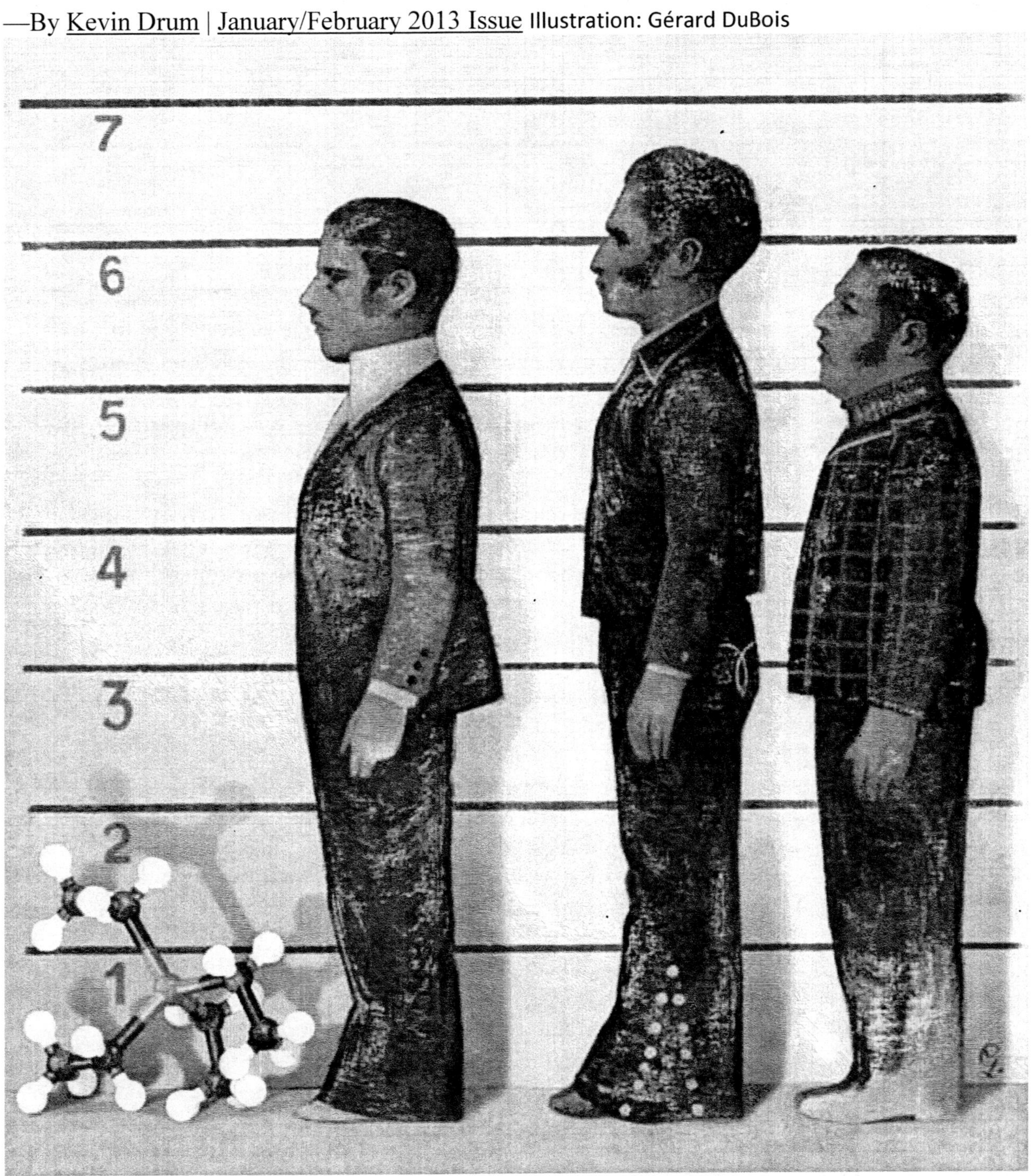

When Rudy Giuliani ran for mayor of New York City in 1993, he campaigned on a platform of bringing down crime and making the city safe again. It was a comfortable position for a former federal prosecutor with a tough-guy image, but it was more than mere posturing. Since 1960, rape rates had nearly quadrupled, murder had quintupled, and robbery had grown fourteenfold. New Yorkers felt like they lived in a city under siege.

- Is There Lead In Your House?
- An Interview With Pioneering Toxicologist Howard Mielke
- How Dangerous Is the Lead in Bullets?
- Does Lead Paint Produce More Crime Too?
- How Your Water Company May Be Poisoning Your Kids

More *MoJo* coverage of the dangers of lead.

Throughout the campaign, Giuliani embraced a theory of crime fighting called "broken windows," popularized a decade earlier by James Q. Wilson and George L. Kelling in <u>an influential article in *The Atlantic.*</u> "If a window in a building is broken and is left unrepaired," they observed, "all the rest of the windows will soon be broken." So too, tolerance of small crimes would create a vicious cycle ending with entire neighborhoods turning into war zones. But if you cracked down on small crimes, bigger crimes would drop as well.

Giuliani won the election, and he made good on his crime-fighting promises by selecting Boston police chief Bill Bratton as the NYPD's new commissioner. Bratton had made his reputation as head of the New York City Transit Police, where he aggressively applied broken-windows policing to turnstile jumpers and vagrants in subway stations. With Giuliani's eager support, he began applying the same lessons to the entire city, going after panhandlers, drunks, drug pushers, and the city's hated squeegee men. And more: He decentralized police operations and gave precinct commanders more control, keeping them accountable with a pioneering system called CompStat that tracked crime hot spots in real time.

The results were dramatic. In 1996, the <u>*New York Times* reported</u> that crime had plunged for the third straight year, the sharpest drop since the end of Prohibition. Since 1993, rape rates had dropped 17 percent, assault 27 percent, robbery 42 percent, and murder an astonishing 49 percent. Giuliani was on his way to becoming America's Mayor and Bratton was on the cover of *Time*. It was a remarkable public policy victory.

But even more remarkable is what happened next. Shortly after Bratton's star turn, political scientist John DiIulio warned that the echo of the baby boom would soon produce a demographic bulge of millions of young males that he famously dubbed "<u>juvenile super-predators.</u>" Other criminologists nodded along. But even though the demographic bulge came right on schedule, crime continued to drop. And drop. And drop. By 2010, violent crime rates in New York City had plunged 75 percent from their peak in the early '90s.

All in all, it seemed to be a story with a happy ending, a triumph for Wilson and Kelling's theory and Giuliani and Bratton's practice. And yet, doubts remained. For one thing, violent crime actually peaked in New York City in 1990, four years before the Giuliani-Bratton era. By the time they took office, it had already dropped 12 percent.

The PB Effect

What happens when you expose a generation of kids to high lead levels? Crime and teen pregnancy data two decades later tell a startling story.

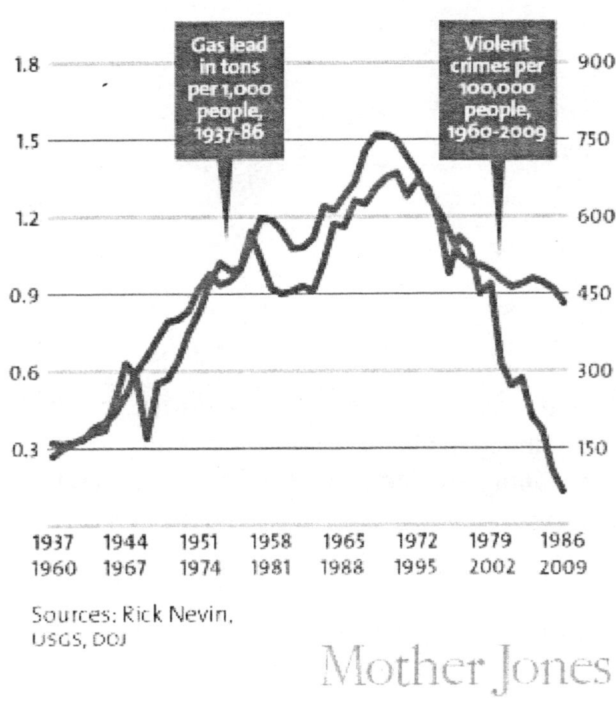

Sources: Rick Nevin, USGS, DOJ

Mother Jones

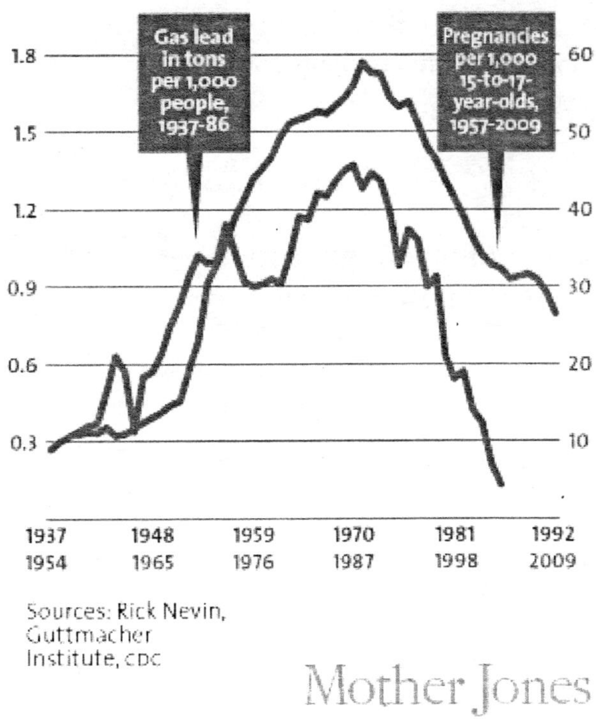

Second, and far more puzzling, it's not just New York that has seen a big drop in crime. In city after city, violent crime peaked in the early '90s and then began a steady and spectacular decline. Washington, DC, didn't have either Giuliani or Bratton, but its violent crime rate has dropped 58 percent since its peak. Dallas' has fallen 70 percent. Newark: 74 percent. Los Angeles: 78 percent.

There must be more going on here than just a change in policing tactics in one city. But what?

There are, it turns out, plenty of theories. When I started research for this story, I worked my way through a pair of thick criminology tomes. One chapter regaled me with the "exciting possibility" that it's mostly a matter of economics: Crime goes down when the economy is booming and goes up when it's in a slump. Unfortunately, the theory doesn't seem to hold water—for example, crime rates have continued to drop recently despite our prolonged downturn.

Another chapter suggested that crime drops in big cities were mostly a reflection of the crack epidemic of the '80s finally burning itself out. A trio of authors identified three major "drug eras" in New York City, the first dominated by heroin, which produced limited violence, and the second by crack, which generated spectacular levels of it. In the early '90s, these researchers proposed, the children of CrackGen switched to marijuana, choosing a less violent and more law-abiding lifestyle. As they did, crime rates in New York and other cities went down.

Another chapter told a story of demographics: As the number of young men increases, so does crime. Unfortunately for this theory, the number of young men increased during the '90s, but crime dropped anyway.

There were chapters in my tomes on the effect of prison expansion. On guns and gun control. On family. On race. On parole and probation. On the raw number of police officers. It seemed as if everyone had a pet theory. In 1999, economist Steven Levitt, later famous as the coauthor of *Freakonomics*, teamed up with John Donohue to suggest that <u>crime dropped because of *Roe v. Wade*</u>; legalized abortion, they argued, led to fewer unwanted babies, which meant fewer maladjusted and violent young men two decades later.

But there's a problem common to all of these theories: It's hard to tease out actual proof. Maybe the end of the crack epidemic contributed to a decline in inner-city crime, but then again, maybe it was really the effect of increased incarceration, more cops on the beat, broken-windows policing, and a rise in abortion rates 20 years earlier. After all, they all happened at the same time.

To address this problem, the field of econometrics gives researchers an enormous toolbox of sophisticated statistical techniques. But, notes statistician and conservative commentator Jim Manzi in his recent book *Uncontrolled*, econometrics consistently fails to explain most of the variation in crime rates. After reviewing 122 known field tests, Manzi found that only 20 percent demonstrated positive results for specific crime-fighting strategies, and none of those positive results were replicated in follow-up studies.

Did Lead Make You Dumber?

Even low levels have a significant effect.

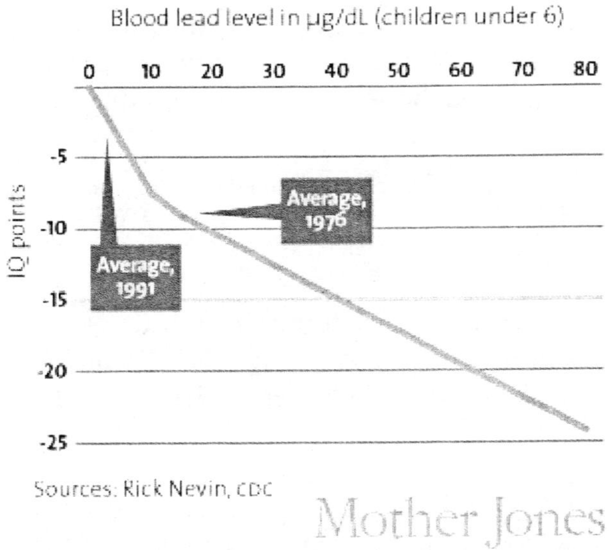

So we're back to square one. More prisons might help control crime, more cops might help, and better policing might help. But the evidence is thin for any of these as the main cause. What are we missing?

Experts often suggest that crime resembles an epidemic. But what kind? Karl Smith, a professor of public economics and government at the University of North Carolina-Chapel Hill, has a good rule of thumb for categorizing epidemics: If it spreads along lines of communication, he says, the cause is information. Think Bieber Fever. If it travels along major transportation routes, the cause is microbial. Think influenza. If it spreads out like a fan, the cause is an insect. Think malaria. But if it's everywhere, all at once—as both the rise of crime in the '60s and '70s and the fall of crime in the '90s seemed to be—the cause is a molecule.

A molecule? That sounds crazy. What molecule could be responsible for a steep and sudden decline in violent crime?

Well, here's one possibility: $Pb(CH_2CH_3)_4$.

In 1994, Rick Nevin was a consultant working for the US Department of Housing and Urban Development on the costs and benefits of removing lead paint from old houses. This has been a topic of intense study because of the growing body of research linking lead exposure in small children with a whole raft of complications later in life, including lower IQ, hyperactivity, behavioral problems, and learning disabilities.

But as Nevin was working on that assignment, his client suggested they might be missing something. A recent study had suggested a link between childhood lead exposure and juvenile delinquency later on. Maybe reducing lead exposure had an effect on violent crime too?

That tip took Nevin in a different direction. The biggest source of lead in the postwar era, it turns out, wasn't paint. It was leaded gasoline. And if you chart the rise and fall of atmospheric lead caused by the rise and fall of leaded gasoline consumption, you get a pretty simple upside-down U: Lead emissions from tailpipes rose steadily from the early '40s through the early '70s, nearly quadrupling over that period. Then, as unleaded gasoline began to replace leaded gasoline, emissions plummeted.

Gasoline lead may explain as much as 90 percent of the rise and fall of violent crime over the past half century.

Intriguingly, violent crime rates followed the same upside-down U pattern. The only thing different was the time period: Crime rates rose dramatically in the '60s through the '80s, and then began dropping steadily starting in the early '90s. The two curves looked eerily identical, but were offset by about 20 years.

So Nevin dove in further, digging up detailed data on lead emissions and crime rates to see if the similarity of the curves was as good as it seemed. It turned out to be even better: In a 2000 paper (PDF) he concluded that if you add a lag time of 23 years, lead emissions from automobiles explain 90 percent of the variation in violent crime in America. Toddlers who ingested high levels of lead in the '40s and '50s really were more likely to become violent criminals in the '60s, '70s, and '80s.

And with that we have our molecule: tetraethyl lead, the gasoline additive invented by General Motors in the 1920s to prevent knocking and pinging in high-performance engines. As auto sales boomed after World War II, and drivers in powerful new cars increasingly asked service station attendants to "fill 'er up with ethyl," they were unwittingly creating a crime wave two decades later.

It was an exciting conjecture, and it prompted an immediate wave of…nothing. Nevin's paper was almost completely ignored, and in one sense it's easy to see why—Nevin is an economist, not a criminologist, and his paper was published in *Environmental Research*, not a journal with a big readership in the criminology community. What's more, a single correlation between two curves isn't all that impressive, econometrically speaking. Sales of vinyl LPs rose in the postwar period too, and then declined in the '80s and '90s. Lots of things follow a pattern like that. So no matter how good the fit, if you only have a single correlation it might just be a coincidence. You need to do something more to establish causality.

As it turns out, however, a few hundred miles north someone was doing just that. In the late '90s, Jessica Wolpaw Reyes was a graduate student at Harvard casting around for a dissertation topic that eventually became a study she published in 2007 as a public health policy professor at Amherst. "I learned about lead because I was pregnant and living in old housing in Harvard Square," she told me, and after attending a talk where future *Freakonomics* star Levitt outlined his abortion/crime theory, she started thinking about lead and crime. Although the association seemed plausible, she wanted to find out whether increased lead exposure *caused* increases in crime. But how?

In states where consumption of leaded gasoline declined slowly, crime declined slowly. Where it declined quickly, crime declined quickly.

The answer, it turned out, involved "several months of cold calling" to find lead emissions data at the state level. During the '70s and '80s, the introduction of the catalytic converter, combined with increasingly stringent Environmental Protection Agency rules, steadily reduced the amount of leaded gasoline used in America, but Reyes discovered that this reduction wasn't uniform. In fact, use of leaded gasoline varied widely among states, and this gave Reyes the opening she needed. If childhood lead exposure really did produce criminal behavior in adults, you'd expect that in states where consumption of leaded gasoline declined slowly, crime would decline slowly too. Conversely, in states where it declined quickly, crime would decline quickly. And that's exactly what she found.

Meanwhile, Nevin had kept busy as well, and in 2007 he published a new paper looking at crime trends around the world (PDF). This way, he could make sure the close match he'd found between the lead curve and the crime curve wasn't just a coincidence. Sure, maybe the real culprit in the United States was something else happening at the exact same time, but what are the odds of that same something happening at several *different* times in several *different* countries?

Nevin collected lead data and crime data for Australia and found a close match. Ditto for Canada. And Great Britain and Finland and France and Italy and New Zealand and West

Germany. Every time, the two curves fit each other astonishingly well. When I spoke to Nevin about this, I asked him if he had ever found a country that didn't fit the theory. "No," he replied. "Not one."

Just this year, Tulane University researcher Howard Mielke published a paper with demographer Sammy Zahran on the correlation of lead and crime at the city level. They studied six US cities that had both good crime data and good lead data going back to the '50s, and they found a good fit in every single one. In fact, Mielke has even studied lead concentrations at the *neighborhood* level in New Orleans and shared his maps with the local police. "When they overlay them with crime maps," he told me, "they realize they match up."

Location, Location, Location

In New Orleans, lead levels can vary dramatically from one neighborhood to the next—and the poorest neighborhoods tend to be the worst hit.

Sources: Howard Mielke, US Census

Mother Jones

Sources: Howard Mielke, US Census

Maps by Karen Minot

Put all this together and you have an astonishing body of evidence. We now have studies at the international level, the national level, the state level, the city level, and even the individual level. Groups of children have been followed from the womb to adulthood, and higher childhood blood lead levels are consistently associated with <u>higher adult arrest rates for violent crimes</u>. All of these studies tell the same story: Gasoline lead is responsible for a good share of the rise and fall of violent crime over the past half century.

When differences of atmospheric lead density between big and small cities largely went away, so did the difference in murder rates.

Like many good theories, the gasoline lead hypothesis helps explain some things we might not have realized even needed explaining. For example, murder rates have always been higher in big cities than in towns and small cities. We're so used to this that it seems unsurprising, but Nevin points out that it might actually have a surprising explanation—because big cities have lots of cars in a small area, they also had high densities of atmospheric lead during the postwar era. But as lead levels in gasoline decreased, the differences between big and small cities largely went away. And guess what? The difference in murder rates went away too. Today, homicide rates are <u>similar in cities of all sizes</u>. It may be that violent crime isn't an inevitable consequence of being a big city after all.

The gasoline lead story has another virtue too: It's the only hypothesis that persuasively explains both the rise of crime in the '60s and '70s and its fall beginning in the '90s. Two other theories— the baby boom demographic bulge and the drug explosion of the '60s—at least have the potential to explain both, but neither one fully fits the known data. Only gasoline lead, with its dramatic rise and fall following World War II, can explain the equally dramatic rise and fall in violent crime.

Unit 4 – Illegal Drugs and Prostitution

CHAPTER 6

Sex, Booze, and Drugs

Before 1914, cocaine was legal in this country. Today it is not. Alcoholic beverages are legal in the United States today. From 1920 to 1933, they were not. Prostitution is legal in Nevada today. In the other 49 states, it is not.[1] All these goods—sex, booze, and drugs—have at least one thing in common: The consumption of each brings together a willing seller with a willing buyer, creating an act of mutually beneficial exchange (at least in the opinion of the parties involved). Partly because of this property, attempts to proscribe the consumption of these goods have met with less than spectacular success and have yielded some peculiar patterns of production, distribution, and usage. Let's see why.

SUPPLY-SIDE ENFORCEMENT

When the government seeks to prevent voluntary exchange, it must generally decide whether to go after the seller or the buyer. In most cases (and certainly where sex, booze, and drugs are concerned), the government targets sellers, because this is where the authorities get the most benefit from their enforcement dollars. A cocaine dealer, even a small retail pusher, often supplies dozens or even hundreds of users each day, as did speakeasies (illegal saloons) during Prohibition; a hooker typically services three to ten "tricks" per day. By incarcerating the supplier, the police can prevent several, or even several hundred, transactions from taking place, which is usually much more cost-effective than going after the buyers one by one. It is not that the police ignore the consumers of illegal goods. Indeed, sting operations, in which the police pose as illicit sellers, often make the headlines. Nevertheless, most enforcement efforts focus on the supply side, and so shall we.

Law enforcement activities directed against the suppliers of illegal goods increase the suppliers' operating costs. The risks of fines, jail sentences, and possibly even violence become part of the costs of doing business and must be taken into account by existing and potential suppliers. Some entrepreneurs will leave the business, turning their talents to other activities. Others will resort to clandestine (and costly) means to hide their operations from the police. Still others will restrict the circle of buyers with whom they are willing to deal to minimize the chances that a customer is a cop. Across the board, the costs of operation are higher, and at any given price, less of the product will be available. There is a reduction in supply, and the result is a higher price for the good.

This increase in price is, in a sense, exactly what the enforcement officials are after, for the consumers of sex, booze, and drugs behave according to the **law of demand:** The higher the price of a good, the lower the amount consumed. So the immediate impact of the enforcement efforts against sellers is to reduce the consumption of the illegal good. There are, however, some other effects.

VIOLENCE EMERGES

First, because the good in question is illegal, people who have a **comparative advantage** in conducting illegal activities will be attracted to the business of supplying (and perhaps demanding) the good. Some may have an existing criminal record and are relatively unconcerned about adding to it. Others may have developed skills in evading detection and prosecution while engaged in other criminal activities. Some may simply look at the illegal activity as another means of thumbing their noses at society. The general point is when an activity is made illegal, people who are good at being criminals are attracted to that activity.

Illegal contracts are usually not enforceable through legal channels (even if they were, few suppliers of illegal goods would be foolish enough to complain to the police about not being paid for their products). Thus, buyers and sellers of illegal goods must frequently resort to private methods of contract enforcement, which often entails violence.[2]

---

1 These statements are not entirely correct. Even today, cocaine may be obtained legally by prescription from a physician. Prostitution in Nevada is legal only in counties that have chosen to permit it. Finally, some counties in the United States remain "dry," prohibiting the sale of beer, wine, and distilled spirits.

2 Fundamentally, violence—such as involuntary incarceration—also plays a key role in the government's enforcement of legal contracts. We often do not think of it as violence, of course, because it is usually cushioned by constitutional safeguards and procedural rules.

Hence, people who are relatively good at violence are attracted to illegal activities and have greater **incentives** to employ their talents. This is one reason why the murder rate in America rose to record levels during Prohibition and then dropped sharply when liquor was again made legal. It also helps explain why the number of drug-related murders soared during the 1980s and why drive-by shootings became commonplace in many drug-infested cities. The Thompson submachine gun of the 1930s and the MAC-10 machine gun of the 1980s were just low-cost means of contract enforcement.

Usage Changes

The attempts of law enforcement officials to drive sellers of illegal goods out of business have another effect. Based on recent wholesale prices, $300,000 worth of pure heroin weighs about 10 pounds, while $300,000 worth of marijuana weighs about 200 pounds. As any drug smuggler can tell you, hiding 10 pounds of contraband is a lot easier than hiding 200 pounds. Thus, to avoid detection and prosecution, suppliers of the illegal good have an incentive to deal in the more valuable versions of their product, which for drugs and booze mean the more potent versions. Bootleggers during Prohibition concentrated on hard liquor rather than on beer and wine. Even today, moonshine typically has roughly twice the alcohol content of legal hard liquor such as bourbon, scotch, or vodka. After narcotics became illegal in this country in 1914, importers switched from the milder opium to its more valuable and more potent derivative, heroin.

The move to the more potent versions of illegal commodities is enhanced by enforcement activities directed against users. Not only do users, like suppliers, find it easier (cheaper) to hide the more potent versions, but there is also a change in relative prices due to user penalties. Typically, the law has lower penalties for using an illegal substance than for distributing it. Within each category (use or sale), however, there is commonly the same penalty regardless of value per unit. For example, during Prohibition, a bottle of wine and a bottle of more expensive, more potent hard liquor were equally illegal. Today, the possession of 1 gram of 90 percent pure cocaine brings the same penalty as the possession of 1 gram of 10 percent pure cocaine. Given the physical quantities, there is a fixed cost (the legal penalty) associated with being caught, regardless of value per unit (and thus potency) of the substance. Hence, the structure of legal penalties raises the relative price of less potent versions, encouraging users to substitute more potent versions—heroin instead of opium, hashish instead of marijuana, and hard liquor instead of beer.

Penalties against users also encourage a change in the nature of usage. Before 1914, cocaine was legal in this country and was used openly as a mild stimulant, much as people today use caffeine. (Cocaine was even an ingredient in the original formulation of Coca-Cola.) This type of usage—small, regular doses over long time intervals—becomes relatively more expensive when the substance is made illegal. Extensive usage (small doses spread over time) is more likely to be detected by the authorities than intensive usage (a large dose consumed at once), simply because possession time is longer and the drug must be accessed more frequently. Thus, when a substance is made illegal, there is an incentive for consumers to switch toward more intensive usage. Rather than ingesting cocaine orally in the form of a highly diluted liquid solution, as was commonly done before 1914, people switched to snorting or injecting it. During Prohibition, people dispensed with cocktails before dinner each night; instead, on the less frequent occasions when they drank, they more often drank to get drunk. The same phenomenon is observed today. People under the age of 21 consume alcoholic beverages less frequently than people over the age of 21. But when they do drink, they are more likely to drink to get drunk. Binge drinking becomes the norm.

Information Costs Rise

Not surprisingly, the suppliers of illegal commodities are reluctant to advertise their wares openly; the police are as capable of reading billboards and watching TV as potential customers are. Suppliers are also reluctant to establish easily recognized identities and regular places and hours of business because to do so raises the chance of being caught by the police. Information about the price and quality of products being sold goes underground, often with unfortunate effects for consumers.

With legal goods, consumers have several means of obtaining information. They can learn from friends, advertisements, and personal experience. When goods are legal, they can be trademarked for identification. The trademark cannot legally be copied and the courts protect it. Given such easily identified brands, consumers can be made aware of the quality and price of each. If their experience does not meet expectations, they can assure themselves of no further contact with the unsatisfactory product by never buying that brand again.

When a general class of products becomes illegal, there are fewer ways to obtain information. Brand names are no longer protected by law, so falsification of well-known brands ensues. When products do not meet expectations, it is more difficult (costly) for consumers to punish suppliers. Frequently, the result is degradation of and uncertainty about product quality. The consequences for consumers of the illegal goods are often unpleasant and sometimes fatal.

DANGEROUS SEX

Consider prostitution. In Nevada counties where prostitution is legal, the prostitutes are required to register with the local authorities, and they generally conduct their business in well-established bordellos. These establishments advertise openly and rely heavily on repeat business. Health officials test the prostitutes weekly for venereal disease and monthly for HIV (the virus that causes AIDS). Contrast this with other areas of the country, where prostitution is illegal. Suppliers are generally streetwalkers, because a fixed, physical location is too easy for the police to detect and raid. They change locations frequently to reduce harassment by police. Repeat business is reported to be minimal. Frequently, customers have never seen the prostitute before and never will again.

The difference in outcomes is striking. In Nevada, the spread of venereal disease by legal prostitutes is estimated to be almost nonexistent. To date, none of the registered prostitutes in Nevada has tested positive for HIV. By contrast, in some major cities outside Nevada, the incidence of venereal disease among prostitutes is estimated to be near 100 percent. In Miami, one study found that 19 percent of all incarcerated prostitutes tested positive for HIV. In Newark, New Jersey, 52 percent of the prostitutes tested were infected with the AIDS virus, and about half of the prostitutes in Washington, D.C., and New York City are also believed to be carrying the AIDS virus. Due to the lack of reliable information in markets for illegal goods, customers frequently do not know exactly what they are getting. As a result, they sometimes get more than they bargained for.

DEADLY DRUGS AND BAD BOOZE

Consider alcohol and drugs. Today, alcoholic beverages are heavily advertised to establish their brand names and are carried by reputable dealers. Customers can readily punish suppliers for any deviation from the expected potency or quality by withdrawing their business, telling their friends, or even bringing a lawsuit. Similar circumstances prevailed before 1914 in this country for the hundreds of products containing opium or cocaine.

During Prohibition, consumers of alcohol often did not know exactly what they were buying or where to find the supplier the next

day if they were dissatisfied. Fly-by-night operators sometimes adulterated liquor with far more lethal methyl alcohol. In tiny concentrations, this made watered-down booze taste like it had more kick, but in only slightly higher concentrations, the methyl alcohol blinded or even killed the unsuspecting consumer. Even in "reputable" speakeasies (those likely to be in business at the same location the next day), bottles bearing the labels of high-priced foreign whiskeys were refilled repeatedly with locally (and illegally) produced rotgut until their labels wore off.

In the 1970s, more than one purchaser of what was reputed to be high-potency Panama Red or Acapulco gold marijuana ended up with low-potency pot heavily loaded with stems, seeds, and maybe even oregano. Buyers of cocaine must worry not only about how much the product has been cut along the distribution chain, but also about what has been used to cut it. In recent years, the purity of cocaine at the retail level has ranged between 10 and 95 percent; for heroin, the degree of purity has ranged from 5 to 50 percent. Cutting agents can turn out to be any of various sugars, local anesthetics, or amphetamines; on occasion, rat poison has been used.

We noted earlier that the legal penalties for the users of illegal goods encourage them to use more potent forms and to use them more intensively. These facts and the uncertain quality and potency of the illegal products yield a deadly combination. During Prohibition, the death rate from acute alcohol poisoning (due to overdose) was more than 30 times higher than today. In 1927 alone, 12,000 people died from acute alcohol poisoning, and many thousands more were blinded or killed by contaminated booze. Today, about 8,000 people per year die as a direct result of consuming either cocaine or heroin. Of that total, it is estimated, roughly 80 percent die from either an overdose caused by an unexpectedly potent product or an adverse reaction to the material used to cut the drug. Clearly, caveat emptor ("let the buyer beware") is a warning to be taken seriously if one is consuming an illegal product.

SUCCESS IS LIMITED

We noted at the beginning of this chapter that one of the effects of making a good illegal is to raise its price. One might well ask, "by how much?" During the early 1990s, the federal government was spending about $2 billion per year in its efforts to stop the importation of cocaine from Colombia. One study concluded that these efforts had hiked the price of cocaine by 4 percent relative to what it would have been, had the federal government done nothing to interdict cocaine imports. The study estimated that the cost of raising the price of cocaine an additional 2 percent would be $1 billion per year. More recently, Nobel Laureate Gary Becker and his colleagues have estimated that America's war on drugs costs at least $100 billion per year. And the results? The prices of heroin and cocaine are at record-low levels.

The government's efforts to halt imports of marijuana have had some success, presumably because marijuana is easier to detect than cocaine. Nevertheless, suppliers have responded by cultivating marijuana domestically instead of importing it or by bringing it in across the relatively open U.S.–Canadian border rather than from elsewhere. The net effect has been an estimated tenfold increase in potency due to the superior farming techniques available in this country and Canada, as well as the use of genetic bioengineering to improve strains.

A few years ago, most states and the federal government began restricting sales of cold medicines containing pseudoephedrine, because that ingredient was widely used for making the illegal stimulant methamphetamine in home laboratories. The restrictions succeeded in reducing home production of "meth." They also led to a huge increase in imports of a far more potent version of meth from Mexico. Overall, it is estimated that neither consumption of nor addiction to methamphetamine was reduced by the restrictions. But overdoses from the drug rose sharply because of the greater purity of the imports. Moreover, the "shake-and-bake" method of domestic production that arose after the crackdown on cold medicines had an unintended and often fatal consequence. The mixing process often goes wrong, and when it does, the ensuing explosion causes horrific and sometimes fatal burns of the head and upper torso. Many emergency rooms and hospital burn centers have been overwhelmed by these casualties.

Consider also the government's efforts to eliminate the consumption of alcohol during the 1920s and 1930s. They failed so badly that the Eighteenth Amendment, which put Prohibition in place, was the first (and so far the only) constitutional amendment ever to be repealed. As for prostitution, it is reputed to be "the oldest profession" and by all accounts continues to flourish today, even in Newark and Miami.

The government's inability to halt the consumption of sex, booze, or drugs does not mean that its efforts have failed. Indeed, the impact of these efforts is manifested in their consequences, ranging from tainted drugs and alcohol to disease-ridden prostitutes. The message instead is that when the government attempts to prevent mutually beneficial exchange, even its best efforts are unlikely to meet with spectacular success.

DISCUSSION QUESTIONS

1. From an economic perspective, is it possible for laws restricting dangerous or destructive activity to be *too* strict? Explain. (*Hint:* Revisit Chapter 3.)

2. In recent years, more than 15 states have passed so-called medical marijuana laws. Typically, these laws permit individuals to lawfully purchase marijuana from licensed stores, provided they have letter from their doctor recommending its use. Use the reasoning in this chapter to predict how the characteristics of medical marijuana will differ from illegal marijuana. Focus specifically on price, quality, variety, and consistency (or predictability).

3. The federal government currently taxes alcohol on the basis of the 100-proof gallon. (Alcohol that is 100 proof is 50 percent pure ethyl alcohol; most hard liquor sold is 80 proof, or 40 percent ethyl alcohol, whereas wine is usually about 24 proof, and most beer is 6–10 proof.) How would alcohol consumption patterns change if the government taxed alcohol strictly on the basis of volume rather than also taking its potency into account?

4. During Prohibition, some speakeasy operators paid bribes to ensure that the police did not raid them. Would you expect the quality of the liquor served in such speakeasies to be higher or lower than in those that did not pay bribes? Would you expect to find differences (e.g., in income levels) between the customers patronizing the two types of speakeasies?

5. The markets for prostitution in Nevada and New Jersey have two important differences: (i) prostitutes in New Jersey face higher costs because of government efforts to prosecute them and (ii) customers in New Jersey face higher risks of contracting diseases from prostitutes because the illegal nature of the business makes reliable information about product quality much more costly to obtain. Given these facts, in which state would you expect the price of prostitution services to be higher? Which state would have the higher amount of services consumed (adjusted for population differences)? Explain your answer.

6. According to the Surgeon General of the United States, nicotine is the most addictive drug known to humanity, and cigarette smoking kills perhaps 300,000–400,000 people per year in the United States. Why then isn't tobacco illegal in America?

ca.news.yahoo.com

What is and is not legal under Canada's new prostitution laws

Matt Coutts

Carol Leigh, a long-time sex worker and advocate for decriminalizing prostitution, poses for a photograph in her office in San Francisco, California July 18, 2014. Calls by Bay Area sex workers for decriminalizing "consensual" prostitution have been spurred anew following the FBI seizure of a West Coast sex services website that prosecutors say hooked up clients with prostitutes and which sex workers saw as a vital forum to screen dangerous clients. Picture taken July 18, 2014. To match Feature USA-SEXWORKERS/SANFRANCISCO REUTERS/Robert Galbraith

(UNITED STATES - Tags: POLITICS CRIME LAW SOCIETY TPX IMAGES OF THE DAY)

Canada's new prostitution laws went into effect over the weekend, and already they are prompting concern and doubt. And confusion — always good when you're at risk of jail time if you don't understand the law.

The Protection of Communities and Exploited Persons Act, which replaces former laws that have been shot down as unconstitutional by the Supreme Court, are meant to give sex workers the ability to protect themselves, and create avenues to help get them out of the industry.

But those on the ground have complained that they still can't tell what is legal and what is not.

"The rules and regulations are still hazy," Cameron Diablo, a Victoria, B.C. sex worker, told the *Victoria Times Colonist.*

"We're unsure about licensing, legality, if we live near schools but work indoors, landlord-tenant regulations with the new law, advertising. The list is endless with the detailed questions my group of colleagues and I have come up with."

It is not a great sign for a set of laws that were written with the intention of clarifying the murky legality of the sex industry in Canada.

Prostitution is legal in Canada, but the country's former set of laws made almost everything around it illegal. The Supreme Court of Canada shot down those laws last year, calling them unconstitutional, and gave the government one year to replace them.

Justice Minister Peter MacKay unveiled the Protection of Communities and Exploited Persons Act earlier this year, which criminalizes buying sex, profiting from the sale of sex, and third-party advertising.

The changes were not well received. Several groups and agencies, including the Canadian AIDS Society and the Native Women's Resource Centre, continue to oppose the new laws.

Ontario Premier Kathleen Wynne says she has asked the province's attorney general to investigate the laws and advise her on their "constitutional validity."

"I am not an expert, and I am not a lawyer, but as premier of this province, I am concerned that this legislation (now the law of the land) will not make sex workers safer," reads Wynne's statement.

Regardless of the confusion and opposition, the bill is now law, and the country's sex industry is bound by them.

So let's take a look at what is legal, illegal and up for debate under the Protection of Communities and Exploited Persons Act:

IT IS LEGAL to communicate with the intention of selling sex, in some circumstances. This is a key change from the previous laws, which made it illegal to negotiate the sale of sex at any time. The change arguably fulfills a key concern raised by the Supreme Court ruling.

IT IS ILLEGAL to sell sex near any area where a person under 18 years of age could reasonably be expected to be present. Notably, school grounds, playgrounds or day care centres. The government says the change balances the Supreme Court's concerns while keeping children from being exposed to prostitution. Opponents say the provision forces sex workers into dangerous and isolated areas which will limit their ability to screen clients and negotiate terms.

IT IS ILLEGAL to purchase sexual services. Or communicate with the intention of buying sex. This is punishable with up to five years in jail and fines that begin at $500 an increase with subsequent offences. Fines double if it is done anywhere kids may be present.

The government says criminalizing those who "create a demand for prostitution" limits the lure for sex workers. Opponents say criminalizing these exchanges push them underground and therefore make the situation more dangerous for sex workers. The Pivot Legal Society says the provision "violates the security of the person rights of sex workers."

IT IS LEGAL, technically, to advertise your own services. Sex workers receive an "immunity" from advertising laws. Though in-person negotiations are subject to the rules above and advertising through media channels, well…

IT IS ILLEGAL to advertise the sale of others' sexual services. It cracks down on back-of-magazine as well as online ads. It targets those who would run the ads, and could extend to publishers and website administrators.

The government argues that such advertisements create a demand for prostitution. Opponents argue that limiting a sex worker's ability to advertise forces her onto the street and would probably be found unconstitutional by Canadian courts.

IT IS ILLEGAL to financially benefit from the sale of sex. This provision makes it illegal to run a business that sells sexual services – such as escort agencies, massage parlours, etc.

IT IS LEGAL to receive financial benefit, or at least the above law does not apply, for those in "legitimate living arrangements" or with "legal or moral obligations" to sex workers. This clarification to the previous law allows sex workers to conduct their own personal affairs. Like anyone else, they can support their children, spouses and roommates. They can hire accountants and pay for security services. However, a "pimp" would not fall under those exemptions.

The Pivot Legal Society says, however, that many of the changes introduced by the federal government have been misrepresented. While the changes are said to offer safety for sex workers, they actually "result in sweeping criminalization of the sex industry, targeting sex workers, clients, and third parties."

The result will not be safer and more secure working conditions, as was requested by the Supreme Court, and will instead make things more difficult, and more dangerous in some cases.

Police in British Columbia have indicated that the new bill will not have a major impact on how they handle the sex trade. Still, some 60 groups are calling for the laws to be repealed. The Toronto Sex Workers' Action Project is calling for decriminalization entirely.

That's not likely to happen. Legal challenges, however, are inevitable. Until then, sex workers are best to read up on what is legal, and what currently is not.

NEWS

Barely illegal: New prostitution laws may drive sex work underground — but can it stop it?

RICHARD WARNICA | May 7, 2015 | Last Updated: May 8 10:21 PM ET
More from Richard Warnica

Republish
Reprint

ex trade work is illegal ... but will it be for much longer?

THE CANADIAN PRESS/Jonathan Hayward /Files

Barely illegal: Canada's vice laws have undergone radical change in the last few years — but it hasn't necessarily affected how Canadians, and the police, behave. In a two-part package, National Post *looks at enforcement (or the lack thereof) around marijuana and prostitution and what it means for the future.*

Raven" sells herself online as "classy, genuine and discreet." She takes "donations" for her time: $160 for 30 minutes or $220 for a ull hour. She can be a "sweet innocent girl," she wrote in a recent posting, "or the one to fulfill all your fantasies." But if you don't ke tattoos, she added, she's not the one for you.

aven, a name she uses professionally, started selling sex in Winnipeg about a year ago. "It's something I enjoy," she says. She isn't rafficked. She wasn't forced into it. She likes the people she meets. "There's nothing wrong with it," she says. "I'm not hurting nybody."

n the last several months, though, Raven, 33, has noticed small changes cropping up in her industry. Clients are becoming more autious, she believes, and advertising more discreet. Online posts — once quite explicit — are slipping into euphemism. "Everything as a to be a lot more quiet now and underground," she says. "People are worried about being busted."

Four months after the federal government brought into force new laws aimed at ending prostitution in this country, the vast grey market for sexual services in Canada remains, unsurprisingly, intact. From Halifax to Victoria and everywhere in between, sex is still being bought and sold in Canada, according to sex workers, police departments, researchers, and common sense.

But that doesn't mean the industry itself hasn't shifted in response to the laws. More importantly, it doesn't mean the problems that prompted the legal change in the first place have gone away.

In interviews with the *National Post*, sex workers in five cities across Canada, all contacted through a popular sexual services website and identified here by their work names, said uncertainty over the new regulations has pushed some clients away and made business harder for them in other ways.

"What's changed is that we're not getting new customers," says "Nicole," 39, who sells sex from her apartment in Toronto. "I used to make quite a bit of money, less now because I think a lot of clients are afraid to call us."

What's changed is that we're not getting new customers. I used to make quite a bit of money, less now because I think a lot of clients are afraid to call us

The new legislation, the *Protection of Communities and Exploited Persons Act*, or just Bill C-36, was the Conservative government's response to Supreme Court's ruling in the "Bedford" case.

In that landmark decision, brought down in 2013, Canada's highest court tossed out several criminal code provisions related to the sale of sex on the grounds they violated sex workers rights to security under the Charter. The court suspended that ruling for 12 months, however, giving the federal government time to craft a new set of, in some ways, even more restrictive laws around sex work.

Bill C-36, for the first time in Canada, explicitly outlawed the buying, but not the selling of sex. It also gave police new powers to prosecute those who advertise sex work and those who exploit or otherwise make money off sex workers in all but a few limited cases.

The explicit goal of the legislation, outlined in a justice department position paper, was to reduce the demand for prostitution by "discouraging entry into it, deterring participation in it and ultimately abolishing it to the greatest extent possible."

MARTIN OESER/AFP/Getty Images

On one, limited, level, that strategy appears to be working. "I think it's changed for the guys since the law's changed," says "Stacy," who works in a massage parlour in Edmonton. "There's one guy I know, he'll only see a girl he's seen before, whereas before he'd go on Back Page [the Kijiji of escort ads] and go and see whoever."

But if, in the short term, some sex buyers are shying away under the new regime, Chris Atchison, a research associate at the University of Victoria, doesn't expect it to last. Atchison, who has spent almost 20 years studying men who buy sex, says what we're seeing now is basically what happens anytime there's any change to the laws around sex work.

Really what we see is initially a lot of fear," he says. Clients become more cautious as they try to gauge the police reaction and the new risks. But the market doesn't go away in the long run.

I've seen it in these various [online] forums," he says. People say they're retiring from "the hobby," as they call it, or taking a break. But I don't think these people ever quit," Atchison says. "They'll walk away long enough to figure out: 'How can I do this safely?'" But eventually, most, if not all of them, will be back.

For Atchison, the worry is that, as the industry recalibrates, it will reform in ways that are less open and thus less safe for sex workers and clients alike. One key risk, he believes, is that, by criminalizing the purchase of sex, the government has created a powerful disincentive for Johns to come forward if they see someone being abused or forced into the trade.

It's not an abstract fear. The Toronto Police Service is currently in the midst of a large-scale crackdown on human trafficking. In two recent high profile busts, investigators were tipped off by Johns, says Detective Sgt. Nunzio Tramontozzi, the head of the department's human trafficking division.

A lot of these girls, what happens is the guys will say that they're 19 or 20 or 21," Tramontozzi says. "But when [the Johns] get to them in the hotel room, they can actually see that they're a lot younger. They're way too young. And they'll say, listen, I'm leaving, but I'm going to the police."

But when [the Johns] get to them in the hotel room, they can actually see that they're a lot younger. They're way too young. And they'll say, listen, I'm leaving, but I'm going to the police

Atchinson says that, under the new laws, that may be less likely to happen. In one recent survey, he asked Johns if they'd report abuse if they saw it. Many would, he said. But among those who wouldn't, the number one reason they gave was fear of arrest or exposure.

Not every sex worker who spoke to the *Post* has seen their business change since the new laws came in. One woman, a grandmother who operates professionally under the name "Submissive Rose" — mostly out of Mississauga hotel rooms — says she and her clients are too discreet to attract much notice.

I'm a bit of an anomaly, because I'm older," she says. "I came into this recently with my eyes wide open."

What seems to exist more than anything among the women interviewed for this story is uncertainty over what exactly the new laws mean and how police plan to enforce them. But police departments contacted across the country indicate little or no change – so far.

In Winnipeg, the police department had already shifted its enforcement focus toward the "wellbeing of women in the sex trade," in 2013, Sgt. Cam Mackid said in an email. That hasn't changed under the new regime. The department will still only charge sex trade workers "as a last resort," Mackid wrote. Instead, investigators focus on anyone "exploiting women:" from traffickers to pimps and Johns.

It's a similar story in Toronto, where the department had already beefed up the number of officers in the human trafficking division last year. Nunzio says investigators have charged individual pimps under the new advertising laws, but otherwise, so far, not much has changed. They are in talks with the Crown about going after websites and newspapers that host sex ads, but "there's no plan in place as of yet" to lay charges, Nunzio says.

In Edmonton, investigators have employed the new advertising laws, but otherwise haven't altered their sex work strategy, says department spokesman Scott Pattison.

In Victoria, too, the "new laws have not changed how we deal with street workers in our jurisdiction," says Const. Mike Russell. "Our approach is one of working collaboratively with outreach agencies and the workers themselves to ensure their safety."

That attitude reflects a sea change in policing in some Canadian cities that predates the Bill C-36 era, says Cecilia Benoit, a professor of Sociology at the University of Victoria and one of the lead researchers behind Understanding Sex Work, perhaps the most comprehensive academic study on the topic ever undertaken in Canada. Benoit worries that, with the new laws, some of that progress — the bridge-building between sex workers and police — might be lost.

Even if it remains static, though, if things stay largely the same under the new laws as they were under the old, there are risks. The Bedford decision did not emerge from a vacuum. The challenge to Canada's old prostitution laws came for several reasons, but the most important one was this: sex trade workers in Canada have, for decades, been subject to horrific levels of violence.

Emily Symons, representing a group called Power, leave Osgoode Hall in Toronto, Ontario, Thursday, June 16, 2011.   Tyler Anderson/National Post

ANOEK DE GROOT/AFP/Getty Images/Files

In one study Benoit conducted, 24% of sex trade workers indicated they had been attacked on the job; 19% said someone had forced or attempted to force them into sex. Robert Pickton, the most prolific serial killer in Canadian history, murdered sex trade workers with impunity for years in B.C. before the police deigned to take notice.

And while many advocates believe policing of the sex trade has improved dramatically in the years since Pickton operated, sex trade workers are still vulnerable in Canada. Cindy Gladue, an Edmonton escort, bled to death from a vaginal wound after sex with a client in 2011. (The client, Bradley Barton, was acquitted of first-degree murder; the Crown has appealed.) Warren Mann, a client, beat Gail Brown, an escort in Ontario, nearly to death in 2012. He was convicted of attempted murder in her case last week.

Rates of workplace violence for sex work are actually lower than they are for several other professions, including emergency room nursing, as Benoit writes in a recent analysis published by the Canadian Institutes for Health Research on Thursday.

What is clear, though, according to the women who spoke for this article and to organizations that work with sex workers in Canada, is that the new laws, despite their focus on buyers not sellers, aren't making things any safer.

"Sex workers are still being quite endangered," says Brenda Belak, the sex work campaign lawyer at the Pivot Legal Society in Vancouver. "They're still feeling that they have to do things in a covert manner to avoid police contact because their clients want to avoid police contact."

"You can't be as open and upfront as before," agrees Raven. "This new law," adds Nicole, "sucks."

◯ Follow

HOW IS A STREET PROSTITUTE LIKE A DEPARTMENT-STORE SANTA?

One afternoon not long ago, on a welcoming cool day toward the end of summer, a twenty-nine-year-old woman named LaSheena sat on the hood of an SUV outside the Dearborn Homes, a housing project on the South Side of Chicago. She had a beaten-down look in her eyes but otherwise seemed youthful, her pretty face framed by straightened hair. She was dressed in a baggy black-and-red tracksuit, the kind she'd worn since she was a kid. Her parents rarely had money for new clothes, so she used to get her male cousins' hand-me-downs, and the habit stuck.

LaSheena was talking about how she earns her living. She described four main streams of income: "boosting," "roosting," cutting hair, and turning tricks.

"Boosting," she explained, is shoplifting and selling the swag. "Roosting" means serving as a lookout for the local street gang that sells drugs. She gets $8 for a boy's haircut and $12 for a man's.

Which job is the worst of the four?

"Turning tricks," she says, with no hesitation.

Why?

"'Cause I don't really like men. I guess it bothers me mentally."

And what if prostitution paid twice as much?

"Would I do it more?" she asks. "Yeah!"

Throughout history, it has invariably been easier to be male than female. Yes, this is an overgeneralization and yes, there are exceptions, but by any important measure, women have had it rougher than men. Even though men handled most of the warfare, hunting, and brute-force labor, women had a shorter life expectancy. Some deaths were more senseless than others. Between the thirteenth and nineteenth centuries, as many as 1 million European women, most of them poor and many of them widowed, were executed for witchcraft, taking the blame for bad weather that killed crops.

Women have finally overtaken men in life expectancy, thanks mainly to medical improvements surrounding childbirth. In many countries, however, being female remains a serious handicap even in the twenty-first century. Young women in Cameroon have their breasts "ironed"—beaten or massaged by a wooden pestle or a heated coconut shell—to make them less sexually tempting. In China, foot binding has finally been done away with (after roughly one thousand years), but females are still far more likely than males to be abandoned after birth, to be illiterate, and to commit suicide. And women in rural India, as we wrote earlier, continue to face discrimination in just about every direction.

But especially in the world's developed nations, women's lives have improved dramatically. There is no comparing the prospects of a girl in twenty-first-century America or Britain or Japan with her counterpart from a century or two earlier. In any arena you look—education, legal and voting rights, career opportunities, and so on—it is far better to be a woman today than at any other point in history. In 1872, the earliest year for which such statistics are available, 21 percent of college students in the United States were female. Today, that number is 58 percent and rising. It has truly been a stunning ascendancy.

And yet there is still a considerable economic price to pay for being a woman. For American women twenty-five and older who hold at least a bachelor's degree and work full-time, the national median income is about $47,000. Similar men, meanwhile, make more than $66,000, a premium of 40 percent. The same is true even for women who attend the nation's elite universities. The economists Claudia Goldin and Lawrence Katz found that women who went to Harvard earned *less than half as much* as the average Harvard man. Even when the analysis included only full-time, full-year employees and controlled for college major, profession, and other variables, Goldin and Katz found that the Harvard women still earned about 30 percent less than their male counterparts.

What can possibly account for such a huge wage gap?

There are a variety of factors. Women are more likely to leave the workforce or downshift their careers to raise a family. Even within high-paying occupations like medicine and law, women tend to choose specialties that pay less (general practitioner, for instance, or in-house counsel). And there is likely still a good amount of discrimination. This may range from the overt—denying a woman a promotion purely because she is not a man—to the insidious. A considerable body of research has shown that overweight women suffer a greater wage penalty than overweight men. The same is true for women with bad teeth.

There are some biological wild cards as well. The economists Andrea Ichino and Enrico Moretti, analyzing personnel data from a large Italian bank, found that female employees under forty-five years old tended to miss work consistently on twenty-eight-day cycles. Plotting these absences against employee productivity ratings, the economists determined that this menstrual absenteeism accounted for 14 percent of the difference between female and male earnings at the bank.

Or consider the 1972 U.S. law known as Title IX. While broadly designed to prohibit sex discrimination in educational settings, Title IX also required high schools and colleges to bring their women's sports programs up to the level of their men's programs. Millions of young women subsequently joined these new programs, and as the economist Betsey Stevenson discovered, girls who play high-school sports are more likely to attend college and land a solid job, especially in some of the high-skill fields traditionally dominated by men. That's the good news.

But Title IX also brought some bad news for women. When the law was passed, more than 90 percent of college women's sports teams had female head coaches. Title IX boosted the appeal of such jobs: salaries rose and there was more exposure and excitement. Like the lowly peasant food that is "discovered" by the culinary elite and promptly migrates from roadside shacks into high-end restaurants, these jobs were soon snapped up by a new set of customers: men. These days, barely 40 percent of college women's sports teams are coached by women. Among the most visible coaching jobs in women's sports are those in the Women's National Basketball Association (WNBA), founded thirteen years ago as a corollary to the men's NBA. As of this writing, the WNBA

has 13 teams and just 6 of them—again, fewer than 50 percent—are coached by women. This is actually an improvement from the league's tenth anniversary season, when only 3 of the 14 coaches were women.

For all the progress women have made in the twenty-first-century labor market, the typical female would come out well ahead if she had simply had the foresight to be born male.

There *is* one labor market women have always dominated: prostitution.

Its business model is built upon a simple premise. Since time immemorial and all over the world, men have wanted more sex than they could get for free. So what inevitably emerges is a supply of women who, for the right price, are willing to satisfy this demand.

Today prostitution is generally illegal in the United States, albeit with a few exceptions and many inconsistencies in enforcement. In the early years of the nation, prostitution was frowned upon but not criminalized. It was during the Progressive Era, roughly from the 1890s to the 1920s, that this leniency ended. There was a public outcry against "white slavery," in which thousands of women were imprisoned against their will to work as prostitutes.

The white slavery problem turned out to be a wild exaggeration. The reality was perhaps scarier: rather than being forced into prostitution, women were choosing it for themselves. In the early 1910s, the Department of Justice conducted a census of 310 cities in 26 states to tally the number of prostitutes in the United States: "We arrive at the conservative figure of approximately 200,000 women in the regular army of vice."

At the time, the American population included 22 million women between the ages of fifteen and forty-four. If the DOJ numbers are to be believed, 1 of every 110 women in that age range was a prostitute. But most prostitutes, about 85 percent, were in their twenties. In that age range, 1 of every 50 American women was a prostitute.

The market was particularly strong in Chicago, which had more than a thousand known brothels. The mayor assembled a blue-ribbon Vice Commission, comprising religious leaders as well as civic, educational, legal, and medical authorities. Once they got their hands dirty, these good people realized they were up against an enemy even more venal than sex: economics.

"Is it any wonder," the commission declared, "that a tempted girl who receives only $6 per week working with her hands sells her body for $25 per week when she learns that there is demand for it and men are willing to pay the price?"

Converted into today's dollars, the $6-per-week shopgirl had an annual salary of only $6,500. The same woman who took up prostitution at $25 a week earned the modern equivalent of more than $25,000 a year. But the Vice Commission acknowledged that $25 per week was at the very low end of what Chicago prostitutes earned. A woman working in a "dollar house" (some brothels charged as little as 50 cents; others charged $5 or $10) took home an average weekly salary of $70, or the modern equivalent of about $76,000 annually.

At the heart of the Levee, the South Side neighborhood that housed block after block of brothels, stood the Everleigh Club, which the Vice Commission described as "the most famous and luxurious house of prostitution in the country." Its customers included business titans, politicians, athletes, entertainers, and even a few anti-prostitution crusaders. The Everleigh's prostitutes, known as "butterfly girls," were not only attractive, hygienic, and trustworthy, but also good conversationalists who could cite classical poetry if that's what floated a particular gentleman's boat. In the book *Sin in the Second City*, Karen Abbott reports that the Everleigh also offered sexual delicacies that weren't available elsewhere—"French" style, for instance, commonly known today as oral sex.

In an age when a nice dinner cost about $12 in today's currency, the Everleigh's customers were willing to pay the equivalent of $250 just to get into the club and $370 for a bottle of champagne. Relatively speaking, the sex was pretty cheap: about $1,250.

Ada and Minna Everleigh, the sisters who ran the brothel, guarded their assets carefully. Butterflies were provided with a healthful diet, excellent medical care, a well-rounded education, and the best wage going: as much as $400 a week, or the modern equivalent of about $430,000 a year.

To be sure, an Everleigh butterfly's wages were off the charts. But why did even a typical Chicago prostitute one hundred years ago earn so much money?

The best answer is that wages are determined in large part by the laws of supply and demand, which are often more powerful than laws made by legislators.

In the United States especially, politics and economics don't mix well. Politicians have all sorts of reasons to pass all sorts of laws that, as well-meaning as they may be, fail to account for the way real people respond to real-world incentives.

When prostitution was criminalized in the United States, most of the policing energy was directed at the prostitutes rather than their customers. This is pretty typical. As with other illicit markets—think about drug dealing or black-market guns—most governments prefer to punish the people who are supplying the goods and services rather than the people who are consuming them.

But when you lock up a supplier, a scarcity is created that inevitably drives the price higher, and that entices more suppliers to enter the market. The U.S. "war on drugs" has been relatively ineffective precisely because it focuses on sellers and not buyers. While drug buyers obviously outnumber drug sellers, more than 90 percent of all prison time for drug convictions is served by dealers.

Why doesn't the public support punishing users? It may seem unfair to punish the little guy, the user, when he can't help himself from partaking in vice. The suppliers, meanwhile, are much easier to demonize.

But if a government really wanted to crack down on illicit goods and services, it would go after the people who demand them. If, for instance, men convicted of hiring a prostitute were sentenced to castration, the market would contract in a hurry.

In Chicago some one hundred years ago, the risk of punishment fell almost entirely on the prostitute. Besides the constant threat of arrest, there was also the deep social stigma of prostitution. Perhaps the greatest penalty was that a woman who worked as a prostitute would never be able to find a suitable husband. Combine these factors and you can see that a prostitute's wages *had* to be high to entice enough women to satisfy the strong demand.

The biggest money, of course, was taken home by the women at the top of the prostitution pyramid. By the time the Everleigh Club was shut down—the Chicago Vice Commission finally got its way—Ada and Minna Everleigh had accumulated, in today's currency, about $22 million.

The mansion that housed the Everleigh Club is long gone. So is the entire Levee district. The very street grid where the Everleigh stood was wiped away in the 1960s, replaced by a high-rise housing project.

But this is still the South Side of Chicago and prostitutes still work there—like LaSheena, in the black-and-red tracksuit—although you can be pretty sure they won't be quoting you any Greek poetry.

LaSheena is one of the many street prostitutes Sudhir Venkatesh has gotten to know lately. Venkatesh, a sociologist at Columbia University in New York, spent his grad-school years in Chicago and still returns there regularly for research.

When he first arrived, he was a naïve, sheltered, Grateful Dead–loving kid who'd grown up in laid-back California, eager to take the temperature of an intense town where race—particularly black and white—played out with great zeal. Being neither black nor white (he was born in India) worked in Venkatesh's favor, letting him slip behind the battle lines of both academia (which was overwhelmingly white) and the South Side ghettos (which were overwhelmingly black). Before long, he had embedded himself with a street gang that practically ran

the neighborhood and made most of its money by selling crack cocaine. (Yes, it was Venkatesh's research that figured prominently in the *Freakonomics* chapter about drug dealers, and yes, we are back now for a second helping.) Along the way, he became an authority on the neighborhood's underground economy, and when he was done with the drug dealers he moved on to the prostitutes.

But an interview or two with a woman like LaSheena can reveal only so much. Anyone who wants to really understand the prostitution market needs to accumulate some real data.

That's easier said than done. Because of the illicit nature of the activity, standard data sources (think of census forms or tax rolls) are no help. Even when prostitutes have been surveyed directly in previous studies, the interviews are often conducted long after the fact and by the kind of agency (a drug-rehab center, for instance, or a church shelter) that doesn't necessarily elicit impartial results.

Moreover, earlier research has shown that when people are surveyed about stigmatizing behavior, they either downplay or exaggerate their participation, depending on what's at stake or who is asking.

Consider the Mexican welfare program Oportunidades. To get aid, applicants have to itemize their personal possessions and household goods. Once an applicant is accepted, a caseworker visits his home and learns whether the applicant was telling the truth.

César Martinelli and Susan W. Parker, two economists who analyzed the data from more than 100,000 Oportunidades clients, found that applicants routinely underreported certain items, including cars, trucks, video recorders, satellite TVs, and washing machines. This shouldn't surprise anyone. People hoping to get welfare benefits have an incentive to make it sound like they are poorer than they truly are. But as Martinelli and Parker discovered, applicants *over*reported other items: indoor plumbing, running water, a gas stove, and a concrete floor. Why on earth would welfare applicants say they had these essentials when they didn't?

Martinelli and Parker attribute it to embarrassment. Even people who are poor enough to need welfare apparently don't want to admit to a welfare clerk that they have a dirt floor or live without a toilet.

Venkatesh, knowing that traditional survey methods don't necessarily produce reliable results for a sensitive topic like prostitution, tried something different: real-time, on-the-spot data collection. He hired trackers to stand on street corners or sit in brothels with the prostitutes, directly observing some facets of their transactions and gathering more intimate details from the prostitutes as soon as the customers were gone.

Most of the trackers were former prostitutes—an important credential because such women were more likely to get honest responses. Venkatesh also paid the prostitutes for participating in the study. If they were willing to have sex for money, he reasoned, surely they'd be willing to talk about having sex for money. And they were. Over the course of nearly two years, Venkatesh accumulated data on roughly 160 prostitutes in three separate South Side neighborhoods, logging more than 2,200 sexual transactions.

The tracking sheets recorded a considerable variety of data, including:

- The specific sexual act performed, and the duration of the trick

- Where the act took place (in a car, outdoors, or indoors)

- Amount received in cash

- Amount received in drugs

- The customer's race

- The customer's approximate age

- The customer's attractiveness (10 = sexy, 1 = disgusting)

- Whether a condom was used

- Whether the customer was new or returning

- If it could be determined, whether the customer was married; employed; affiliated with a gang; from the neighborhood

- Whether the prostitute stole from the customer

- Whether the customer gave the prostitute any trouble, violent or otherwise

- Whether the sex act was paid for, or was a "freebie"

So what can these data tell us?

Let's start with wages. It turns out that the typical street prostitute in Chicago works 13 hours a week, performing 10 sex acts during that period, and earns an hourly wage of approximately $27. So her weekly take-home pay is roughly $350. This includes an average of $20 that a prostitute steals from her customers and acknowledges that some prostitutes accept drugs in lieu of cash—usually crack cocaine or heroin, and usually at a discount. Of all the women in Venkatesh's study, 83 percent were drug addicts.

Like LaSheena, many of these women took on other, non-prostitution work, which Venkatesh also tracked. Prostitution paid about four times more than those jobs. But as high as that wage premium may be, it looks pretty meager when you consider the job's downsides. In a given year, a typical prostitute in Venkatesh's study experienced a dozen incidents of violence. At least 3 of the 160 prostitutes who participated died during the course of the study. "Most of the violence by johns is when, for some reason, they can't consummate or can't get erect," says Venkatesh. "Then he's shamed—'I'm too manly for you' or 'You're too ugly for me!' Then the john wants his money back, and you definitely don't want to negotiate with a man who just lost his masculinity."

Moreover, the women's wage premium pales in comparison to the one enjoyed by even the low-rent prostitutes from a hundred years ago. Compared with them, women like LaSheena are working for next to nothing.

Why has the prostitute's wage fallen so far?

Because demand has fallen dramatically. Not the demand for *sex*. That is still robust. But prostitution, like any industry, is vulnerable to competition.

Who poses the greatest competition to a prostitute? Simple: any woman who is willing to have sex with a man for free.

It is no secret that sexual mores have evolved substantially in recent decades. The phrase "casual sex" didn't exist a century ago (to say nothing of "friends with benefits"). Sex outside of marriage was much harder to come by and carried significantly higher penalties than it does today.

Imagine a young man, just out of college but not ready to settle down, who wants to have some sex. In decades past, prostitution was a likely option. Although illegal, it was never hard to find, and the risk of arrest was minuscule. While relatively expensive in the short term, it provided good long-term value because it didn't carry the potential costs of an unwanted pregnancy or a marriage commitment. At least 20 percent of American men born between 1933 and 1942 had their first sexual intercourse with a prostitute.

Now imagine that same young man twenty years later. The shift in sexual mores has given him a much greater supply of unpaid sex. In his generation, only 5 percent of men lose their virginity to a prostitute.

And it's not that he and his friends are saving themselves for marriage. More than 70 percent of the men in his generation have sex before they marry, compared with just 33 percent in the earlier generation.

So premarital sex emerged as a viable substitute for prostitution. And as the demand for paid sex decreased, so too did the wage of the people who provide it.

If prostitution were a typical industry, it might have hired lobbyists to fight against the encroachment of premarital sex. They would have pushed to have premarital sex criminalized or, at the very least, heavily taxed. When the steelmakers and sugar producers of America began to feel the heat of competition—in the form of cheaper goods from Mexico, China, or Brazil—they got the federal government to impose tariffs that protected their homegrown products.

Such protectionist tendencies are nothing new. More than 150 years ago, the French economist Frédéric Bastiat wrote "The Candlemakers' Petition," said to represent the interests of "the Manufacturers of Candles, Tapers, Lanterns, Candlesticks, Street Lamps, Snuffers, and Extinguishers" as well as "the Producers of Tallow, Oil, Resin, Alcohol, and Generally Everything Connected with Lighting."

These industries, Bastiat complained, "are suffering from the ruinous competition of a foreign rival who apparently works under conditions so far superior to our own for the production of light that he is flooding the domestic market with it at an incredibly low price."

Who was this dastardly foreign rival?

"None other than the sun," wrote Bastiat. He begged the French government to pass a law forbidding all citizens to allow sunlight to enter their homes. (Yes, his petition was a satire; in economists' circles, this is what passes for radical high jinks.)

Alas, the prostitution industry lacks a champion as passionate, even in jest, as Bastiat. And unlike the sugar and steel industries, it holds little sway in Washington's corridors of power—despite, it should be said, its many, many connections with men of high government office. This explains why the industry's fortunes have been so badly buffeted by the naked winds of the free market.

Prostitution is more geographically concentrated than other criminal activity: nearly half of all Chicago prostitution arrests occur in less than one-third of 1 percent of the city's blocks. What do these blocks have in common? They are near train stations and major roads (prostitutes need to be where customers can find them) and have a lot of poor residents—although not, as is common in most poor neighborhoods, an overabundance of female-headed households.

This concentration makes it possible to take Venkatesh's data and merge it with the Chicago Police Department's citywide arrest data to estimate the scope of street prostitution citywide. The conclusion: in any given week, about 4,400 women are working as street prostitutes in Chicago, turning a combined 1.6 million tricks a year for 175,000 different men. That's about the same number of prostitutes who worked in Chicago a hundred years ago. Considering that the city's population has grown by 30 percent since then, the per-capita count of street prostitutes has fallen significantly. One thing that hasn't changed: for the customer at least, prostitution is only barely illegal. The data show that a man who solicits a street prostitute is likely to be arrested about once for every 1,200 visits.

The prostitutes in Venkatesh's study worked in three separate areas of the city: West Pullman, Roseland, and Washington Park. Most of these neighborhoods' residents are African American, as are the prostitutes. West Pullman and Roseland, which adjoin each other, are working-class neighborhoods on the far South Side that used to be almost exclusively white (West Pullman was organized around the Pullman train factory).

Washington Park has been a poor black neighborhood for decades. In all three areas, the race of the prostitutes' clientele is mixed.

Monday is easily the slowest night of the week for these prostitutes. Fridays are the busiest, but on Saturday night a prostitute will typically earn about 20 percent more than on Friday.

Why isn't the busiest night also the most profitable? Because the single greatest determinant of a prostitute's price is the specific trick she is hired to perform. And for whatever reason, Saturday customers purchase more expensive services. Consider the four different sexual acts these prostitutes routinely performed, each with its own price tag:

SEXUAL ACT	AVERAGE PRICE
MANUAL STIMULATION	$26.70
ORAL SEX	$37.26
VAGINAL SEX	$80.05
ANAL SEX	$94.13

It's interesting to note that the price of oral sex has plummeted over time relative to "regular" sexual intercourse. In the days of the Everleigh Club, men paid double or triple for oral sex; now it costs less than half the price of intercourse. Why?

True, oral sex imposes a lower cost on the prostitute because it eliminates the possibility of pregnancy and lessens the risk of sexually transmitted disease. (It also offers what one public-health scholar calls "ease of exit," whereby a prostitute can hurriedly escape the police or a threatening customer.) But oral sex *always* had those benefits. What accounted for the price difference in the old days?

The best answer is that oral sex carried a sort of taboo tax. At the time, it was considered a form of perversion, especially by religious-minded folks, since it satisfied the lust requirements of sex without fulfilling the reproductive requirements. The Everleigh Club was of course happy to profit from this taboo. Indeed, the club's physician avidly endorsed oral sex because it meant higher profits for the establishment and less wear and tear on the butterflies.

But as social attitudes changed, the price fell to reflect the new reality. This shift in preferences has not been confined to prostitution. Among U.S. teenagers, oral sex is on the rise while sexual intercourse and pregnancy have fallen. Some might call it coincidence (or worse), but we call it economics at work.

The lower price for oral sex among prostitutes has been met by strong demand. Here is a breakdown of the market share of each sex act performed by the Chicago prostitutes:

SEXUAL ACT	SHARE OF ALL TRICKS
ORAL SEX	55%
VAGINAL SEX	17%
MANUAL STIMULATION	15%
ANAL SEX	9%
OTHER	4%

Included in the "other" category are nude dancing, "just talk" (an extremely rare event, observed only a handful of times over more than two thousand transactions), and a variety of acts that are the complete opposite of "just talk," so far out of bounds that they would tax the imagination of even the most creative reader. If nothing else, such acts suggest a prime reason that a prostitution market still thrives despite the availability of free sex: men hire prostitutes to do things a girlfriend or wife would never be willing to do. (It should also be said, however, that some of the most deviant acts in our sample actually *include* family members, with every conceivable combination of gender and generation.)

Prostitutes do not charge all customers the same price. Black customers, for instance, pay on average about $9 less per trick than white customers, while Hispanic customers are in the middle. Economists have a name for the practice of charging different prices for the same product: *price discrimination.*

In the business world, it isn't always possible to price-discriminate. At least two conditions must be met:

- Some customers must have clearly identifiable traits that place them in the willing-to-pay-more category. (As identifiable traits go, black or white skin is a pretty good one.)

- The seller must be able to prevent resale of the product, thereby destroying any arbitrage opportunities. (In the case of prostitution, resale is pretty much impossible.)

If these circumstances can be met, most firms will profit from price discriminating whenever they can. Business travelers know this all too well, because they routinely pay three times more for a last-minute airline ticket than the vacationer in the next seat. Women who pay for a salon haircut know it too, since they pay twice as much as men for what is pretty much the same haircut. Or consider the online health-care catalog Dr. Leonard's, which sells a Barber Magic hair trimmer for $12.99 and, elsewhere on its site, the Barber Magic Trim-a-Pet hair trimmer for $7.99. The two products appear to be identical—but Dr. Leonard seems to think that people will spend more to trim their own hair than their pet's.

How do the Chicago street prostitutes price-discriminate? As Venkatesh learned, they use different pricing strategies for white and black customers. When dealing with blacks, the prostitutes usually name the price outright to discourage any negotiation. (Venkatesh observed that black customers are more likely than whites to haggle—perhaps, he reasoned, because they're more familiar with the neighborhood and therefore know the market better.) When doing business with white customers, meanwhile, the prostitute makes the *man* name a price, hoping for a generous offer. As evidenced by the black-white price differential in the data, this strategy seems to work pretty well.

Other factors can knock down the price customers pay a Chicago prostitute. For instance:

	AVERAGE DISCOUNT
PROSTITUTE PAID IN DRUGS RATHER THAN CASH	$7.00
SEX ACT PERFORMED OUTDOORS	$6.50
CUSTOMER USES A CONDOM	$2.00

The drug discount isn't much of a shock considering that most of the prostitutes are drug addicts. The outdoors discount is partially a time discount because tricks performed outdoors tend to be faster. But also, prostitutes charge more for an indoor trick because they usually have to pay for the indoor space. Some women rent a bedroom in someone's home or keep a mattress in the basement; others use a cheap motel or a dollar store that has closed for the night.

The small discount for condom use *is* surprising. Even more surprising is how seldom condoms are used: less than 25 percent of the time even when counting only vaginal and anal sex. (New customers were more likely to use condoms than repeat customers; black customers were less likely than others.) A typical Chicago street prostitute could expect to have about 300 instances of unprotected sex a year. The good news, according to earlier research, is that men who use street prostitutes have a surprisingly low rate of HIV infection, less than 3 percent. (The same is not true for male customers who hire male prostitutes; their rate is above 35 percent.)

So a lot of factors influence a prostitute's pricing: the act itself, certain customer characteristics, even the location.

But amazingly, prices at a given location are virtually the same from one prostitute to the next. You might think one woman would charge more than another who is less desirable. But that rarely happens. Why?

The only sensible explanation is that most customers view the women as what economists call *perfect substitutes,* or commodities that are easily interchanged. Just as a shopper in a grocery store may see one bunch of bananas as pretty much identical to the rest, the same principle seems to hold true for the men who frequent this market.

One surefire way for a customer to get a big discount is to hire the prostitute directly rather than dealing with a pimp. If he does, he'll get the same sex act for about $16 less.

This estimate is based on data from the prostitutes in Roseland and West Pullman. The two neighborhoods are located next to each other and are similar in most regards. But in West Pullman, the prostitutes used pimps, whereas those in Roseland did not. West Pullman is slightly more residential, which creates community pressure to keep prostitutes off the streets. Roseland, meanwhile, has more street-gang activity. Even though Chicago's gangs don't typically get involved in pimping, they don't want anyone else horning in on their black-market economy.

This key difference allows us to measure the impact of the pimp (henceforth known as the *pimpact*). But first, here's an important question: how can we be sure the two populations of prostitutes are in fact comparable? Perhaps the prostitutes who work with pimps have different characteristics than the others. Maybe they're savvier or less drug addicted. If that were the case, we'd merely be measuring two different populations of women rather than the pimpact.

But as it happened, many of the women in Venkatesh's study went back and forth between the two neighborhoods, sometimes working with a pimp and sometimes solo. This enabled us to analyze the data in such a way that isolates the pimpact.

As just noted, customers pay about $16 more if they go through a pimp. But the customers who use pimps also tend to buy more expensive services—no manual stimulation for these gents—which further bumps up the women's wages. So even after the pimps take their typical 25 percent commission, the prostitutes earn more money while turning fewer tricks:

PROSTITUTE	WEEKLY SALARY	AVERAGE TRICKS PER WEEK
WORKING SOLO	$ 325	7.8
WITH PIMP	$ 410	6.2

The secret to the pimps' success is that they go after a different clientele than the street prostitutes can get on their own. As Venkatesh learned, the pimps in West Pullman spent a lot of their time recruiting customers, mostly white ones, in downtown strip clubs and the riverboat casinos in nearby Indiana.

But as the data show, the pimpact goes well beyond producing higher wages. A prostitute who works with a pimp is less likely to be beaten up by a customer or forced into giving freebies to gang members.

So if you are a street prostitute in Chicago, using a pimp looks to be all upside. Even after paying the commission, you come out ahead on just about every front. If only every agent in every industry provided this kind of value.

Consider a different sales environment: residential real estate. Just as you can sell your body with or without the aid of a pimp, you can sell your house with or without a Realtor. While Realtors charge a much lower commission than the pimps—about 5 percent versus 25 percent—the Realtor's cut is usually in the tens of thousands of dollars for a single sale.

So do Realtors earn their pay?

Three economists recently analyzed home-sales data in Madison, Wisconsin, which has a thriving for-sale-by-owner market (or FSBO, pronounced "FIZZ-bo"). This revolves around the website FSBOMadison.com, which charges homeowners $150 to list a house, with no commission when the home is sold. By comparing FSBO sales in Madison with Realtor-sold homes in Madison along several dimensions—price, house and neighborhood characteristics, time on market, and so on—the economists were able to gauge the Realtor's impact (or, in the interest of symmetry, the *Rimpact*).

What did they find?

The homes sold on FSBOMadison.com typically fetched about the same price as the homes sold by Realtors. That doesn't make the Realtors look very good. Using a Realtor to sell a $400,000 house means paying a commission of about $20,000—versus just $150 to FSBOMadison.com. (Another recent study, meanwhile, found that flat-fee real-estate agents, who typically charge about $500 to list a house, also get about the same price as full-fee Realtors.)

But there are some important caveats. In exchange for the 5 percent commission, someone else does all the work for you. For some home sellers, that's well worth the price. It's also hard to say if the Madison results would hold true in other cities. Furthermore, the study took place during a strong housing market, which probably makes it easier to sell a home yourself. Also, the kind of people who choose to sell their houses without a Realtor may have a better business head to start with. Finally, even though the FSBO homes sold for the same average price as those sold by Realtors, they took twenty days longer to sell. But most people would probably consider it worth $20,000 to live in their old home for an extra twenty days.

A Realtor and a pimp perform the same primary service: marketing your product to potential customers. As this study shows, the Internet is proving to be a pretty powerful substitute for the Realtor. But if you're trying to sell street prostitution, the Internet isn't very good—not yet, at least—at matching sellers to buyers.

So once you consider the value you get for each of these two agents, it seems clear that a pimp's services are considerably more valuable than a Realtor's. Or, for those who prefer their conclusions rendered mathematically:

PIMPACT > RIMPACT

During Venkatesh's study, six pimps managed the prostitution in West Pullman, and he got to know each of them. They were all men. In the old days, prostitution rings in even the poorest Chicago neighborhoods were usually run by women. But men, attracted by the high wages, eventually took over—yet another example in the long history of men stepping in to outearn women.

These six pimps ranged in age from their early thirties to their late forties and "were doing pretty well," Venkatesh says, making roughly $50,000 a year. Some also held legit jobs—car mechanic or store manager—and most owned their homes. None were drug addicts.

One of their most important roles was handling the police. Venkatesh learned that the pimps had a good working relationship with the police, particularly with one officer, named Charles. When he was new on the beat, Charles harassed and arrested the pimps. But this backfired. "When you arrest the pimps, there'll just be fighting to replace them," Venkatesh says, "and the violence is worse than the prostitution."

So instead, Charles extracted some compromises. The pimps agreed to stay away from the park when kids were playing there, and to keep the

prostitution hidden. In return, the police would leave the pimps alone—and, importantly, they wouldn't arrest the prostitutes either. Over the course of Venkatesh's study, there was only one official arrest of a prostitute in an area controlled by pimps. Of all the advantages a prostitute gained by using a pimp, not getting arrested was one of the biggest.

But you don't necessarily need a pimp to stay out of jail. The average prostitute in Chicago will turn 450 tricks before she is arrested, and only 1 in 10 arrests leads to a prison sentence.

It's not that the police don't know where the prostitutes are. Nor have the police brass or mayor made a conscious decision to let prostitution thrive. Rather, this is a graphic example of what economists call *the principal-agent problem*. That's what happens when two parties in a given undertaking seem to have the same incentives but in fact may not.

In this case, you could think of the police chief as the principal. He would like to curtail street prostitution. The cop on the street, meanwhile, is the agent. He may also want to curtail prostitution, at least in theory, but he doesn't have a very strong incentive to actually make arrests. As some officers see it, the prostitutes offer something far more appealing than just another arrest tally: sex.

This shows up loud and clear in Venkatesh's study. Of all the tricks turned by the prostitutes he tracked, roughly 3 percent were freebies given to police officers.

The data don't lie: a Chicago street prostitute is more likely to have sex with a cop than to be arrested by one.

It would be hard to overemphasize how undesirable it is to be a street prostitute—the degradation, the risk of disease, the nearly constant threat of violence.

Nowhere were the conditions as bad as in Washington Park, the third neighborhood in Venkatesh's study, which lies about six miles north of Roseland and West Pullman. It is more economically depressed and less accessible to outsiders, especially whites. The prostitution is centered around four locations: two large apartment buildings, a five-block stretch of busy commercial street, and in the park itself, a 372-acre landmark designed in the 1870s by Frederick Law Olmsted and Calvert Vaux. The prostitutes in Washington Park work without pimps, and they earn the lowest wages of any prostitutes in Venkatesh's study.

This might lead you to think that such women would rather be doing anything else but turning tricks. But one feature of a market economy is that prices tend to find a level whereby even the worst conceivable job is worth doing. As bad off as these women are, they would seem to be worse off without prostitution.

Sound absurd?

The strongest evidence for this argument comes from an unlikely source: the long-loved American tradition known as the family reunion. Every summer around the Fourth of July holiday, Washington Park is thronged with families and other large groups who get together for cookouts and parties. For some of these visitors, catching up with Aunt Ida over lemonade isn't quite stimulating enough. It turns out that the demand for prostitutes in Washington Park skyrockets every year during this period.

And the prostitutes do what any good entrepreneur would do: they raise prices by about 30 percent and work as much overtime as they can handle.

Most interestingly, this surge in demand attracts a special kind of worker—a woman who steers clear of prostitution all year long but, during this busy season, drops her other work and starts turning tricks. Most of these part-time prostitutes have children and take care of their households; they aren't drug addicts. But like prospectors at a gold rush or Realtors during a housing boom, they see the chance to cash in and jump at it.

As for the question posed in this chapter's title—*How is a street prostitute like a department-store Santa?*—the answer should be obvious: they both take advantage of short-term job opportunities brought about by holiday spikes in demand.

We've already established that demand for prostitutes is far lower today than it was sixty years ago (if offset a bit by holiday surges), in large part because of the feminist revolution.

If you found that surprising, consider an even more unlikely victim of the feminist revolution: schoolchildren.

Teaching has traditionally been dominated by women. A hundred years ago, it was one of the few jobs available to women that didn't involve cooking, cleaning, or other menial labor. (Nursing was another such profession, but teaching was far more prominent, with six teachers for every nurse.) At the time, nearly 6 percent of the female workforce were teachers, trailing only laborers (19 percent), servants (16 percent), and laundresses (6.5 percent). And by a large margin it was the job of choice among college graduates. As of 1940, an astonishing 55 percent of all college-educated female workers in their early thirties were employed as teachers.

Soon after, however, opportunities for smart women began to multiply. The Equal Pay Act of 1963 and the Civil Rights Act of 1964 were contributing factors, as was the societal shift in the perception of women's roles. As more girls went off to college, more women emerged ready to join the workforce, especially in the desirable professions that had been largely off-limits: law, medicine, business, finance, and so on. (One of the unsung heroes of this revolution was the widespread use of baby formula, which allowed new mothers to get right back to work.)

These demanding, competitive professions offered high wages and attracted the best and brightest women available. No doubt many of these women would have become schoolteachers had they been born a generation earlier.

But they didn't. As a consequence, the schoolteacher corps began to experience a brain drain. In 1960, about 40 percent of female teachers scored in the top quintile of IQ and other aptitude tests, with only 8 percent in the bottom. Twenty years later, fewer than half as many were in the top quintile, with more than twice as many in the bottom. It hardly helped that teachers' wages were falling significantly in relation to those of other jobs. "The quality of teachers has been declining for decades," the chancellor of New York City's public schools declared in 2000, "and no one wants to talk about it."

This isn't to say that there aren't still a lot of great teachers. Of course there are. But overall teacher skill declined during these years, and with it the quality of classroom instruction. Between 1967 and 1980, U.S. test scores fell by about 1.25 grade-level equivalents. The education researcher John Bishop called this decline "historically unprecedented," arguing that it put a serious drag on national productivity that would continue well into the twenty-first century.

But at least things worked out well for the women who went into other professions, right?

Well, sort of. As we wrote earlier, even the best-educated women earn less than their male counterparts. This is especially true in the high-flying financial and corporate sectors—where, moreover, women are vastly underrepresented. The number of female CEOs has increased roughly eightfold in recent years, but women still hold less than 1.5 percent of all CEO positions. Among the top fifteen hundred companies in the United States, only about 2.5 percent of the highest-paying executive positions are held by women. This is especially surprising given that women have earned more than 30 percent of all the master's in business administration (MBA) degrees at the nation's top

colleges over the past twenty-five years. Their share today is at its highest yet, 43 percent.

The economists Marianne Bertrand, Claudia Goldin, and Lawrence Katz tried to solve this wage-gap puzzle by analyzing the career outcomes of more than 2,000 male and female MBAs from the University of Chicago.

Their conclusion: while gender discrimination may be a minor contributor to the male-female wage differential, it is desire—or the lack thereof—that accounts for most of the wage gap. The economists identified three main factors:

- Women have slightly lower GPAs than men and, perhaps more important, they take fewer finance courses. All else being equal, there is a strong correlation between a finance background and career earnings.

- Over the first fifteen years of their careers, women work fewer hours than men, 52 per week versus 58. Over fifteen years, that six-hour difference adds up to six months' less experience.

- Women take more career interruptions than men. After ten years in the workforce, only 10 percent of male MBAs went for six months or more without working, compared with 40 percent of female MBAs.

The big issue seems to be that many women, even those with MBAs, love kids. The average female MBA with no children works only 3 percent fewer hours than the average male MBA. But female MBAs *with* children work 24 percent less. "The pecuniary penalties from shorter hours and any job discontinuity among MBAs are enormous," the three economists write. "It appears that many MBA mothers, especially those with well-off spouses, decided to slow down within a few years following their first birth."

This is a strange twist. Many of the best and brightest women in the United States get an MBA so they can earn high wages, but they end up marrying the best and brightest men, who *also* earn high wages— which affords these women the luxury of not having to work so much.

Does this mean the women's investment of time and money in pursuing an MBA was poorly spent? Maybe not. Perhaps they never would have *met* such husbands if they hadn't gone to business school.

There's one more angle to consider when examining the male-female wage gap. Rather than interpreting women's lower wages as a failure, perhaps it should be seen as a sign that a higher wage simply isn't as meaningful an incentive for women as it is for men. Could it be that men have a weakness for money just as women have a weakness for children?

Consider a recent pair of experiments in which young men and women were recruited to take an SAT-style math test with twenty questions. In one version, every participant was paid a flat rate, $5 for showing up and another $15 for completing the test. In the second version, participants were paid the $5 show-up fee and another $2 for each correct answer.

How'd they do?

In the flat-rate version, the men performed only slightly better, getting 1 more correct answer out of 20 than the women. But in the cash-incentive version, the men blew away the women. The women's performance barely budged when compared with the flat-rate version, whereas the average man scored an extra 2 correct questions out of the 20.

Economists do the best they can by assembling data and using complex statistical techniques to tease out the reasons why women earn less than men. The fundamental difficulty, however, is that men and women differ in so many ways. What an economist would *really* like to do is perform an experiment, something like this: take a bunch of women and clone male versions of them; do the reverse for a bunch of men; now sit back and watch. By measuring the labor outcomes of each gender group against their own clones, you could likely gain some real insights.

Or, if cloning weren't an option, you could take a bunch of women, randomly select half of them, and magically switch their gender to male, leaving everything else about them the same, and do the opposite with a bunch of men.

Unfortunately, economists aren't allowed to conduct such experiments. (Yet.) But individuals can if they want to. It's called a sex-change operation.

So what happens when a man decides to employ surgery and hormone therapy to live as a woman (a so-called MTF, or male-to-female transgender) or when a woman decides to live as a man (an FTM, or female-to-male)?

Ben Barres, a Stanford neurobiologist, was born Barbara Barres and became a man in 1997, at the age of forty-two. Neurobiology, like most math and science disciplines, is heavily populated by men. His decision "came as a surprise to my colleagues and students," he notes, but they "have all been terrific about it." Indeed, his intellectual stature seems to have increased. Once, after Barres gave a seminar, a fellow scientist turned to a friend of Barres's in the audience and issued this left-handed compliment: "Ben Barres's work is much better than his sister's." But Barres doesn't have a sister; the commenter was slighting Barres's former, female self.

"It is much harder for men to transition to women than for women to transition to men," Barres admits. The problem, he says, is that males are presumed to be competent in certain fields—especially areas like science and finance—while females are not.

On the other hand, consider Deirdre McCloskey, a prominent economist at the University of Illinois at Chicago. She was born a male, Donald, and decided to become a woman in 1995, at the age of fifty-three. Economics, like neuroscience, is a heavily male field. "I was prepared to move to Spokane and become a secretary in a grain elevator," she says. That proved unnecessary, but McCloskey did "detect a queerness penalty toward me in some of the economics profession. I reckon I'd make a little more money now if I were still Donald."

McCloskey and Barres are just two data points. A pair of researchers named Kristen Schilt and Matthew Wiswall wanted to systematically examine what happens to the salaries of people who switched gender as adults. It is not quite the experiment we proposed above—after all, the set of folks who switch gender aren't exactly a random sample, nor are they the typical woman or man before or after—but still, the results are intriguing. Schilt and Wiswall found that women who become men earn slightly more money after their gender transitions, while men who become women make, on average, nearly one-third less than their previous wage.

Their conclusion comes with a number of caveats. For starters, the sample set was very small: just fourteen MTFs and twenty-four FTMs. Furthermore, the people they studied were mainly recruited at transgender conferences. That puts them in the category of what Deirdre McCloskey calls "professional gender crossers," who aren't necessarily representative.

"One could easily believe," she says, "that people who do not just become women and then get on with their lives, but keep looking back, are not going to be the most successful people in the workplace." (She may have changed gender, but once an economist, always an economist.)

Back in Chicago, in a chic neighborhood just a few miles from where the street prostitutes work, lives someone who was born female, stayed that way, and makes more money than she ever thought possible.

She grew up in a large and largely dysfunctional family in Texas and left home to join the military. She trained in electronics and worked in research and development on navigation systems. When she rejoined the civilian world seven years later, she took a job in computer programming with one of the world's largest corporations. She made a solid five-figure salary and married a man who earned well into six figures as a mortgage broker. Her life was a success, but it was also—well, it was boring.

She got divorced (the couple had no children) and moved back to Texas, in part to help care for a sick relative. Working once again as a computer programmer, she remarried but this marriage also failed.

Her career wasn't going much better. She was smart, capable, technically sophisticated, and she also happened to be physically attractive, a curvaceous and friendly blonde whose attributes were always well appreciated in her corporate setting. But she just didn't like working all that hard. So she became an entrepreneur, launching a one-woman business that enabled her to work just ten or fifteen hours a week and earn five times her old salary. Her name is Allie, and she is a prostitute.

She fell into the profession by accident, or at least on a lark. Her family was devout Southern Baptist, and Allie had grown up "very straitlaced," she says. As an adult, she was the same. "You know, yard-of-the-month in the suburbs, no more than two beers a night and *never* before seven." But as a young divorcée, she started visiting online dating sites—she liked men, and she liked sex—and just for fun listed "escort" on her profile. "I mean, it was so instantaneous," she recalls. "I just thought I'd put it up and see what happens."

Her computer was instantly flooded with replies. "I started hitting *minimize, minimize, minimize,* just so I could keep up!"

She arranged to meet a man at two o'clock on a weekday afternoon at a hotel, in the southwest corner of its parking lot. He'd be driving a black Mercedes. Allie had no idea what to charge. She was thinking about $50.

He was a dentist—physically unintimidating, married, and perfectly kind. Once inside the room, Allie undressed nervously. She can no longer recall the particulars of the sex ("it's all a big blur by this point," she says) but does remember that "it was nothing really kinky or anything."

When they were done, the man put some money on the dresser. "You've never done this before, have you?" he asked.

Allie tried to fib, but it was useless.

"Okay," he said, "this is what you need to do." He began to lecture her. She had to be more careful; she shouldn't be willing to meet a stranger in a parking lot; she needed to know something in advance about her clients.

"He was the perfect first date," Allie says. "To this day, I remain grateful."

Once he left the room, Allie counted the cash on the dresser: $200. "I'd been giving it away for years, and so the fact that someone was going to give me even a penny—well, that was shocking."

She was immediately tempted to take up prostitution full-time, but she was worried her family and friends would find out. So she eased into it, booking mainly out-of-town liaisons. She curtailed her programming hours but even so found the job stultifying. That's when she decided to move to Chicago.

Yes, it was a big city, which Allie found intimidating, but unlike New York or Los Angeles, it was civil enough to make a southern girl feel at home. She built a website (those computer skills came in handy) and, through intensive trial and error, determined which erotic-

services sites would help her attract the right kind of client and which ones would waste her ad dollars. (The winners were Eros.com and BigDoggie.net.)

Running a one-woman operation held several advantages, the main one being that she didn't have to share her revenues with anyone. In the old days, Allie probably would have worked for someone like the Everleigh sisters, who paid their girls handsomely but took enough off the top to make themselves truly rich. The Internet let Allie be her own madam and accumulate the riches for herself. Much has been said of the Internet's awesome ability to "disintermediate"—to cut out the agent or middleman—in industries like travel, real estate, insurance, and the sale of stocks and bonds. But it is hard to think of a market more naturally suited to disintermediation than high-end prostitution.

The downside was that Allie had no one but herself to screen potential clients and ensure they wouldn't beat her up or rip her off. She hit upon a solution that was as simple as it was smart. When a new client contacted her online, she wouldn't book an appointment until she had secured his real name and his work telephone number. Then she'd call him the morning of their date, ostensibly just to say how excited she was to meet him.

But the call also acknowledged that she could reach him at will and, if something were to go wrong, she could storm his office. "Nobody wants to see the 'crazy ho' routine," she says with a smile. To date, Allie has resorted to this tactic only once, after a client paid her in counterfeit cash. When Allie visited his office, he promptly located some real money.

She saw clients in her apartment, mainly during the day. Most of them were middle-aged white men, 80 percent of whom were married, and they found it easier to slip off during work hours than explain an evening absence. Allie loved having her evenings free to read, go to the movies, or just relax. She set her fee at $300 an hour—that's what most other women of her caliber seemed to be charging—with a few discount options: $500 for two hours or $2,400 for a twelve-hour sleepover. About 60 percent of her appointments were for a single hour.

Her bedroom—"my office," she calls it with a laugh—is dominated by a massive Victorian four-poster, its carved mahogany pillars draped with an off-white silk crepe. It is not the easiest bed to mount. When asked if any of her clients have difficulty doing so, she confesses that one portly gentleman actually broke the bed not long ago.

What did Allie do?

"I told him that the damn thing was already broken, and I was sorry I hadn't gotten it fixed."

She is the kind of person who sees something good in everyone—and this, she believes, has contributed to her entrepreneurial success. She genuinely likes the men who come to her, and the men therefore like Allie even beyond the fact that she will have sex with them. Often, they bring gifts: a $100 gift certificate from Amazon.com; a nice bottle of wine (she Googles the label afterward to determine the value); and, once, a new MacBook. The men sweet-talk her, and compliment her looks or the decor. They treat her, in many ways, as men are expected to treat their wives but often don't.

Most women of Allie's pay grade call themselves "escorts." When Allie discusses her friends in the business, she simply calls them "girls." But she isn't fussy. "I like *hooker*, I like *whore*, I like them all," she says. "Come on, I know what I do, so I'm not trying to butter it up." Allie mentions one friend whose fee is $500 an hour. "She thinks she's nothing like the girls on the street giving blow jobs for $100, and I'm like, 'Yes, honey, you're the same damn thing.'"

About this, Allie is likely wrong. Although she views herself as similar to a street prostitute, she has less in common with that kind of woman than she does with a trophy wife. Allie is essentially a trophy wife who is

rented by the hour. She isn't really selling sex, or at least not sex alone. She sells men the opportunity to trade in their existing wives for a younger, more sexually adventurous version—without the trouble and long-term expense of actually having to go through with it. For an hour or two, she represents the ideal wife: beautiful, attentive, smart, laughing at your jokes and satisfying your lust. She is happy to see you every time you show up at her door. Your favorite music is already playing and your favorite beverage is on ice. She will never ask you to take out the trash.

Allie says she is "a little more liberal" than some prostitutes when it comes to satisfying a client's unusual request. There was, for instance, the fellow back in Texas who still flew her in regularly and asked her to incorporate some devices he kept in a briefcase in a session most people wouldn't even recognize as sex per se. But she categorically insists that her clients wear a condom.

What if a client offered her $1 million to have sex without a condom?

Allie pauses to consider this question. Then, exhibiting a keen understanding of what economists call *adverse selection*, she declares that she still wouldn't do it—because any client crazy enough to offer $1 million for a single round of unprotected sex must be so crazy that he should be avoided at all costs.

When she started out in Chicago, at $300 an hour, the demand was nearly overwhelming. She took on as many clients as she could physically accommodate, working roughly thirty hours a week. She kept that up for a while, but once she paid off her car and built up some cash reserves, she scaled back to fifteen hours a week.

Even so, she began to wonder if one hour of her time was more valuable to her than another $300. As it was, a fifteen-hour workload generated more than $200,000 a year in cash.

Eventually she raised her fee to $350 an hour. She expected demand to fall, but it didn't. So a few months later, she raised it to $400. Again, there was no discernible drop-off in demand. Allie was a bit peeved with herself. Plainly she had been charging too little the whole time. But at least she was able to strategically exploit her fee change by engaging in a little price discrimination. She grandfathered in her favorite clients at the old rate but told her less-favorite clients that an hour now cost $400—and if they balked, she had a handy excuse to cut them loose. There were always more where they came from.

It wasn't long before she raised her fee again, to $450 an hour, and a few months later to $500. In the space of a couple of years, Allie had increased her price by 67 percent, and yet she saw practically no decrease in demand.

Her price hikes revealed another surprise: the more she charged, the less actual sex she was having. At $300 an hour, she had a string of one-hour appointments with each man wanting to get in as much action as he could. But charging $500 an hour, she was often wined and dined—"a four-hour dinner date that ends with a twenty-minute sexual encounter," she says, "even though I was the same girl, dressed the same, and had the same conversations as when I charged $300."

She figured she may have just been profiting from a strong economy. This was during 2006 and 2007, which were go-go years for many of the bankers, lawyers, and real-estate developers she saw. But Allie had found that most people who bought her services were, in the language of economics, *price insensitive*. Demand for sex seemed relatively uncoupled from the broader economy.

Our best estimate is that there are fewer than one thousand prostitutes like Allie in Chicago, either working solo or for an escort service. Street prostitutes like LaSheena might have the worst job in America. But for elite prostitutes like Allie, the circumstances are completely different: high wages, flexible hours, and relatively little risk of violence or arrest. So the real puzzle isn't why someone like Allie becomes a prostitute, but rather why *more* women don't choose this career.

Certainly, prostitution isn't for every woman. You have to like sex

enough, and be willing to make some sacrifices, like not having a husband (unless he is very understanding, or very greedy). Still, these negatives just might not seem that important when the wage is $500 an hour. Indeed, when Allie confided to one longtime friend that she had become a prostitute and described her new life, it was only a few weeks before the friend joined Allie in the business.

Allie has never had any trouble with the police, and doesn't expect to. The truth is that she would be distraught if prostitution were legalized, because her stratospherically high wage stems from the fact that the service she provides *cannot* be gotten legally.

Allie had mastered her domain. She was a shrewd entrepreneur who kept her overhead low, maintained quality control, learned to price-discriminate, and understood well the market forces of supply and demand. She also enjoyed her work.

But all that said, Allie began looking for an exit strategy. She was in her early thirties by now and, while still attractive, she understood that her commodity was perishable. She felt sorry for older prostitutes who, like aging athletes, didn't know when to quit. (One such athlete, a future Hall of Fame baseball player, had propositioned Allie while she was vacationing in South America, not knowing that she was a professional. Allie declined, uninterested in a busman's holiday.)

She had also grown tired of living a secret life. Her family and friends didn't know she was a prostitute, and the constant deception wore her out. The only people with whom she could be unguarded were other girls in the business, and they weren't her closest friends.

She had saved money but not enough to retire. So she began casting about for her next career. She got her real-estate license. The housing boom was in full swing, and it seemed pretty simple to transition out of her old job and into the new, since both allowed a flexible schedule. But too many other people had the same idea. The barrier to entry for real-estate agents is so low that every boom inevitably attracts a swarm of new agents—in the previous ten years, membership in the National Association of Realtors had risen 75 percent—which has the effect of depressing their median income. And Allie was aghast when she realized she'd have to give half of her commission to the agency that employed her. That was a steeper cut than any pimp would dare take!

Finally Allie realized what she really wanted to do: go back to college. She would build on everything she'd learned by running her own business and, if all went well, apply this newfound knowledge to some profession that would pay an insanely high wage without relying on her own physical labor.

Her chosen field of study? Economics, of course.

Unit 5 – (Crime and) Punishment

On the Economics of Capital Punishment

GARY S. BECKER

Posner provides a good discussion of the various issue related to capital punishment. I will concentrate my comments on deterrence, which is really the crucial issue in the acrimonious debate over capital punishment. I support the use of capital punishment for persons convicted of murder because, and only because, I believe it deters murders. If I did not believe that, I would be opposed because revenge and the other possible motives that are mentioned and dis-

Gary Becker is a Regular Columnist for the Economists' Voice. He won the Nobel Prize in 1992 and is a Senior Fellow at the Hoover Institution and a University Professor of Economics and Sociology at the University of Chicago. He is internationally recognized for pioneering work on human capital, discrimination, the economic analysis of crime, and the economics of the family. A.B., Princeton, 1951; A.M., 1952, Ph.D., 1955, University of Chicago.

cussed by Posner, should not be a basis for public policy.

As Posner indicates, serious empirical research on capital punishment began with Isaac Ehrlich's pioneering paper. Subsequent studies have sometimes found much weaker effects than he found, while others, including a recent one cited by Posner, found a much larger effect than even that found by Ehrlich. The available data are quite limited, however, so one should not base any conclusions solely on the econometric evidence. Still, I believe the preponderance of evidence does indicate that capital punishment deters, although a recent article by John J. Donahue and Justin Wolfers in the Stanford Law Review reaches the opposite conclusion after a

review of many studies on the subject. In correspondence I gave them some reasons why I believe they understate the evidence that capital punishment deters.

Of course, public policy on punishments cannot wait until the evidence is perfect. Even with the limited quantitative evidence available, there are good reasons to believe that capital punishment deters murders. Most people, and murderers in particular, fear death, especially when it follows swiftly and with considerable certainty following the commission of a murder. David Hume said in discussing suicide that "no man ever threw away life, while it was worth living. *For such is our natural horror of death…*" (emphasis added). Schopenhauer added also in discussing suicide "…as soon as the terrors of life reach a point at which they outweigh the terrors of death, a man will put an end to his life. *But the terrors of death offer considerable resistance…"* (emphasis added).

As Posner indicates, the deterrent effect of capital punishment would be greater if the delays on its implementation were much shortened, and if this punishment was more certain to be used in the appropriate cases. But I agree with Posner that capital punishment has an important deterrent effect even with the way the present system actually operates.

TRADING OFF LIVES IS INEVITABLE

Opponents of capital punishment frequently proclaim that the State has no moral right to take the life of anyone, including that of a most reprehensible murderer, even if we assume that the deterrent effect on murders is "sizeable". Yet that is absolutely the wrong conclusion for anyone who believes that capital punishment deters. To show why, suppose that for each murderer executed (instead of say receiving life imprisonment), the number of murders is reduced by three, which is a much lower number than Ehrlich's and some other estimates of the deterrent effect. This implies that for each murderer not given capital punishment, three generally innocent victims would die. This argument means that the government would indirectly be "taking" many lives if it did not use capital punishment. The lives so taken are usually much more worthwhile than that of the murderers who would be spared execution. For this reason, the State has a "moral" obligation to use capital punishment if such punishment significantly reduces the number of murders and saves lives of innocent victims.

Saving three other lives for every person executed seems like a very attractive trade-off. Even two lives saved per execution seem like a persuasive benefit-cost ratio for capital punishment. But let us go further and suppose only one life was saved for each murderer executed. Wouldn't the trade-off still be desirable if the life saved is much better than the life taken, which would usually be the case? As the deterrent effect of capital punishment is made smaller, at some point even I would shift to the anti-capital punishment camp.

Admittedly, the argument gets less clear-cut as the number of lives saved per execution falls from two to lower values, say, for example, to one life saved per execution. Many readers of the Posner-Becker blog have objected to this comparison of the qualities of the life saved and the life taken. Yet I do not see how to avoid making such a comparison. Consider a person with a long criminal record who holds up and kills a victim who led a decent life and left several children and a spouse behind. Suppose it would be possible to save the life of an innocent victim by executing such a criminal. To me it is obvious that saving the lives of such a victim has to count for more than taking the life of such a criminal. To be sure, not all cases are so clear-cut, but I am just trying to establish the principle that a comparison of the qualities of individual lives has to be part of any reasonable social policy.

Why capital punishment is not appropriate for lesser crimes

The above argument helps explain why capital punishment should only be used for some murders, and not for theft, robbery, and other lesser crimes. For then the trade off is between taking lives and reducing property theft, and the case in favor of milder punishments is strong. However, severe assaults, including some gruesome rapes, may approach in severity some murders, and might conceivably at times call for capital punishment, although I do not support its use in these cases.

A powerful argument for reserving capital punishment for murders is related to what is called marginal deterrence in the crime and punishment literature. If perpetrators of assaults were punished with execution, an assaulter would have an incentive to kill the victims in order to reduce the likelihood that he would be discovered. That is a major reason more generally why the severity of punishments should be matched to the severity of crimes. One complication is that capital punishment may make a murderer fight harder to avoid being captured, which could lead to more deaths. That argument has to be weighed in judging the case for capital punishment. While marginal deterrence is important, I believe the resistance of murderers to being captured, possibly at the expense of their own lives, is really indirect evidence that criminals do fear capital punishment.

The problem of executing the innocent

Of course I am worried about the risk of executing innocent persons for murders committed by others. In any policy toward crime, including capital punishment, one has to compare errors of wrongful conviction with errors of failing to convict guilty persons. My support for capital punishment would weaken greatly if the rate of killing innocent persons were as large as that claimed by many. However, I believe along with Posner that the appeal process offers enormous protection not so much against wrongful conviction as against wrongful execution, so that there are very few, if any, documented cases of wrongful execution. And this process has been strengthened enormously with the development of DNA identification. However, lengthy appeals delay the execution of guilty murderers, and that can only lower the deterrent effect of capital punishment.

Final comments

European governments are adamantly opposed to capital punishment, and some Europeans consider the American use of this punishment to be barbaric. But Europeans have generally been "soft" on most crimes during the past half-century. For a long time they could be smug because their crime rates were well below American rates. But during the past twenty years European crime has increased sharply while American rates have fallen-in part because American apprehension and conviction rates have increased considerably. Now some European countries have higher per capita property crime rates than the United States does, although violent crimes are still more common in the United States. At the same time that America was reducing crime significantly in part by greater use of punishments, many European intellectuals continued to argue that not just capital

Economists' Voice www.bepress.com/ev March, 2006

punishments, but punishments in general, do not deter.

To repeat, the capital punishment debate comes down in essentials to a debate over deterrence. I can understand that some people are skeptical about the evidence, although I believe they are wrong both on the evidence and on the common sense of the issue. It is very disturbing to take someone's life, even a murderer's life, but sometimes highly unpleasant actions are necessary to deter even worse behavior that takes the lives of innocent victims.

Letters commenting on this piece or others may be submitted at http://www.bepress.com/cgi/submit.cgi?context=ev

REFERENCES AND FURTHER READING

Donohue, John J. and Justin Wolfers, "Uses and Abuses of the Evidence in the Death Penalty Debate," 58 Stanford Law Review 791, 2005.

Ehrlich, Isaac. "The Deterrent Effect of Capital Punishment: A Question of Life and Death," American Economic Review, vol. 65(3), pp. 397-417, 1975.

Becker, Gary, "Further Comments on Capital Punishment," December 25, 2005, available at http://www.becker-posner-blog.com/archives/2005/12/.

Posner, Richard, "The Economics of Capital Punishment," The Economists' Voice, March 2006, available at www.bepress.com/ev.

Posner, Richard, "The Economics of Capital Punishment," available at http://www.becker-posner-blog.com/archives/2005/12/25.

ACKNOWLEDGEMENTS

To create this column, Gary Becker combined two of his blog entries from the discussion between Judge Richard Posner and himself on capital punishment in their weekly blog (Becker-Posner-blog.com; December 18 and 25, 2005).

Human organs -- another Chinese export

Executed prisoners provide vast harvest of 'fresh' body parts for sale
Published: 07/03/2000 at 1:00 AM

"They told me my kidney came from an executed prisoner because you get them fresh that way. From the taking out of the kidney, it is only a few hours to get it transplanted in me."

So said one of six patients recovering from a transplant operation at Huaxi University of Medical Sciences in Chengdu, China, whose comments were recorded secretly on videotape in 1994 by Chinese dissident and former political prisoner Harry Wu.

Five other patients in the room had also received a "fresh" kidney that day. It is unlikely that it was a mere coincidence that, on that same day, the Chinese government carried out a mass execution only 10 miles away.

The People's Republic of China has long used mass executions for political and criminal justice purposes, but it now appears that there is another purpose to mass executions: to bring in revenue for the Chinese government through the harvesting and sale of the organs from executed "criminals."

In Zhengzhou City, a hospital worker who had many times extracted organs at execution sites, told Wu, "A shot in his head, blow away his brain, and the guy is brain dead. He has no more thinking, ceases to be a human being, just a thing, and we use the waste."

T. Kumar of Amnesty International USA testified on the organ harvesting at a 1998 hearing before the House Government Reform and Oversight Committee.

"Amnesty International reported on this practice in 1993 and called at that time for the Chinese government to ban the use of organs from executed prisoners without their free and informed consent," said Kumar. "However, the use of organs from this source continues in China, reportedly on a widespread scale."

Executed prisoners
The Chinese apply the death penalty to a much broader set of crimes than in Western nations.

"In China," Kumar testified, "there are about 68 offenses punishable by death, including reselling value-added tax receipts, theft, burglary, hooliganism, seriously disrupting public order, pimping, trafficking of women, taking of bribes, corruption, forgery and tax evasion."

Ninety percent of the organs used for transplants in China, Kumar said, come "from executed prisoners."

The use of prisoners' organs for transplant raises the obvious issue of donor consent. If ordinary, law-abiding Chinese are not free to decide their own destiny when they are alive, is it credible that Chinese prisoners are free to determine the destiny of their organs when they are executed?

On paper, the Chinese have covered themselves on this issue. A 1984 Chinese government document Wu smuggled out of the country outlined the "Official Administrative Regulations" for collecting organs from executed prisoners. One regulation stipulates that organ harvesting can be done only "with the consent of the prisoner or his family, or in cases where the body is uncollected."

Wu points out, however, that poor prisoners in China are often executed far from their home territories, where it is impossible for their families to collect their bodies.

Yet, Gao Pei Qi, the onetime deputy chief of the Public Security Bureau in Shenzhen, China, told the Senate Foreign Relations Committee in 1995, "In the 10 years that I worked for the Public Security Bureau, I never saw or heard anything to suggest that death-row prisoners were asked for consent before donating organs. Nor was the family asked. In fact, more often than not, the prisoner's family would be held under house arrest while the executions were taking place. Only by agreeing to pay the authorities for the urn would they be able to collect the ashes."

In 1994, posing as a businessman seeking a kidney for a relative, Wu took a hidden video camera to an organ-marketing office in Hong Kong. In a room complete with sales brochures, a saleswoman assured Wu that "all organs [for sale] are from brain-dead people and have been donated voluntarily."

'Easily arranged'
At First University Hospital in Chengdu, Wu videotaped a Chinese doctor making a sales pitch to someone he thought was a prospective organ buyer.

"The quality of our kidneys is better than in America," said the doctor, "because we can remove the kidney fast and at the appropriate time. Basically, as soon as we know the donor is brain dead, we can get at the kidney with the minimum of fuss and we can guarantee several kidneys in one month. The distance between where we remove the kidney and the transplant is short. We can do it in, oh, less than 10 hours. In America it takes more than 20 hours."

According to Wu, there are 90 hospitals in China capable of performing kidney and cornea transplants. The going price for kidneys is $30,000, and several hospitals are now doing a more complicated (and far more lucrative) liver transplant procedure.

On Jan. 9, the South China Morning Post reported, "Organs from executed prisoners are being offered for up to $300,000 each to Hong Kong liver transplant patients who travel to a mainland hospital."

A reporter from the paper, inquiring about the possibility of a liver transplant for a friend, was told by a doctor at Sun Yat Sen University of Medical Sciences in Chengdu, "[T]he organs are of good quality as they come from young prisoners."

The doctor went on to say, "I cannot make it too clear … if you miss this chance [before Lunar New Year], you may have to wait until Labor Day. Some prisoners have been sentenced earlier. We will have some organs this month. Of course, we have to match the patient's blood type, but no need to worry. There will be lots."

At a hospital in Guangzhou, a doctor told a Morning Post reporter: "A liver transplant can be easily arranged, and consent is not an issue. There is no provision in mainland law for prisoners to give consent to donate organs."

What happened to the 1984 "consent" regulations smuggled out by Wu? There have never been any provisions made for their enforcement.

In October 1997, ABC's "Prime Time Live" aired a segment titled "Blood Money," that utilized videotape of two Chinese nationals in New York attempting to sell human organs to Wu. The Chinese nationals were arrested for allegedly violating a U.S. law that prohibits organ selling, but prosecutors eventually dropped the charges.

The overall U.S. response to Chinese organ harvesting has been tepid. The 1999 State Department "Country Report on Human Rights Practices in China" does acknowledge that "credible reports have alleged that organs from some executed prisoners were removed, sold and transplanted" and that "[t]here have been credible reports in the past that patients from abroad had undergone organ transplant operations on the mainland, using organs removed from executed prisoners."

But Amnesty International's Kumar told Congress in 1998, "We are not aware of any concrete steps taken by the Clinton administration to raise the issue with Chinese authorities."

China to end use of prisoners' organs for transplants in mid-2014

HANGZHOU, CHINA | BY LI HUI AND BEN BLANCHARD

Inmates listen to a speech at Taiyuan No.1 prison in Taiyuan, Shanxi province September 1, 2010.
REUTERS/STRINGER

China, the only country that still systematically takes organs from executed prisoners for use in transplant operations, plans to end the controversial practice by the middle of next year, a senior official said on Saturday.

By mid-2014, all hospitals licensed for organ transplants will be required to stop using organs from executed prisoners and only use those voluntarily donated and allocated through a fledging national system, said Huang Jiefu, a former deputy health minister who heads the organ transplant reform.

The supply of human organs falls far short of demand in China due in part to a traditional belief that bodies should be buried or cremated intact. An estimated 300,000 patients are wait-listed every year for organ transplants, and only about one in 30 ultimately receives a transplant.

That shortage has driven a trade in illegal organ trafficking, and in 2007 the government banned transplants from living donors, except spouses, blood relatives and step- or adopted family members.

Huang, an Australian-trained transplant surgeon, admitted the problem of an organ black market was not something China would be able to easily resolve.

"The illegal trade of human organs will be inevitable in Chinese society in the years to come. The huge demand for organs is one of the causes. As long as there's a gap between supply and demand, illegal organ trafficking won't disappear, but the government will continue to crack down on it," he told Reuters.

INTERNATIONAL CRITICISM

Beijing said in August it would begin to phase out the practice of using executed prisoners' organs this month. Huang did not give an exact date for a ban on their use.

"Using executed prisoners' organs for transplants does not meet with the ethical standards universally accepted, and has always received criticism from the international community," Huang told a meeting of health and hospital officials in the eastern city of Hangzhou. "China's organ transplant reform is the government's political commitment to the people, and the world."

"There has never been a law that regulates the use of prisoners' organs. Enforcement of the policy has many loopholes, and there have been a lot of scandals that tarnish the image of the Chinese government," Huang said.

Courts, which oversee executions, have been told they are no longer allowed to offer organs to hospitals, Huang later told Reuters, noting a trend in China anyway for fewer executions. "China has meted out fewer and fewer death sentences, so reliance on death-row inmates' donations will become a dead end. So we must rely on voluntary donations," he said.

China does not publish the numbers of people it executes, though the World Coalition Against The Death Penalty estimates it was about 4,000 last year.

VOLUNTEER PROGRAMMES

To cut back on its dependency on prisoners' organs, China has launched pilot volunteer organ donor programs in 25 provinces and municipalities since February, with the aim of creating a nationwide voluntary scheme by the end of this year.

The number of transplants using donated organs has jumped to more than 900 cases in the first seven months of this year from 245 in 2011, but is still less than half the number of organs from death-row inmates, according to data provided by Huang.

Rights groups say many organs are taken from prisoners without their consent or their family's knowledge, something the government denies.

A decrease in organ supply will also put more pressure on China's nascent donation system.

A transplant surgeon at Saturday's meeting from the nearby city of Nanjing, who asked to be identified by his last name, Li, said it was likely the new rules would limit the number of transplants they were able to carry out.

"There might be a temporary shortage of organs. If so, we will just have to do fewer transplants. There's nothing we can do about that. Other countries haven't solved that problem either," he said.

(Ben Blanchard reported from Beijing; Editing by Ian Geoghegan)

Does America Imprison Too Many People? Posner

A society can be thought of as a collection of private and public systems. At present a number of these systems in American society are under stress: the medical system, the educational system (other than elite private schooling and elite university education), the political system (especially at the legislative level), the finance industry, the fiscal system (including taxation, borrowing, and spending at all levels of government), transportation infrastructure, the regulation and assimilation of immigrants, and perhaps others. In contrast, foreign affairs, the military (and national security generally), and industries such as retailing, the production of intellectual property, computer technology, and the production of pharmaceuticals and medical technology are areas of great national strength.

Another troubled American system is that of criminal justice, with particular emphasis on the astrounding growth and level of imprisonment. Some statistics: the incarceration rate had been 118 per 100,000 in 1950, and actually fell in 1972 to 93 per 100,00. By 2000 it had reached 469 and only since the advent of the economic crisis has it begun to decline as states try to reduce expenditures. Between 1950 and 2000 the white imprisonment rate increased by 184 percent and the black imprisonment rate by 355 percent; today 40 percent of prison and jail inmates are black, although blacks are only 13 percent of the overall population. Even though the U.S. crime rate fell by a third in the 1990s (and by two-thirds in many large cities)— the murder rate by more than 40 percent—the inmate population continued growing during this period, an increase that cannot be explained by population growth, since the population grew by much less than a third in the 1990s.

The inmate population started its rapid growth in the early 1970s, largely in response to sharply rising crimes rates in the 1960s, a decade of domestic unrest. In 1960 the homicide rate was 4.6 per 100,000 persons; in 1970, 7.9; in 1980, 10.2; in 1990, 9.4—but by 2000 it had dropped 5.5 and it is about the same today, which is to say that it is almost back to where it was in 1960, before crime became a big issue. Crime rates are higher than they were in the 1950s but they are tolerable, yet the incarcerated percentage of the population remains much higher now than then.

The economist Steven Levitt, after correcting for other factors that have been proposed as explanations for the decline in crime rates since 1980, has attributed the leveling of and then decline in those rates to the increase in the prison population, along with increases in the number of police, a decline (largely, it seems, independently of law enforcement) in the consumption of crack cocaine, and the legalization of abortion in the early 1970s. Legalization resulted (Levitt argues, though his statistical evidence has been questioned) in a decline in crime rates twenty years later; unwanted children are more likely to be neglected, brought up badly, and as a result get into trouble as young adults than wanted children.

The striking thing is that although the criminal sentences are considerably more severe in the United States than in our peer countries, which one expect to have a substantial deterrent effect, the percentage of the American population that is incarcerated is the highest of any country in the world—at 2.3 million, it is about .8 percent (eight-tenths of 1 percent), which is 4 to 7 times the percentage of any of our peer countries—and our crime rates are generally no lower than in those countries and our murder rate is much higher. Although we have a larger black population than those countries, and our blacks are disproportionately engaged in crime, as noted earlier, even if their crime rate were no higher than that of the rest of the population our overall crime rate would still greatly exceed that of the other countries, because it would fall by only 27 percent from its present level, or to about 1.8 million, which is .6 percent of the population, compared to its current level of.8 percent.

Long prison sentences should deter crime, or if not deter then incapacitate the criminals and thus prevent them from committing crimes (outside the prison itself) for a long period of time. We might therefore expect to have lower crime rates than our peer countries, and, given the deterrent effect of heavy sentences, lower rates of imprisonment. The fact that instead the U.S. imprison more persons in prison than foreign countries do, yet has no lower a crime rate, calls for explanation. If the demand for crime in the U.S. were no higher than in those countries, and the supply price no lower, we would expect the the United States to have a lower crime rate if it imprisons more persons. So the fact that our crime rate isn't lower requires investigation. The investigation might show for example that we criminalize more activity, which is the equivalent of increasing the demand for crime. If an activity is criminalized, this increases the amount of crime unless the criminalization of the activity drives its level to zero.

There are a number of other possible explanations for the conjunction of a high rate of imprisonment with a high crime rate. One is not enough police, or intelligent enough police, to prevent and detect crime effectively. Another is a high elasticity of supply for criminal activity, so that discouraging or preventing one person from committing crimes induces someone else to enter the crime industry. Another (suggested above) is that we define crime too broadly, criminalizing activities that in other countries are lawful; our high rate of sexual offenses against minors is a function in part of a high age of consent (18). Or we may make too little use of fines, and of regulatory and private-litigation alternatives to criminal punishment. The prevalence of gun ownership may be a factor, along with the proximity to the United States of countries in Latin America that are large producers of illegal drugs. And finally crime rates are particularly high in the southern states of the United States, and that may have deep cultural roots.

Reform is difficult when the causes of a problem are multiple or unknown. And because the direct monetary costs of the criminal justice system are not very great by current standards (only about $40 billion a year), and there is strong hostility among the general public to criminals (another cultural fact, perhaps), and because our huge prison system provides a great deal of employment, there is no pressure for reform. Yet the indirect costs of high levels of incarceration must be very great, in the form of the lost output of the large number of prisoners, most of whom are of working age.

Feds studying private prisons as way to save money

Ottawa Bureau Chief Robert Fife and Field Producer Philip Ling, CTV News
Published Friday, September 21, 2012 10:02PM EDT
Last Updated Friday, September 21, 2012 11:58PM EDT

OTTAWA -- The Harper government has been quietly studying private prisons in other countries as a possible model to save money in federal penitentiaries, CTV News has learned.

The government hired the consulting firm Deloitte & Touche to examine prisons in seven countries aimed at building an "understanding of various models, approaches and experiences," according the 1,400-page report obtained by CTV News under the Access to Information Act.

The massive report was kept secret from Canada's Correctional Investigator Howard Sapers, who expressed concerns about for-profit prisons in Canada.

"This study came as a surprise. I wasn't aware that they had commissioned this study," Sapers said. "I'm always concerned when Corrections is treated just like another business. It's hard to find profit in that kind of enterprise."

Deloitte studied in detail 10 prisons in Canada, the United Kingdom, Australia, New Zealand, Ireland, Spain and Belgium -- providing an assessment and recommendation on each prison's "relevancy to Canadian market" and their "relation to Correctional Services Canada."

Some of those prisons in the Deloitte study were fully operated by private firms, while other institutions hired companies for basic services such as cleaning, laundry and food preparation services.

Public Safety Minister Vic Toews acknowledged he discussed the idea of private prisons with his British counterpart in a meeting in May, but said he ended up ruling it out.

"Britain indicates . . . that there were benefits. I've examined that myself, but I don't see there are sufficient benefits to change over an entire system," Toews said.

"I didn't feel there was any benefit to going toward a privatization model, that is the private supervision of prisoners," he said. "We have no interest in going to a private model which would put the supervision of prisoners in private hands."

But critics question why the government commissioned the reports, which were completed between October 2011 and this March.

"This raises the question: why would you do this kind of investigation if you don't plan to implement private prisons in Canada?" said Liberal MP Geoff Reagan. "The government should clearly bring this forward for discussion and have an open debate in Canada, instead of doing this behind closed doors."

NDP MP Paul Dewar said his party is against private prisons because the experience in other countries "has been a disaster."

"The problem with privatizing prisons is it's all about profits and not rehabilitation," he said. "What we need to know is: what is the real agenda? The government -- are they going to privatize prisons or not?"

Toews did say he is open to limited private-sector involvement, adding that "there are private services being offered in prisons already." He pointed out Canadian institutions already have private dental, medical and psychiatric services.

"We're always looking at ways ensure that we can provide services at the best cost for the taxpayer," he said.

The government is trying to cut spending, while imposing tougher sentences on criminals.

The Conservative government has passed a number of tough-on-crime laws since taking power in 2006, including a controversial omnibus crime bill in March.

Ottawa is spending about $600 million to build 2,700 new cells in the coming years. It is also closing two federal prisons -- the Kingston Penitentiary and the Leclerc Institution -- a move that the government says will save $120 million per year.

The Deloitte study comes as U.S. private prison firms have been lobbying a number of government departments in Ottawa for fresh opportunities.

Representatives from Florida-based GEO group met in August 2011 with Public Safety officials to promote the company's services. The company even offered to set up a tour of its Australian facilities, but the offer was declined. Records also show that Toews was lobbied by a consultant representing GEO Group in October of that year.

United States, United Kingdom and Australia have already turned to the private companies to manage prison facilities. More than 200 institutions worldwide are operated privately, according to data from the Association of Private Correctional and Treatment Organizations.

Pennsylvania rocked by 'jailing kids for cash' scandal

By Stephanie Chen
CNN

(CNN) -- At a friend's sleepover more than a year ago, 14-year-old Phillip Swartley pocketed change from unlocked vehicles in the neighborhood to buy chips and soft drinks. The cops caught him.

There was no need for an attorney, said Phillip's mother, Amy Swartley, who thought at most, the judge would slap her son with a fine or community service.

But she was shocked to find her eighth-grader handcuffed and shackled in the courtroom and sentenced to a youth detention center. Then, he was shipped to a boarding school for troubled teens for nine months.

"Yes, my son made a mistake, but I didn't think he was going to be taken away from me," said Swartley, a 41-year-old single mother raising two boys in Wilkes-Barre, Pennsylvania.

CNN does not usually identify minors accused of crimes. But Swartley and others agreed to be named to bring public attention to the issue.

As scandals from Wall Street to Washington roil the public trust, the justice system in Luzerne County, in the heart of Pennsylvania's struggling coal country, has also fallen prey to corruption. The county has been rocked by a kickback scandal involving two elected judges who essentially jailed kids for cash. Many of the children had appeared before judges without a lawyer.

The nonprofit Juvenile Law Center in Philadelphia said Phillip is one of at least 5,000 children over the past five years who appeared before former Luzerne County President Judge Mark Ciavarella.

Ciavarella pleaded guilty earlier this month to federal criminal charges of fraud and other tax charges, according to the U.S. attorney's office. Former Luzerne County Senior Judge Michael Conahan also pleaded guilty to the same charges. The two secretly received more than $2.6 million, prosecutors said.

The judges have been disbarred and have resigned from their elected positions. They agreed to serve 87 months in prison under their plea deals. Ciavarella and Conahan did not return calls, and their attorneys told CNN that they have no comment.

Ciavarella, 58, along with Conahan, 56, corruptly and fraudulently "created the potential for an increased number of juvenile offenders to be sent to juvenile detention facilities," federal court documents alleged. Children would be placed in private detention centers, under contract with the court, to increase the head count. In exchange, the two judges would receive kickbacks.

The Juvenile Law Center said it plans to file a class-action lawsuit this week representing what they say are victims of corruption. Juvenile Law Center attorneys cite a few examples of harsh penalties Judge Ciavarella meted out for relatively petty offenses:

• Ciavarvella sent 15-year-old Hillary Transue to a wilderness camp for mocking an assistant principal on a MySpace page.

• He whisked 13-year-old Shane Bly, who was accused of trespassing in a vacant building, from his parents and confined him in a boot camp for two weekends.

• He sentenced Kurt Kruger, 17, to detention and five months of boot camp for helping a friend steal DVDs from Wal-Mart.

Several other lawsuits on behalf of the juveniles who have appeared in Ciavarella's courtroom have emerged.

The private juvenile detention centers, owned by Mid Atlantic Youth Services Corp., are still operating and are not a target of the federal investigation, according court documents. The company cooperated in the investigation, the documents said.

A spokesman from the company denied that its current owner, Gregory Zappala, knew about the kickbacks.

Ciavarella assured the community that he could provide justice. Elected to the bench in 1996, he once ran for judge on the promise that he would punish "people who break the law," according to local reports.

The corruption began in 2002, when Conahan shut down the state juvenile detention center and used money from the Luzerne County budget to fund a multimillion-dollar lease for the private facilities. Despite some raised eyebrows from the community, county commissioners approved the deal.

The federal government began investigating in 2006.

"It's been a dark cloud hanging over the county for a very, very long time," said Luzerne County Commissioner Maryanne C. Petrilla, whose office approved the judges' budgets during the corruption. "I'm looking forward to the ship turning around now and us moving in the right direction."

The kickback scandal highlights a major problem in the juvenile justice system in Luzerne County and across the country, attorneys say. They say hundreds of children who appeared before Ciavarella didn't have lawyers.

"Kids think very much in the present, and they have limited abilities to understand long-term consequences," said Robin Dahlberg, an attorney at the American Civil Liberties Union in New York who specializes in juvenile issues.

Dahlberg's recent study in Ohio revealed that some of the counties had as many as 90 percent of children going through the court system without a lawyer.

"This Pennsylvania case is a sad reminder of why kids need an attorney," she said.

A 1967 Supreme Court ruling says children have a right to counsel. However, many states allow children and their parents to appear without an attorney by completing a waiver.

Pennsylvania is among about half of the states in the country that allow waivers to be signed for juveniles to appear before a judge without an attorney, legal experts say.

In Luzerne County, teens who waived counsel were at greater risk of being sent to placement center than those with representation.

About 50 percent of the children who waived counsel before Ciavarella were sent to some kind of placement, the Philadelphia-based Juvenile Law Center reports. In comparison, the Juvenile Court Judges' Commission in Pennsylvania found that 8.4 percent of juveniles across the state wind up in placement.

"When you have this many kids waiving counsel, then that's way out of line," said Marsha Levick, an attorney at the Juvenile Law Center. "There was no record [Ciavarella] was assuring the child and parent about the consequences of not having representation."

Minors charged with nonviolent crimes were often given harsher sentences than what probation officers recommended, court documents say. Other investigators say the trials lasted a few minutes at most.

All four of the teens cited in this story say they appeared before Ciavarella without lawyers.

"I was sort of shocked and taken aback," Hillary Transue, the MySpace offender who is now 17, said of her experience in Ciavarella's courtroom in April 2007. "I didn't really understand what was going on."

The Juvenile Law Center says it first red-flagged Ciavarella in 1999 after discovering that a 13-year-old boy was detained without being read his rights and had appeared in court without a lawyer. When the case became public, Ciavarella promised the public that every minor in his courtroom would have a lawyer.

Judges must verbally explain the consequences of appearing in court without counsel to minors and parents, lawyers say. Juvenile Law Center officials say Ciavarella neglected to do so in many cases.

Yet in the past five years, attorneys, law enforcement officials and other judges did not report Ciavarella's behavior to the Judicial Conduct Board of Pennsylvania, says Joseph A. Massa Jr., chief counsel at the board.

Privatizing detention facilities is a growing in popularity among governments because the companies say they offer lower rates than the state.

Pennsylvania has the second highest number of private facilities after Florida, accounting for about 11 percent of the private facilities in the United States, according to the National Center for Juvenile Justice in Pittsburgh, Pennsylvania.

Critics say private prisons lack transparency because they don't go through the same inspections and audits as a state facility, and this may have allowed payoffs to go so long without being noticed.

"Once somebody is going to make more money by holding more kids, there is a pretty good predictable profit motive," said criminal justice consultant Judith Greene, who heads a nonprofit group called Justice Strategies. "It's predictable that companies are going to tolerate certain behaviors they shouldn't."

An audit draft obtained by the Philadelphia Inquirer showed that Luzerne County was spending more than $1.2 million in expenses that weren't allowed under state regulations. The Pennsylvania Department of Public Welfare, the agency overseeing the audits, says the audit drafts are not final.

The audits also allege that two people paid the judges. Attorneys for former Mid-Atlantic owner Robert Powell say that their client is one of those people but that he was pressured by the judges to make payments. The attorneys say Powell never offered to pay the judges, never sought to influence any juvenile case and is now cooperating with the investigation. Zappala and Powell were partners until Zappala bought out Powell in 2008.

Senior Judge Arthur E. Grim of Berks County is reviewing the cases for minors who appeared before Ciavarella. Court officials say some children may have their records expunged or be granted new hearings.

The Philadelphia Bar Association has expressed outrage, assuring the public that the rest of the judges on the state's bench are "composed of highly qualified, honorable and honest people, who take their responsibilities to the public very seriously."

But some of the children -- many who, like Phillip Swartley, are now young adults -- have become jaded and believe that their cases were tainted in Ciavarella's courtroom.

After being sent to boarding school, Phillip, now 15, became withdrawn and depressed, his mother says.

"What do these kids see of the legal system and of authority figures?" Amy Swartley asked.
"These kids see people who abuse their power. Now, we have a whole county and generation of children who have lost trust in the system.

Module 3 - Individual Legal but Risky Behaviour

Unit 6 – Obesity

Perspective

APRIL 30, 2009

Ounces of Prevention — The Public Policy Case for Taxes on Sugared Beverages

Kelly D. Brownell, Ph.D., and Thomas R. Frieden, M.D., M.P.H.

> Sugar, rum, and tobacco are commodities which are nowhere necessaries of life, which are become objects of almost universal consumption, and which are therefore extremely proper subjects of taxation.
>
> Adam Smith, *The Wealth of Nations*, 1776

The obesity epidemic has inspired calls for public health measures to prevent diet-related diseases. One controversial idea is now the subject of public debate: food taxes.

Forty states already have small taxes on sugared beverages and snack foods, but in the past year, Maine and New York have proposed large taxes on sugared beverages, and similar discussions have begun in other states. The size of the taxes, their potential for generating revenue and reducing consumption, and vigorous opposition by the beverage industry have resulted in substantial controversy. Because excess consumption of unhealthful foods underlies many leading causes of death, food taxes at local, state, and national levels are likely to remain part of political and public health discourse.

Sugar-sweetened beverages (soda sweetened with sugar, corn syrup, or other caloric sweeteners and other carbonated and uncarbonated drinks, such as sports and energy drinks) may be the single largest driver of the obesity epidemic. A recent meta-analysis found that the intake of sugared beverages is associated with increased body weight, poor nutrition, and displacement of more healthful beverages; increasing consumption increases risk for obesity and diabetes; the strongest effects are seen in studies with the best methods (e.g., longitudinal and interventional vs. correlational studies); and interventional studies show that reduced intake of soft drinks improves health.[1] Studies that do not support a relationship between consumption of sugared beverages and health outcomes tend to be conducted by authors supported by the beverage industry.[2]

Sugared beverages are marketed extensively to children and adolescents, and in the mid-1990s, children's intake of sugared beverages surpassed that of milk. In the past decade, per capita intake of calories from sugar-sweetened beverages has increased by nearly 30% (see bar graph)[3]; beverages now account for 10 to 15% of the calories consumed by children and adolescents. For each extra can or glass of sugared beverage consumed per day, the likelihood of a child's becoming obese increases by 60%.[4]

Taxes on tobacco products have been highly effective in reducing consumption, and data indicate that higher prices also reduce soda consumption. A review conducted by Yale University's Rudd Center for Food Policy and Obesity suggested that for every 10% increase in price, consumption decreases by 7.8%. An industry trade publication reported even larger reductions: as prices of carbonated soft drinks increased by 6.8%, sales dropped by 7.8%, and as Coca-Cola prices increased by 12%, sales dropped by 14.6%.[5] Such studies — and the economic principles that support their findings — suggest that a tax on sugared beverages would encourage consumers to switch to more healthful beverages, which would lead to reduced caloric intake and less weight gain.

The increasing affordability of soda — and the decreasing affordability of fresh fruits and vegetables (see line graph) — probably contributes to the rise in obesity in the United States. In 2008, a group of child and health care advocates in New York proposed a one-penny-per-ounce excise tax on sugared beverages, which would be expected to reduce consumption by 13% — about two servings per week per person. Even if one quarter of the calories consumed from sugared beverages are replaced by other food, the decrease in consumption would lead to an estimated reduction of 8000 calories per

person per year — slightly more than 2 lb each year for the average person. Such a reduction in calorie consumption would be expected to substantially reduce the risk of obesity and diabetes and may also reduce the risk of heart disease and other conditions.

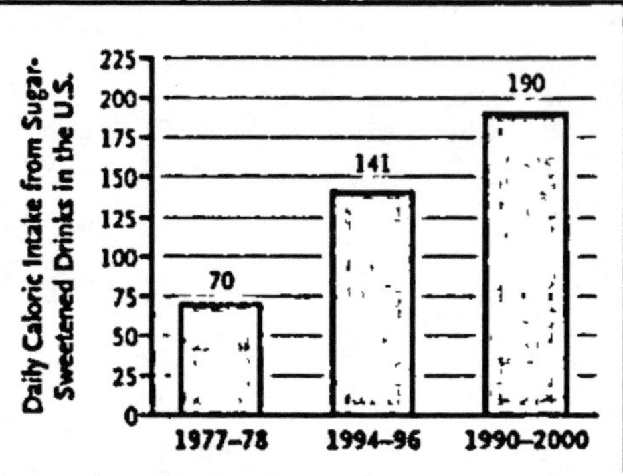

Daily Caloric Intake from Sugar-Sweetened Drinks in the United States.

Data are from Nielsen and Popkin.[3]

Some argue that government should not interfere in the market and that products and prices will change as consumers demand more healthful food, but several considerations support government action. The first is externality — costs to parties not directly involved in a transaction. The contribution of unhealthful diets to health care costs is already high and is increasing — an estimated $79 billion is spent annually for overweight and obesity alone — and approximately half of these costs are paid by Medicare and Medicaid, at taxpayers' expense. Diet-related diseases also cost society in terms of decreased work productivity, increased absenteeism, poorer school performance, and reduced fitness on the part of military recruits, among other negative effects.

The second consideration is information asymmetry between the parties to a transaction. In

the case of sugared beverages, marketers commonly make health claims (e.g., that such beverages provide energy or vitamins) and use techniques that exploit the cognitive vulnerabilities of young children, who often cannot distinguish a television program from an advertisement.

A third consideration is revenue generation, which can further increase the societal benefits of a tax on soft drinks. A penny-per-ounce excise tax would raise an estimated $1.2 billion in New York State alone. In times of economic hardship, taxes that both generate this much revenue and promote health are better options than revenue initiatives that may have adverse effects.

Objections have certainly been raised: that such a tax would be regressive, that food taxes are not comparable to tobacco or alcohol taxes because people must eat to survive, that it is unfair to single out one type of food for taxation, and that the tax will not solve the obesity problem. But the poor are disproportionately affected by diet-related diseases and would derive the greatest benefit from reduced consumption; sugared beverages are not necessary for survival; Americans consume about 250 to 300 more calories daily today than they did several decades ago, and nearly half this increase is accounted for by consumption of sugared beverages; and though no single intervention will solve the obesity problem, that is hardly a reason to take no action.

The full impact of public policies becomes apparent only after they take effect. We can estimate changes in sugared-drink con-

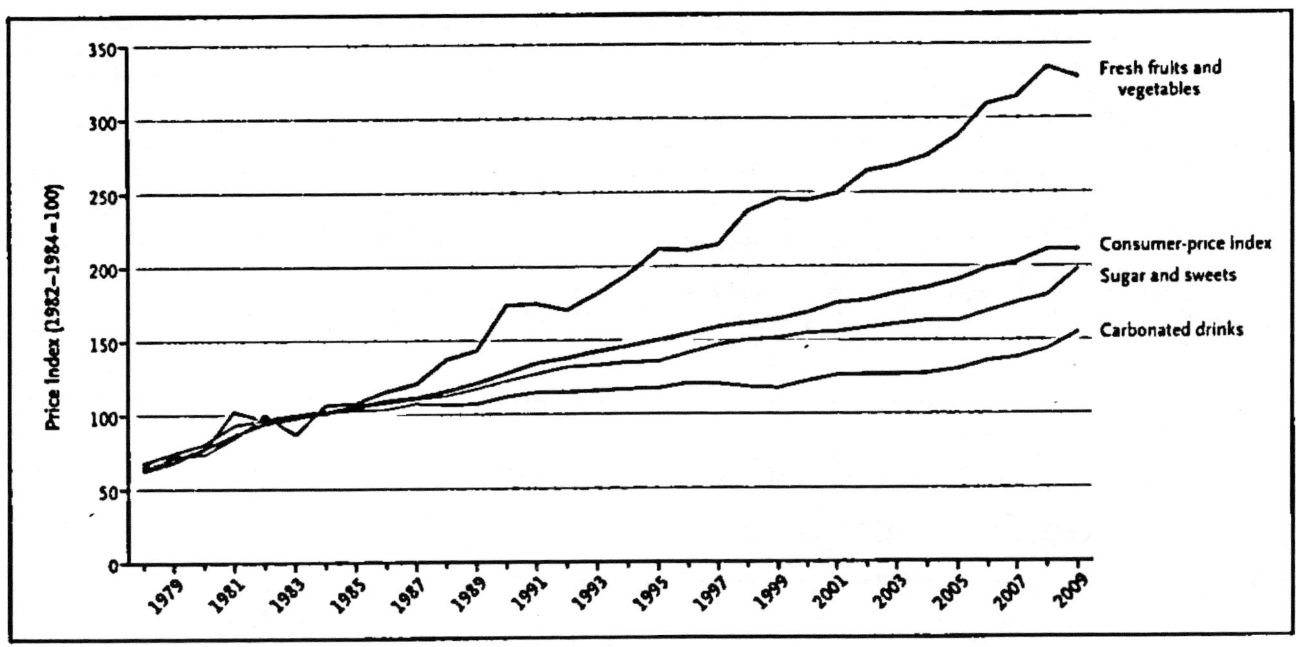

Relative Price Changes for Fresh Fruits and Vegetables, Sugars and Sweets, and Carbonated Drinks, 1978–2009.
Data are from the Bureau of Labor Statistics and represent the U.S. city averages for all urban consumers in January of each year.

sumption that would be prompted by a tax, but accompanying changes in the consumption of other foods or beverages are more difficult to predict. One question is whether the proportions of calories consumed in liquid and solid foods would change. And shifts among beverages would have different effects depending on whether consumers substituted water, milk, diet drinks, or equivalent generic brands of sugared drinks.

Effects will also vary depending on whether the tax is designed to reduce consumption, generate revenue, or both; the size of the tax; whether the revenue is earmarked for programs related to nutrition and health; and where in the production and distribution chain the tax is applied. Given the heavy consumption of sugared beverages, even small taxes will generate substantial revenue, but only heftier taxes will significantly reduce consumption.

Sales taxes are the most common form of food tax, but because they are levied as a percentage of the retail price, they encourage the purchase of less-expensive brands or larger containers. Excise taxes structured as a fixed cost per ounce provide an incentive to buy less and hence would be much more effective in reducing consumption and improving health. In addition, manufacturers generally pass the cost of an excise tax along to their customers, including it in the price consumers see when they are making their selection, whereas sales taxes are seen only at the cash register.

Although a tax on sugared beverages would have health benefits regardless of how the revenue was used, the popularity of such a proposal increases greatly if revenues are used for programs to prevent childhood obesity, such as media campaigns, facilities and programs for phys-

ical activity, and healthier food in schools. Poll results show that support of a tax on sugared beverages ranges from 37 to 72%; a poll of New York residents found that 52% supported a "soda tax," but the number rose to 72% when respondents were told that the revenue would be used for obesity prevention. Perhaps the most defensible approach is to use revenue to subsidize the purchase of healthful foods. The public would then see a relationship between tax and benefit, and any regressive effects would be counteracted by the reduced costs of healthful food.

A penny-per-ounce excise tax could reduce consumption of sugared beverages by more than 10%. It is difficult to imagine producing behavior change of this magnitude through education alone, even if government devoted massive resources to the task. In contrast, a sales tax on sugared drinks would generate considerable rev-

125

enue, and as with the tax on tobacco, it could become a key tool in efforts to improve health.

No potential conflict of interest relevant to this article was reported.

Dr. Brownell is a professor and director of the Rudd Center for Food Policy and Obesity, Yale University, New Haven, CT. Dr. Frieden is the health commissioner for the City of New York.

This article (10.1056/NEJMp0902392) was published at NEJM.org on April 8, 2009

1. Vartanian LR, Schwartz MB, Brownell KD. Effects of soft drink consumption on nutrition and health: a systematic review and meta-analysis. Am J Public Health 2007;97 667-75.
2. Forshee RA, Anderson PA, Storey ML. Sugar-sweetened beverages and body mass index in children and adolescents: a meta-analysis. Am J Clin Nutr 2008 87.1662-71.
3. Nielsen SJ, Popkin BM. Changes in beverage intake between 1977 and 2001. Am J Prev Med 2004,27:205-10. [Erratum, Am J Prev Med 2005,28 413]
4. Ludwig DS, Peterson KE, Gortmaker SL. Relation between consumption of sugar-sweetened drinks and childhood obesity: a prospective, observational analysis. Lancet 2001;357.505-8.
5. Elasticity: big price increases cause Coke volume to plummet. Beverage Digest. November 21, 2008 3-4.

GLOBAL HEALTH

Rationing Antiretroviral Therapy in Africa — Treating Too Few, Too Late

Nathan Ford, D.H.A., Edward Mills, Ph.D., and Alexandra Calmy, M.D.

Related article, p. 1815

The past 6 years have seen striking advances in access to antiretroviral therapy in Africa. From 2002 onward, the international drive to scale up antiretroviral treatment gained considerable momentum, most notably with the establishment of the Global Fund to Fight AIDS, Tuberculosis, and Malaria, the "3 by 5" Initiative of the World Health Organization (WHO), and the U.S. President's Emergency Plan for AIDS Relief (PEPFAR). Today, an estimated 3 million people in the developing world are receiving antiretroviral therapy.

The momentum has now begun to wane, with various groups arguing that the focus on AIDS has had its day and that health care funding should now be redirected to other areas, such as maternal and child health and primary care. But before the international community gives up on prioritizing care for patients with HIV infection, we believe that on-the-ground discussions must address not only whether enough has been done to scale up treatment but also whether

the treatment that patients are receiving is good enough.

The standard approach to HIV treatment in Africa is to wait until people are visibly sick, treat them with effective but poorly tolerated drugs, and then wait until they are sick again before switching regimens. There are several problems with this approach.

The first is that too few people are receiving treatment. The 3 million people receiving antiretroviral therapy are usually said to account for about 30% of the need for such treatment, but even this rate reflects the use of stringent eligibility criteria that have been abandoned in wealthier countries.

Second, we are waiting until people are symptomatic before they are treated. In most African countries, patients begin receiving treatment when the CD4+ count falls below 200 cells per cubic millimeter, at which point most patients already have symptomatic and severe (WHO stage 3 or 4) infection. In the United States and Europe, treatment is initiated earlier — as

soon as the CD4+ count reaches 350 cells per cubic millimeter — and increasingly, experts are arguing that even that is too late.

In many patients in Africa, the CD4+ count takes only about a year to decline from the cutoff for such early initiation to that for the later initiation now practiced in developing countries.[1] Although delaying therapy may mean saving money on drugs during this period, the long-term cost of such delays is increased substantially by the need for more intensive clinical care, decreased income, and likely regimen switches. Cost is thus no longer a tenable justification for delaying therapy. More important, recent observational data presented by Kitahata et al. in this issue of the *Journal* (pages 1815–1826) show that the risk of death increases by 69% when the initiation of therapy is delayed until the CD4+ count drops below 350 cells per cubic millimeter. Patients' immunologic nadir — how low their CD4+ count is allowed to drop — is predictive of the degree of benefit they will

HEALTH POLICY REPORT

The Public Health and Economic Benefits of Taxing Sugar-Sweetened Beverages

Kelly D. Brownell, Ph.D., Thomas Farley, M.D., M.P.H., Walter C. Willett, M.D., Dr.P.H.,
Barry M. Popkin, Ph.D., Frank J. Chaloupka, Ph.D., Joseph W. Thompson, M.D., M.P.H.,
and David S. Ludwig, M.D., Ph.D.

The consumption of sugar-sweetened beverages has been linked to risks for obesity, diabetes, and heart disease[1-3]; therefore, a compelling case can be made for the need for reduced consumption of these beverages. Sugar-sweetened beverages are beverages that contain added, naturally derived caloric sweeteners such as sucrose (table sugar), high-fructose corn syrup, or fruit-juice concentrates, all of which have similar metabolic effects.

Taxation has been proposed as a means of reducing the intake of these beverages and thereby lowering health care costs, as well as a means of generating revenue that governments can use for health programs.[4-7] Currently, 33 states have sales taxes on soft drinks (mean tax rate, 5.2%), but the taxes are too small to affect consumption and the revenues are not earmarked for programs related to health. This article examines trends in the consumption of sugar-sweetened beverages, evidence linking these beverages to adverse health outcomes, and approaches to designing a tax system that could promote good nutrition and help the nation recover health care costs associated with the consumption of sugar-sweetened beverages.

CONSUMPTION TRENDS AND HEALTH OUTCOMES

In recent decades, intake of sugar-sweetened beverages has increased around the globe; for example, intake in Mexico doubled between 1999 and 2006 across all age groups.[8] Between 1977 and 2002, the per capita intake of caloric beverages doubled in the United States across all age groups[9] (Fig. 1). The most recent data (2005–2006) show that children and adults in the United States consume about 172 and 175 kcal daily, respectively, per capita from sugar-sweetened beverages.

The relationship between the consumption of sugar-sweetened beverages and body weight has been examined in many cross-sectional and longitudinal studies and has been summarized in systematic reviews.[1,2] A meta-analysis showed positive associations between the intake of sugar-sweetened beverages and body weight — associations that were stronger in longitudinal studies than in cross-sectional studies and in studies that were not funded by the beverage industry than in those that were.[2] A meta-analysis of studies involving children[10] — a meta-analysis that was supported by the beverage industry — was interpreted as showing that there was no evidence of an association between consumption of sugar-sweetened beverages and body weight, but it erroneously gave large weight to several small negative studies; when a more realistic weighting was used, the meta-analysis summary supported a positive association.[11] A prospective study involving middle-school students over the course of 2 academic years showed that the risk of becoming obese increased by 60% for every additional serving of sugar-sweetened beverages per day.[12] In an 8-year prospective study involving women, those who increased their consumption of sugar-sweetened beverages at year 4 and maintained this increase gained 8 kg, whereas those who decreased their intake of sugar-sweetened beverages at year 4 and maintained this decrease gained only 2.8 kg.[13]

Short-term clinical trials provide an experimental basis for understanding the way in which sugar-sweetened beverages may affect adiposity. Tordoff and Alleva[14] found that as compared with total energy intake and weight during a 3-week period in which no beverages were provided, total energy intake and body weight increased when subjects were given 530 kcal of sugar-sweetened beverages per day for 3 weeks but decreased when

127

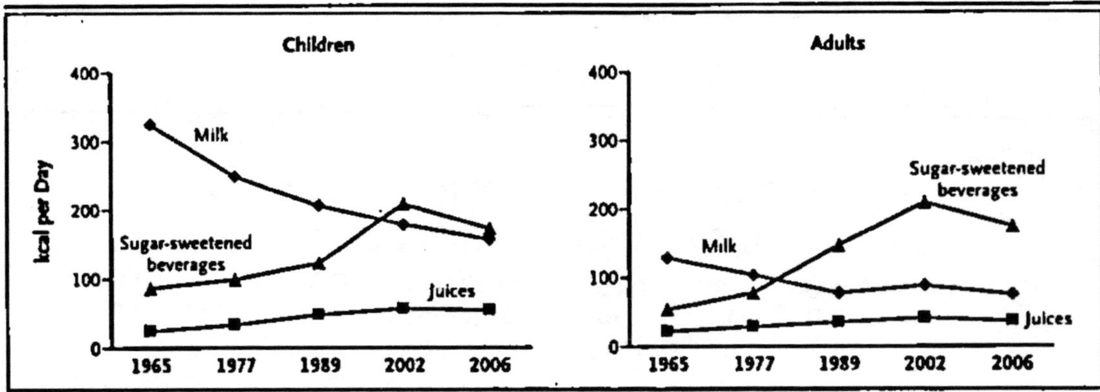

Figure 1. U.S. Trends in Per Capita Calories from Beverages.

Data are for U.S. children 2 to 18 years of age and adults 19 years of age or older. Data have been weighted to be nationally representative, with the use of methods that generate measures of each beverage that are comparable over time. Data for 1965–2002 are from Duffey and Popkin[9]; data for 2005–2006 have not been published previously.

subjects were given noncaloric sweetened beverages for the same length of time. Raben et al.[15] reported that obese subjects gained weight when they were given sucrose, primarily in the form of sugar-sweetened beverages, for 10 weeks, whereas they lost weight when they were given noncaloric sweeteners for the same length of time.

Four long-term, randomized, controlled trials examining the relationship between the consumption of sugar-sweetened beverages and body weight have been reported; the results showed the strongest effects among overweight persons. A school-based intervention to reduce the consumption of carbonated beverages was assessed among 644 students, 7 to 11 years of age, in the United Kingdom with the use of a cluster design.[16] After 1 year, the intervention group, as compared with the control group, had a nonsignificantly lower mean body-mass index (the weight in kilograms divided by the square of the height in meters) and a significant 7.7% lower incidence of obesity. In a study involving 1140 Brazilian schoolchildren, 9 to 12 years of age, that was designed to discourage the consumption of sugar-sweetened beverages, no overall effect on body-mass index was observed during the 9-month academic year.[17] Among students who were overweight at baseline, the body-mass index was nonsignificantly decreased in the intervention group as compared with the control group; the difference was significant among overweight girls. In another clinical trial, 103 high-school students in Boston were assigned to a control group or to an intervention group that received home delivery of noncaloric beverages for 25 weeks. The body-mass index was nonsignificantly reduced in the overall intervention group, but among students in the upper third of body-mass index at baseline, there was a significant decrease in the body-mass index in the intervention group, as compared with the control group (a decrease of 0.63 vs. an increase of 0.12).[18] The effects of replacing sugar-sweetened beverages with milk products were examined among 98 overweight Chilean children.[19] After 16 weeks, there was a nonsignificantly lower increase in the percentage of body fat in the intervention group than in the control group (0.36% and 0.78% increase, respectively), whereas there was a significantly greater increase in lean mass in the intervention group (0.92 vs. 0.62 kg).

Three prospective, observational studies — one involving nurses in the United States, one involving Finnish men and women, and one involving black women — each showed positive associations between the consumption of sugar-sweetened beverages and the risk of type 2 diabetes.[13,20,21] Among the 91,249 women in the Nurses' Health Study II who were followed for 8 years, the risk of diabetes among women who consumed one or more servings of sugar-sweetened beverages per day was nearly double the risk among women who consumed less than one serving of sugar-sweetened beverages per month[13]; about half the excess risk was accounted for by greater body weight. Among black women, excess weight accounted for most of the excess risk.

Among 88,520 women in the Nurses' Health

Study, the risk of coronary heart disease among women who consumed one serving of sugar-sweetened beverages per day, as compared with women who consumed less than one serving per month, was increased by 23%, and among those who consumed two servings or more per day, the risk was increased by 35%.[3] Increased body weight explained some, but not all, of this association.

MECHANISMS LINKING SUGAR-SWEETENED BEVERAGES WITH POOR HEALTH

A variety of behavioral and biologic mechanisms may be responsible for the associations between the consumption of sugar-sweetened beverages and adverse health outcomes, with some links (e.g., the link between intake of sugar-sweetened beverages and weight gain) better established than others. The well-documented adverse physiological and metabolic consequences of a high intake of refined carbohydrates such as sugar include the elevation of triglyceride levels and of blood pressure and the lowering of high-density lipoprotein cholesterol levels, which would be expected to increase the risk of coronary heart disease.[22] Because of the high glycemic load of sugar-sweetened beverages, consumption of these beverages would be expected to increase the risk of diabetes by causing insulin resistance and also through direct effects on pancreatic islet cells.[23] Observational research has shown that consumption of sugar-sweetened beverages, but not of noncalorically sweetened beverages, is associated with markers of insulin resistance.[24]

Intake of sugar-sweetened beverages may cause excessive weight gain owing in part to the apparently poor satiating properties of sugar in liquid form. Indeed, adjustment of caloric intake at subsequent meals for energy that had been consumed as a beverage is less complete than adjustment of intake for energy that had been consumed as a solid food.[25] For example, in a study involving 323 adults, in which 7-day food diaries were used, energy from beverages added to total energy intake instead of displacing other sources of calories.[26] The results of a study of school-age children were consistent with the data from adults and showed that children who drank 9 oz or more of sugar-sweetened beverages per day consumed nearly 200 kcal per day more than those who did not drink sugar-sweetened beverages.[27]

Short-term studies of the effect of beverage consumption on energy intake support this mechanism. Among 33 adults who were given identical test lunches on six occasions but were given beverages of different types (sugar-sweetened cola, noncaloric cola, or water) and amounts (12 oz [355 ml] or 18 oz [532 ml]),[28] the intake of solid food did not differ across conditions; the result was that there was significantly greater total energy consumption when the sugar-sweetened beverages were served.

Sugar-sweetened beverages may also affect body weight through other behavioral mechanisms. Whereas the intake of solid food is characteristically coupled to hunger, people may consume sugar-sweetened beverages in the absence of hunger, to satisfy thirst or for social reasons. Sugar-sweetened beverages may also have chronic adverse effects on taste preferences and food acceptance. Persons — especially children — who habitually consume sugar-sweetened beverages rather than water may find more satiating but less sweet foods (e.g., vegetables, legumes, and fruits) unappealing or unpalatable, with the result that their diet may be of poor quality.

ECONOMIC RATIONALE

Economists agree that government intervention in a market is warranted when there are "market failures" that result in less-than-optimal production and consumption.[29,30] Several market failures exist with respect to sugar-sweetened beverages. First, because many persons do not fully appreciate the links between consumption of these beverages and health consequences, they make consumption decisions with imperfect information. These decisions are likely to be further distorted by the extensive marketing campaigns that advertise the benefits of consumption. A second failure results from time-inconsistent preferences (i.e., decisions that provide short-term gratification but long-term harm). This problem is exacerbated in the case of children and adolescents, who place a higher value on present satisfaction while more heavily discounting future consequences. Finally, financial "externalities" exist in the market for sugar-sweetened beverages in that consumers do not bear the full costs of their consumption decisions. Because of the contribution of the consumption of sugar-sweetened beverages to obesity, as well as the health consequences that are independent of weight, the consumption of sugar-sweetened beverages generates excess health care costs. Medical costs for overweight and obesity alone are estimated to be $147 billion — or 9.1% of U.S. health care expenditures — with half these costs paid for publicly through the Medicare and Medicaid programs.[31]

AN EFFECTIVE TAX POLICY AND PROJECTED EFFECTS

Key factors to consider in developing an effective policy include the definition of taxable beverages, the type of tax (sales tax or excise tax), and the tax rate. We propose an excise tax of 1 cent per ounce for beverages that have any added caloric sweetener. An alternative would be to tax beverages that exceed a threshold of grams of added caloric sweetener or of kilocalories per ounce. If this approach were used, we would recommend that the threshold be set at 1 g of sugar per ounce (30 ml) (32 kcal per 8 oz [237 ml]). Another option would be a tax assessed per gram of added sugar, but such an approach would be difficult to administer. The advantage of taxing beverages that have any added sugar is that this kind of tax is simpler to administer and it may promote the consumption of no-calorie beverages, most notably water; however, a threshold approach would also promote calorie reductions and would encourage manufacturers to reformulate products. A consumer who drinks a conventional soft drink (20 oz [591 ml]) every day and switches to a beverage below this threshold would consume approximately 174 fewer calories each day.

A specific excise tax (a tax levied on units such as volume or weight) per ounce or per gram of added sugar would be preferable to a sales tax or an ad valorem excise tax (a tax levied as a percentage of price) and would provide an incentive to reduce the amount of sugar per ounce of a sugar-sweetened beverage. Sales taxes added as a percentage of retail cost would have three disadvantages: they could simply encourage the purchase of lower-priced brands (thus resulting in no calorie reduction) or of large containers that cost less per ounce; consumers would become aware of the added tax only after making the decision to purchase the beverage; and the syrups

that are used in fountain drinks, which are often served with multiple refills, would remain untaxed. A number of states currently exempt sugar-sweetened beverages from sales taxes along with food, presumably because food is a necessity. This practice should be eliminated, whether or not an excise tax is enacted.

Excise taxes could be levied on producers and wholesalers, and the cost would almost certainly be passed along to retailers, who would then incorporate it into the retail price; thus, consumers would become aware of the cost at the point of making a purchase decision. Taxes levied on producers and wholesalers would be much easier to collect and enforce than taxes levied on retailers because of the smaller number of businesses that would have to comply with the tax; in addition, the sugar used in syrups could be taxed — a major advantage because of the heavy sales of fountain drinks. Experience with tobacco and alcohol taxes suggests that specific excise taxes have a greater effect on consumption than do ad valorem excise taxes and can also generate more stable revenues because they are less dependent on industry pricing strategies.[32] In addition, tax laws should be written with provisions for the regular adjustment of specific excise taxes to keep pace with inflation, in order to prevent the effect of the taxes on both prices and revenues from eroding over time.

A tax of 1 cent per ounce of beverage would increase the cost of a 20-oz soft drink by 15 to 20%. The effect on consumption can be estimated through research on price elasticity (i.e., consumption shifts produced by price). The price elasticity for all soft drinks is in the range of −0.8 to −1.0.[33] (Elasticity of −0.8 suggests that for every 10% increase in price, there would be a decrease in consumption of 8%, whereas elasticity of −1.0 suggests that for every 10% increase in price, there would be a decrease in consumption of 10%.) Even greater price effects are expected from taxing only sugar-sweetened beverages, since some consumers will switch to diet beverages. With the use of a conservative estimate that consumers would substitute calories in other forms for 25% of the reduced calorie consumption, an excise tax of 1 cent per ounce would lead to a minimum reduction of 10% in calorie consumption from sweetened beverages, or 20 kcal per person per day, a reduction that is sufficient for weight loss and reduction in risk (unpublished data). The benefit would be larger among consumers who consume higher volumes, since these consumers are more likely to be overweight and appear to be more responsive to prices.[7] Higher taxes would have greater benefits.

A controversial issue is whether to tax beverages that are sweetened with noncaloric sweeteners. No adverse health effects of noncaloric sweeteners have been consistently demonstrated, but there are concerns that diet beverages may increase calorie consumption by justifying consumption of other caloric foods or by promoting a preference for sweet tastes.[34] At present, we do not propose taxing beverages with noncaloric sweeteners, but we recommend close tracking of studies to determine whether taxing might be justified in the future.

REVENUE-GENERATING POTENTIAL

The revenue generated from a tax on sugar-sweetened beverages would be considerable and could be used to help support childhood nutrition programs, obesity-prevention programs, or health care for the uninsured or to help meet general revenue needs. A national tax of 1 cent per ounce on sugar-sweetened beverages would raise $14.9 billion in the first year alone. Taxes at the state level would also generate considerable revenue — for example, $139 million in Arkansas, $183 million in Oregon, $221 million in Alabama, $928 million in Florida, $937 million in New York, $1.2 billion in Texas, and $1.8 billion in California. A tax calculator that is available online can generate revenue numbers for states and 25 major cities.[35]

OBJECTIONS, INDUSTRY REACTION, PUBLIC SUPPORT, AND FRAMING

One objection to a tax on sugar-sweetened beverages is that it would be regressive. This argument arose with respect to tobacco taxes but was challenged successfully by proponents of the taxes, who pointed out that the poor face a disproportionate burden of smoking-related illnesses, that nearly all smokers begin to smoke when they are teenagers, and that both groups are sensitive to price changes.[7] In addition, some of the tobacco revenue has been used for programs developed specifically for the poor and for youth. The poor are most affected by illnesses that are related to unhealthful diets, and brand loyalties for beverages tend to be set by the teenage years. In addition, sugar-sweetened beverages are not necessary for survival, and an alternative (i.e., water) is available at little or no cost; hence, a tax that shifted intake from sugar-sweetened beverages to water would benefit the poor both by improving health and by lowering expenditures on beverages. Designating revenues for programs promoting childhood nutrition, obesity prevention, or health care for the uninsured would preferentially help those most in need.

A second objection is that taxing sugar-sweetened beverages will not solve the obesity crisis and is a blunt instrument that affects even those who consume small amounts of such beverages. Seat-belt legislation and tobacco taxation do not eliminate traffic accidents and heart disease but are nevertheless sound policies. Similarly, obesity is unlikely to yield to any single policy intervention, so it is important to pursue multiple opportunities to obtain incremental gains. Reducing caloric intake by 1 to 2% per year would have a marked impact on health in all age groups, and the financial burden on those who consumed small amounts of sugar-sweetened beverages would be minimal.

Opposition to a tax by the beverage industry is to be expected, given the possible effect on sales; opposition has been seen in jurisdictions that have considered such taxes and can be predicted from the behavior of the tobacco industry under similar circumstances.[36] PepsiCo threatened to move its corporate headquarters out of New York when the state considered implementing an 18% sales tax on sugar-sweetened beverages.[37] The tobacco industry fought policy changes by creating front groups with names that suggested community involvement. The beverage industry has created Americans Against Food Taxes.[38] These reactions suggest that the beverage industry believes that a tax would have a substantial impact on consumption.

Public support for food and beverage taxes to address obesity has increased steadily. Questions about taxes in polls have been asked in various ways, and the results are therefore not directly comparable from year to year, but overall trends are clear. Support for food taxes rose from 33% in 2001 to 41% in 2003 and then to 54% in 2004.[39] A 2008 poll of New York State residents showed that 52% of respondents support a soda tax; 72% support such a tax if the revenue is used to support programs for the prevention of obesity in children and adults. The way in which the issue is framed is essential; support is highest when the tax is introduced in the context of promoting health and when the revenues are earmarked for programs promoting childhood nutrition or obesity prevention.

CONCLUSIONS

The federal government, a number of states and cities, and some countries (e.g., Mexico[8]) are considering levying taxes on sugar-sweetened beverages. The reasons to proceed are compelling. The science base linking the consumption of sugar-sweetened beverages to the risk of chronic diseases is clear. Escalating health care costs and the rising burden of diseases related to poor diet create an urgent need for solutions, thus justifying government's right to recoup costs.

As with any public health intervention, the precise effect of a tax cannot be known until it is implemented and studied, but research to date suggests that a tax on sugar-sweetened beverages would have strong positive effects on reducing consumption.[5,33] In addition, the tax has the potential to generate substantial revenue to prevent obesity and address other external costs resulting from the consumption of sugar-sweetened beverages, as well as to fund other health-related programs. Much as taxes on tobacco products are routine at both state and federal levels because they generate revenue and they confer a public health benefit with respect to smoking rates, we believe that taxes on beverages that help drive the obesity epidemic should and will become routine.

Supported in part by grants from the Rudd Foundation (to Dr. Brownell), the National Institutes of Health (R01-CA121152, to Dr. Popkin), and the Robert Wood Johnson Foundation (to Dr. Chaloupka).

No potential conflict of interest relevant to this article was reported.

From the Rudd Center for Food Policy and Obesity, Yale University, New Haven, CT (K D B); the Department of Health and Mental Hygiene, City of New York, New York (T.F); the Department of Nutrition, Harvard School of Public Health (W C.W), and the Optimal Weight for Life Program, Children's Hospital, and Harvard Medical School (D S L.) — all in Boston; the Department of Nutrition and the University of North Carolina Interdisciplinary Obesity Center, University of North Carolina, Chapel Hill (B M P); the Department of Economics and the University of Illinois at Chicago Health Policy Center, University of Illinois, Chicago (F J C.); and the University of Arkansas for Medical Sciences and the Surgeon General's Office, State of Arkansas, Little Rock (J W T)

This article (10.1056/NEJMhpr0905723) was published on September 16, 2009, and was updated on March 31, 2010, at NEJM org

1. Malik VS, Schulze MB, Hu FB. Intake of sugar-sweetened beverages and weight gain: a systematic review. Am J Clin Nutr 2006;84:274-88.
2. Vartanian LR, Schwartz MB, Brownell KD. Effects of soft drink consumption on nutrition and health: a systematic review and meta-analysis. Am J Public Health 2007,97.667-75.
3. Fung TT, Malik V, Rexrode KM, Manson JE, Willett WC, Hu FB. Sweetened beverage consumption and risk of coronary heart disease in women. Am J Clin Nutr 2009,89:1037-42.
4. Brownell KD. Get slim with higher taxes. New York Times. December 15, 1994:A29.
5. Brownell KD, Frieden TR. Ounces of prevention — the public policy case for taxes on sugared beverages. N Engl J Med 2009; 360:1805-8.
6. Jacobson MF, Brownell KD. Small taxes on soft drinks and snack foods to promote health. Am J Public Health 2000;90: 854-7.
7. Powell LM, Chaloupka FJ. Food prices and obesity: evidence and policy implications for taxes and subsidies. Milbank Q 2009; 87:229-57.
8. Barquera S, Hernandez-Barrera L, Tolentino ML, et al. Energy intake from beverages is increasing among Mexican adolescents and adults. J Nutr 2008;138:2454-61.
9. Duffey KJ, Popkin BM. Shifts in patterns and consumption of beverages between 1965 and 2002. Obesity (Silver Spring) 2007; 15:2739-47.
10. Forshee RA, Anderson PA, Storey ML. Sugar-sweetened beverages and body mass index in children and adolescents: a meta-analysis. Am J Clin Nutr 2008,87:1662-71. [Erratum, Am J Clin Nutr 2009,89.441-2.]
11. Malik VS, Willett WC, Hu FB. Sugar-sweetened beverages and BMI in children and adolescents: reanalyses of a meta-analysis. Am J Clin Nutr 2009,89:438-9.
12. Ludwig DS, Peterson KE, Gortmaker SL. Relation between consumption of sugar-sweetened drinks and childhood obesity: a prospective, observational analysis. Lancet 2001;357:505-8.
13. Schulze MB, Manson JE, Ludwig DS, et al. Sugar-sweetened beverages, weight gain, and incidence of type 2 diabetes in young and middle-aged women. JAMA 2004;292:927-34.
14. Tordoff MG, Alleva AM. Effect of drinking soda sweetened with aspartame or high-fructose corn syrup on food intake and body weight. Am J Clin Nutr 1990,51.963-9.
15. Raben A, Vasilaras TH, Moller AC, Astrup A. Sucrose compared with artificial sweeteners: different effects on ad libitum food intake and body weight after 10 wk of supplementation in overweight subjects. Am J Clin Nutr 2002;76:721-9.
16. James J, Thomas P, Cavan D, Kerr D. Preventing childhood obesity by reducing consumption of carbonated drinks: cluster randomised controlled trial. BMJ 2004;328.1237. [Erratum, BMJ 2004;328:1236.]
17. Sichieri R, Paula Trotte A, de Souza RA, Veiga GV. School randomised trial on prevention of excessive weight gain by discouraging students from drinking sodas. Public Health Nutr 2009;12:197-202.
18. Ebbeling CB, Feldman HA, Osganian SK, Chomitz VR, Ellenbogen SJ, Ludwig DS. Effects of decreasing sugar-sweetened beverage consumption on body weight in adolescents: a randomized, controlled pilot study. Pediatrics 2006;117:673-80.
19. Albala C, Ebbeling CB, Cifuentes M, Lera L, Bustos N, Ludwig DS. Effects of replacing the habitual consumption of sugar-sweetened beverages with milk in Chilean children. Am J Clin Nutr 2008,88.605-11.
20. Montonen J, Jarvinen R, Knekt P, Heliövaara M, Reunanen A.

Consumption of sweetened beverages and intakes of fructose and glucose predict type 2 diabetes occurrence. J Nutr 2007;137: 1447-54.

21. Palmer JR, Boggs DA, Krishnan S, Hu FB, Singer M, Rosenberg L. Sugar-sweetened beverages and incidence of type 2 diabetes mellitus in African American women. Arch Intern Med 2008;168 1487-92.

22. Appel LJ, Sacks FM, Carey VJ, et al. Effects of protein, monounsaturated fat, and carbohydrate intake on blood pressure and serum lipids: results of the OmniHeart randomized trial. JAMA 2005;294-2455-64.

23. Ludwig DS. The glycemic index: physiological mechanisms relating to obesity, diabetes, and cardiovascular disease. JAMA 2002;287:2414-23.

24. Yoshida M, McKeown NM, Rogers G, et al. Surrogate markers of insulin resistance are associated with consumption of sugar-sweetened drinks and fruit juice in middle and older-aged adults. J Nutr 2007;137:2121-7.

25. Mourao DM, Bressan J, Campbell WW, Mattes RD. Effects of food form on appetite and energy intake in lean and obese young adults. Int J Obes (Lond) 2007;31:1688-95.

26. De Castro JM. The effects of the spontaneous ingestion of particular foods or beverages on the meal pattern and overall nutrient intake of humans. Physiol Behav 1993;53:1133-44.

27. Harnack L, Stang J, Story M. Soft drink consumption among US children and adolescents: nutritional consequences. J Am Diet Assoc 1999;99-436-41.

28. Flood JE, Roe LS, Rolls BJ. The effect of increased beverage portion size on energy intake at a meal. J Am Diet Assoc 2006; 106:1984-90.

29. Cawley J. An economic framework for understanding physical activity and eating behaviors. Am J Prev Med 2004;27:117-25.

30. Finkelstein EA, Ruhm CJ, Kosa KM. Economic causes and consequences of obesity. Annu Rev Public Health 2005;26:239-57.

31. Finkelstein EA, Trogdon JG, Cohen JW, Dietz W. Annual medical spending attributable to obesity: payer-and-service-specific estimates. Health Aff (Millwood) 2009;28.w822-w831.

32. Chaloupka FJ, Peck RM., Tauras JA, Yurekli A. Cigarette excise taxation: the impact of tax structure on prices, revenues, and cigarettes smoking. Geneva: World Health Organization (in press).

33. Andreyeva T, Long MW, Brownell KD. The impact of food prices on consumption: a systematic review of research on price elasticity of demand for food. Am J Public Health (in press).

34. Mattes RD, Popkin BM. Nonnutritive sweetener consumption in humans: effects on appetite and food intake and their putative mechanisms. Am J Clin Nutr 2009;89:1-14.

35. Rudd Center for Food Policy and Obesity. Revenue calculator for soft drink taxes. (Accessed September 24, 2009, at http://www.yaleruddcenter.org/sodatax.aspx.)

36. Brownell KD, Warner KE. The perils of ignoring history: big tobacco played dirty and millions died: how similar is big food? Milbank Q 2009;87:259-94.

37. Hakim D, McGeehan P. New York vulnerable to poaching in recession. New York Times. March 1, 2009.

38. Americans Against Food Taxes home page. (Accessed September 24, 2009, at http.//nofoodtaxes.com.)

39. Brownell KD. The chronicling of obesity: growing awareness of its social, economic, and political contexts. J Health Polit Policy Law 2005;30.955-64.

Unit 7 – Risky Pastimes

growth and change

Growth and Change
Vol. 45 No. 1 (March 2014), pp. 98–120

DOI: 10.1111/grow.12034

Access to Legal Gambling and the Incidence of Crime: Evidence from Alberta

BRAD R. HUMPHREYS AND BRIAN P. SOEBBING

ABSTRACT   Much research examines the positive and negative impacts of gambling in specific areas, including the relationship between gambling, such as casinos and electronic gaming, on crime. Since Grinols and Mustard, the academic literature finds a mixed relationship. The present research examines the relationship between video lottery terminals (VLTs) and casino gambling and crime in the province of Alberta from 1977 to 2008 using data from the Uniform Crime Reporting Survey Estimates from a two-way fixed effect regression indicate little association between gambling and crime. However, some positive and negative crime-specific effects are found for both casinos and VLTs.

Introduction

A small, growing literature examines the relationship between access to legal gambling and crime. Much of this evidence comes from the U.S. No consensus exists regarding the nature of this relationship; some studies found a positive association, whereas others found no association. The gambling–crime relationship has important public policy implications because communities across North America have been expanding access to legal gambling to increase the government revenues generated by these activities (Kearney 2005). However, increased crime associated with casinos could increase costs in the jurisdiction to fight the increase in crime (Eadington 1999).

Research on the relationship between access to legal gambling and crime occurs within the larger context of evaluating the overall costs and benefits to society generated by gambling (Kearney 2005). Walker (2007) argued that accounting for legal and justice costs (and benefits) of gambling based on government provision of judicial and

Brad R. Humphreys is an associate professor in the College of Business & Economics, West Virginia University, Morgantown, WV 26506, USA. His e-mail address is: brhumphreys@wvu.edu. Brian P. Soebbing is an assistant professor in the School of Kinesiology, Louisiana State University, 112 Huey P. Long Field House, Baton Rouge, LA 70803, USA. His e-mail address is: bsoebb1@lsu.edu. We acknowledge the financial support of the Alberta Gambling Research Institute for this research. Some results in this paper appear in Humphreys, B. R., Soebbing, B. P., Wynne, H., Turvey, J., and Lee, Y. S. (2011). University of Alberta SEIGA research team: Final report to the Alberta Gaming Research Institute on the socio-economic impact of gambling in Alberta. May 25, 2011. We thank Harold Wynne, Yang Seung Lee and John Turvey for their assistance and support, and acknowledge their contribution to the earlier report that informs this research.

Submitted May 2012; revised December 2012; accepted March 2013.

police services is problematic. Thus, researchers should examine data from specific jurisdictions using information about individual crimes and not government financial accounts.

The present study examines the relationship between legal gambling, in the form of casinos and video lottery terminals (VLTs) in bars and taverns, in the Canadian Province of Alberta. Alberta represents an interesting setting, as a large number of casinos and VLTs are scattered throughout the province. The numbers of VLTs that are operated throughout the province are limited and have not changed over time. However, VLT locations changed as existing machines moved to different communities, providing a good empirical setting to examine the relationship between access to VLTs and crime. Finally, violent crime is less common in Canada compared to the U.S., where much of the previous research was based. The present research examines the relationship between access to VLTs and casinos over time in communities and nine different types of crime using data from the Canadian Uniform Crime Report (UCR) from 1977 to 2008. The sample period encompasses time both before and after legalized gambling existed in the province. Based on Walker's (2007) observations, the present research focuses only on estimating the statistical relationship between gambling and crime in Alberta, and does not attempt to estimate a monetary value of the benefits and costs of crime.

Results from a reduced form regression model of the determination of the incidence of nine types of crime find little statistical association between access to legal gambling and crime. However, the introduction of VLTs is associated with an increase in credit card fraud and a decrease in prostitution and shoplifting. The introduction of casinos is also associated with an increase in robberies and a decrease in shoplifting. The addition of lags and leads to the empirical model, like in Grinols and Mustard (2006), shows declines in the incidence rates of many of these types of crimes following the opening of a new casino in a community. These results provide new evidence on the relationship between legal gambling and crime, and show that the relationship is not necessarily positive.

Literature Review

A large body of research exists on the overall costs and benefits generated by increased access to legal gambling, where crime represents an important source of costs. Kearney (2005) documented the increase in access to legal gambling over the past 30 years in North America and demonstrated the importance of assessing the costs and benefits of this increased access. Walker (2003) pointed out the problems inherent in any full cost–benefit accounting of gambling in society. Researchers generally focus on the relationship between legal gambling and specific costs and benefits, including the effect of casinos on property values (Wenz 2007), bankruptcy rates (Koo, Rosentraub, and Horn 2007), individuals' quality of life (Wenz 2008), and fatal alcohol-related traffic accidents (Cotti and Walker 2010).

This research is theoretically motivated by the routine activities and rational choice theories. Rey, Mack, and Koschinsky (2012) stated that these two theories are complementary when explaining crime. In rational choice, "Crime is assumed a priori to involve rational calculation and is viewed essentially as an economic transaction or a question of occupational choice" (Clarke and Cornish 1985: 156). Becker's (1968) seminal model of crime is rooted in rational choice theory. In his model, committing a crime is a utility maximizing choice made by individuals who compare the expected costs and benefits of committing a crime and engage in criminal behavior if the expected benefits outweigh the expected costs. Since Becker's theoretical model, crime has been extensively studied as an economic activity in the economics literature.

Routine activities theory addresses the environment that a crime is being committed (Rey, Mack, and Koschinsky 2012). Cohen and Felson (1979) defined routine activities as "any recurrent and prevalent activities which provide for basic population and individual needs, whatever their biological or cultural origins" (p. 593). Specifically dealing with crime, the theory predicts that a crime is likely to be committed due to the convergence of three factors in one location: a person who is likely to commit a crime, a target, and the absence of protection that would deter a person to commit a crime (Rey, Mack, and Koschinsky 2012). Routine activities theory is especially useful when examining casinos and access to legal gambling in the broader context of economic development. Policy makers in communities may use gambling as a way to attract tourists to an area, increasing the opportunities for crime (Giacopassi and Stitt 1993). Both rational choice and routine activities theories explain how the presence of legal gambling can affect crime and why the impact may differ across types of legal gambling and categories of crime. In Alberta, VLTs exist in bars and taverns located near other businesses and residential areas in small and large communities so many VLT gamblers may arrive on foot and gamblers may be difficult to distinguish from other patrons; casinos tend to be relatively large venues located away from other businesses; many gamblers drive and park at the facility and few non-gamblers are present. In terms of rational choice theory, VLT gamblers may have a different expected benefit than casino gamblers for criminals, as they can be difficult to distinguish from non-gambling bar and tavern patrons and may be on foot, reducing the expected benefit of some crimes such as robbery in contrast to casinos where gamblers arrive by car and park in large underground parking lots potentially carrying large amounts of cash.

In terms of routine activities theory, casino gamblers congregate in large numbers at casinos which provides an increase in the number of likely targets which may attract individuals more likely to commit certain crimes such as robbery but not others such as drug use or shoplifting. Rational choice theory also predicts that different crimes may have different expected costs, especially in light of the locational differences for VLTs and casinos. VLTs located in high-traffic areas may increase the likelihood of detection of a crime, increasing the total costs of commission, relative to casinos with large, often underground, parking lots. VLTs in bars and taverns may be located near other commercial establishments, increasing the ability to commit crimes such as shoplifting. Both theories predict that the relationship between different forms of legal gambling and different types of crime should not be uniform; VLT gambling might be expected to increase shoplifting, for example, if many bars with VLTs are located near convenience stores; casino gambling might be expected to increase robbery if the presence of large number of casino gamblers carrying large sums of cash attracted more individuals intent on committing robbery.

Gambling and crime.   Typically, casinos are chosen to examine the relationship between legal gambling and crime. This relationship has considerable interest for many stakeholders because the initial development of casino gambling in the U.S. was linked to organized crime and crime continues to be a visible measure of the quality of life in a community. Early research by Giacopassi and Stitt (1993) examined the impact of casino gambling on crime in Biloxi, Mississippi, and found that larceny and motor vehicle theft were the only categories of crime associated with the introduction of casinos. However, no significant effect was found for violent crimes.

Grinols and Mustard (2006) performed an extensive statistical analysis of the relationship between casinos and crime in the U.S. They concluded that approximately 8 percent of the crimes occurring in the U.S. counties with casinos were attributable to the presence of casinos. The crimes affected by casino openings included several types of violent crimes (aggravated assault, robbery, rape), burglary, and auto theft. The crime rates increased 3 to 5 years after the opening of a casino in a county.

Grinols and Mustard's (2006) results attracted considerable attention. Walker (2008a,b) criticized Grinols and Mustard on methodological grounds, whereas Reece (2010) raised additional issues regarding the methodology and cast doubt on the conclusion that casinos cause crime to increase. He found that the presence of hotels near casinos, an omitted variable from the Grinols and Mustard study, made inviting targets for criminals committing crimes such as robbery, car theft, and prostitution. Reece (2010) also examined the temporal lag between the opening of a casino and the increase in crime, and showed that hotels were built and opened several years after casinos opened in communities, providing an alternative to Grinols and Mustard's explanation for the temporal lag.

Clark and Walker (2009) found a positive and significant relationship between the amount young adults lost while gambling and the likelihood of committing a crime. Wheeler, Round, and Wilson (2011) examined the relationship between expenditure on electronic gaming and crime in the state of Victoria in Australia. Their research grouped crimes into income-generating crimes (such as robbery, fraud, and theft) and non–income-generating crimes (defined as all other crimes committed). Increased spending on electronic gaming was associated with increased rates of income-generating and non–income-generating crimes in 1996, 2001, and 2006. Hyclak (2011) examined the relationship between the presence of casinos and crimes committed on nearby college campuses in four Midwestern U.S. states. Car thefts increased on campuses close to casinos, but robberies and burglaries did not.

Overall, the strong positive relationship between casinos and crime reported by Grinols and Mustard (2006) has not been found in other settings while this body of research casts considerable doubt on their results. Little attention has been paid to the relationship between other forms of legal gambling, such as electronic gaming, and crime. The lack of consensus about the relationship between legal gambling and crime in the literature suggests that additional research in other settings needs to be conducted. The present research focuses on the province of Alberta.

Legal gambling in Alberta.   In 1980, Alberta's first private casino opened in Calgary. The Criminal Code of Canada was modified in 1985 to transfer legal gambling authority from federal control to the provinces, in addition to legalizing VLT and slot machine gambling. Seven years after the change, VLTs were introduced in Alberta. The province initially authorized 6,000 VLTs, and the number authorized has remained constant, although the location of VLTs, and the precise number in operation, has changed over time. In 2011, 5,694 VLTS were installed and operated at 1,030 bars and taverns. Although successful as a form of entertainment and an important source of gambling revenue, many communities viewed VLTs with hostility. In response to plebiscites, and despite the objections of retailers, VLTs were voted to be "removed" from seven communities in Alberta by its citizens. For example, in Fort McMurray, VLTs were eliminated from bars and lounges due to increased concerns related to problem gambling, and concentrated in the casino. They effectively remained in the community, but as slot machines (permitted in casinos since 1996). The most recent change in Alberta's gambling environment was the construction of First Nations casinos on tribal reserve land. Currently, five First Nations casinos exist in Alberta, all of which comply with the Alberta Gaming and Liquor Commission (AGLC) charitable gaming model, but with provisions that allow flexibility to provide additional financial resources in terms of revenues and jobs to addressing issues within First Nations' communities.

A wide array of legal gambling activities are available in Alberta, including casino gambling at both private charity casinos and casinos on First Nations reserve land with table games and slot machines, horse race gambling and slot machines at "racinos," VLTs in bars and pubs, and other traditional legal gambling activities such as lottery and bingo. We focus on VLTs and casinos because of the variation in the availability of these forms of legal gambling over the period for which crime data exist; bingo, lottery outlets, and horse racing venues did not change much over the sample period, making them less interesting from an empirical perspective. Table 1 summarizes the availability of casino, racino, and slot machine gambling in the province in 2008. Note that the casinos in Kananaskis and Whitecourt opened in 2008 on First Nations reserve lands after the sample period ends, so these casinos are not included in the analysis.

The AGLC has the responsibility for regulating gaming and managing the distribution of gambling revenues in Alberta. The AGLC also regulates the operation of casinos and the location and operation of VLTs. Under its oversight, a charitable gaming model was established to ensure that the proceeds and benefits of legalized gambling were

TABLE 1. CASINOS AND RACINOS IN ALBERTA FOR 2008.

Community	Casinos	Racinos	Slot machines
Calgary	7	—	4,591
Camrose	1	—	200
Cold Lake	1	—	150
Edmonton	6	1	4,296
Fort McMurray	1	—	399
Grande Prairie	1	1	491
Kananaskis	1	—	300
Lethbridge	1	1	398
Medicine Hat	1	—	230
Red Deer	2	—	598
St. Albert	1	—	240
Whitecourt	1	—	250
Total	**24**	**3**	**12,143**

Source: Various websites, Alberta Gaming and Liquor Commission Website and Annual Reports.

returned to the citizens of Alberta. The charitable gaming model in Alberta allows charity and non-profit organizations to benefit from legal gambling in Alberta. Charitable gambling revenues are distributed to community organizations through two mechanisms: the Alberta Lottery Fund and event licenses granted to individual organizations for casino, bingo, and instant win gambling activities. This model could have an impact on the relationship between legal gambling and crime since gambling revenues explicitly benefit good causes in the province and could affect the expected costs and benefits of crime. Since VLT and casino location are tightly regulated, and the number of VLTs in the province has been constant, this can also mitigate potential correlation between the presence of legal gambling in a community and unobservable factors affecting crime rates as provincial regulators attempt to maximize gambling revenues generated for charitable causes.

Charitable gambling revenues generated by ticket lotteries, slot machines, keno, and VLTs are distributed to community groups through the Alberta Lottery Fund. In 2007–2008, $1.62 billion in gambling revenues were transferred to the Alberta Lottery Fund according to the AGLC Annual Report. This money is then paid out in the form of grants to community organizations—an estimated $465 million during 2007–2008. Access to charitable gaming revenues requires that a charitable, religious, or non-profit group apply for a license and provide volunteers from their membership to contribute labor for operating charity casinos.

Researchers from different backgrounds have analyzed the impacts of legalized gambling on communities. One common impact studied is the relationship between legalized gambling and crime. The results from previous research have been mixed, increasing the importance of studying the relationship in additional jurisdictions. The present research examines the province of Alberta due to the importance of gambling revenues within the province for both the government and the charitable organizations but also the wide availability for the citizens throughout the large province. Based on the history of the legalization of gambling in Canada and the change in regulation policy over the past decades, examining the relationship before and after the regulation change provides additional information to researchers and public policy makers.

Empirical Analysis of VLTs, Casinos, and Crime Rates

Following the general practice in the literature, the present research estimates reduced form regression models that explain the determination of crimes committed in specific areas in Alberta over time. These models include variables that reflect access to legal gambling opportunities, in this case VLTs and casinos, in each area. Alberta has a relatively large number of casinos and horse racing tracks with slot machines, 27 by the end of the sample, and almost 6,000 VLTs located in bars and taverns throughout the province. Casinos and racinos opened over the last 30 years, and the number and location of VLTs has changed, providing variation in the availability of these forms of legal gambling across areas and over time.

Crime in Alberta.   The crime data source used, the UCR, comes from Statistics Canada in association with the Canadian Centre for Justice Statistics (CCJS). The UCR is an annual census based on all incidents of crime reported to the policing community in jurisdictions in Canada. Detailed historical crime data are available for a large number of communities in Alberta in the UCR. The CCJS cooperates with various police agencies to collect crime statistics through the UCR. The data reflect reported crimes substantiated by police investigation. The crime data in the UCR are available annually over the period 1977–2008, providing an opportunity to examine crime before and after the casinos and VLTs were legally established in the province.

The present research uses data from the UCR1 survey, an aggregate survey for reporting incidents across jurisdictions throughout Canada. An "incident" is the basis for counting a reported crime and is defined as a set of connected crime-related events usually constituting an occurrence report and represents a single event that may include multiple crimes. To avoid double counting of crimes, an incident that involves the commission of multiple crimes is identified only once in the UCR, based on the most serious offence committed. Under the most serious offense procedure, an incident containing a non-violent crime, say breaking and entering, and a violent crime, say assault, will be recorded only as an assault; this procedure can result in undercounts of crimes related to gambling. The UCR data contain information on the number of criminal incidents, incidence rates (per 100,000 population), and the clearance rate—percent of incidents where a suspect was identified—of those incidents from 1977 to 2007.

The geographic unit of observation in the UCR to analyze the relationship between gambling and crime in Alberta is a Royal Canadian Mounted Police (RCMP) Division or a metropolitan police force jurisdiction. After eliminating observations from RCMP Divisions and municipal police forces with missing data, the sample included crime data from 78 communities in Alberta. Table 2 lists the communities and the number of observations from each community in the sample. The communities that have one or more casinos, and the eight communities that do not have VLTs are identified in Table 2. Note that the present research only analyzes data from the urban part of the police jurisdictions in the UCR. The UCR contains data on incidents from the rural part of RMCP Divisions in Alberta beginning in 2002, but does not contain information on the population of these rural areas. Since the literature clearly identifies population as an important determinant of crime (the larger the population in an area, the more potential criminals and victims), a thorough statistical analysis cannot be performed. While this limitation is recognized to limit the results somewhat, if the relationship between gambling and crime in rural areas is similar to the relationship in urban areas, then the results can be generalized to the entire province. In any event, the vast majority of crime incidents take place in the urban part of RCMP Divisions.

Although Grinols and Mustard (2006) found that casino openings were related to increases in violent crimes in the U.S., violent crime rates in Canada are substantially lower, and research by Smith and Wynne (1999) reported that most of the crimes associated with gambling in Western Canada are non-violent in nature. The availability of legal gambling could affect the propensity to commit any crime to the extent that legal gambling changes either the total expected cost or benefit of committing a crime. According to Grinols and Mustard, local labor market conditions can change after the opening of a casino in a community, affecting the relative return to crime compared to work. Humphreys and Marchand (2012) developed evidence that opening new casinos had positive effects on local labor markets in Canada over this period. Since different crimes have different expected returns, labor market effects could have a differential impact on rate of commission of crimes. The focus of this analysis is on nine specific non-violent crimes identified in the UCR data: breaking and entering, credit card fraud, drug possession, illegal gambling, other fraud, prostitution, robbery, shoplifting over $5,000, and shoplifting under $5,000. In Canada, frauds are "Every one who, by deceit, falsehood or other fraudulent means, whether or not it is a false pretense within the meaning of this Act, defrauds the public or any person, whether ascertained or not, of any property, money or valuable security or any service." The "other fraud" category includes writing bad checks, selling goods or services that were never produced, or other deceitful actions. This list of crimes includes many crimes associated with gambling in Western Canada identified by Smith and Wynne and other less serious crimes that could be plausibly linked to legal gambling.

Figure 1 shows the annual incidence rate per 100,000 persons for these nine crimes in Alberta over the period 1977–2008. The red vertical lines identify three important

TABLE 2. ALBERTA COMMUNITIES IN THE SAMPLE.

Community	Observations	% sample
Airdrie	31	1.45
Athabasca	27	1.26
Banff	14	0.65
Barrhead	29	1.35
Beaumont	14	0.65
Blairmore[a]	3	0.14
Bonnyville	31	1.45
Brooks	31	1.45
Calgary[b]	31	1.45
Camrose[b]	31	1.45
Canmore	31	1.45
Cardston[a]	28	1.31
Chestermere	3	0.14
Claresholm	28	1.31
Coaldale	27	1.26
Cochrane	31	1.45
Cold Lake[b]	31	1.45
Coleman[a]	2	0.09
Crowsnest Pass[a]	27	1.26
Devon	31	1.45
Didsbury	28	1.31
Drayton Valley	31	1.45
Drumheller	31	1.45
Edmonton[b]	31	1.45
Edson	31	1.45
Fairview	28	1.31
Fort Macleod	28	1.31
Fort McMurray[b]	31	1.45
Fort Saskatchewan	31	1.45
Fox Creek	28	1.31
Grande Cache	28	1.31
Grande Prairie[b]	31	1.45
Grimshaw	28	1.31
Hanna	28	1.31
High Level	28	1.31
High Prairie	28	1.31
High River	31	1.45
Hinton	32	1.49
Hobbema[a]	3	0.14
Innisfail	31	1.45
Lac La Biche	28	1.31
Lacombe	31	1.45

TABLE 2. (CONTINUED)

Community	Observations	% sample
Leduc	31	1.45
Lesser Slave Lake[a]	4	0.19
Lethbridge[b]	31	1.45
Louis Bull[a]	21	0.98
Medicine Hat[b]	31	1.45
Morinville	31	1.45
Okotoks	31	1.45
Olds	31	1.45
Peace River	31	1.45
Pincher Creek	28	1.31
Ponoka	31	1.45
Raymond[a]	28	1.31
Red Deer[b]	31	1.45
Redcliff[a]	16	0.75
Redwater	28	1.31
Rimbey	29	1.35
Rocky Mt. House	31	1.45
Sherwood Park	31	1.45
Slave Lake	31	1.45
Spruce Grove	31	1.45
St. Albert[b]	31	1.45
St. Paul	31	1.45
Stettler	31	1.45
Stony Plain	31	1.45
Strathmore	31	1.45
Swan Hills	28	1.31
Sylvan Lake	31	1.45
Taber	31	1.45
Three Hills	28	1.31
Valleyview	27	1.26
Vegreville	31	1.45
Vermilion	28	1.31
Wainwright	31	1.45
Westlock	28	1.31
Wetaskiwin	31	1.45
Whitecourt[b]	31	1.45

[a] No video lottery terminals in community.

[b] Casino in community.

Source: Uniform Crime Reporting Survey.

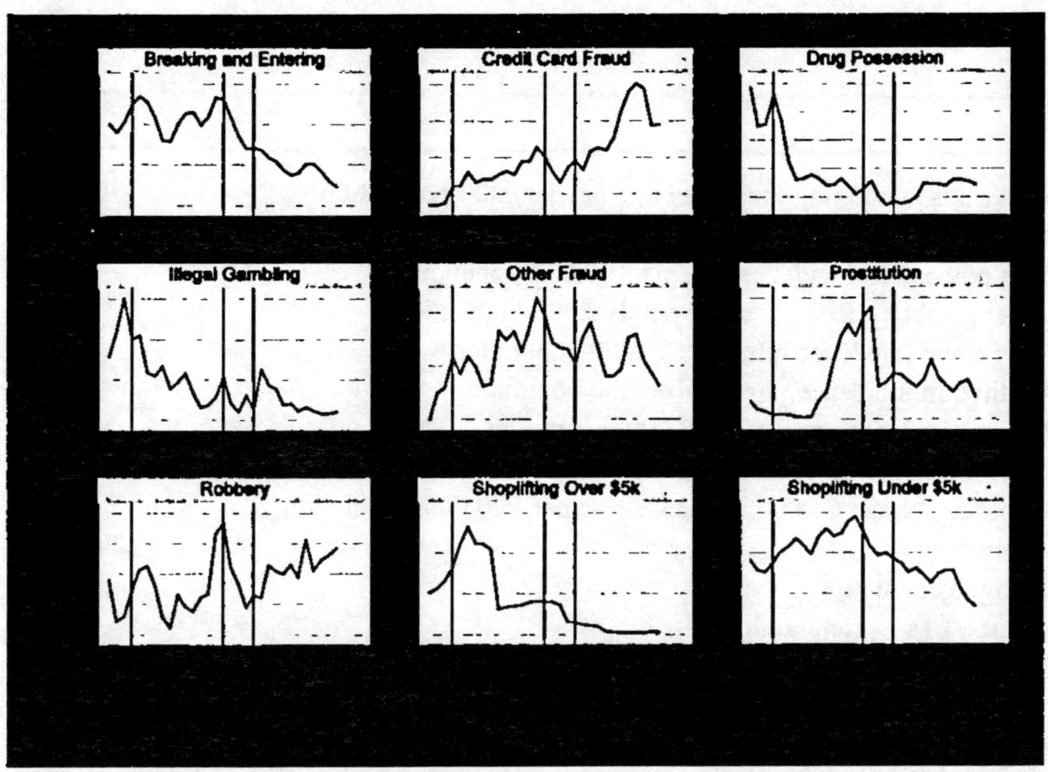

FIGURE 1. CRIME INCIDENCE RATES IN ALBERTA 1977–2008.
Source: Authors calculations based on data from the Uniform Crime Reporting Survey.

gambling-related events: the opening of casinos (1980), the introduction of VLTs (1992), and the introduction of slot machines in casinos (1996).

Figure 1 provides a general picture of the incidence rates and trends in crimes committed in Alberta. These are incidence rates so they indicate the number of crimes of each type reported to the police and determined to be genuine. Some of these crimes, including breaking and entering, drug possession, illegal gambling, and shoplifting, show clear downward trends in the incidence rates over the sample period. Others, including credit card fraud and robbery, show upward trends. There is also quite a bit of year-to-year variation in the sample period.

Detailed data on the number of VLTs in each UCR community in Alberta, as well as the dates of the opening of all casinos, were obtained from the AGLC. These data annually identify the number of VLT machines and casinos in each community. Eight communities in the sample (Blairmore, Cardston, Coleman, Crowsnest Pass, Hobbema, Lesser Slave Lake, Louis Bull, Raymond, and Redcliff) had no VLTs. One or more casinos exist in 10 communities. Since the crime data begin before the introduction of VLTs and casinos in the province, this analysis constitutes a "before and after" statistical analysis similar to Grinols and Mustard (2006). The results from the

TABLE 3. SAMPLE MEANS, CRIME INCIDENCE RATES, AND OTHER VARIABLES, 1977–2008.

Variable	Mean
Breaking and entering incidence rate per 100,000 population	1,095
Credit card fraud incidence rate per 100,000 population	54
Drug possession incidence rate per 100,000 population	397
Illegal gambling incidence rate per 100,000 population	2
Other fraud incidence rate per 100,000 population	295
Prostitution incidence rate per 100,000 population	3
Robbery incidence rate per 100,000 population	31
Shoplifting over $5,000 incidence rate per 100,000 population	16
Shoplifting under $5,000 incidence rate per 100,000 population	390
Community population	29,214
Unemployment rate	7.0
No. of VLTs in community	31

Source: Authors Calculations based on data from the Uniform Crime Reporting Survey.
VLTs, video lottery terminals.

present research reflect conditional crime rate estimates before and after the introduction of VLTs and casinos, between communities with and without VLTs and casinos, and within communities with VLTs and casinos, since the number of VLTs and casinos in communities varies over the sample period.

The focus here is on the statistical relationship between crime and VLTs and casinos. While many other types of legal gambling exist, including lottery, sports betting, bingo, and horse racing, casino gambling and VLTs generally receive most of attention within the literature on gambling and crime. Casino gambling and VLTs, unlike bingo and horse racing, has increased in popularity in recent years in Alberta, and policy makers face pressure to increase the number of venues and machines in the province.

Table 3 shows the sample means for the nine crime incidence rates per 100,000 in population and the other key variables in the analysis. Illegal gambling is relatively rare in the province. Keep in mind that these are incidence rates, not the rate of commission of crimes. Every crime committed is not reported to authorities, so incident rates understate the rate at which crimes are committed.

The introduction of VLTs and the changes in the number of VLTs in communities over time provide variation in the access to VLT gambling in each community and variation within each community over time. The regression model exploits this variation to quantify the relationship between crime and legal gambling, conditional on other observable and unobservable factors that affect crime.

Methodology

The present study analyzes the relationship between the opening of casinos in the province and the introduction of VLTs in bars and taverns and historical crime incidence rates in each of the 78 communities in the sample over the period 1977–2008 using reduced form regression models. This regression approach explains observed variation in crime incidence rates across communities and over time with observed variation in other factors that have been shown to affect crime rates in the literature, including economic factors such as the unemployment rate, demographic factors such as the population, and variation in gambling opportunities across communities and over time. The regression models control for unobservable heterogeneity in the communities and years in the sample, as well as the effect of factors known to affect crime such as the unemployment rate in the province and the population of each community, and province wide trends in crime.

A panel data model is estimated to explain observed variation in crime. The dependent variable (Y_{it}) is the crime incidence rate per 100,000 population for the nine crimes identified above in the 78 UCR communities. The dependent variables vary both across the $i = 1, 2, 3, \ldots, N (= 78)$ communities over $t = 1, 2, 3, \ldots, T (= 31)$ years. Formally, the regression models estimated take the form:

$$Y_{it} = \alpha_i + \alpha_t + \beta G_{it} + \gamma EX_{it} + e_{it} \tag{1}$$

and contain both a vector of explanatory variables that vary over cross-sectional units and time, EX_{it}, and a gambling-related explanatory variable, G_{it}, that also varies over the cross-sectional units and time. α_i, α_t, and γ are vectors of unknown parameters to be estimated. α_i is a vector of cross-sectional unit specific intercepts that capture unobservable heterogeneity in the communities. α_t is a vector of time-period specific intercepts that capture unobservable heterogeneity in each year in the sample. This could include the business cycle in the province, the regulatory environment, the effects of demographic changes, or other time varying effects. Estimates of α_i and α_t are not reported. β, the key unknown parameter of interest, captures the relationship between the gaming-related explanatory variable, G_{it}, and the outcome variable.

e_{it} is an unobservable equation error term that captures the effects of all other unobservable factors that affect the outcome variable of interest. By assumption, e_{it} is a mean zero independent and identically distributed random variable with constant variance σ_e that is uncorrelated with α_i, α_t, G_{it}, and EX_{it}. Under this assumption, ordinary least squares (OLS) applied to equation (1) produces unbiased, efficient, and consistent estimates of the population parameters of interest. We use the White-Huber "sandwich" correction for heteroscedasticity, in the form of different σ_e's for different communities and also cluster correct the estimated standard errors at the community level, to account for potential within-community correlation of the unobservable equation error term (Greene 2000).

Results

Tables 4 and 5 contain the parameter estimates, p-values, and other summary statistics from equation (1) using data on the number of casinos in each community as the gambling-related explanatory variable of interest. Recall that only 10 of the UCR communities (Calgary, Camrose, Cold Lake, Edmonton, Fort McMurray, Grand Prairie, Lethbridge, and Medicine Hat) had casinos present in one or more years in the sample period. This is a relatively simplistic measure of legal gambling opportunities, since it treats all casinos as equal in terms of their potential to affect crime rates. Since casino handle and patronage varies, a better approach would use a measure of the gambling activity that takes place inside casinos instead of a variable containing the number of casinos in each community. However, the data to perform this type of analysis are not available during the sample period. These results represent a local effect of casinos on crime because it assumes that the effect of the casino on crime does not extend beyond the nearby community.

From Tables 4 and 5, equation (1) does a somewhat mixed job in explaining the variation in the incidence of these nine crimes in communities in Alberta. Population is not related to the incidence rate of most of these crimes. Prostitution, credit card fraud, and illegal gambling respond to business cycle conditions, as captured by the provincial unemployment rate, but other crimes do not. Grinols and Mustard (2006) discussed how the commission of different crimes could respond differently to changes

TABLE 4. TWO-WAY FIXED EFFECTS REGRESSION RESULTS: CASINOS AND CRIME I.

Model Variable/crime	1 B&E	2 Credit card fraud	3 Drugs	4 Illegal gambling	5 Other fraud
Population	−6.269	−0.069	−3.111	−0.059	−2.994
	(0.264)	(0.855)	(0.147)	(0.180)	(0.032)
Population²	0.00314	−0.00000557	0.00173	0.0000377	0.00187
	(0.322)	(0.980)	(0.156)	(0.160)	(0.027)
Unemployment rate	−207	−19.93	6.697	−3.049	−94.82
	(0.092)	(<0.001)	(0.936)	(0.020)	(0.265)
Casino	24.06	19.28	8.02	0.34	14.21
	(0.741)	(0.084)	(0.767)	(0.432)	(0.459)
Time trend	200.6	21.2	−24.4	2.98	102.3
	(0.090)	(<0.001)	(0.760)	(0.016)	(0.212)
R^2	0.643	0.199	0.494	0.096	0.206

$n = 2{,}166$; p-values shown in parentheses below parameter estimates.
Source: Authors Calculations based on data from the Uniform Crime Reporting Survey.

component and, following the introduction of casinos, individuals who would have satisfied this desire for a "thrill" by shoplifting instead satisfy it by gambling in casinos.

Another explanation for the observed negative statistical relationship between casinos and crime is that the regression model is mis-specified. There may be important variables that were omitted that affects the incident rate of crime and also happens to be correlated with the presence of casinos. For example, Reece (2010) showed the importance of hotels nearby casinos in explaining the relationship between casinos and crime. Data on the presence of hotels at the casinos in the sample were not available for the sample period. Alternatively, the regression model may fail to adequately account for the clear downward secular trend in shoplifting in Alberta after 1990 visible in Figure 1, despite the presence of a time trend variable in equation (1).

The present research also examines statistical association between the number of VLTs in a community and crime. VLT gambling differs from casino gambling in important ways, so the relationship between VLT gambling and crime can be expected to differ from the casino–crime relationship. Tables 6 and 7 show parameter estimates, p-values, and other regression summary statistics from estimation of equation (1) when the gambling variable was defined as the number of VLTs in a community. The

TABLE 6. TWO-WAY FIXED EFFECTS REGRESSION RESULTS: VIDEO LOTTERY TERMINALS AND CRIME I.

Model	1	2	3	4	5
Variable/crime	B&E	Credit card fraud	Drugs	Illegal gambling	Other fraud
Population	−3.818	0.399	−2.563	−0.049	−2.742
	(0.323)	(0.392)	(0.106)	(0.200)	(0.023)
Population^2	0.00239	−0.00028	0.00151	0.0000332	0.00166
	(0.321)	(0.314)	(0.119)	(0.172)	(0.035)
Unemployment rate	−318.5	−20.28	−17.6	−2.105	−120.7
	(0.014)	(<0.001)	(0.832)	(0.268)	(0.041)
Number of VLTs	−0.253	0.057	−0.0264	0.00044	0.0662
	(0.232)	(0.038)	(0.583)	(0.650)	(0.250)
Time trend	307	21.41	−1.189	2.065	127.2
	(0.012)	(<0.001)	(0.988)	(0.268)	(0.041)
R^2	0.628	0.197	0.492	0.095	0.204

$n = 2{,}143$; p-values shown in parentheses below parameter estimates.
Source: Authors Calculations based on data from the Uniform Crime Reporting Survey.

TABLE 7. TWO-WAY FIXED EFFECTS REGRESSION RESULTS: VIDEO LOTTERY TERMINALS AND CRIME II.

Model Variable/crime	1 Prostitution	2 Robbery	3 Shoplifting < 5k	4 Shoplifting > 5k
Population	0.856	0.606	−0.309	−1.562
	(0.003)	(0.005)	(0.012)	(0.291)
Population²	−0.00046	−0.00033	0.00022	0.00124
	(0.014)	(0.028)	(0.007)	(0.186)
Unemployment rate	−2.46	−10.50	9.32	39.55
	(0.001)	(0.093)	(0.132)	(0.683)
Number of VLTs	−0.030	−0.015	−0.020	−0.169
	(0.022)	(0.221)	(0.005)	(0.001)
Time trend	1.772	9.924	−4.935	−30.23
	(0.001)	(0.094)	(0.410)	(0.683)
R^2	0.589	0.489	0.236	0.538

$n = 2,143$; p-values shown in parentheses below parameter estimates.
Source: Authors Calculations based on data from the Uniform Crime Reporting Survey.

significance of the estimated parameters on the population, unemployment, and time trend variables were identical to those in Tables 4 and 5.

The regression results in Tables 6 and 7 indicate little relationship between VLTs and crime in communities in Alberta since the introduction of VLTs in the early 1990s. There is no statistical association between the number of VLTs in communities and breaking and entering, drug possession, illegal gambling, fraud, and robbery. Credit card fraud is slightly higher in communities with VLTs, but the effect was small, since 100 additional VLTs were associated with an increase of about 5 additional incidences of credit card frauds per 100,000 population.

Interestingly, the association between the presence of VLTs and prostitution and the two types of shoplifting was negative. The incident rate of both types of shoplifting tended to decline after VLTs were introduced in communities, although the effects were small. In the case of shoplifting under $5,000, there were about two fewer incidences of these crimes per year for each additional 100 VLTs in a community. Again, these estimates are not causal, so the results do not mean that introducing VLTs caused the incidence rate of these crimes to fall in communities; it simply means that VLTs were statistically associated with lower crime. One explanation for the observed relationship between VLTs and prostitution is that some individuals have a "vice" budget that they spend on illicit behavior. When VLTs are introduced to a community, some individuals with preferences for illicit behavior may substitute VLT gambling for dealings with prostitutes. One explanation for the relationship between VLTs and shoplifting is that shoplifting has a "thrill" component in the total utility generated by committing this crime, and after the introduction of VLTs individuals who would have satisfied this desire for a "thrill" by shoplifting instead satisfy it by playing VLTs.

Another explanation for the observed negative statistical relationship between VLTs and crime is that the regression model is mis-specified. There could be some important variables that were omitted that affect the incident rate of crime and happen to be correlated with VLTs. Alternatively, the regression model may fail to adequately account for the clear downward secular trend in prostitution and shoplifting in Alberta after 1990 visible in Figure 1. The regression model contains a time trend variable that should capture this downward trend, but the trend in the model is linear and the actual trend could be non-linear. Alternatively, VLTs may have been placed in communities that experienced relatively large declines in prostitution and shoplifting by chance.

Robustness checks.   For the results reported in Tables 4–7, several robustness checks were performed. Both Grinols and Mustard (2006) and Reece (2010) emphasized the importance of temporal leads and lags when estimating the relationship between access to legal gambling and crime. The inclusion of lags and leads variables reflecting access to legal gambling in an area is related to the potential for endogeneity in the observed relationship between access to legal gambling and crime. Walker (2008b) and Grinols and Mustard (2008) discussed the issue of endogenous siting of casinos in detail. The idea is straightforward: The error term in equation (1) captures all factors that affect crime in an area other than the explanatory variables on the right hand side of equation (1). There could be factors captured in this error term that are observable by decision makers who determine the location of casinos and other forms of legal gambling that affect the decision to put a casino in a specific area. The idea that casinos may be intentionally located in high-crime areas is one example of this problem; Grinols and Mustard addressed this point. If a specific area can "self-select" into the category of areas with a casino, and the self-selection depends on unobservable factors captured in the error term in equation (1), then OLS parameter estimates from equation (1) may suffer from econometric problems. Grinols and Mustard investigated this possibility by including leads and lags of the indicator variable for the presence of a casino in a county in their econometric model.

In Alberta, the regulation of casinos and the charity gambling model used in the province mitigate the potential that casinos are intentionally located in high-crime areas. Under the charity gambling model, casinos are viewed as an important source of funds for local charitable organizations, and these organizations are granted casino "licenses" that allows them to keep the profits generated from casino gambling (net of operation costs) on one or two specific dates in exchange for providing the casino with unskilled labor on those dates. Since the provincial casino regulators want to maximize the funds going to charitable organizations from a casino, and recognize that members of these charitable organizations will go to the casino to work, it is unlikely that these casinos would be intentionally placed in high-crime areas.

The province also regulates the location and quantity of VLTs in communities. The number of VLTs in communities changed over time as the AGLC shifted VLTs around in the province and some communities eliminated them. Conversations with AGLC staff indicated that changes in VLT location in the province reflect changes in the demand for VLT gambling in communities, and not community pressure to remove them. All of the observed reallocation of VLTs in the sample was from low- to high-revenue generating locations. It is unlikely that VLT location has any relationship to crime rates in the surrounding community.

However, casino location may still be influenced by unobservable factors captured in the equation error term in equation (1), and the impact of casinos on crime in an area may happen over time. To explore these factors, we added leads and lags of the variable indicating presence of a casino in a community, G_{it}, to equation (1), like the specification used by Grinols and Mustard (2006) and re-estimated the regression model. Table 8 contains the parameter estimates and p-values on the casino indicator variables and other summary statistics for eight of the categories of crime analyzed here.[1]

From Table 8, very few of the parameter estimates on the leads are statistically significant; casinos do not appear to have been located in areas where crime was high in the years leading up to the opening of these casinos. The contemporaneous relationship between the opening of a new casino and the eight types of crime are similar to those reported in Tables 4 and 5; most are not statistically different from zero, some are positive and one is negative, indicating a mixed relationship. Interestingly, the estimated parameter on the first lag variable is negative and statistically different from zero in all cases. The incidence rate of all these types of crime declined in the year following the opening of a casino in communities in Alberta. These results differ markedly from those reported in Grinols and Mustard (2006), who found increases in crime rates after the opening of casinos in the U.S. counties. The second lags are generally not statistically different from zero, and those that are significantly different from zero are generally negative.

One interpretation of these results is that the presence of a new casino either decreases the expected benefits of committing crimes or increases the expected costs, reducing the incentive to commit crimes in the community. Grinols and Mustard (2006) discussed improvements in the local labor market, in terms of increased prospects for employment, as one mechanism through which this might happen. Humphreys and Marchand (2012) showed that new casinos in Canada had positive effects in local labor markets. However, these negative and significant parameter estimates may still reflect econometric problems. Adding leads and lags will not correct for endogeneity. Instrumental variables is the appropriate econometric correction for this problem. Unfortunately, we lack an instrument to identify the opening of a new casino. Also, the results reported in Tables 4–8 are not causal; they simply reflect correlation between expanding opportunities for legal gambling and crime in a community.

TABLE 8. REGRESSION RESULTS—LEADS AND LAGS.

Variable	Breaking/entering		Credit card fraud		Drug possession		Other fraud	
	Parameter estimate	p-value	Parameter estimate	p-value	Parameter estimate	p-value	Parameter estimate	p-value
Lead 1	−40.7	0.312	4.639	0.628	8.242	0.772	19.05	0.670
Lead 2	77.8	0.169	17.18	0.062	3.429	0.920	4.101	0.889
Open	562.3	0.161	28.48	0.018	226.45	0.080	426.12	0.002
Lag 1	−905.2	<0.001	−31.89	<0.001	−236.51	<0.001	−521.93	<0.001
Lag 2	−48.8	0.859	−35.65	0.002	−13.08	0.647	−160.03	0.417
N/R2	1,846	0.646	1,846	0.192	1,846	0.499	1,846	0.206

Variable	Prostitution		Robbery		Shoplifting over $5k		Shoplifting under $5k	
	Estimate	p-value	Estimate	p-value	Estimate	p-value	Estimate	p-value
Lead 1	−8.941	0.008	−1.437	0.785	−6.904	0.024	−32.35	0.105
Lead 2	10.08	0.019	8.946	0.003	1.322	0.605	−25.37	0.339
Open	0.029	0.976	27.57	<0.001	−46.24	0.054	449.18	<0.001
Lag 1	−2.071	0.015	−17.79	<0.001	−15.16	0.023	−381.18	<0.001
Lag 2	−1.803	0.006	−17.27	0.037	81.28	0.029	−124.29	0.241
N/R2	1,846	0.593	1,846	0.469	1,846	0.252	1,846	0.532
Year effects	Yes	Yes	Yes	Yes	Yes	Yes	Yes	Yes
Area effects	Yes	Yes	Yes	Yes	Yes	Yes	Yes	Yes
Cluster correction	Yes	Yes	Yes	Yes	Yes	Yes	Yes	Yes

Source: Authors calculations based on data from the Uniform Crime Reporting Survey.

Since casinos draw patrons from all over the province, it is possible that the relationship between casinos and crime extends outside the immediate vicinity of casinos. To investigate this relationship, the present research aggregated the crime and population data to a larger area, the Census Division. Aggregating to Census Divisions reduced the number of cross-sectional units in the sample to 19. The results using more aggregated spatial areas showed no relationship between variation in crime incidence rates and the presence of a casino in Census Divisions in Alberta, suggesting that the association between casinos and crime was localized.

Summary and Conclusions

The present research used data from the Statistics Canada Uniform Crime Reporting Survey (UCRS) to analyze the relationship between access to legal gambling and crime in Alberta. The relationship between incidence rates for nine types of crimes in 78 Alberta communities and the opening of casinos in Alberta and the introduction of VLTs in bars and lounges was examined and provided the following conclusions about the impact of gambling on crime.

The results indicated little relationship between the presence of VLTs and crime since the introduction of VLTs in the early 1990s. There was no statistical association between the number of VLTs in communities and breaking and entering, drug possession, illegal gambling, fraud, and robbery. Credit card fraud was slightly higher in communities with VLTs, but the effect was small, since 100 additional VLTs were associated with an increase of about 5 incidences of credit card fraud per 100,000 population per year.

The association between the presence of VLTs and prostitution and shoplifting was negative. The incidence rate of these crimes tended to decline slightly after VLTs were introduced. These results are similar to what one might hypothesize using the routine activities theory as these crimes generally occur in areas of large economic activity. Bars and restaurants that have VLTs may not be located in areas where much economic activity occurs. Again, these estimates are not causal, so the results do not mean introducing VLTs caused the incidence rate of these crimes to fall in communities.

There was no association between the opening of casinos in communities and local crime incidence for breaking/entering, credit card fraud, drug possession, illegal gambling, and prostitution. There is a slight increase in the local incidence of robbery and, in contrast, a slight decrease in shoplifting over $5,000.

In general, the results here suggest a weaker association between access to legal gambling, in the form of VLTs and casinos, and crime in Alberta. Unlike previous research, the results here suggest a negative association between legal gambling and some types of crime. One reason for this difference may be the charity gambling model used in Alberta. Gamblers know that a portion of their losses at casinos, and in VLTs, will be returned to charitable organizations in their community, which could have an effect on the propensity to commit crimes. In the case of casino gambling, criminals may be less likely to prey on people at charity casinos since they are effectively making a donation to charitable organizations in the province. In the context of Becker's (1968) model of crime, potential criminals might perceive the expected utility from committing crimes against charity casino patrons as lower, or the expected costs as higher.

The negative association between the presence of VLTs and the "victimless" crimes of prostitution and shoplifting highlights the importance of the entertainment aspect of VLT gambling. Many of the communities in this sample are small rural towns or villages with limited entertainment options compared with larger cities. In such communities, VLTs may represent an important entertainment option for those interested in entertainment activities with an important "thrill" component. In this sense, VLT gambling could be a substitute for activities such as minor shoplifting.

In any event, the results here indicate that the association between access to legal gambling and crime does not have to be positive. For some types of crime, the association can be negative. This may be due to the charity gambling model used in Alberta, or it could reflect econometric issues. Additional research using techniques, like instrumental variables, that correct for confounding factors, like reverse causality, will help to assess the robustness of these results.

NOTE

1. We omit the results for illegal gambling. All parameter estimates on casino indicator variables were not statistically different from zero for that category of crime, like in Table 4. We also included three lags of these variables. Those results were very similar to those reported in Table 8.

REFERENCES

Becker, G.S. 1968. Crime and punishment: An economic approach. *The Journal of Political Economy* 76: 169–217.

Clark, C., and D.M. Walker. 2009. Are gamblers more likely to commit crimes? An empirical analysis of a nationally representative survey of US young adults. *International Gambling Studies* 9: 119–134.

Clarke, R.V., and D.B. Cornish. 1985. Modeling offenders' decisions: A framework for research and policy. *Crime and Justice* 6: 147–185.

Cohen, L.E., and M. Felson. 1979. Social change and crime rate trends: A routine activity approach. *American Sociological Review* 44: 588–608.

Cotti, C.D., and D.M. Walker. 2010. The impact of casinos on fatal alcohol-related traffic accidents in the United States. *Journal of Health Economics* 29: 788–796.

Eadington, W.R. 1999. The economics of casino gambling. *The Journal of Economic Perspectives* 13: 173–192.

Giacopassi, D., and B.G. Stitt. 1993. Assessing the impact of casino gambling on crime in Mississippi. *American Journal of Criminal Justice* 18: 117–131.

Greene, W.H. 2000. *Econometric analysis*, 4th ed. Upper Saddle, NJ: Prentice-Hall.

Grinols, E.L., and D.B. Mustard. 2006. Casino, crime, and community costs. *The Review of Economics and Statistics* 88: 28–45.

———. 2008. Correctly critiquing casino-crime causality. *Econ Journal Watch* 5: 21–31.

Humphreys, B.R., and J. Marchand. 2012. *New casinos and local labor markets: Evidence from Canada.* Working Papers 2012-16, University of Alberta, Department of Economics.

Hyclak, T. 2011. Casinos and campus crime. *Economics Letters* 112: 31–33.

Kearney, M.S. 2005. The economic winners and losers of legalized gambling. *National Tax Journal* 58: 281–302.

Koo, J.K., M.S. Rosentraub, and A. Horn. 2007. Rolling the dice? Casinos, tax revenues, and the social costs of gaming. *Journal of Urban Affairs* 29: 367–381.

Reece, W.S. 2010. Casinos, hotels, and crime. *Contemporary Economic Policy* 28: 145–161.

Rey, S.J., E.A. Mack, and J. Koschinsky. 2012. Exploratory space-time analysis of burglary patterns. *Journal of Quantitative Criminology* 28: 509–531.

Smith, G., and H. Wynne. 1999. Gambling and crime in Western Canada: Exploring myth and reality. A report prepared for the Canada West Foundation.

Walker, D.M. 2003. Methodological issues in the social cost of gambling studies. *Journal of Gambling Studies* 19: 149–184.

———. 2007. Problems in quantifying the social costs and benefits of gambling. *American Journal of Economics and Sociology* 66: 609–645.

———. 2008a. Do casinos really cause crime? *Econ Journal Watch* 5: 4–20.

———. 2008b. Evaluating crime attributable to casinos in the U.S.: A closer look at Grinols and Mustard's "Casinos, crime, and community costs". *Journal of Gambling Business and Economics* 2: 23–52.

Wenz, M. 2007. The impact of casino gambling on housing markets: A hedonic approach. *Journal of Gambling Business and Economics* 1: 101–120.

———. 2008. Matching estimation, casino gambling and the quality of life. *The Annals of Regional Science* 42: 235–249.

Wheeler, S.A., D.K. Round, and J.K. Wilson. 2011. The relationship between crime and electronic gaming expenditure: Evidence from Victoria, Australia. *Journal of Quantitative Criminology* 27: 315–338.

Government **Gouvernement**
of Canada **du Canada**

Canada

Department of Justice (/eng/index.html)

Home → Reports and Publications → Criminal Justice

Victims of Crime Research Digest, Issue No. 7

← Previous Page (p5.html)   Table of Contents (toc-tdm.html)   Next Page →

The Human Cost of Impaired Driving in Canada

André Solecki with Katie Scrim

The decline of impaired driving crime in Canada is an example of the progress that can be made when government and civil society work together to change harmful social behaviour and, in this instance, save lives. Half a century ago, impaired driving was, to some extent, a tolerated behaviour in Western society (The Breathalyzer Team 2010). Today, public awareness campaigns and education in schools seek to prevent impaired driving; criminal and civil penalties seek to punish and prevent the act from occurring; and driver spot checks, such as the Reduced Impaired Driving Everywhere program (RIDE), seek to deter drinking and driving and to catch and remove impaired drivers from roads. Nevertheless, fatalities continue to occur as a result of impaired driving on Canadian roads and highways every year.

While there have been many positive changes in both the attitudes and behaviours of Canadians, impaired driving continues to be a widespread problem with a tragic human cost. This article attempts to determine the extent of this human cost by looking at the data available in Canada on the number of fatalities caused by impaired driving.

Background

The Canadian *Criminal Code* defines impaired driving in a variety of ways. Drivers are said to be criminally impaired if they have more than 80 milligrams of alcohol per 100 millilitres of blood in their system. This ratio is commonly referred to as .08% Blood Alcohol Concentration (BAC). A driver can also be impaired if he or she is under the influence of narcotics or prescription medication. A driver's impairment poses an immediate risk of death or injury to the driver, to passengers, to other drivers on the road, to cyclists, and to pedestrians.

Over the summer of 2013, the federal Minister of Justice addressed the issue of impaired driving, expressing a desire to amend the existing relevant legislation. The Minister is supported by various victims' advocacy groups, including Families for Justice, which supports this legal redefinition (Chamberlain 2013), and Mothers Against Drunk Driving (MADD), which supports various legislative changes that would institute mandatory minimum penalties, as well as the implementation of random breath testing (MADD 2012).[1]

In Canada, the two primary sources of data on impaired driving causing death are Statistics Canada's Uniform Crime Reporting (UCR) survey and the Traffic Injury Research Foundation (TIRF) survey. The UCR is used to present police-reported data concerning impaired driving causing death, by alcohol or drug use. The UCR survey is virtually 100% representative of police-reported crime as it is completed every time a police officer can substantiate the occurrence of a crime. The UCR collects data that can be used to present crime visually on a map and provides information on the demographics of victims and accused. A limitation of the UCR is that it relies on police reporting: not all crimes are reported to, or are substantiated by, the police. This means that the UCR may not present the true extent of impaired driving causing death in Canada.[2] The second data source comes from TIRF, an organization that has conducted numerous studies of alcohol-related road accident fatalities. TIRF's data show the proportion of drivers killed in motor vehicle accidents where alcohol was involved. The two data sources differ in so far as one collects police-reported data on impaired driving causing death, and the other collects information on drivers killed in alcohol-related road accidents. Combined they present an estimate of the number of people killed in Canada by impaired driving.

Statistics on impaired driving

Police are amongst the first responders to fatal vehicle accidents and are usually responsible for recommending a criminal charge when the circumstances warrant it. Police officers reported 793 incidents of impaired driving causing death over the five-year period of 2008 to 2012. It is important to emphasize that these incidents do not include incidents where only the impaired driver was killed.[3] The majority of incidents resulted in a driver being charged: police identified a driver to be charged in 665 incidents (84%). For 78 incidents (10%), charges were cleared for other reasons.[4] The remaining 6% of incidents were not cleared for charges, either due to the escape of the accused or the inability of the police to locate an accused.

The UCR collects information about the age and gender of victims of impaired driving causing death and of those accused of the crime. Data available from 2009 to 2012, the only years for which data are available, reveal that 598 people were killed by an impaired driver over the four-year period. The majority of victims were adult males. While 88% of victims were over the age of 18, 53% of adult victims were between the ages of 18 and 35, showing that victims of impaired driving causing death are typically younger than middle age. A total of 67 youth were fatally injured by this crime between 2009 and 2012, with 4 victims under the age of 12. The demographic characteristics were similar for those accused of impaired driving causing death. Accused persons were mainly young adult males. The vast majority (95%) of accused were adults; more than two-thirds (68%) were between the ages of 18 and 35. In total, 26 youth aged 12 to 17 were charged with impaired driving causing death between 2009 and 2012.

Table 1 presents incident counts of impaired driving causing death and the rate of incidents per 100,000 population,[5] for the years 2008 to 2012. Note that an incident can have one or more victims. The five-year trend of police-reported incidents of impaired driving causing death indicates a 30% reduction in incidents of impaired driving causing death over the period of 2008 to 2012. In addition, the rate has declined from .59 to .40 incidents per 100,000 population. Nevertheless, police-reported impaired driving causing death remains a problem in all Canadian jurisdictions.

Table 1: Incident counts and rates of impaired driving causing death, 2008 - 2012

Region	2008		2009		2010		2011		2012	
	Incidents	Rate	Incidents	Rate	Incidents	Rate	Incidents	Rate	Incidents	Rate
N.L.	3	0.59	0	0	1	0.2	1	0.19	0	0
P.E.I.	0	0	1	0.71	0	0	1	0.69	3	2.05
N.S.	2	0.21	2	0.21	3	0.32	5	0.53	3	0.32
N.B.	3	0.4	2	0.27	6	0.8	7	0.93	8	1.06
Que.	52	0.67	51	0.65	53	0.67	26	0.33	15	0.19
Ont.	35	0.27	26	0.2	28	0.21	23	0.17	23	0.17
Man.	11	0.91	9	0.74	11	0.89	16	1.28	17	1.34
Sask.	25	2.47	12	1.17	14	1.34	14	1.32	22	2.04
Alta.	34	0.95	34	0.93	27	0.73	20	0.53	27	0.7
B.C.	29	0.66	19	0.43	23	0.51	16	0.35	18	0.39
Y.T.	1	3.02	0	0	2	5.78	1	2.83	1	2.77
N.W.T.	2	4.58	1	2.29	1	2.28	0	0	1	2.31
Nvt.	0	0	2	6.21	0	0	0	0	0	0
CANADA	197	0.59	159	0.47	169	0.49	130	0.38	138	0.40

Source: Statistics Canada, *The Uniform Crime Reporting Survey.*

Incident counts of impaired driving causing death are high in the more populous provinces. However, there are a few examples of high counts of incidents and high rates in less populated provinces. In 2012, for example, Saskatchewan, Manitoba, and New Brunswick all report rates of impaired driving causing death higher than the national rate of .40, whereas Québec, Ontario, Alberta, and British Columbia have recorded rates lower than the national rate.

The following map depicts the number of police-reported incidents of impaired driving causing death for the 2012 calendar year, distinguished by whether they occurred within a Census Metropolitan Area (CMA) or outside of one. CMAs can be considered major urban areas. They are formed by one or more adjacent municipalities centred on a population centre, known as the core. A CMA must have a total population of at least 100,000, of which 50,000 or more live in the core (Statistics Canada 2012a). There were 33 CMAs in Canada according to the 2011 Census (Statistics Canada 2012b). While some non-CMAs can still be considered urban,[6] distinguishing the locations of incidents between CMAs and non-CMAs provides an interesting comparison of where incidents of impaired driving causing death have occurred.

<u>Figure 1: Police-reported incidents of impaired driving causing death in Canada in 2012, by Census Metropolitan Area and Non-Census Metropolitan Area (fig1p6.html)</u>

Geographically plotting police-reported incidents of impaired driving causing death helps to illustrate an interesting finding: 70% of all incidents of impaired driving causing death in 2012 occurred in non-CMA areas. Since roughly 7 out of 10 Canadians lived in a CMA in 2011, incidents of impaired driving causing death are overrepresented in non-CMAs (Statistics Canada 2012a). Given the wide-spread availability of alternate means of transportation in major urban centres, such as taxis and buses, this is not entirely surprising. This geographic distinction shows that drivers, passengers, cyclists, and pedestrians in rural or non-CMA urban regions face a greater likelihood of being killed by an impaired driver than drivers, passengers, cyclists, and pedestrians in CMAs.

The second source of data is the report of the Traffic Injury Research Foundation (TIRF) of Canada entitled *Alcohol-Crash Problem in Canada: 2010* (TIRF 2013). This report contains information on fatally wounded drivers with alcohol detected in their blood and presents data that show that alcohol and driving result in many more fatalities than the UCR reports. TIRF collects BAC data from police reports and coroner reports relating to fatal motor vehicle crashes. TIRF data show how prevalent alcohol use and driving deaths are by looking beyond the criminal instances of impaired driving causing death, presenting a more complete estimate of the number of drivers killed in alcohol-related road accidents. Unlike the UCR, no narcotics-related fatal accidents are included. A limitation of the TIRF data is that it still underestimates how many Canadians are killed by alcohol-related accidents as it does not relate other victims killed to those drivers killed in alcohol-related road accidents.

For the latest year of data available (2010), TIRF recorded 1,621 drivers killed in a motor vehicle accident. Of these fatally wounded drivers, 36% (590) had alcohol detected in their blood. From a human cost perspective, the TIRF data show that the problem of alcohol-related deaths on Canada's highways and streets is a greater problem than homicide: there were more alcohol-related driver fatalities in 2010 than homicides (554).

Some characteristics of fatally wounded drivers with alcohol detected in their blood are reported by TIRF. Fatally wounded drivers were mostly male (84%) and generally between the ages of 20 and 35 (44%). The BAC levels of fatally injured drivers were also reported by TIRF. Over four fifths (83%) of fatally injured drivers with alcohol detected in their blood had BAC levels above the criminal limit of .08% BAC. Crashes involving fatally wounded drivers with alcohol detected in their blood were typically found to be single vehicle crashes.

Regionally, the TIRF data mimic the police-reported data. Figure 2 presents the number of driver fatalities related to alcohol for the latest TIRF reporting year (2010) by jurisdiction.

<u>Figure 2: Number of alcohol-related driver fatalities by province and territory, 2010 (fig2p6.html)</u>

Not surprisingly, the counts of fatally wounded drivers with alcohol detected in their blood are higher in the more populated provinces. Nevertheless, smaller provinces, such as New Brunswick, Nova Scotia, Manitoba, and Saskatchewan show high numbers for relatively small populations.

International comparisons can be made to the TIRF data, as two nations conduct similar surveys. A report by the Australian Transport Council (2011), entitled *National Road Safety Strategy: 2011-2020*, notes that 30% of Australian crashes resulting in a fatality were related to impaired driving. New Zealand reports that of the 227 drivers killed in a road crash in 2010, 26% (59 drivers) were killed in an alcohol-related accident (ANZPAA 2010). From TIRF's perspective, Canada's alcohol-related crash fatality problem is comparable, if not more serious, than in nations with comparable legal systems and cultures.

An analysis of the TIRF data shows how broad the problem of fatal, alcohol-related road accidents is in Canadian jurisdictions. However, these data only present the number of drivers who died as a result of their drinking and do not present the numbers of other victims, such as passengers, other drivers, cyclists, and pedestrians. Ultimately, this means that the death toll of impaired driving is much greater than either the UCR or TIRF sources estimate.

The full extent of victimization by impaired drivers in Canada is not known. In order to measure the full extent, it would be necessary to test all drivers and victims of all motor vehicle accidents for impairing substances. Currently, Canadians know only the number of incidents that are reported to, and are substantiated by, the police and the number of fatal road accidents that are alcohol-related. However, one advocacy group, Mothers Against Drunk Driving (MADD) Canada, has generated its own estimate of the number of people killed in Canada as a result of impaired driving. MADD estimated that 1,082 individuals died as a result of impaired driving in 2010, but the group suspects the true number may be closer to 1,500 fatalities per year when off-road vehicles, such as boats and all terrain vehicles, are included (MADD 2013). Using these figures, another MADD Canada report has attempted to estimate the economic cost of impaired driving in Canada. The authors estimate that impaired driving causing death cost Canadians over $16 billion in 2010 alone (Pitel and Solomon 2013).

The human cost

There is no doubt that impaired driving causing death exacts a devastating cost. Not only are lives lost, but survivors bear the costs of grieving for the family and friends they have lost. In the devastating instances where the impaired driver survives and the passengers do not, that individual bears the grief that accompanies being responsible for a friend or family member's death.

Various advocacy and lobby groups provide victim services to those individuals affected by the criminal actions of an impaired driver. MADD, the largest of such groups, organizes and participates in victim conferences and support networks, and lobbies provincial and federal governments for changes in the laws relating to alcohol and vehicle use. MADD has chapters located across Canada where trained volunteers provide court accompaniment services, support services, and assistance to victims and their family members in writing and delivering victim impact statements. MADD also produces information materials for victims and their family members. These materials concern bereavement and how to navigate the criminal justice system, amongst other issues. The agency also operates a victim support line for those seeking help. Victim Services are also available in every province and territory and such services provide information and support to victims of crime, their families, and their friends.

Conclusion

Impaired driving is totally preventable, yet every year hundreds of motorists, passengers, cyclists, and pedestrians are killed in alcohol-related accidents. The exact number of fatalities as a result of impaired driving is actually not known, given the lack of available comprehensive data. Statistical data cannot prevent alcohol-related accidents. However, developing more comprehensive data and analyzing regional and local trends in impaired driving would provide a clearer picture of the full extent of the human cost of impaired driving and would help police, policy makers, and legislators combat this crime and bring about a much greater reduction in the number of Canadians killed by impaired driving.

References

Australian Transport Council. 2011. *National Road Safety Strategy 2011-2020*. Accessed October 8, 2013, from http://www.infrastructure.gov.au/roads/safety/national_road_safety_strategy/files /NRSS_2011_2020_15Aug11.pdf.

Australia New Zealand Policing Advisory Agency (ANZPAA). 2010. *Road policing statistics*. Victoria: ANZPAA. Accessed October 8, 2013, from http://www.anzpaa.org.au/current-initiatives/operation-crossroads/road-policing-statistics.

Chamberlain, Jason. 2013. Families for Justice seeks harsher penalties for drunk drivers. *The Athabasca Advocate*. Accessed October 8, 2013, from http://www.athabascaadvocate.com/article /20130115/ATH0801/301159990/-1/ath08/families-for-justice-seeks-harsher-penalties-for-drunk-drivers.

Mothers Against Drunk Driving (MADD) Canada. 2012. *Sentencing for impaired driving*. Oakville: MADD Canada. Accessed October 8, 2013, from http://www.madd.ca/media /docs/MADD_Canada_Sentencing_Framework_FINAL.pdf.

Mothers Against Drunk Driving (MADD) Canada. 2013. *The magnitude of the alcohol/drug-related crash problem in Canada: Overview*. Oakville: MADD Canada. Accessed October 9, 2013, from http://www.madd.ca/madd2/en/impaired_driving/impaired_driving_statistics.html.

Pitel, Stephen, and Robert Solomon. 2013. *Estimating the number and cost of impairment-related traffic crashes in Canada: 1999 to 2010*. Oakville: MADD Canada. Accessed October 9, 2013, from http://madd.ca/media/docs/estimating_presence.pdf.

Statistics Canada. 2012a. *Census Dictionary*. Ottawa: Statistics Canada. Accessed December 4, 2013, from http://www5.statcan.gc.ca/bsolc/olc-cel/olc-cel?catno=98-301-X&lang=eng.

Statistics Canada. 2012b. *The Canadian Population in 2011: Population counts and growth*. Ottawa: Statistics Canada, 2012. Accessed December 4, 2013, from http://www12.statcan.gc.ca/census-recensement/2011/as-sa/98-310-x/98-310-x2011001-eng.cfm#a4.

The Breathalyzer Team. 2010. Social attitudes towards drunk driving are changing for the better. *Breathalyzer Canada*. Accessed October 10, 2013, from http://www.breathalyzercanada.com /DUI-social-attitudes-and-impact.html.

Traffic Injury Research Foundation of Canada (TIRF). 2013. *Alcohol-crash problem in Canada: 2010*.

CCMTA Road Safety Report Series. Ottawa: Traffic Injury Research Foundation of Canada. Accessed October 8, 2013, from http://tirf.ca/publications/PDF_publications /2010_Alcohol_Crash_Problem_Report_4_FINAL.pdf.

[1] Random breath testing legislation would give police officers the power to pull over any driver, at any time, to demand a sobriety test and/or a breath test.

[2] The *Criminal Code* violation of impaired driving causing death does not tend to be subject to a high degree of underreporting to the UCR.

[3] The UCR's reported figures on impaired driving causing death do not capture incidents where only the impaired driver was killed; they include only incidents that involve the death of passengers, drivers of other vehicles and pedestrians. For more information, see http://www.statcan.gc.ca /pub/85-002-x/2013001/article/11739-eng.htm#n1 (http://www.statcan.gc.ca/pub/85-002-x/2013001 /article/11739-eng.htm#n1).

[4] Other reasons include the death of the accused following or after the incident, the committal of the accused to a mental hospital, the diplomatic immunity of the accused, or because the accused was no longer in Canada and could not be returned.

[5] The rate measures the number of incidents of a crime relative to the population of a region or country. The rate is often considered a better measurement of criminal activity than incident counts as one can gauge the relative prevalence of a crime in society and make comparisons across social and geographic boundaries.

[6] Charlottetown, P.E.I., for example may be considered an urban area, but it is not a CMA.

André Solecki, LLB, PhD, is Principal Researcher with the Research and Statistics Division, Department of Justice Canada, in Ottawa. She is responsible for victims of crime research in the Department and has extensive research experience on a range of victim issues.

Katie Scrim is a policy analyst with the Policy Centre for Victim Issues, Department of Justice Canada, in Ottawa. She is responsible for the Children's Advocacy Centres initiative at the PCVI and also provides policy input on a range of Victims Fund projects as well as general oversight to the Victims Fund.

Date modified:
2015-01-07

Alcohol

Fact sheet
Updated May 2014

Key facts [1]

- Worldwide, 3.3 million people die every year due to harmful use of alcohol,[2] this represent 5.9 % of all deaths.
- The harmful use of alcohol is a causal factor in more than 200 disease and injury conditions.
- Overall 5.1 % of the global burden of disease and injury is attributable to alcohol, as measured in disability- adjusted life years (DALYs).[3]
- Alcohol consumption causes death and disability relatively early in life. In the age group 20 – 39 years approximately 25 % of the total deaths are alcohol-attributable.
- There is a causal relationship between harmful use of alcohol and a range of mental and behavioural disorders, other noncommunicable conditions as well as injuries.
- The latest causal relationships have been established between harmful drinking and incidence of infectious diseases such as tuberculosis as well as the course of HIV/AIDS.
- Beyond health consequences, the harmful use of alcohol brings significant social and economic losses to individuals and society at large.

Alcohol is a psychoactive substance with dependence-producing properties that has been widely used in many cultures for centuries. The harmful use of alcohol causes a large disease, social and economic burden in societies.

Alcohol impacts people and societies in many ways and it is determined by the volume of alcohol consumed, the pattern of drinking, and, on rare occasions, the quality of alcohol consumed. In 2012, about 3.3 million deaths, or 5.9 % of all global deaths, were attributable to alcohol consumption.

The harmful use of alcohol can also result in harm to other people, such as family members, friends, co-workers and strangers. Moreover, the harmful use of alcohol results in a significant health, social and economic burden on society at large.

Alcohol consumption is a causal factor in more than 200 disease and injury conditions. Drinking alcohol is associated with a risk of developing health problems such as mental and behavioural disorders, including alcohol dependence, major noncommunicable diseases such as liver cirrhosis, some cancers and cardiovascular diseases, as well as injuries resulting from violence and road clashes and collisions.

The latest causal relationships are those between alcohol consumption and incidence of infectious diseases such as tuberculosis as well as the course of HIV/AIDS. Alcohol consumption by an expectant mother may cause fetal alcohol syndrome and pre-term birth complications. A significant proportion of the disease burden attributable to harmful drinking arises from unintentional and intentional injuries, including those due to road traffic crashes, violence, and suicides. Fatal injuries attributable to alcohol consumption tend to occur in relatively younger age groups.

Factors affecting alcohol consumption and alcohol-related harm

A variety of factors have been identified at the individual and the societal level, which affect the levels and patterns of alcohol consumption and the magnitude of alcohol-related problems in populations.

Environmental factors include economic development, culture, availability of alcohol, and the comprehensiveness and levels of implementation and enforcement of alcohol policies. For a given level or pattern of drinking, vulnerabilities within a society are likely to have similar differential effects as those between societies. Although there is no single risk factor that is dominant, the more vulnerabilities a person has, the more likely the person is to develop alcohol-related problems as a result of alcohol consumption.

Conceptual causal model of alcohol consumption and health outcomes

[1] Quality of the alcohol consumed can also be a factor
[2] Development of health and welfare system, and economy as a whole
Source: Based on Rehm et al., 2010 and Blas et al., 2010

The impact of alcohol consumption on chronic and acute health outcomes in populations is largely determined by 2 separate but related dimensions of drinking:

- the total volume of alcohol consumed, and
- the pattern of drinking.

The context of drinking plays an important role in occurrence of alcohol-related harm, particularly associated with health effects of alcohol intoxication, and, on rare occasions, also the quality of alcohol consumed. Alcohol consumption can have an impact not only on the incidence of diseases, injuries and other health conditions, but also on the course of disorders and their outcomes in individuals.

There are gender differences in alcohol-related mortality, morbidity, as well as levels and patterns of alcohol consumption. The percentage of alcohol-attributable deaths among men amount to 7.6 % of all global deaths, compared to 4.0 % of all deaths among women Total alcohol per capita consumption in 2010 among male and female drinkers worldwide was on average 21.2 litres for males and 8.9 litres of pure alcohol for females.

Ways to reduce the burden from harmful use of alcohol

The health, safety and socioeconomic problems attributable to alcohol can be effectively reduced and requires actions on the levels, patterns and contexts of alcohol consumption and the wider social determinants of health.

Countries have a responsibility for formulating, implementing, monitoring and evaluating public policies to reduce the harmful use of alcohol. Substantial scientific knowledge exists for policy-makers on the effectiveness and cost–effectiveness of the following strategies:

- regulating the marketing of alcoholic beverages (in particular to younger people);
- regulating and restricting availability of alcohol;
- enacting appropriate drink-driving policies;
- reducing demand through taxation and pricing mechanisms;
- raising awareness of public health problems caused by harmful use of alcohol and ensuring support for effective alcohol policies;
- providing accessible and affordable treatment for people with alcohol-use disorders; and
- implementing screening and brief interventions programmes for hazardous and harmful drinking in health services.

WHO response

WHO aims is to reduce the health burden caused by the harmful use of alcohol and, thereby, to save lives, prevent injuries and diseases and improve the well-being of individuals, communities and society at large.

WHO emphasizes the development, implementation and evaluation of cost-effective interventions for harmful use of alcohol as well as creating, compiling and disseminating scientific information on alcohol use and dependence, and related health and social consequences.

In 2010, the World Health Assembly approved a resolution to endorse a global strategy to reduce the harmful use of alcohol. The resolution urged countries to strengthen national responses to public health problems caused by the harmful use of alcohol.

The global strategy to reduce the harmful use of alcohol represents a collective commitment by WHO Member States to reduce the global burden of disease caused by harmful use of alcohol. The strategy includes evidence-based policies and interventions that can protect health and save lives if adopted, implemented and enforced. The strategy also contains a set of principles to guide the development and implementation of policies; it sets priority areas for global action, recommends target areas for national action and gives a strong mandate to WHO to strengthen action at all levels.

The policy options and interventions available for national action can be grouped into 10 recommended target areas, which are mutually supportive and complementary. The 10 areas are:

- leadership, awareness and commitment
- health services' response
- community action
- drink–driving policies and countermeasures
- availability of alcohol
- marketing of alcoholic beverages
- pricing policies
- reducing the negative consequences of drinking and alcohol intoxication
- reducing the public health impact of illicit alcohol and informally produced alcohol
- monitoring and surveillance.

The Global Information System on Alcohol and Health (GISAH) has been developed by WHO to dynamically present data on levels and patterns of alcohol consumption, alcohol-attributable health and social consequences and policy responses at all levels.

Successful implementation of the strategy will require action by countries, effective global governance and appropriate engagement of all relevant stakeholders. By effectively working together, the negative health and social consequences of alcohol can be reduced.

Footnotes

- Based on the Global status report on alcohol and health 2014.
- The Global strategy refers only to public-health effects of alcohol consumption, without prejudice to religious beliefs and cultural norms in any way. The concept of "harmful use of alcohol" in this context is different from "harmful use of alcohol" as a diagnostic category in the ICD-10 Classification of Mental and Behavioural Disorders (WHO, 1992).
- The disability-adjusted life year (DALY) extends the concept of potential years of life lost due to premature death to include equivalent years of "healthy" life lost by virtue of being in states of poor health or disability.

Unit 8 – Smoking

Is Smoking a Positive Fiscal Externality?

Posted on October 7, 2013 by Noah Carl

In this post, I will examine the question of whether smoking is a positive fiscal externality in the UK. A person's fiscal contribution is equal to the total taxes she pays minus the total public money that is spent on her during her lifetime. If taking-up smoking leads to an increase in the average person's fiscal contribution, then smoking is a positive fiscal externality; if taking-up smoking leads to a decrease in her fiscal contribution, then it is a negative externality. Smoking affects a person's fiscal contribution in a number of ways: it affects her income taxes (via its impact on her productivity in the labour market), it affects her consumption taxes, it affects her healthcare expenses, and it affects her pension contributions and benefits. In addition, it may affect other people's fiscal contributions via passive smoking.

Cigarettes are subject to very high tax rates in the U.K. Taxes account for 77% of the price of a pack of premium cigarettes and more than 90% of the price of a pack of cheap cigarettes (TMA, 2013a). Comparatively, VAT accounts for only 20% of the price of most consumer goods. Indeed, one of the main arguments for taxing cigarettes at such high rates is that smoking is an externality under the NHS (e.g., Reed, 2010). In particular, because the NHS is funded by the taxpayer and smoking increases a person's lifetime healthcare expenses (or so it is assumed), someone who smokes is externalising the costs of his behaviour onto the taxpayer, and should therefore be taxed. In order to evaluate this argument and answer the more general question with which I began, I will briefly review the literature on the fiscal impact of smoking. My conclusion will be that smoking probably is a positive fiscal externality. This implies that efforts to curb smoking are likely to bring down tax revenues and push up public spending.

One effect of smoking is to reduce a person's productivity in the labour market. Smokers may call in sick more often, take more cigarette breaks, or simply work less efficiently. What matters is whether taking-up smoking leads to a decrease in a person's lifetime taxable output. If every smoker would earn substantially more during her lifetime if she didn't smoke, then smoking reduces income tax revenues, all else being equal. However, it is possible that unobserved factors causing people to smoke make them less productive in the workplace, meaning that smokers wouldn't be any more productive if they didn't smoke. Furthermore, since in many professions output does not accumulate uniformly over time, a smoker's cigarette breaks do not necessarily represent a loss of production. Sloan *et al.* (2004, p.255) attempt to estimate the external cost of smoking on worker productivity in the U.S, yet they calculate total wages lost (a partly private cost), rather than total income tax revenues lost. Using cohort data from Finland, Tiihonen *et al.* (2012) estimate a loss in income tax revenues due to smoking of €12,700 per smoker.

Another effect of smoking is to alter a person's lifetime healthcare expenses. Although smoking increases the risk of some diseases that are expensive to treat (e.g., lung cancer), it reduces life expectancy and thereby lowers health expenditures at advanced ages. Consequently, it is not clear *prima facie* whether taking-up smoking increases or decreases a person's lifetime healthcare expenses. Overall, the empirical literature on this question is quite mixed; some studies find that smokers' lifetime healthcare expenses are higher than those of non-smokers, while others find that they are lower. However, more of the recent studies do seem to find that smokers incur lower lifetime healthcare expenses.

One reason to suspect that smokers incur lower lifetime healthcare expenses is that, counter to intuition, prophylactic medicine tends to increase healthcare costs. In a review paper, Cohen *et al.* (2008) obtained cost-effectiveness ratios of various medical interventions from 599 articles published between 2000 and 2005, and found that the great majority of preventative interventions were not cost-saving. Cohen *et al.*'s conclusions are reiterated by Russell (2009), Rappange *et al.* (2009) and Temple (2011). As Russell puts it, "Over the last four decades since cost-effectiveness analysis was first applied to health and medicine, hundreds of studies have shown that prevention usually adds to medical costs instead of reducing them." Considering the healthcare costs of smoking itself, some early studies find that smokers' lifetime healthcare expenses are higher than non-smokers' (Hodgson, 1992; Miller *et al.,* 1999), but others find that they are lower (Lippiat, 1990; Barendregt et al., 1997). Among more recent studies, Rasmussen *et al.* (2004) find that smokers' incur higher lifetime healthcare expenses, whereas Van Baal *et al.* (2008) find the opposite. Two recent prospective studies, one conducted in Japan and one in Finland, both document lower lifetime healthcare expenses among smokers (Hayashida *et al.*, 2010; Tiihonen *et al.*, 2012).

Smoking affects not only a person's healthcare expenses but also her pension contributions and benefits. Studies find that taking-up smoking reduces the total benefits a person receives to a much greater extent than it reduces the total contributions she makes. Because smokers tend to die younger than non-smokers, they receive pension benefits for fewer years. Indeed, from the perspective of the state pension system, the ideal situation is for a person to work as productively as possible during her lifetime and then to die immediately upon reaching retirement. That way, she pays into the system throughout her working life, but does not take anything from the system once she has retired. Sloan *et al.* estimate that, in the U.S., female smokers put in around $1,500 more to Social Security than they get out, while male smokers put in around $6,500 more than they get out (p.153). Tiihonen *et al.* estimate that, in Finland, smokers receive approximately €127,000 less in after-tax pension benefits than non-smokers. However, they do not differentiate between payouts from private pensions and those from the state pension.

Although taking-up smoking reduces the amount of income tax a person pays, it increases the amount of consumption tax he pays. A simple back-of-the-envelope calculation yields the amount of tax revenue that smoking generates per smoker. The U.K. government takes in about £6 in tax revenue each time a pack of 20 cigarettes is purchased (TMA, 2013b). Under the conservative assumption that the average smoker consumes 10 cigarettes per day, he pays approximately £1,100 in cigarette taxes every year. Assuming that if he didn't smoke he would spend his money on goods taxed at only 20%, the government collects about £840 more in taxes from him than it would do if he didn't smoke. Over a lifetime of smoking (i.e., 50 years), this adds up to an additional £42,000 in consumption taxes; assuming he smokes 20 cigarettes a day, the figure is closer to £84,000. Note that eliminating smoking from society lowers consumption tax revenues because (under reasonable assumptions) it is equivalent to reducing the average rate of consumption tax.

There have been a number of attempts to gauge the overall fiscal impact of smoking. Although the literature is, again, somewhat mixed, the evidence seems to suggest that smoking has a positive fiscal impact. Manning *et al.* (1989) estimate that, in the U.S., smokers confer an external benefit on society of $1 per pack at a zero discount rate, but confer an external cost of $0.15 per pack at a 5% discount rate. They conclude that "smokers probably pay their way at the current level of excise taxes on cigarettes". Viscussi (1995) also analyses data from the U.S., and estimates that smokers save society $0.1–0.5 per pack, which translates into $900–4,600 over the lifetime of a smoker consuming 10 cigarettes per day. On the other hand, Sloan et al. estimate the external cost of smoking to be $1.44 per pack, which translates into $13,100 over a smoker's lifetime (p.255).

An unpublished report produced by the U.K. government, which was leaked to The Guardian in 1980, estimated that a public anti-smoking campaign would cause a substantial fall in tax revenues and a substantial rise in pension outlays (Phillips, 1980; Temple, 2010). A report produced by Arthur D. Little for the Czech government in 2001, which was commissioned by Philip Morris, estimated that smoking has a moderate positive impact on public finances in the Czech Republic (Philip Morris, 2000; Tiihonen *et al.,* 2012). Given that the report was commissioned by a tobacco company, its findings should obviously be interpreted with a fair amount of scepticism. Yang *et al.* (2011) estimate that smoking confers net costs on the Chinese economy, yet they do not attempt to quantify any of the potential benefits of smoking. Finally, Tiihonen *et al.* estimate that, in Finland, the average smoker's fiscal contribution is around €133,000 greater than the average non-smoker's.

In conclusion, the weight of the evidence suggests that smoking is a positive fiscal externality. Smokers pay less in income taxes than non-smokers, yet pay considerably more in consumption taxes. Their lifetime healthcare costs are probably slightly lower than those of non-smokers. And they take far less from the pension system than non-smokers, relative to what they pay in. There are several important caveats to my conclusion. First, it is tentative. At least one major study, namely Sloan et al., reaches the opposite conclusion. Second, it may only apply to the U.K. (and other similar countries), where healthcare and pensions are largely financed by the state, and taxes on cigarettes are very high. Third, as many authors have noted, the fact that smoking may have a positive fiscal impact does not imply that efforts to curtail smoking reduce social welfare. Indeed, if each QALY is assumed to be worth €14,600, then Tiihonen *et al.*'s finding reverses, and smoking becomes a net cost for society.

- Barendregt, J. *et al.* (1997). The health care costs of smoking. *NEJM*, 337:1052-1057.

- Bonneux, L. *et al.* (1998). Preventing fatal diseases increases healthcare costs: cause elimination life table approach. *BMJ*, 316:26-29.

- Cohen, J. (2008). Does preventative care save money? Health economics and the presidential candidates. *NEJM*, 358:661-663.

- Hayashida, K. *et al.* (2010). Difference in lifetime medical expenses between male smokers and non-smokers. *Health Policy*, 94:84-89.

- Hodgson, T. (1992). Cigarette smoking and lifetime medical expenditures. *The Milbank Quarterly*, 70:81- 125.

- Sloan, F. *et al.* (2004). Price of Smoking. MIT Press, Cambridge, MA.

- Lippiat, B. (1990). Measuring medical cost and life expectancy impacts of changes in cigarette sales. *Preventative Medicine*, 19:515-532.

- Manning, W. *et al.* (1989). The taxes of sin: do smokers and drinkers pay their way? *JAMA*, 261:1604-1609.

- Miller, V. *et al.* (1999). Smoking-attributable medical care costs in the USA. *Social Science and Medicine*, 48:375-391.

- Phillips, M. (1980). Why smoking, not health, wins the day: governments have failed to mount a public campaign against smoking. *The Guardian*, May 6th.

- Philip Morris. (2000). Public finance balance of smoking in the Czech Republic. Philip Morris CR. http://www.ash.org.uk/files/documents/ASH_719.pdf.

- Rappange, D. *et al.* (2009). Lifestyle intervention: from cost savings to value for money. *Journal of Public Health*, 32:440-447.

- Rasmussen, S. *et al.* (2004). The total lifetime costs of smoking. European *Journal of Public Health*, 14:95- 100.

- Reed, H. (2010). The effects of increasing tobacco taxation: a cost benefit and public finances analysis. *Action on Smoking and Health*. http://www.ash.org.uk/tax/analysis.

- Russell, L. (2009). Preventing chronic disease: an important investment but don't count on cost savings. *Health Affairs*, 28:42-45.

- Temple, N. (2010). Governments, pay for smoking cessation. *CMAJ*, 182:1761-1762.

- Temple, N. (2011). Why prevention can increase healthcare spending. *European Journal of Public Health*, 22:618-619.

- Tiihonen, J. *et al.* (2012). The net effect of smoking on healthcare and welfare costs. A cohort study. *BMJ Open*, 2:1-5.

- TMA. (2013a). Tobacco taxation briefing. *Tobacco Manufacturers Association.* http://www.the-tma.org.uk/~thetma/wp-content/uploads/2012/11/TMA-Tobacco-Tax-Briefing.pdf.

- TMA. (2013b). UK cigarette prices. *Tobacco Manufacturers Association.* http://www.the-tma.org.uk/tma-publications-research/facts-figures/uk-cigarette-prices/.

- Van Baal, P. *et al.* (2008). Lifetime medical costs of obesity: prevention no cure for increasing health expenditure. *PLOS Medicine*, 5:e29.

- Viscussi, W. (1995). Cigarette taxes and the social consequences of smoking. *Tax Policy and the Economy*, 9:51-101.

- Yang, L. et al. (2011). Economic costs attributable to smoking in China: update and an 8-year comparison, 2000-2008. *Tobacco Control*, 20:266-272.

Taxes and their impact on smoking across the lifespan: Is the consensus shifting?

Introduction

In this fact sheet, I discuss the impact of cigarette excise taxation on smoking behaviour, focusing on the impact of taxes across the lifespan. However, I first provide some necessary background, including the economic rationale for using a tax to affect smoking behaviour as well as some statistics on cigarette taxation in Canada and the United States. Next, I discuss the conventional wisdom—the idea that youth smoking is more sensitive to higher cigarette prices than adult smoking—and the early research upon which it is based. Finally, I discuss more recent work, including my own research with co-authors which, when considered as a whole, begins to challenges this conventional wisdom and implies that more work is needed before potentially making unwarranted conclusions and hence unwarranted policy decisions.

Why and how cigarette taxes might reduce smoking

Economists have long recognized that price is a mechanism by which scare resources are allocated. This implies that prices can affect the choices that consumers take. More recently, they have suggested price changes in the context of policy interventions intended to improve public health. For example, economists have often called for lowering the price of goods considered "healthy" (i.e., subsidizing their consumption) and raising the price of ones considered "unhealthy" (i.e., taxing their consumption) beyond the price determined by market forces that affect supply and demand. The underlying assumption is that the healthy or unhealthy nature of the good in question is somehow not reflected in the market price. For example, perhaps consumers do not realize the full costs or benefits of consumption or, alternatively, individuals other than the person consuming the good are affected by that individual's consumption.[1]

Economic rationale aside, the idea is that by changing prices, the amount of a good consumed might be altered. Consider a per-unit tax on cigarettes.[2] Conceptually, the price increase might affect consumption via two mechanisms. First, the tax increases the price of cigarettes relative to other goods. To the extent that reasonable substitutes for cigarettes exist, and their price is unaffected by the tax, one would expect a reduction in the consumption of cigarettes.[3] Second, to the extent that the smoker does not adjust his or her smoking behaviour, or adjusts it only slightly, the smoker now has less real income.[4] In principle, this may reduce the consumption of cigarettes, but also perhaps

---

[1] Economists refer to this latter scenario as an "externality in consumption". Either scenario may apply to cigarette smoking.

[2] Cigarette taxes tend to be per-unit, usually per pack of twenty cigarettes, as opposed to a fixed percentage tax as is the case with most sales taxes, though some jurisdictions add sales taxes to the purchase price. Prior research shows that cigarette taxes tend to raise cigarette prices in a one-to-one fashion. In other words, if the tax increase is one dollar per pack of twenty cigarettes, the price will increase by that amount.

[3] Economists refer to this as a "substitution" or "relative price" effect.

[4] Economists refer to this as an "income" or "wealth" effect. Of course, if a smoker quit smoking altogether in response to higher taxes, then his or her real income would actually increase.

the consumption of other goods as well, since there is less income generally available to make other purchases.[5]

Independent of the mechanisms, two types of smoking behaviour might be affected. In particular, existing smokers might be induced to stop smoking altogether (i.e., smoking cessation) or reduce their consumption of cigarettes, while continuing as a smoker. Moreover, younger individuals might be deterred from starting to smoke cigarettes (i.e., smoking initiation).[6] Changes in the initiation and cessation of smoking are referred to as changes on the "extensive" margin or changes in smoking "participation", while changes in the amount of cigarettes smoked, usually per day, are referred to as changes on the "intensive" margin or changes in "conditional demand". Jargon aside, the idea is that higher tax-induced cigarette prices might reduce smoking in two ways: first, in terms of the fraction of individuals who smoke and, second, for the set of remaining smokers, their level of smoking.

The role of government and the scope of public policy

Governments are able to affect the price of goods via direct subsidies or taxation.[7] Nearly all governments have general sales taxes which are used to raise revenues for government operations, but most also tax goods considered unhealthy or otherwise undesirable; often these are referred to as "sin" taxes. Cigarettes are a prime example of such a good. In Canada and the United States, cigarettes are taxed by federal and provincial/state governments and these taxes can be substantial. Since they create variation between individuals living in different areas, researchers focus on area-specific variation that usually involves provincial or state-level taxation. Between 1982 and 1993, Canadian provinces increased cigarette taxes from roughly fifty cents per pack of twenty cigarettes to nearly $3.50 per pack, before a set of provinces reduced them sharply after concern with smuggling from the United States (Gruber, Sen and Stabile, 2003). Since about 1996, Canadian cigarette taxes have started to trend back upwards (Sen and Fatima, 2010). The U.S. experience is somewhat different. As the concern about smuggling suggests, the United States did not experience large cigarette tax increases in the 1980s and early 1990s as had Canada. Instead, the U.S. has experienced these increases more recently, beginning around 2001 (DeCicca and McLeod, 2008). Indeed, over the past ten years, U.S. state cigarette taxes have roughly doubled, reaching and exceeding Canadian levels in some states.

Estimating the impact of price on smoking behaviour

Economists and other researchers use variation in cigarette taxes to understand the extent to which price affects consumption on both the extensive and intensive margins. In other words, economists are interested in smoking initiation and cessation as well as the

---

[5] This is there is concern with the regressivity of cigarette taxes (e.g., Colman and Remler, 2008). That is, there is concern that they fall disproportionately on lower income individuals.

[6] Indeed, this latter case is often put forth as the strongest rationale for the taxation of cigarettes.

[7] Of course, they are also able to affect prices indirectly. In the present context, subsidies to tobacco growers might ultimately reduce the retail price of cigarettes.

cigarette consumption of smokers. Earlier work on the impact of cigarette taxation on smoking behaviour used cross-sectional variation (i.e., variation in tax rates across provinces or states at a point in time) to estimate the impact of price. Over time, researchers recognized that such variation was problematic since cigarette taxes likely reflect, at least to some extent, the sentiment residents have towards smoking.[8] More recent work uses within-area (e.g., province or state) changes in cigarette taxes to estimate the impact of price on smoking behaviour.[9] In principle, this is a more valid approach, to the extent that there is "enough" such variation to allow for credible estimation. Finally, note that economists tend to report their findings via elasticities. These unitless measures tell us the percent reduction in smoking (on either the extensive or intensive margins) associated with a given percentage increase in cigarette price.[10]

Conventional wisdom on the impact of cigarette taxation across the lifespan

Generally speaking, conventional wisdom implies that the smoking of younger individuals is more responsive to tax-induced price increases than older ones. Ostensibly, the logic is compelling. Before individuals start to smoke, they are not exposed to nicotine, the substance that leads to smokers to become addicted, and thus less sensitive to price. Moreover, economists believe that the income effect associated with any tax-induce price increase might be larger for young people who tend to have lower incomes than adults. The rationale works in reverse for older individuals. Since most individuals start smoking before age eighteen, the older individuals of concern are established smokers.[11] Overall, though likely to a varying degree, they are more addicted to the nicotine that cigarette consumption provides than younger individuals who are either not yet smokers or are relatively new smokers. As a result, they may be less responsive to price than those with a lower level of addiction (i.e., younger individuals). Moreover, older individuals tend to have relatively higher and more stable incomes and are thought to be better able to "afford" any tax increase, relative to younger individuals.

While sensible, these arguments are not air-tight. For example, youth smokers are much more likely to smoke more expensive, brand-name cigarettes than older smokers who are more likely to purchase generic or contraband cigarettes or cross borders to save money (Cummings et al., 2007; DeCicca, Kenkel and Liu, 2010a; DeCicca, Kenkel and Liu, 2010b). These stylized facts argue against the notion that younger individuals will have larger income effects, perhaps because their lower income is disproportionately

---

[8] For example, places with relatively few smokers might enact a high tax since most individuals are not affected. All else equal, this would tend to induce the researcher to find a falsely strong inverse relationship between taxes and smoking behaviour in cross-sectional data.

[9] The level of variation (i.e., province or state) is important since these taxes differ for individuals in a given country, as opposed to federal-level taxes which are uniform across all places, and therefore do not allow the researcher to estimate their impact.

[10] Studies now often also provide the absolute implied reduction in smoking associated with a hypothetical increase in the level of the cigarette tax (e.g., the absolute reduction associated with a one-dollar per pack increase). In some sense, this is preferred to an elasticity, especially a participation elasticity, which is sensitive to the level of smoking in the relevant sample.

[11] More recent work suggests that there are substantial smoking dynamics between the ages of 18 and 24. For example, DeCicca, Kenkel and Mathios (2008) find that nearly half of smokers at age 24 had not started smoking by age 18.

"disposable" in nature. That is, it is earmarked for discretionary consumption, rather than the fixed costs typically associated with adulthood. Moreover, there is a strong association between parental and child smoking. To the extent that new smokers (i.e., youth) are exposed to substantial amounts of second-hand smoke by their parents or others in close proximity, it is possible that they exhibit reasonably high levels of addiction that might mitigate against the effectiveness of higher tax-induced prices in preventing them from becoming smokers. Ultimately, the impact of price on smoking behaviour across the age distribution is an empirical question, so I turn next to the early evidence and then to more recent work, including my own work with co-authors.

Existing evidence

In general, research prior to the late 1990s tends to support the conventional wisdom that youth smoking is more sensitive to price than adult smoking behaviour; indeed their findings contributed largely to this stylized fact. The majority of age-related work focuses on the impact of higher tax-induced prices on youth smoking, particularly on smoking initiation, rather than on adult smoking. This is understandable for reasons presented above. Moreover, it involves an appealing scenario from a public policy perspective: preventing smoking initiation precludes a lifetime of smoking and the associated health and financial costs.[12]

Building a consensus

The earliest empirical papers on the potential impact of cigarette taxation on smoking date to the early 1980s (Lewit, Coate and Grossman, 1981; Lewit and Coate, 1982). Though some time had elapsed, these two papers, coupled with a renewed interest in the potentially harmful effects of smoking, spurred a great deal of research on youth smoking in the 1990s. For the most part, these studies used cross-sectional variation in taxes to estimate the impact of price on youth smoking behaviour taking advantage of the large differences in cigarette taxes across U.S. states. In general, these studies found a strong inverse relationship between higher cigarette taxes and youth smoking (Lewit, Coate and Grossman, 1981; Lewit and Coate, 1982; Chaloupka and Grossman, 1996; Chaloupka and Wechsler, 1997; Lewit et al., 1997; Chaloupka and Pacula, 1999; Harris and Chan, 1999). That is, their findings implied that higher taxes could reduce youth smoking participation and therefore lifetime smokers.[13] By the late 1990s, this research had led to a widely held consensus that youth smoking was particularly sensitive to the impact of taxation. For example, during the debate leading up to what became the Master Settlement Agreement in the United States, policy analysts at the U.S. Treasury Department wrote, "...a consensus view is that for every ten percent increase in price, at

---

[12] Of course, this scenario assumes that higher cigarette taxes actually prevent initiation and do not just delay it to older ages, as suggested by Glied (2002). Also, it assumes that there are not unintended consequences associated with reduced smoking rates such as greater rates of obesity which presumably would reduce any financial savings.

[13] Two notable exceptions were Wasserman et al., 1991 and Douglas and Hariharan, 1994 which found no evidence of a systematic relationship.

today's prices, seven percent fewer youths will smoke" (U.S. Treasury, p.14, 1998). In other words, the price elasticity of youth smoking participation was thought to be around -0.7. This was consistent with other governmental and institutional reviews around the same time, and a consensus was effectively established (Congressional Budget Office, 1998; General Accounting Office, 1998; Institute of Medicine, 1998).

As noted earlier, youth smoking has been of much greater interest than that of adults who, for the most part, are established smokers by their mid-twenties. It is important to note that this implies that the smoking behaviour of interest is smoking cessation, since initiation is not a relevant phase for most adult smokers. In other words, any changes in smoking behaviour among adults will involve smoking cessation, not smoking initiation. Until a recent study which I will discuss later, the dearth of existing work tends to find very small to no effect of cigarette taxation on adult smoking, with most papers finding an implied price elasticity of smoking participation between zero and -0.2 which is much smaller than the corresponding estimate for youth smoking participation (CDC, 1998; Farrelly et al., 2001 and Tauras, 2006). While there were no large-scale governmental or institutional reviews of the adult literature, a consensus seemed to emerge among researchers that adult smoking was rather immutable to higher taxes, at least in the context of the tax increases we had observed governments implement at that time.

Newer research: A consensus in flux?

One trend in health-related research, as well as in other areas, is the emergence of longitudinal data. Longitudinal data contains a time component, either following the same individual over time (i.e., panel data) or following different individuals in the same area over time (i.e., repeated cross-sectional data). In principle, these types of data allow the researcher to implement more valid research designs, relative to cross-sectional data.[14] Such data should allow for less biased estimates of the relationship of interest.

The importance of research design is seen most clearly in the youth smoking literature. DeCicca, Kenkel and Mathios (2002) was the first smoking study to employ longitudinal data on current smoking behaviour. Using data from the early 1990s, these authors were able to observe smoking behaviour of youths at ages 13, 15 and 17, a time during which many youth initiate smoking. They first estimated cross-sectional models of smoking participation, similar to work in the 1990s, and found similar results. That is, they found a strong inverse relationship between cigarette taxes and smoking at these three ages. Next, using the panel nature of their data, they directly examined smoking initiation behaviour with models that allowed for the use of within-area variation in cigarette taxes, rather than cross-sectional variation. When they did this, DeCicca, Kenkel and Mathios (2002) found essentially no relationship between taxes and youth smoking initiation, contrary to existing work and their own cross-sectional estimates which were designed to mimic earlier work.

---

[14] Though, by themselves they are not sufficient. Most importantly, it is important to have enough within-area variation in the variable of interest; in this context, that would be cigarette taxes.

More recent work tends to employ the type of empirical strategy used by DeCicca, Kenkel and Mathios (2002). For example, Carpenter and Cook (2008), using more recent, repeated cross-sectional data, find a somewhat larger and statistically precise relationship between cigarette taxes and youth smoking participation.[15] Their estimates imply a price elasticity of youth smoking participation between -0.2 and -0.5, a range which does not include the consensus estimate of -0.7. Even more recent work suggests a youth smoking participation elasticity between -0.3 and -0.4, or about half of the earlier consensus (Sen et al., 2010). Beyond youth smoking, my co-authors and I have begun to examine the dynamics of smoking in young adulthood. Descriptively, our work challenges the notion that most individuals start smoking prior to age eighteen. In particular, we found that roughly half of smokers at about age twenty-four were not smokers at age eighteen, and of those who were smokers at age eighteen only about two-thirds remained so by age twenty-four (DeCicca, Kenkel and Mathios, 2008). More to the point, these authors found no evidence that taxes prevented "late" smoking initiation between the ages of eighteen and twenty-four and only limited evidence that they encouraged smoking cessation among those who had started by age eighteen.

Consistent with the paucity of earlier work on adult smoking, there has been little new research on adult smoking. One exception is DeCicca and McLeod (2008) which examines the impact of relatively large post-2001 tax increases in the U.S. on the smoking behaviour of older adults. Using repeated cross-sectional data, these authors find evidence of substantial cessation in response to these higher taxes. In particular, we find that a one-dollar increase in the cigarette tax leads to between a 1.0 and 1.5 percentage point reduction in smoking participation among individuals aged forty-five to fifty-nine, a decrease in smoking participation of roughly six to eight percent. Though still in process, I am presently undertaking work with my graduate student, Cong Li, and our early estimates using data over roughly the same period as DeCicca and McLeod (2008) tend to confirm the notion that adult smoking participation may be more responsive to higher prices than conventional wisdom would suggest. That said, much more work is needed in this area before any definitive conclusions are made.

Final remarks

More recent work on the impact of tax-induced price increases on smoking behaviour, including my work with co-authors, collectively begins to challenge the conventional wisdom that youth are price-sensitive while adult smokers are not. Understanding this relationship is important to making useful public policy. For example, if taxes are not as effective in preventing youth smoking as is now thought, there will be a tendency to ignore other policy options, especially since taxes typically are not as costly as other interventions like anti-tobacco education, information campaigns, etc. Similarly, if taxes

---

[15] These authors also use data from 1991 to 2006, which include some relatively large tax increases by U.S. states, especially in the last five years of their data. In principle, these larger increases should provide better policy variation with which to estimate the relationship between taxes and smoking.

are more effective than thought in encouraging smoking cessation among established adult smokers, this is important information that may imply a smaller weight be placed on regressivity concerns in raising cigarette taxes. More work is needed and the recent large increases in cigarette taxes should provide analysts with the policy variation necessary to better understand these relationships.

References

Carpenter, Chistopher, Cook, Philip (2008). "Cigarette taxes and youth smoking: new evidence from national, state and local Youth Risk Behaviour Studies." *Journal of Health Economics,* 27 (2), 287–299.

Centers for Disease Control (1998). "Response to Increases in Cigarette Prices by Race/ Ethnicity, Income, and Age Groups—United States, 1976–1993." *Morbidity and Mortality Weekly Report* 47: 605–608.

Chaloupka, Frank J., and Grossman, Michael (1996). "Price, Tobacco Control Policies and Youth Smoking." NBER Working Paper no. 5740. Cambridge, MA.

Chaloupka, Frank J., and Pacula, Rosalie L. (1999). "Sex and Race Differences in Young People's Responsiveness to Price and Tobacco Control Policies." *Tobacco Control* 8: 373–377.

Chaloupka, Frank J., and Warner, Kenneth E. (2000). "The Economics of Smoking." In *Handbook of Health Economics,* vol. 1B, edited by Joseph P. Newhouse and Anthony J. Culyer. Amsterdam: North-Holland.

Chaloupka, Frank J., and Wechsler, Henry (1997). "Price, Tobacco Control Policies and Smoking among Young Adults." *Journal of Health Economics.* 16: 359–373.

Colman, Gregory J. and Dahlia K. Remler (2008). Vertical equity consequences of very high cigarette tax increases: If the poor are the ones smoking, how could cigarette tax increases be progressive? Journal of Policy Analysis and Management 27 (2): 376 - 400.

Congressional Budget Office (1998). "The Proposed Tobacco Settlement: Issues from a Federal Perspective." Manuscript. CBO: Washington, DC.

Cummings, K. Michael, Hyland, Andrew, Pechacek, Terry, Orlandi, Mario, and William Lynn (2007). Comparisons of recent trends in adult and adolescent cigarette smoking behavior and brand preferences. *Tobacco Control* 6 (Supplement 2): S31 – S37.

DeCicca, Philip, Kenkel, Donald S. and Alan D. Mathios (2002). Putting out the fires: will higher taxes reduce the onset of youth smoking? *Journal of Political Economy,* 110 (1), 144–169.

DeCicca, Philip, Kenkel, Donald S., Mathios, Alan D., Shin, Y.-J. and J.-Y. Lim (2006). Youth smoking, cigarette prices and anti-smoking sentiment. NBER Working Paper #12458.

DeCicca, Philip, Kenkel, Donald S. and Alan D. Mathios (2008). Cigarette taxes and the transition from youth to adult smoking. *Journal of Health Economics*, 27(4): 904-917.

DeCicca, Philip and Logan McLeod (2008). "Cigarette taxes and older adult smoking: Evidence from recent large tax increases", *Journal of Health Economics*, 27(4): 918-929.

DeCicca, Philip, Kenkel, Donald S. and Feng Liu (2010a). Excise tax avoidance: the case of state cigarette taxes. NBER Working Paper #15941.

DeCicca, Philip, Kenkel, Donald S. and Feng Liu (2010b). Who pays cigarette taxes? The impact of consumer price search. NBER Working Paper #15942.

Douglas, Stratford, and Hariharan, Govind (1994). "The Hazard of Starting Smoking: Estimates from a Split Population Duration Model." *Journal of Health Economics*, 13: 213–30.

Farrelly, Matthew C., Bray, Jeremy W., Pechacek, Terry, and Trevor Woollery (2001). Responses by adults to increases in cigarette prices by sociodemographic characteristics. *Southern Economic Journal* 68 (1), 156–165.

General Accounting Office (1998). *Tobacco: Issues Surrounding a National Tobacco Settlement.* GAO: Washington, DC.

Glied, Sherry. (2002). "Youth tobacco control: reconciling theory and empirical evidence." *Journal of Health Economics*, 21(1): 117-135.

Gruber, Jonathan (2000). "Youth Smoking in the U.S.: Prices and Policies." NBER Working Paper No. 7506. Cambridge, MA.

Gruber, J., Zinman, J. (2001). Youth smoking in the U.S.: evidence and implications. In: Gruber, J. (Ed.), Risky Behaviour Among Youth: An Economic Analysis. University of Chicago Press, Chicago, pp. 69–120.

Gruber, Jonathon, Sen, Anindya, and Mark Stabile (2003). "Estimating price elasticities when there is smuggling: the sensitivity of smoking to price in Canada", *Journal of Health Economics*, 22(5): 821-842.

Harris, Jeffrey E., and Chan, Sandra W. (1999). "The Continuum-of-Addiction: Cigarette Smoking in Relation to Price among Americans Aged 15–29." *Health Economics*, 8: 81–86.

Institute of Medicine. National Cancer Policy Board (1998). *Taking Action to Reduce Tobacco Use*. National Academy Press: Washington, DC.

Lewit, Eugene M., and Coate, Douglas (1982). "The Potential for Using Excise Taxes to Reduce Smoking." *Journal of Health Economics*, 1: 121–545.

Lewit, Eugene M.; Coate, Douglas; and Grossman, Michael (1981). "The Effects of Government Regulation on Teenage Smoking." *Journal of Law and Economics*, 24: 545–569.

Lewit, Eugene M.; Hyland, Andrew; Kerrebrock, Nancy; and Cummings, K. Michael. (1997). "Price, Public Policy, and Smoking in Young People." *Tobacco Control* 6 (S2): S2-17–S2-24.

Sen, Anindya and Nafeez Fatima (2010). "Do lower cigarette taxes lead to more smoking?" Evidence from the Canadian National Experiment, forthcoming in *Canadian Tax Journal*.

Sen, Anindya and Tony Wirjanto (2010). "Estimating the impact of cigarette taxes on youth smoking participation, initiation and persistence: Evidence from Canada", *Health Economics*, 19(11): 1264-1280.

Sen, Anindya, Ariizumi, Hideki, and Daciana Driambe (2010). "Do changes in cigarette taxes impact youth smoking?", *Forum for Health Economics and Policy*, 13(2).

Tauras, John A. (2006). Smoke-free air laws, cigarette prices and adult cigarette demand. *Economic Inquiry*, 44(2): 333–342.

Wasserman, Jeffrey; Manning, Willard G.; Newhouse, Joseph P.; and Winkler, John D. (1991). "The Effects of Excise Taxes and Regulations on Cigarette Smoking." *Journal of Health Economics*, 10: 43–64.

Despite their popularity, government-mandated smoking bans are not justified.

The Case Against Smoking Bans

THOMAS A. LAMBERT
University of Missouri–Columbia School of Law

In recent months, dozens of localities and a number of states have enacted sweeping smoking bans. The bans generally forbid smoking in "public" places, which are defined to include not only publicly owned facilities but also privately owned properties to which members of the public are invited (e.g., bars, restaurants, hotel lobbies, etc.). Proponents of the bans insist that they are necessary to reduce risks to public health and welfare and to protect the rights of nonsmoking patrons and employees of the regulated establishments.

Specifically, ban advocates have offered three justifications for government-imposed bans: First, they claim that such bans are warranted because indoor smoking involves a "negative externality," the market failure normally invoked to justify regulation of the ambient environment. In addition, advocates assert that smoking bans shape individual preferences against smoking, thereby reducing the number of smokers in society. Finally, proponents argue that smoking bans are justified, regardless of whether any market failure is present, simply because of the health risks associated with inhalation of environmental tobacco smoke (ETS), commonly referred to as "secondhand smoke."

This article contends that government-imposed smoking bans cannot be justified as responses to market failure, as means of shaping preferences, or on risk-reduction grounds. Smoking bans reduce public welfare by preventing an optimal allocation of nonsmoking and smoking-permitted public places. A laissez-faire approach better accommodates heterogeneous preferences regarding public smoking.

THE EXTERNALITY ARGUMENT

The conventional justification for regulation of the ambient environment (i.e., outdoor air and water) is that it is necessary

Thomas A. Lambert is associate professor at the University of Missouri–Columbia School of Law. He may be contacted by e-mail at lambertt@missouri.edu.

to combat the inefficiencies created by negative externalities. Negative externalities are costs that are not borne by the party in charge of the process that creates them. For example, the owner of a smoke-spewing factory does not fully bear the costs associated with the smoke, stench, and health risks his factory produces; many of those costs are foisted onto the factory's neighbors. When conduct involves negative externalities, participants will tend to engage in that conduct to an excessive degree, for they bear the full benefits, but not the full costs, of their activities. Quite often, then, government intervention (e.g., taxing the cost-creating behavior or limiting the amount permitted) may be desirable as a means of ensuring that the cost-creator does not engage to an excessive degree in the conduct at issue.

Advocates of smoking bans insist that indoor smoking involves negative externalities. First, ban advocates argue that nonsmoking patrons and employees of establishments that allow smoking are forced to bear costs over which they have no control. In addition, smokers impose negative externalities in the form of increased healthcare costs, a portion of which is paid from the public fisc. Thus, taxpayers are required to foot the bill for some of the costs associated with smoking in general. Examined closely, each of these externality-based arguments for smoking bans fails.

PATRONS AND EMPLOYEES Outdoor air pollution involves the sort of negative externality likely to result in both an inoptimal (i.e., excessive) amount of the polluting activity and a violation of pollution victims' rights. When it comes to indoor air pollution, by contrast, there is no such externality. That is because the individual charged with determining how much, if any, smoking is permitted in an indoor space ultimately bears the full costs of his or her decision and is thus likely to select the optimal level of air cleanliness. Moreover, nonsmokers' "rights" are not violated, because they are compen-

Tragedy of the Commons), the air inside a building is, in essence, "owned" by the building owner. That means that the building owner, who is in a position to control the amount of smoking (if any) that is permitted in the building, has an incentive to permit the "right" amount of smoking — that is, the amount that maximizes the welfare of individuals within the building. Depending on the highest and best use of the space and the types of people who patronize the building, the optimal level of smoking may be zero (as in an art museum), or "as much as patrons desire" (as in a tobacco lounge), or something in-between (as in most restaurants, which have smoking and nonsmoking sections). Because patrons select establishments based on the benefits and costs of patronage, they will avoid establishments with air policies they do not like or will, at a minimum, reduce the amount they are willing to pay for goods and services at such places. Owners of public places thus bear the full costs and benefits of their decisions regarding air quality and can be expected to select the optimal level of air cleanliness. Moreover, customers who do not like the air policy a space-owner has selected will patronize the space only if they are being otherwise

sated for the inconveniences and risks they suffer.

One might wonder how this could be. Because smokers in a public space impose costs on nonsmoking patrons, who cannot order the smokers to stop, will indoor smoking not entail both the inefficiency (an excessive level of pollution) and the injustice (an infringement of non-polluters' rights to enjoy clean air) associated with outdoor air pollution? In a word, no. There is a crucial difference between outdoor and indoor air, and that difference alleviates the inefficiencies and rights-violations normally associated with air pollution.

The crucial difference is property rights. Whereas outdoor air is common property (and thus subject to the famous

compensated by some positive attribute of the space at issue — say, cheap drinks or a particularly attractive clientele. They are, in other words, compensated for any "rights" violation. The de facto property rights that exist in indoor air, then, prevent the inefficiencies and injustices that accompany outdoor air pollution.

But what about workers at businesses that permit smoking? Is there not an externality in that they are forced to bear costs (and assume risks) over which they have no control? Again, the answer is no. Workers exercise control by demanding higher pay to compensate them for the risks and unpleasantries they experience because of the smoke in their workplaces. Adam Smith theorized about such "risk premiums" when he wrote in *The Wealth of Nations:*

> The whole of the advantages and disadvantages of the different employments of labor and stock must, in the same neighborhood, be either perfectly equal or tending to equality.... [T]he wages of labor vary with the ease or hardship, the honorableness or dishonorableness of employment.

He was right. A vast body of empirical evidence, including most notably that produced by economist W. Kip Viscusi, demonstrates that employers do in fact pay a premium for exposing their workers to risks and unpleasantries. Such risk/unpleasantry premiums motivate employers to select the optimal amount of smoke in their restaurants. They also alleviate any injustices occasioned by what might otherwise appear to be a violation of employees' rights. Thus, smoking in public establishments does not, in any meaningful sense, impose genuine negative externalities in the form of risks and unpleasantries to the patrons and employees of such establishments. Any externalities produced are merely "pecuniary" externalities — that is, externalities that are mitigated by the price mechanism and thus do not create inefficiencies and injustices.

PUBLIC COSTS Ban advocates also seek to justify prohibitions by pointing to externalities in the form of public healthcare expenditures. The argument here proceeds as follows:

- Smokers face disproportionately high health care costs.
- A portion of such costs is borne not by smokers themselves but by the public at large.
- Smokers thereby externalize some of the costs of their behavior and thus will tend to engage in "too much" smoking.
- Therefore, smoking bans are justified as an effort to cut back on the level of smoking that would otherwise exist.

This argument suffers from several weaknesses. First and most importantly, the initial premise is unsound. According to a comprehensive study in the *New England Journal of Medicine* in 1997, smoking probably has the effect of reducing overall health care costs because smokers die earlier than nonsmokers. The study's authors concluded that in a population in which no one smoked, health care costs would be 7 percent higher among men and 4 percent higher among women than the costs in the current mixed population of smokers and nonsmokers. The authors further determined that if all smokers were to quit, health care costs would be lower at first, but after 15 years they would become higher than at present.

Even if smoking were shown to increase public health care expenditures, the argument here would seem to prove too much. If increased healthcare costs could justify government imposition of a smoking ban in privately owned places, could they not similarly justify governmental regulation of menus at fast food restaurants or mandatory exercise regimens? Seri-

ous liberty interests would be at stake if a government were to make its citizens "be healthy" so as not to impose health care costs on others.

Finally, the assumption that public smoking bans reduce the incidence of smoking seems suspect. As discussed below, widespread smoking bans may actually increase the incidence of smoking among young people. Externalities in the form of increased public health care costs, then, likely cannot justify widespread bans on smoking in public spaces.

THE PREFERENCE-SHAPING ARGUMENT

The argument above concludes that smoking bans are unnecessary because market processes will ensure either that patrons' and employees' preferences regarding smoking are honored or that those individuals are compensated for not receiving their preferences. That argument assumes, though, that individuals' preferences are unaffected by the legal rule itself. A number of scholars have disputed the notion of "exogenous preferences." Instead, they claim that individuals' preferences regarding activities like smoking are influenced by the background legal rules themselves. Some theorists have therefore sought to justify smoking bans on grounds that they make smokers less likely to want to smoke and/or make nonsmokers more likely to appreciate smoke-free environments and thus more willing to pay a premium for such environments. In the end, neither preference-shaping argument can justify widespread bans on public smoking.

SHAPING ATTITUDES In recent years, legal scholars have produced a voluminous literature on the role of law in indirectly controlling conduct by shaping social norms and individual preferences. Smoking bans provide one of the favorite "success stories" of those who laud the use of legal rules to change norms and preferences. According to these scholars, smoking bans affect behavior, even if under-enforced, because they change the social norm regarding smoking in public. With the advent of smoking bans, nonsmokers who previously felt embarrassed about publicly expressing their distaste for ETS are speaking up. By providing a de facto community statement that public smoking is unacceptable, the bans embolden nonsmokers to confront smokers who are inconveniencing them. Facing heightened public hostility toward their habits, smokers are likely to revise their preferences regarding smoking. Thus, by making smoking more socially costly, the theory goes, bans reduce the number of smokers.

Of course, this is a good thing only if actual social utility is increased by reducing the incidence of smoking. Ban advocates assume that reducing smoking is welfare-enhancing for the obvious reason that smoking carries serious health risks. But ban advocates generally are not in a position to judge the cost side of reducing smoking because they do not know the degree of utility smokers experience by smoking. Smokers themselves, who these days are aware of the risks of smoking, appear to believe that the benefits they experience from the activity outweigh the costs. It is thus not at all clear that eliminating smoking will enhance social welfare.

But even if it were clear that society would be better off with less smoking, attempting to use smoking bans to influence social norms may not represent wise policy. Sweeping smoking bans may actually increase the incidence of smoking. A large percentage of smokers acquire the habit at a young age, and they frequently do so because smoking is "cool." Smoking is cool, of course, because it is rebellious. The harder anti-smoking forces work to coerce people into quitting smoking, and the more they engage the government and other establishment institutions in their efforts, the more rebellious — and thus the "cooler" — smoking becomes. Even advocates of the use of smoking regulation to alter social norms acknowledge that overly intrusive regulations may result in this sort of "norm backlash." As an empirical matter, then, it is not clear whether sweeping smoking bans — highly intrusive regulatory interventions — actually reduce the incidence of smoking in the long run.

WILLINGNESS TO PAY   The preference-shaping argument analyzed above focuses on the potential for smoking bans to shape the preferences of smokers (and potential smokers) by manipulating social norms. Insights from cognitive psychol-

porting to demonstrate an "endowment effect," whereby an individual's valuation of an asset is determined, in part, by whether or not she owns that asset. The general finding is that people attach a greater value to things they own than they would attach to those things if they did not own them and had to purchase them. In other words, ownership enhances subjective value.

With regard to smoking bans, ban advocates may argue that legal prohibitions effectively endow nonsmokers with the right to smoke-free air, causing them to value it more than they would if they had to "buy" it. If that is indeed the case, then the laissez-faire approach to indoor smoking appears troubling, for it is not, as its advocates maintain, merely a neutral policy that facilitates satisfaction of existing preferences. Rather than providing a level playing field on which privately adopted nonsmoking and smoking-permitted policies can compete, it biases the outcome of competition in favor of smoking-permitted policies. Because a truly neutral market solution is really impossible, ban advocates may call for the government to weigh in on the side of public health and force

There is no need for government to force establishments to go nonsmoking; the market will provide an optimal number of nonsmoking choices.

ogy suggest that smoking bans might similarly influence the preferences of nonsmokers, making them more willing to pay a premium for smoke-free environments and thereby encouraging more business owners to adopt no-smoking policies.

Advocates of a laissez-faire approach to the issue of indoor smoking maintain that an unregulated market will produce an optimal number of smoking and smoke-free establishments as business owners respond to the demands of patrons and employees. If patrons and employees are willing to pay more for a smoke-free environment (via, respectively, higher prices for the business's goods and services, or lower wages) than smokers are willing to pay for the right to smoke, then business owners will be motivated to ban smoking. Otherwise, they will not. Thus, there is no need for the government to force establishments to go nonsmoking; the market will provide an optimal number of nonsmoking facilities.

This argument assumes, though, that nonsmokers' willingness to pay for smoke-free environments is unaffected by the smoking laws themselves. If the laissez-faire approach depresses the amount nonsmokers are willing to pay for a smoke-free environment, then intervention in the market in the form of smoking bans may be justified.

So why might the background rules on when and where smoking is permitted affect nonsmokers' willingness to pay for smoke-free environments? In recent decades, cognitive psychologists have conducted a number of experiments pur-

the no-smoking policies that will be under-produced by the inherently biased free market.

There are several problems with this analysis. First, there is a great deal of debate over the extent to which the endowment effect really exists and the extent to which it applies to ownership of intangible rights (e.g., the right to smoke-free air) as well as to ownership of tangible property. In addition, given the number of public establishments that have already gone smoke-free, thereby "endowing" their patrons with the right to smoke-free air, the argument is a little out of date. Nonsmokers have now been exposed to enough facilities in which they have been endowed with the "right" to smoke-free air that they likely have adjusted upward their subjective valuation of that commodity (assuming endowment would, in fact, occasion an upward adjustment). Finally, the endowment effect argument would support, at most, temporary smoking bans — i.e., bans that persisted long enough to move the amount nonsmokers would be willing to pay to avoid smoke from a "willingness to pay" measure to a "willingness to accept" measure. If the justification for the bans is a need to enhance nonsmokers' valuation of smoke-free spaces so as to encourage market creation of such spaces, then the bans need not be permanent.

THE RISK ARGUMENT

The first two arguments for smoking bans focus, to some degree, on citizens' preferences: the externality argument focuses on a purported market failure that allegedly prevents the satisfaction of preferences regarding smoking, and the preference-shaping argument focuses on the law's inevitable role in shaping those preferences. By contrast, the third common argument for smoking bans ignores citizens' smoking preferences altogether. That argument asserts that smoking should be banned in public places, regardless of individuals' smoking preferences, because the health risks it presents are simply too great. In other words, smoking bans are justified on risk-based grounds even if there is no need to remedy a market failure or to correct a preference-shaping bias in the law.

Policymakers frequently invoke excessive risk as a sufficient ground for regulating an activity, even when that activity does not involve a market failure or reflect preferences that have been skewed by the background legal rules. Consider, for example, mandatory seatbelt laws. There is not much of an externality involved in the failure to wear a seatbelt because the costs of the conduct are borne by the person deciding to engage in it. While mandatory seatbelt laws may have the effect of altering preferences, there is no reason to think that the background legal rule had previously biased preferences against wearing seatbelts, and risk-avoidance is the sole reason for altering citizen preferences in the first place. Thus, the predominant justification for mandatory seatbelt laws, which have been enacted in every state except "Live Free or Die" New Hampshire, is risk-reduction — not externalities or a need to shape preferences for some end other than risk-reduction. Similarly, ban advocates argue, public smoking bans may be justified solely on grounds of risk-avoidance.

But a purely risk-based argument likely cannot justify a sweeping smoking ban. While risk, standing alone, is sometimes deemed sufficient to justify government prohibition of private conduct, such prohibition seems appropriate only when the harm avoided is relatively great and the regulation's intrusion on personal liberty is relatively small. Again, consider mandatory seatbelt laws. The risk associated with not wearing a seatbelt is huge, and the regulation's intrusion on personal liberty is minor — no more than a slight inconvenience. Hence, the laws may be justifiable on risk-reduction grounds. Consider, by comparison, whether the government could invoke risk as a legitimate basis for banning driving after 1:00 a.m. Such behavior certainly presents a heightened risk (late-night drivers are far more likely to fall asleep at the wheel), but the magnitude of risk presented does not justify the degree of liberty intrusion occasioned by the regulation. Smoking bans look more like late-night driving bans than mandatory seatbelt laws and thus likely cannot be justified solely with reference to risk.

To see why this is so, we must first isolate the relevant risk. Because public smoking bans do not prohibit smoking altogether and may not even reduce its incidence, the risk the bans aim to avert is not the risk to smokers themselves. It is instead the risk to nonsmokers — i.e., the risks associated with inhalation of ETS. The key question, then, is whether these risks are of sufficient magnitude to justify a significant intrusion on the personal liberty of private business owners and their customers.

If one were to rely on the stated conclusions of federal agencies (and/or the media reports discussing those conclusions), one might conclude that the risks associated with ETS inhalation do justify significant liberty restrictions. First consider the Environmental Protection Agency's 1992 report, *Respiratory Health Effects of Passive Smoking: Lung Cancer and Other Disorders*. That study, which concluded that ETS is a Class A (known human) carcinogen, purported to show that inhalation of ETS causes 3,000 lung cancer deaths per year. Not surprisingly, the study fueled efforts to impose smoking bans.

As it turns out, the study hardly amounted to sound science. A congressional inquiry into the methods the EPA used in the study found that "the process at every turn [was] characterized by both scientific and procedural irregularities," including "conflicts of interest by both Agency staff involved in the preparation of the risk assessment and members of the Science Advisory Board panel selected to provide a supposedly independent evaluation of the document." The congressional inquiry further concluded that "the Agency ha[d] deliberately abused and manipulated the scientific data in order to reach a predetermined, politically motivated result."

The findings of the EPA's 1992 study have also been undermined by court opinion. Charged with evaluating the agency's risk assessment in determining that ETS constitutes a Class A carcinogen, a federal district judge in the case *Flue-Cured Tobacco Coop. Stabilization Corp. v. U.S. EPA* criticized the agency's analysis in terms that can best be described as scathing. The court concluded:

> [The EPA] publicly committed to a conclusion before research had begun; . . . adjusted established procedure and scientific norms to validate the Agency's public conclusion[;] . . . disregarded information and made findings on selective information; did not disseminate significant epidemiologic information; deviated from its Risk Assessment Guidelines; failed to disclose important findings and reasoning; and left significant questions without answers.

Thus, the EPA's purported finding that ETS poses a serious cancer risk — a "finding" that has been extremely influential in motivating state and local smoking bans throughout the United States, should be discounted.

Apparently undeterred by these congressional and judicial reprimands, the U.S. surgeon general recently released a report entitled *The Health Consequences of Involuntary Exposure to Tobacco Smoke*, which purports to settle once and for all the debate over the risks of ETS inhalation. In releasing the report, Surgeon General Richard Carmona confidently proclaimed:

> The scientific evidence is now indisputable: secondhand smoke is not a mere annoyance. It is a serious health hazard that can lead to disease and premature death in children and nonsmoking adults.

In presenting the report, the surgeon general's office emphasized to the news media that even brief exposure to ETS poses immediate and significant health risks. The press release accompanying the report stated that "there is no risk-free level of exposure to secondhand smoke" and that "even brief exposure to secondhand smoke has immediate adverse effects on the cardiovascular system and increases risk for heart disease and lung cancer." In his remarks to the media, the surgeon general stated, "Breathing secondhand smoke for even a short time can damage cells and set the cancer process in motion." In a "fact sheet" accompanying the report, the surgeon general explained, "Breathing secondhand smoke for even a short time can have immediate adverse effects on the cardiovascular system." These and similar statements, faithfully repeated by the news media, create the impression that science has determined that simply being in a smoke-filled room exposes one to significant health risks.

Examined closely, the surgeon general's report established

begin with. A 20 percent increase in a tiny risk is, well, really tiny — certainly too tiny to justify the substantial liberty infringement involved in smoking bans. Indeed, risk alone has not justified a ban on smoking itself, an activity that increases the risk of heart disease by 100 to 300 percent and that of lung cancer by 900 percent. How, then, could a much smaller risk justify highly intrusive regulation of the voluntary actions of individuals gathered on private property?

This analysis even assumes that the conclusions of the surgeon general's report are accurate. In fact, they probably are not. The report is a meta-analysis, meaning that the authors did not collect their own epidemiological data but instead combined the results of previously published ETS studies. Meta-analyses are useful analyses, but they are no more compelling than the underlying studies upon which they are based.

The question is whether the risks of secondhand smoke justify a significant intrusion on the personal liberty of business owners and their customers.

no such proposition. The underlying studies upon which the surgeon general's report was based considered the effects of chronic exposure to ETS on individuals, such as long-time spouses of smokers. The studies simply did not consider the health effects of sporadic exposure to ETS and thus cannot provide empirical support for the surgeon general's statements about short-term ETS exposure.

Moreover, those statements are theoretically unsound, for they conflict with the basic toxicological principle that "the dose makes the poison." According to a study published in the *New England Journal of Medicine* in 1975, when many more individuals smoked and there were much higher ETS concentrations in public places, exposure to an hour's worth of prevailing levels of ETS was equivalent to smoking 0.004 cigarettes. Put differently, one would have to breathe smoke-filled air for 4,000 hours in order to inhale as much tobacco smoke as a smoker inhales in a single cigarette. Given those concentration levels, it seems implausible that short-term exposure to ETS poses serious health risks. Possessing neither empirical foundation nor theoretical plausibility, the Surgeon General's public statements about the health risks of brief exposure to ETS were misleading.

But what about the actual findings of the surgeon general's report, as opposed to the hyperbolic (and widely reported) accompanying statements? Those findings — even taken at face value — do not provide a risk-based rationale for highly intrusive smoking bans. The report concludes that chronic ETS exposure increases the risks of lung cancer and heart disease by 20 to 30 percent. While those numbers sound fairly large, one must remember that the underlying risks of lung cancer and heart disease in nonsmokers are quite small to

In this case, the meta-analysis rests on findings from a number of discredited studies, including the 1992 EPA study. Moreover, the analysis treats all studies equally, regardless of their scope and rigor. A number of the underlying studies purporting to document correlations between chronic ETS exposure and cancer or heart disease were quite small, and most employed "case study" methodologies in which individuals with diseases were polled regarding spousal smoking habits or the presence of ETS at their workplaces. A superior study would involve a large number of subjects — some routinely exposed to ETS, some not — and would follow them over time. This sort of "cohort study" is more difficult to perform than after-the-fact case studies, but it is also more accurate.

In fact, an extremely large cohort study has recently been conducted. In 2003, James Enstrom of UCLA and Geoffrey Kabat of the State University of New York, Stony Brook, published a study of the health histories of more than 35,000 never-smoking Californians who were married to smokers. Using information gathered by the American Cancer Society, the researchers collected data on the never-smokers for 39 years (from 1959 to 1998). Their investigation revealed no heightened lung cancer risk among study subjects. In fact, the authors found no "causal relationship between exposure to [ETS] and tobacco-related mortality," though they acknowledged that "a small effect" cannot be ruled out. Enstrom and Kabat's massive study, which has been vociferously criticized by anti-smoking forces, was not even included in the surgeon general's meta-analysis, which covered only studies published through 2002.

The bottom line is that the research on ETS reveals, at most, that even chronic ETS exposure creates only a negligible absolute risk of cancer and heart disease. Advocates of smoking bans must therefore base their risk arguments on non-disease risks.

Some have acknowledged that the purported link between ETS and cancer or heart disease is dubious but have nonetheless maintained that other health risks justify sweeping bans. For example, Dr. Elizabeth Whelan of the pro-ban American Council on Science and Health chastised her fellow ban advocates for "threaten[ing]" their cause with "hyperbole about the likely effects of ETS" — i.e., claims that ETS causes cancer and heart disease. Maintaining that the advocates should have "simply stated that ETS caused irritation of the eyes, nose and respiratory tract and aggravated preexisting asthma," she insisted, that "surely that is enough of a reason to justify the protection of all workers" via a sweeping smoking ban.

Surely it is not. As noted above, paternalistic regulations aimed solely at reducing risks, not at correcting a legitimate market failure, are justifiable only when the risk is relatively serious and the liberty intrusion occasioned by the regulation is relatively minor. Here, the potential harms at issue (a greater number of watery eyes and runny noses, and aggravation of complications among asthmatics who voluntarily patronize establishments where smoking is permitted) do not seem great enough to justify a governmental command that private business owners force their invitees to refrain from an activity that affects only other invitees. Hence, widespread smoking bans are not justifiable solely on risk-based grounds.

THE SUPERIORITY OF LAISSEZ-FAIRE

Controversies over smoking in public places are ultimately controversies over property rights. Does a smoker have the right to fill the air with his or her smoke, or do nonsmokers have the right to smoke-free air? In other words, who "owns" the air? A smoking ban effectively gives nonsmoking patrons the right to the air. By contrast, the laissez-faire approach effectively permits the owner of the establishment to determine the proper allocation of air rights within his or her space. The owner may choose to give the rights to smoking patrons (by permitting smoking), nonsmokers (by banning smoking), or to try to accommodate both by designating some parts of the establishment nonsmoking but permitting smoking elsewhere within the space.

However owners allocate the right to air among smokers and nonsmokers, there will be some "winners" whose preferred policy is adopted and whose happiness is therefore increased, and some "losers" whose preferred policy is rejected and whose happiness is therefore diminished. There is thus, as Ronald Coase explained, an unavoidable reciprocal harm inherent in any allocation of the right to the indoor air at issue. Adoption of a smoking-permitted policy harms nonsmokers, but adoption of a no-smoking policy harms smokers.

In light of this unavoidable, reciprocal harm, social welfare would be maximized if smoking policies were set to favor the group whose total happiness would be most enhanced by implementation of its favored policy. So, if smoking customers value the right to smoke in a particular place more than nonsmoking customers value the right to be free from such smoke, that place should allow smoking. Conversely, if nonsmoking patrons value an establishment's clean air more than smoking patrons value the right to light up, the establishment should ban smoking.

It should thus be clear why a laissez-faire approach of permitting establishment owners to set their own smoking policies will create more welfare than a ban on smoking in public places. Under the laissez-faire approach, a business owner, seeking to maximize his or her profits, will set the establishment's smoking policy to accommodate the patrons who most value their preferred policy (and thus are most willing to pay a premium to be in the proprietor's space). This will result in a variety of smoking policies at different establishments, as business owners respond to the preferences of their customers.

Under a smoking ban, by contrast, business owners are not permitted to cater to smoking patrons' demands even when those patrons value the right to smoke more than nonsmoking patrons (and employees) value the right to be free from smoke. A smoking ban, then, is less likely to maximize social welfare than a laissez-faire approach, which ensures that the right to any particular public place's air is allocated to the group that values it most.

CONCLUSION

Government-imposed smoking bans are unwise. Considered closely, the arguments used to justify them falter. The externality argument fails because indoor smoking creates, at worst, a pecuniary externality that will be mitigated by the price mechanism. Preference-shaping arguments are weak because heavy-handed government restrictions create a substantial risk of "norm backlash." Risk-based arguments are insufficient because the slight risks associated with ETS cannot justify the substantial privacy intrusion occasioned by sweeping smoking bans. In the end, a laissez-faire policy that would permit private business owners to tailor their own smoking policies according to the demands of their patrons is most likely to maximize social welfare by providing an optimal allocation of both smoking and smoke-free establishments. ▪

Readings

- "The Anti-Tobacco Campaign of the Nazis: A Little Known Aspect of Public Health in Germany, 1933–45," by Robert N. Proctor. *British Medical Journal,* Vol. 313 (1996).

- "Concentrations of Nicotine and Tobacco Smoke in Public Places," by W. C. Hinds and M. W. First. *New England Journal of Medicine,* Vol. 292 (1975).

- "Environmental Tobacco Smoke and Tobacco-Related Mortality in a Prospective Study of Californians, 1960-98," by James E. Enstrom and Geoffrey C. Kabat. *British Journal of Medicine,* Vol. 326 (2003).

- "Gentle Nudges vs. Hard Shoves: Solving the Sticky Norms Problem," by Dan M. Kahan. *University of Chicago Law Review,* Vol. 67 (2000).

- "The Health Care Costs of Smoking," by Jan J. Barendregt et al. *New England Journal of Medicine,* Vol. 337 (1997).

- "Willingness to Pay vs. Willingness to Accept: Legal and Economic Implications," by Elizabeth Hoffman and Matthew L. Spitzer. *Washington University Law Quarterly,* Vol. 71 (1993).

Module 4 - Corporate Bad Behaviour

Unit 9 – Insider Trading, Corporate Governance, Pollution

Notes on "corporate financial crime"

Mike Veall, Department of Economics, McMaster University

A common "share" of a corporation represents a part-ownership. Suppose a corporation has only one type of common share and there are a million such shares issued. Then if A owns one share, she/he owns one one-millionth of the corporation. A will receive one one-millionth of any dividends the corporation issues and if the corporation were sold in its entirety, A would receive one one-millionth of the selling price.

Note that I didn't write that A would receive one one-millionth of the annual profits. That is because the corporation is run by a Board of Directors who decides whether the profits are distributed to shareholders (as dividends) or re-invested in the company (as retained earnings). Each share has a vote so A has one of the million votes as to who is on the Board of Directors, but aside from that A has little influence.

Obviously the corporation's executives and members of the Board of Directors will receive corporate information before A does. Suppose for example, executives learn adverse news about the corporation and sell their stock immediately, or tell their friends to sell the stock. That is called "insider trading". It is illegal. While I believe the vast majority of executives and Directors are honest, the study by Bris I mention in the interview does argue that Canada has a fair amount of insider trading. The study is getting somewhat out of date, however, and I know of no newer studies.

Another issue in corporate governance is that the Board of Directors has to decide how much to pay the executives of the company. In this negotiation, the Board is supposed to represent the interests of the shareholders who do not want the executives paid excessively. While it is hard to judge how well the Board fulfills that responsibility, there have been some cases of clearly illegal behaviour involving "options backdating".

Many executives are paid partly in options. Essentially "options backdating" undervalues the option, so that the executive is actually being paid more than is stated publicly. To understand further, an understanding of options is required.

An option is a right to buy a stock at a stated price. Say the current stock price of company XYZ is $17 and, as part of her/his pay packet, an executive in XYZ is granted an option to buy 200,000 shares of stock at the price of $20. The idea is that the executive will now work for what shareholders most want: a higher share price. If the share price eventually goes to say $25, the executive will use the option to buy 200,000 shares at the $20 option price and if desired sell them immediately for $25 and gain $5 a share, or in total $5 × 200,000 = $1m.   The higher the stock price is when the option is used, the bigger the gain to the executive.

At the time the option is granted, the option will be worth more the higher the current price of the share. To see this, stay with our example of an option to buy the stock at $20 a share and consider three possible current share prices: $23, $20 and $17.

Of these three possibilities, the option is most valuable if the current share price is $23 because it can be used for an instant profit of $3 a share.

The option is not as valuable if the current share price is $20 *but it is still valuable* because there is a chance that the share price will go up above $20 and the option can be used to turn a profit.

The option is the least valuable if the current share price is $17 *but it is still valuable* because there is still a chance that the share price will go above $20. It just is a little less likely and may take longer than if the share price is $20.

Clearly by this logic the option will be worth still less if the current share price is $14.

"Option backdating" occurs when the option is actually issued when the share price is say $17 (or even $20 or $23) but it is falsely dated as if it was issued when the share price was $14. The option is then really worth more to the executive than has been publicly stated. The executive has illegally been paid more than entitled.

It's Nice to Be an Insider in Canada

In the 1980s, studies by Eckbo (1986; 1988) raised eyebrows by contrasting stock price movements around corporate takeovers in Canada versus in the United States. The solid grey line in Figure 5 epitomizes the well-known pattern in the United States (Westin, Mitchell, and Mulherin 2004), tracing out how the target firm's share price moves relatively little until the bidder makes a public announcement that a takeover is in the offing, whereupon the target firm's stock price shoots up — often by 30 percent or more within minutes.

The economics behind this price increase are complicated, but in many cases boil down to the acquirer firm's top mangers being expected to operate the target firm more efficiently, or at least less inefficiently.[1] Except in leveraged buyouts in the 1980s and 1990s, this efficiency gain does not seem detrimental to workers — acquired firms do not fire workers or cut wages relative to otherwise similar firms that remain independent (Shleifer and Summers 2000; Westin, Mitchell, and Mulherin 2004). Overall, the empirical evidence shows that shareholders do better, and workers no worse, if firms are more vulnerable to takeovers.

---

[1] For a full explanation of the economics, theory and evidence, supporting this view, see Westin, Mitchell, and Mulherin (2004).

FIGURE 5
Corporate Takeovers in Canada and the United States

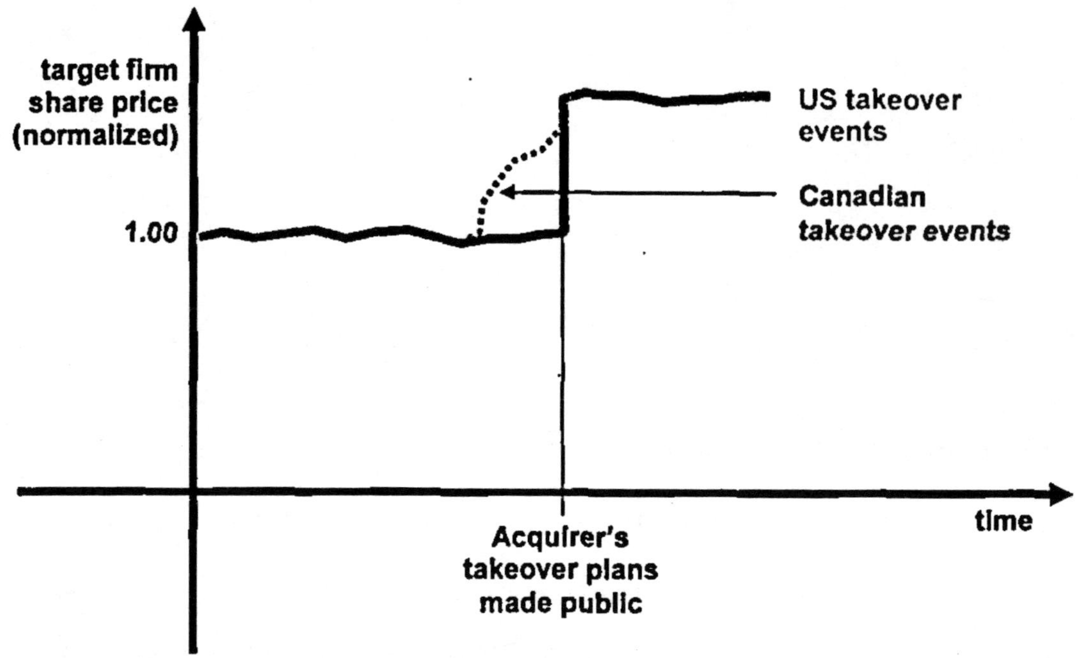

Upon the news that it may be a takeover target, a firm's share price rises markedly. In the United States this increase occurs in the minutes or hours immediately following the announcement. In Canada the target price generally begins rising sooner. *Source:* Graphical summary of findings in Bris (2005); Eckbo (1986; 1988); Jensen and Ruback (1983).

For our purposes, the key revelation is that the target firm's share price holds steady and then shoots up once investors learn that a control change is in the works. This contrasts markedly with the dotted black line that traces out a stylized Canadian corporate takeover. Here the target's share price slowly levitates upward during the two to three months before the takeover is announced and then moves relatively little when the plans are made public. Eckbo (1986, 1988) interprets this as evidence of more energetic and lucrative insider trading in Canada.

Remarkably, a recent study (Bris 2005) shows little change in two decades. In fact, after comparing statistically meaningful samples of takeovers on each of the world's active stock exchanges, he reports that Canada permits the most lucrative insider trading in any developed economy. American courts routinely prosecute top corporate insiders for trading on inside information, and even jail the occasional home decorating guru like Martha Stewart. But Canada, with insider trading laws that read much like those in the United States, did not see its first genuine criminal conviction for insider trading until 2010.[2]

After I mentioned this anomaly in a seminar for senior Canadian business leaders, one explained why it was good for the country. First, he clarified, if shareholders really didn't like it, they could sanction the corporate insiders at the next shareholders meeting. Second, he continued, since Canadian top corporate insiders make a bit extra on the side by trading in their firm's stocks, they accept lower salaries. Neither point, unfortunately, can be tested. Canadian top corporate executives, unlike their American peers, have not faced firm requirements to disclose their insider trades until 2010, and still need not make public their individual compensation packages.

Limits on Shareholder Democracy in Canada

Shareholder democracy in Canada is free of staggered boards – one of its major constraints in the United States. Staggered boards let shareholders elect a third of the board to a three year term each year, and have gained popularity with US corporate insiders seeking to limit the power of outside shareholders. By forcing dissidents to wait two years to replace a majority of the board and three years to replace it entirely, staggered boards effectively entrench insiders to an extent sufficient to significantly depress shareholder value in the affected firms (Bebchuk and Cohen 2008).

---

[2] See In The Matter of the Securities Act, R.S.O. 1990, C. S.5, As Amended v. Stanko Joseph Grmovsek and Gil I. Cornblum, 2009). A mining company executive was previously convicted of insider trading as a lesser charge to fraud and, upon appeal, sentenced to 6 months and fined C$1 M (In the Matter of the Securities Act R.S.O. 1990 c. S 5, as amended v. Glenn Harvey Harper, 2004) in connection with a mining stock fraud, whose principal perpetrators remain unknown (Sergeant 2006, p. 64).

11

In Canada, staggered boards are ineffective because federal and provincial corporations laws let shareholders demand emergency meetings at any time, at which all directors can be replaced; and these provisions trump any charter amendment to the contrary. This enhances the power of shareholders against hired managers. However, if the managers please controlling shareholders, outsider shareholders can be ignored in many cases. A far greater proportion of major firms have controlling shareholders in Canada than in either the United States or United Kingdom, so unhindered shareholder power to hire and fire the board might properly be translated as unhindered power for the controlling shareholder to appoint the board.

This has implications for the Canadian economy because previous work shows that firms with entrenched controlling shareholders underperform (Morck, Shleifer and Vishny 1988; McConnell and Servaes 1990: Morck, Stangeland and Yeung 2000) and that economies in which most large firms have controlling shareholders underperform (Morck and Yeung 2004; Morck, Weinstein and Yeung 2005; Fogel 2007).

Shareholder value is especially compromised where the controlling shareholder commands a dominant block of votes without actually owning a proportionate fraction of the firm's shares (Smith and Amoako-Adu 1995; Gompers, Ishi and Metrick 2010). This happens in two ways in Canada.

First, a number of Canadian firms have used so-called dual class shares (Amoako-Adu and Smith 1995, 2001) to magnify insider shareholders' voting power until it eclipses that of outsider shareholder.[3] The firm sells one class of shares, usually called *restricted voting shares*, to the general public. These shares might give their owners one vote per share at the firm's shareholder meeting. The firm simultaneously provides its insiders with a different class of

---

[3] Dual class shares also exist in the United States and elsewhere. However, they were prohibited on the New York Stock Exchange for many decades, and so fell out of favour among firms desiring a "blue chip" reputation. See Gompers, Ishii, and Metrick (2010).

shares, usually *called superior voting shares*, which give their owners many votes per share. This practice means that even if the majority of a company's shareholders dislike the company's top insiders, they can lack the voting power to do anything about it. Insiders increasingly disproportionate voting in dual class firms has attracted criticism, and pressure to unify their equity into a single class (Smith and Amoako-Adu 2001).

Such a case played out in 2010, Ontario courts and regulators let Magna controlling shareholder Frank Stronach cash in his superior voting shares at a 1,800% premium after 57% shareholder vote to allow it, despite the vocal objections of pensions funds with stock in the firm. The problem with a simple vote on such an issue is that, even if insiders cannot vote, they frame the question: the issue was not to eliminate the insiders' superior voting rights or not, but to eliminate them with a huge payment to the insiders or retain disproportionate insider control for the foreseeable future. We cannot know how shareholders might have voted given a third option, such as the removal of the insiders'' superior voting rights at a premium set by a disinterested third party.

Second, many Canadian firms without dual class shares still have controlling shareholders, typically very wealthy and well-connected, old-moneyed families. These families sometimes command an effective majority through direct ownership of a large voting block, but often employ a practice called *pyramiding*, to enhance their voting power.

Figure 6 explains how pyramiding magnifies substantial fortunes into control over large groups of seemingly distinct corporations that, together, are worth vastly more. A wealthy individual or family controls enough stock to dominate the shareholder meeting of one listed firm – that at the apex in the figure. This firm, in turn, controls equity blocks sufficient to dominate the shareholder meetings of a second tier of listed firms. These, in turn, each hold

13

control blocks in listed firms in a third tier. As many tiers can be added as the apex firm's controlling shareholder desires, and each additional tier exponentially increases the corporate assets that shareholder controls. Pyramiding thus creates artificial controlling shareholders in firms that are really primarily capitalized by outside shareholders such as pension funds and small investors.

Pyramidal groups of this form are the structures that let small cliques of oligarchic families control the economies of many countries in Latin America, Asia, and continental Europe – especially Eastern Europe and Russia. This practice is essentially unknown in both the United States and United Kingdom, but widespread in Canada and throughout Asia, Latin America, and continental Europe (La Porta et al. 1998).

FIGURE 6
Pyramiding Basics

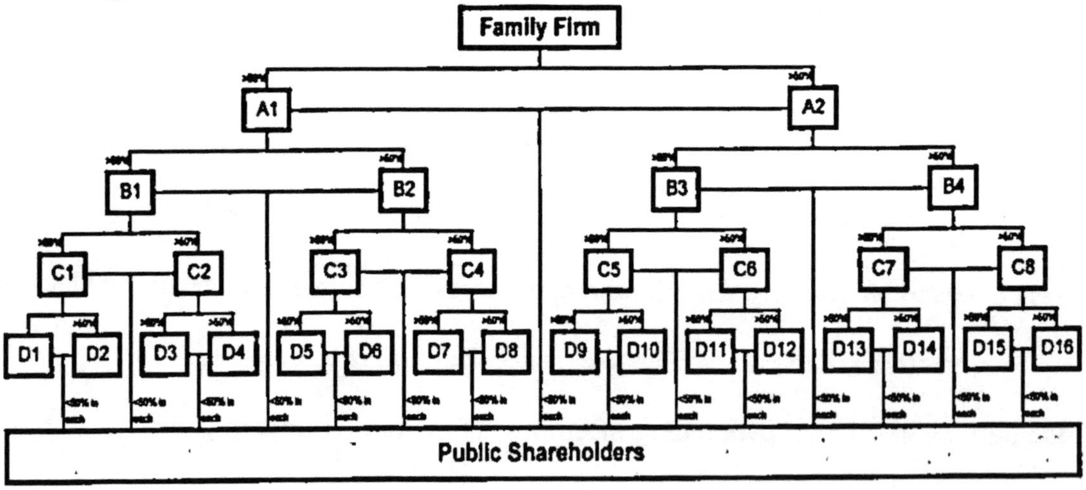

A family firm controls listed firms, each of which controls more listed firms, each of which control yet more listed firms. Remaining shares in each firms are held by public investors.

A third type of explanation emphasizes executive compensation practices. One possibility within this type (e g. Jensen and Meckling, 1976 and Jensen

12 There were other countries with clear surges, including Australia, New Zealand, and Ireland, where perhaps it is important that these countries have a legal system with British roots or that they are English-speaking and hence are closer culturally to the United States. (On the latter point, see the previous discussion of globalization and different trends for English and French speakers in Quebec.) There are other countries where the evidence suggests very small surges, for example, Spain, Switzerland, Sweden, and Denmark. The German case is complicated, but it appears as if top share inequality and wage inequality trends may be different. The data in the World Top Incomes Database are from Dell (2007), are based on taxfiler data, and end in 1998. No surge is reported for the top 1%, top 0.1%, or top 0.01% shares in the 1980s and 1990s. Bach, Corneo, and Steiner (2009) report similar results up to 2003, but find a surge in the top 0.001% and 0.0001% shares. However, over roughly this same period, Fabbri and Marin (2012) find increasing CEO salaries using executive compensation data, and Dustmann, Ludsteck, and Schonberg (2009) find increasing wage inequality using (right-censored) social security data.

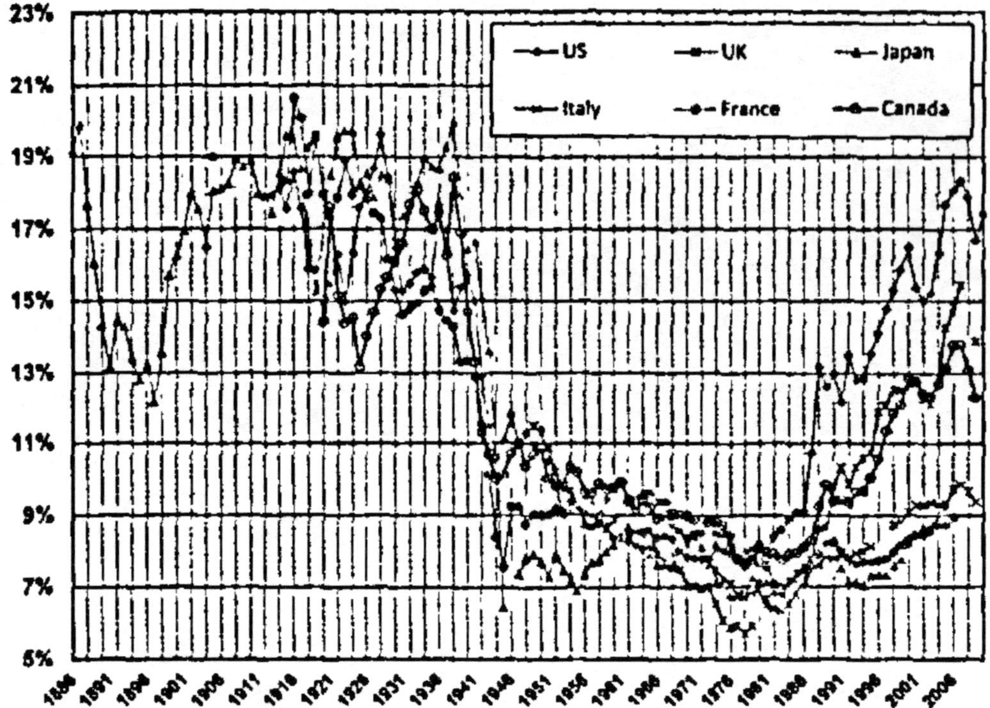

FIGURE 5 Top income shares by countries, 1886–2010
SOURCE: Alvaredo et al. (2012), The World Top Incomes Database.
http://gmond parisschoolofeconomics.eu/topincomes, World Top Incomes Database,
http://g-mond parisschoolofeconomics.eu/topincomes/ as accessed 17 May 2012.

and Murphy, 1990) is that increased executive compensation can be an efficient consequence of an attempt to align top management salaries with those of
shareholders. Gabaix and Landier (2008) emphasize the role of increasing firm
size in explaining the increase in executive compensation, although Lemieux
(2008, fn5) points out that the finding is sensitive to specification, and Gor-
don and Dew-Becker (2008) argue that it is sensitive to measures of firm size
and choice of time period. A very different possibility is that of Bebchuk, Fried
and Walker, 2002 and Bebchuk and Fried, 2004 who argue that higher CEO
salaries are largely a result of the CEO's co-opting corporate governance by in-
fluencing the choice of company directors. Jensen and Murphy (2004) do not
dismiss these concerns and indeed make a series of recommendations that might
mitigate these effects including one that corporations 'change the structural, social and psychological environment of the board so that directors (even those
who fulfill the requirements of independence) no longer see themselves as effectively the employees of the CEO.' However Jensen and Murphy (2004) maintain that these arguments do not explain what they believe is the over-use of
options and the tendency for boards to pay more for CEOs hired externally.
Bebchuk and Fried (2004) and Jensen and Murphy (2004) both emphasize that
CEOs have strong incentives to control the information that determines their

13 Martin (2011) and Brooks and McQuaig (2010) also argue against methods currently used to determine CEO compensation, the latter strongly maintaining it is excessive in both Canada and the United States. Frydman and Saks (2010), who examine U.S. CEO compensation directly, argue that there is no corporate governance explanation that lines up well with the timing of the U.S. surge. However, while speculative, one possibility might be the technological developments that allowed a more liquid options market; for example, the Chicago Board Options Exchange opened for a limited number of stock call options in 1973.

14 Relatedly, a common explanation of the crisis of 2008 is that subordinate financial managers in some financial entities in the United States were rewarded for increasing the valuations of assets in their accounts, with insufficient adjustment for risk. As the values of the accounts of individual managers were aggregated as part of the valuation of the firms themselves, CEOs rewarded by such valuations had a disincentive to question the underreporting of risk or the acquisition of more risk. From this viewpoint, what happened next is well captured by the aphorism attributed to John Kenneth Galbraith: 'Recessions catch what auditors miss.' A very different explanation of the crisis also related to top share inequality is that of Kumhof and Rancière (2010). In their model the desire of those with high incomes to save can only be matched by lending to those with low incomes who eventually take on more than they can repay, leading to collapse of the financial system.

15 Piketty and Saez (2006) suggest that cultural explanations may go beyond corporate culture. For example there may be a constraint as to what level of compensation may be socially acceptable.

16 McNally and Smith (2003) reported poor disclosure of insider trading at the Toronto Stock Exchange with McNally and Smith (2010) reporting marked improvement. Compton, Sandler and Tedds (2009) raise serious issues regarding options backdating in Canada which Compton, Nicholls, Sandler and Tedds (2012) study further in a taxation context. Tedds, Compton, Morrison, Nicholls and Sandler (2011) find shortcomings in public disclosure of granted options in Canada.

Of these the first is the area of corporate governance. As discussed earlier, it has been estimated that Canada has a relatively high prevalence of insider trading and it has not been immune to practices such as backdating options. Morck (2010) writes, 'In practice, the typical big Canadian corporation is arguably *less democratic than in the past, and less democratic than its peers in both America and Great Britain. This is because corporate insiders dominate the shareholder meetings of listed Canadian firms to an extent generally not seen in either the United States or the United Kingdom, and because Canadian legislatures, courts, regulators, and exchanges accept and passively perpetuate this.'* An environment of insider control seems likely to foster excessive CEO compensation, in which case high compensation may be a symptom of something far worse, as Morck continues, *'a large and growing body of evidence shows Canadian corporations underperforming across the board'* and that this is *'no coincidence, for much empirical evidence links shareholder democracy to firm and economy performance.'*

Therefore 'say on pay' laws, where shareholders must approve CEO compensation packages (as in, e.g., Australia and the United States) or be given an opportunity for a non-binding vote (as in, e.g , the United Kingdom and Germany), are unlikely to be sufficient. In any case a number of Canadian corporations are voluntarily adopting such measures (perhaps thereby increasing their share prices; see Trottier 2011). Morck argues for the reduction of the power of controlling shareholders through measures to make non-voting shares and pyramiding[31] less attractive, and to ensure the independence of pension fund trustees. He also supports national securities regulation to prevent a race to the

29 As an example of a consequence of income and wealth polarization in the United States, Drutman and Phelps-Goodman (2012) calculate that for the United States the top 0 01% of donors made close to 25% of all contributions to political campaigns. Hacker and Pierson (2010) argue that the U.S. surge is rooted in a more effective use of lobbying and campaign funding by business interests, beginning in the late 1970s. Acemoglu and Robinson (2012) argue that there is the potential for a vicious circle if increasing wealth enables the wealthy to influence policy in ways that favour the wealthy.

30 Largely focusing on the United States, Stiglitz (2012) argues that, along with agency problems in corporate governance, much of the increase in top shares is due to successful rent-seeking within the political process, at the expense of economic growth.

31 'Pyramiding' is the practice of a firm holding a controlling interest in a number of other firms, which in turn can hold controlling interests in other firms, and so on. It can concentrate corporate power in the hands of a few. Morck explains that tax and other laws essentially have eliminated this practice in the United States and the United Kingdom, although it is common elsewhere.

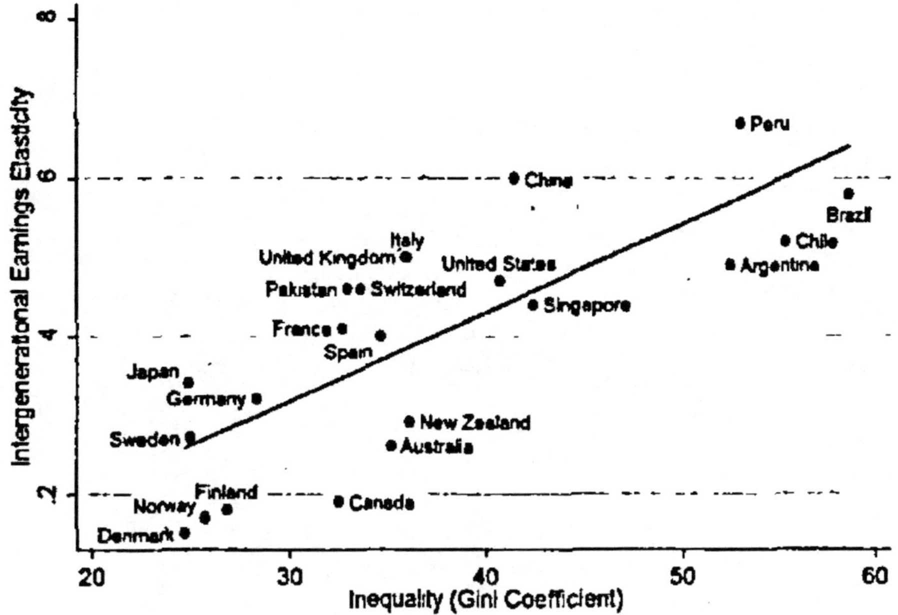

FIGURE 6 The relationship between earnings inequality and intergenerational earnings mobility across countries
SOURCE: Corak (2012)

bottom among provincial securities regulators. Policies that limit the power of insiders (on all matters, but including executive compensation) can aid the raising of capital (by acting as commitment devices for the raisers) as well as promoting a more vigorous market for corporate control and hence better management, capital allocation and growth.[32]

32 While in my view government intervention in the actions of a corporation should be kept to the minimum, government policies that mandate accountability and transparency are akin to consumer-protection regulation in that they can reduce agency problems and hence be of value to all market participants.

What Is Environmental Economics?

Environmental economics is the study of environmental problems with the perspective and analytical ideas of economics. Economics is the study of how and why people—whether they are consumers, firms, non-profit organizations, or government agencies—make decisions about the use of valuable resources. Economics is about making choices. It is divided into *microeconomics,* the study of the behaviour of individuals or small groups, and *macroeconomics,* the study of the economic performance of economies as a whole. Environmental economics draws from both sides, but primarily from microeconomics. The study of environmental economics, like all economics courses, is concerned with the fundamental issue of allocating scarce resources among competing uses. The concepts of **scarcity, opportunity costs, trade-offs, marginal benefits, marginal costs, efficiency,** and **equity** are key ingredients to understanding environmental problems and what can be done about them.

Environmental economics makes use of many familiar concepts in economics. What is different about environmental economics compared to other economic subjects is the focus on how economic activities affect our natural environment—the atmosphere, water, land, and an enormous variety of living species. Economic decisions made by people, firms, and governments can have many deleterious effects on the natural environment. For example, the dumping of waste products into the natural environment creates pollution that harms humans and other living things, production, and degrades ecosystems—the planet's air, water, and land. It leads to wasteful use of resources and threatens the sustainability of both our environment and economy. We ask:

- Why don't people take into account the effects of their economic activity on the natural environment?
- What inhibits economic systems from using its resources wisely and efficiently to protect the sustainability of our planet and people's livelihoods over time?

Environmental economics examines these questions by focusing on ways society can reduce its degradation of the natural environment. Equally as important, environmental economics investigates and assesses different methods of reaching an efficient and equitable use of all resources (including environmental ones) from the viewpoint of society, not just individual decision makers as is the typical focus in economic analysis.

To accomplish these tasks, a simple but powerful analytical model is developed that builds on, but modifies and extends standard economic principles, in particular, the marginal valuations that involve trade-offs between marginal costs and marginal benefits.

2

While **economic efficiency** remains the central criterion for evaluating outcomes and policies, environmental economists also examine other criteria for choosing among alternative policies that attempt to improve the environment—for example, **equity** or fairness. If economic efficiency cannot be obtained, and environmental targets are established using other criteria, an economic approach can still greatly assist decision makers in reaching whatever target is set. This book focuses on how individual actions give rise to environmental degradation and what can be done about these actions. Another branch of economics—*natural resource economics*—examines ways to achieve efficient use of our natural environment over time—energy, forests, land, and harvested species such as fish stocks. We look more closely at the distinction between environmental and natural resource economics in Chapter 2.

The objective of this chapter is to acquaint you with some of the basic ideas and analytical tools of microeconomics that are used in environmental economics. We will illustrate how environmental economics helps answer important questions about our environment and economy with real-world examples. We first consider briefly what we mean by the "economic approach," then turn to two pressing environmental problems; starting first with a local and regional concern—motor vehicle pollution, then turning to a global threat—greenhouse gas emissions. In Chapter 2 we will take a look at the broad linkages existing between economy and environment and define a number of important pollution terms. After that we will be ready to study the economic principles we will need.

ECONOMIC EFFICIENCY

Economic efficiency is all about using resources wisely. An outcome is said to be economically efficient if all resources are put to their highest value use, or equivalently, the economy reaches a desired outcome using the fewest resources. Chapter 4 develops efficiency concepts fully, but for now, consider this illustration.

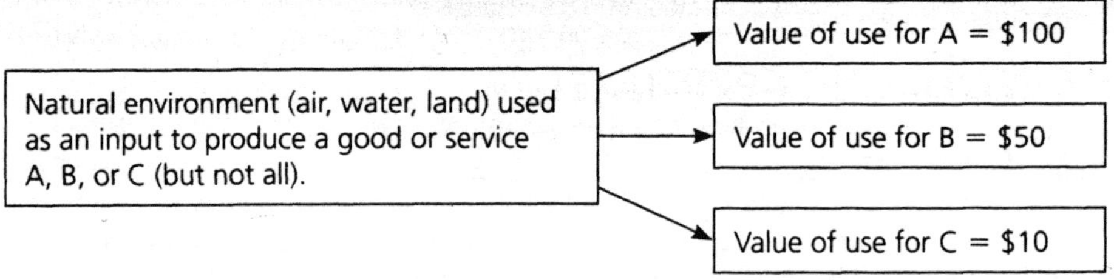

Should we pick A, B, or C? An economically efficient choice would be to pick A. Good or service A maximizes the value of the end use for which resources are being put. In using economic efficiency as an objective, economists are making a value judgment as well as empirical observation. The value judgment (known as a 'normative' approach—see Chapter 5) is that something has value if someone wants it. That 'something' can be a computer or the ability to always take a walk in a forest—it need not be a good that is produced and sold in the marketplace. Both the computer and the walk in the forest use inputs from the natural environment—minerals for the computer components, the ecosystem supporting the forest environment for the walk. Environmental economics emphatically asserts that if individuals value the forest for taking walks more than the computer, than it is the highest value use, even if there is no explicit market for walks in the forest. The empirical observation behind efficiency is hundreds of years of observing people make decisions that indicate they are looking for maximum value such as profit maximization by the owners of firms, or utility maximization by individuals. Environmental economists may have a broader definition of what constitutes utility—walks in the forest count, not just buying goods, but the notion of maximizing or making the best use of what resources are available is still fundamental to how outcomes are assessed.

<table>
<tr><td>

EQUITY

</td><td>

Equity is about how the economic 'pie' is divided up. Who gets how much income or wealth? Dictionary definitions of equity talk about ideals of being "just, impartial, and fair," but who decides what is fair or just? We are in normative/subjective territory again. Think about the following: suppose our government decided that every adult should earn exactly the same income; it will take the total earnings of everyone in the economy and divide them by the total number of workers. Is this equitable? In one sense it is. Everyone is treated equally regardless of circumstances. But what if a person's circumstances differ and as a society we want to take that into account. We may want to divide up the country's total income according to age, number of children people have, whether they are able to work or not due to factors beyond their control such as illness or accidents. The dilemma is that there are many possible ways to divide things up and people may have very different notions of what is or is not equitable. Economists, philosophers, and many other disciplines wrestle with the notions of fairness going back hundreds of years to the early writings in moral philosophy and economics. Environmental economics uses a number of different definitions of equity to help evaluate economic outcomes (efficient or not). These include:

- *Horizontal equity* treats similarly situated people the same way. For example, an environmental program that has the same impact on an urban dweller with $20,000 of income as on a rural dweller with the same income is horizontally equitable.
- *Vertical equity* refers to how a policy impinges on people who are in different circumstances, in particular on people who have different income levels.
- *Intergenerational equity* looks at whether future generations have the same opportunities as current ones. How does society trade off using its resources today when their loss may affect the ability of future generations to enjoy the same quality of life?

Subsequent chapters return to equity as one of the vital criteria in assessing how well the economy is doing.

</td></tr>
</table>

THE ECONOMIC APPROACH

Why do people behave in ways that cause environmental destruction? There are several types of answers to this question. One goes like this: Environmental degradation comes about from human behaviour that is unethical or immoral. Thus, for example, the reason people pollute is because they lack the moral and ethical strength to refrain from the type of behaviour that causes environmental degradation. If this is true, then the way to get people to stop polluting is somehow to increase the general level of environmental morality in the society. In fact, the environmental movement has led a great many people to focus on questions of environmental ethics, exploring the moral dimensions of human impacts on the natural environment. These moral questions are obviously of fundamental concern to any civilized society. Certainly one of the main reasons environmental issues have been put on the front burner of social concern is the sense of moral responsibility that has led people to take their concerns into the political arena.

But there are problems with relying on moral reawakening as our main approach to combating pollution. People don't necessarily have readily available moral buttons to push, and environmental problems are too important to wait for a long process of moral rebuilding. Nor does a sense of moral outrage by itself help us make decisions about all the other social issues that also have ethical dimensions: poverty, housing, health care, education, crime, and so on. In a world of competing objectives we have to worry about very practical questions: are we targeting the right environmental objectives; can we really enforce certain policies; are we getting the most impact for our money; and so on.

But the biggest problem with basing our approach to pollution control strictly on the moral argument is the basic assumption that people pollute because they are somehow morally underdeveloped. It is not moral underdevelopment that leads to environmental destruction; rather, it is the way we have arranged the economic system within which people go about the job of making their livings.

So, a second way of approaching the question of why people pollute is to look at the way the economy and its institutions are set up, and how they lead people to make decisions that result in environmental destruction. Economists argue that

> *people pollute because it is the cheapest way they have of solving a certain very practical problem: how to dispose of the waste products remaining after production and consumption of a good.*

People make these decisions on production, consumption, and disposal within a certain set of economic and social institutions;[1] these institutions structure the incentives that lead people to make decisions in one direction and not in another. An **incentive** is something that attracts or repels people and leads them to modify their behaviour in some way. An "economic incentive" is something in the economic world that leads people to channel their efforts at production and consumption in certain directions. Economic incentives are often viewed as consisting of payoffs in terms of material wealth; people have an incentive to behave in ways that provide them with increased wealth. But there are also many non-material incentives that lead people to modify their economic behaviour; for example, self-esteem, the desire to preserve a beautiful visual environment, or the desire to set a good example for others. Happiness is not a function solely of material wealth. What we will study is

- how incentive processes work, and
- how to restructure them so that people will be led to make decisions and develop lifestyles that have more benign environmental implications.

One simplistic incentive-type statement that you often hear is that pollution is a result of the profit motive. According to this view, in private-enterprise economies of industrialized nations people are rewarded for maximizing profits, the difference between the value of what is produced and the value of what is used up in the production process. Furthermore, the thinking goes, the profits that entrepreneurs try to maximize are strictly monetary profits. In this headlong pursuit of monetary profits, entrepreneurs give no thought to the environmental impacts of their actions because it "doesn't pay." Thus, in this uncontrolled striving for monetary profits, the only way to reduce environmental pollution is to weaken the strength of the profit motive.

But this proposition doesn't stand up to analysis. It is not only "profit-motivated" corporations that cause pollution and threaten the environment with their activities; individual consumers are also guilty when they do things like pour paint thinner down the drain, use anti-bacterial soap, or leave all the chargers for their electronic gadgets plugged in. Since individuals don't keep profit-and-loss statements, it can't be profits per se that lead people to environmentally damaging activities. The same can be said of government agencies, which have sometimes been serious polluters even though they are not profit-motivated. But the most persuasive argument against the view that the search for profits causes pollution comes from political events in Eastern Europe and the former USSR. With the

---

[1] By "institutions," we mean the fundamental set of public and private organizations, customs, laws, and practices that a society uses to structure its economic activity. Markets are an economic institution, for example, as are corporations, a body of commercial law, public agencies, and so on.

collapse of these formerly Communist regimes, we have become aware of the enormous environmental destruction that has occurred in some of these regions—heavily polluted air and water resources in many areas, with major impacts on human health and ecological systems. Many of these problems exceed some of the worst cases of environmental pollution experienced in market-driven countries. But they have happened in an economic system where the profit motive has been entirely lacking. Which means, quite simply, that the profit motive in itself is not the main cause of environmental destruction.

In the sections and chapters that follow, incentives will play a major role in the analysis of how economic systems operate. *Any* system will produce destructive environmental impacts if the incentives within the system are not structured to avoid them. We have to look more deeply into any economic system to understand how its incentive systems work and how they may be changed so that we can have a reasonably progressive economy without disastrous environmental side effects. Two concepts that are important to an understanding of the incentives that exist regarding the environment are **external effects** (also called **externalities**) and **property rights.** These concepts are illustrated in the following two examples and explained in detail in later chapters. Essentially, they involve the question of a lack of ownership of environmental resources. A fundamental point is that

lack of ownership rights to environmental resources means that there are few incentives to take the environmental consequences of our actions into account.

EXTERNALITIES AND PROPERTY RIGHTS

In Section 4, we will examine the role of property rights in reaching a **socially efficient level of pollution.** Property rights—or the lack thereof—are crucial in understanding why we have today's environmental problems. The basic point is that environmental resources generally do not have well-defined property rights. No one owns the atmosphere, our oceans, or large underground aquifers. Two examples illustrate how externalities are connected to property rights.

Auto emissions. *When an SUV releases carbon monoxide and carbon dioxide into the atmosphere, you cannot jump out in front of the vehicle and shout "Stop! You are polluting my air and releasing greenhouse gases that contribute to global climate change!" We all breathe the same air in our communities and GHGs travel to our global atmosphere. For externalities that involve many different sources of pollution, perhaps spread over large areas, there is no effective way to reach any sort of private agreement to limit the emissions. Designing environmental policy is more challenging the more pervasive the externality is across regions or countries and for different sources.*

Dog waste. *You detect your neighbour's dog leaving its waste products on your lawn. This too is an externality. The dog and its owner do not take into account the impact dog waste is having on your lawn when they go about their activities. Contrary to the case of automobile air contaminants and GHG emissions, you and your neighbour would find it relatively easy to negotiate a mutually agreeable resolution to this problem. The neighbour might agree to keep the dog on a leash or to pick up its waste. You may build a fence, or get the neighbour to pay for it. The dog externality is internalized through discussion and negotiation. A solution that is mutually agreeable to both parties can be worked out; the only difference in possible outcomes is who pays for them. That is a function of our bargaining strengths and other factors.*

Why is the dog case different from the auto emissions case? You own your property and the dog is essentially trespassing. Laws say you can keep others off your property. There is also just one other person to bargain with—the dog owner. This case could be more like urban smog if you don't know whose dog is dumping on your lawn. Then you must incur search costs, set up dog surveillance, and so on to detect the perpetrator.

Our most serious environmental problems are closer to the vehicle smog case than the case of the wandering dog. They involve lots of possible polluters, with perhaps very little knowledge about even the source of emissions or the link between emissions and environmental impact. Society members may not recognize that an activity they have been doing for years has a deleterious impact on the environment. For example, manufacturers of leather products in eastern Canada used to use mercury in the tanning process. They would simply dump their wastes in streams or on the ground. Over the years, the mercury percolated into groundwater and contaminated people's drinking water. But people didn't know at the time how toxic mercury is. The tanners themselves suffered from mercury poisoning. This is where the term "mad as a hatter" emerged—mercury poisoning affects brain function. The leather manufacturers are now gone, but mercury still remains a dangerous pollutant in our ecosystem. How can today's population engage in any sort of negotiation with the leather producers of 100 years ago to reach a mutually agreeable level of waste disposal and compensation for disease, shorter lifespans, and contaminated water and soils? This example illustrates the difficulties inherent in depending on individuals who act in their own self-interest to reach a socially efficient outcome. Information about potential problems may be imperfect or non-existent. People today cannot be counted on to make decisions that maximize the well-being of generations who follow. When these conditions exist, some form of government intervention is necessary.

PRACTICAL ILLUSTRATION #1: SMOG AND MOTOR VEHICLES

Each year in Canada, automobiles and light duty trucks discharge approximately 11.5 percent of Canada's total carbon dioxide emissions, 21 percent of nitrogen oxides, 50 percent of volatile organic compounds, 47 percent of carbon monoxide, and 4 percent of fine particulate matter (PM-2.5).[2] These compounds, known as air contaminants contribute to urban smog, acid precipitation, and global climate change. In turn, these environmental conditions adversely affect the health of people and our ecosystem, the survival of many species, the cost of producing goods and services, and our overall enjoyment of our surroundings. Environment Canada[3] estimates that 6,000 Canadians die prematurely each year due to air pollution, while tens of thousands more suffer from bronchitis exacerbated by pollution. Exposure to urban smog may increase the likelihood of cancers in children by up to 25 percent and raise the chance of getting childhood asthma by 400 percent. Acid precipitation changes aquatic and land-based ecosystems, killing fish, amphibians, and other aquatic species and affecting forest growth. Global warming, while a controversial topic, could lead to massive ecosystem changes with worldwide impact. Motor vehicle use contributes to congestion on our roads. Congestion increases driving times, promotes accidents, and generally makes people very crabby, contributing to "road rage."

[2] See Government of Canada, Environment Canada (*2010 National Inventory Report, 2010*), *1990–2008 Greenhouse Gas Sources and Sinks in Canada* for data on greenhouse gases and www.ec.gc.ca/air for information on air contaminants.

[3] See Environment Canada's Web site (www.ec.gc.ca), then go to the Air Quality page for information about the impact of air pollution on health.

Environment Canada:
www.ec.gc.ca

Driving one's car or truck thus affects all sorts of other people (whether they too drive a motor vehicle or not) and our environment. This is an *external effect.* When you drive to school or work or to the beach, you get the direct benefit of transportation services. Others—bystanders—receive the negative impacts of your driving: air pollution, congestion, and associated impacts. The bystanders don't control your driving. And the price you pay for driving your car, your direct costs in the form of gasoline, maintenance, and monthly car payments, do not reflect the negative impacts you impose on others—hence the words *externality* or *external effects* to describe this situation. An externality occurs when the actions of one or more individuals affects the well-being of other individuals without any compensation taking place. While externalities can be positive as well as negative (think enjoying viewing your neighbour's flower garden), pollutants such as air contaminants are negative externalities. We will examine in detail in Section 4 what sorts of initiatives, both individual and with the help of government, can be used to address externalities. For now, let's think a bit more about motor vehicle externalities and what can be done about them. To do so, we look at the concept of incentives.

Incentives: Households and Vehicle Use

When you drive your car, sport-utility vehicle (SUV), or truck, the price you pay per kilometre travelled reflects your **private costs**—gasoline, oil, insurance, and so on. These prices do not take into account the damage the emissions from your car impose on others and the environment; rather, they reflect costs of producing gasoline, retailer markups, and so on. You will respond to changes in these private costs, for example, by driving more when gasoline prices fall and less when they rise. What sort of positive incentive could we contemplate that would induce drivers to reduce the number of emissions they release? A simple relationship may help us see where incentives could enter.

Total quantity of emissions = Number of vehicles × Average kilometres travelled × Emissions per kilometre

Incentives can target the number of vehicles on the road, the average number of kilometres travelled, and emissions per kilometre. In addition, we might want to consider where people drive their vehicles. A car driven in downtown Toronto, Montreal, or Vancouver will have a larger impact on urban smog than that same vehicle being driven in Moose Jaw, Saskatchewan. The release of carbon dioxide will, however, contribute to global warming regardless of where the vehicle is driven.

What are some possible incentives to alter people's behaviour? In greater Vancouver, all older model cars, SUVs, and light trucks must pass an AirCare test once every two years. This test checks to see that motor vehicle exhaust is not emitting more pollutants than consistent with government standards. The policy goal is to create an incentive for vehicle owners to regularly service and maintain their vehicles and thereby reduce emissions per kilometre.

AirCare:
www.aircare.ca

How would we influence the number of kilometres travelled? The economic answer is to increase the cost of driving per kilometre. This provides an incentive for people every time they drive their vehicle to minimize the number of trips, thereby reducing their direct costs. An example of a direct incentive to increase costs of driving is to tax people on the number of kilometres travelled. This could be done using a tax that is payable annually as people renew their vehicle licence. An indirect incentive is to tax gasoline, thereby increasing the costs of driving. How would we influence the number of vehicles on the road? This could be done with an annual tax on vehicle ownership or a buyback program that pays people to retire their older vehicles. Old vehicles contribute far more per kilometre travelled to air emissions than do newer, more fuel-efficient and less pollution-intensive vehicles. We might also want to think about other incentives that might change behaviour.

These could include advertising and education programs that inform people about how their driving decisions affect air quality and, hence, their well-being. Are there others?

Incentives for Businesses

Incentives can also apply to businesses. Think about the producers of motor vehicles and vehicle parts. All industrial firms work within a given set of incentives: to increase profits if they are firms in market economies. Firms have an incentive to take advantage of whatever factors are available to better their performance in terms of these criteria. One way they have been able to do this historically is to use the services of the environment for waste disposal. The motivation for this practice is that these services have essentially been free, and by using free inputs as much as possible a firm obviously can increase its profits. The challenge is to find incentives to alter firms' behaviour so they treat environmental services as a costly activity rather than a free good.

One policy approach is to introduce and then try to enforce laws or regulations that direct the amount of pollution a firm can emit. Canada has company average fuel consumption (CAFC) guidelines for all new cars and light trucks produced in Canada. Vehicle manufacturers have agreed to design their cars and light trucks to meet a voluntary target level of gasoline consumption averaged over their entire fleet of vehicles produced each year. Guidelines were introduced for cars in 1978 at 13.1 litres per 100 kilometres, and then were tightened to 8.6 litres per 100 kilometres in 1986, where they remain today. Guidelines for light trucks were not introduced until 1990 (at 11.8 litres per 100 kilometres) and were gradually tightened to 10.0 litres per 100 kilometres in 2010. In January 2008, the federal government announced that Canada will adopt the same fuel efficiency standards as the United States as its target for 2020. The U.S. standards require a combined corporate average (for all makes and models of vehicles sold each year) of 35 miles per gallon (6.72 litres per 100 kilometres). Fuel efficiency of all cars on the road has increased from approximately 15 litres per 100 kilometres in 1965 to 6.7 litres per 100 kilometres in 2010.[4] Light duty trucks were estimated to average 8.6 litres per 100 kilometres in 2010.

Natural Resources Canada, Office of Energy Efficiency Initiative: http://oee.nrcan.gc.ca/ english/index.cfm?attr=0

The CAFC guidelines are voluntary, not compulsory. Vehicle manufacturers meet the standards because the United States has the same type of policy and it is compulsory in that country. The North American automobile industry is completely integrated—cars and light trucks produced in Canada are exported to the United States and vice versa. Canadian cars that do not meet the U.S. fuel efficiency standards cannot be sold there. There is a clear profit incentive for Canadian manufacturers to comply with the voluntary standard. Note that CAFC standards require the auto manufacturer to meet the standard *on average* across all its cars or trucks produced each year. If automakers produce a lot of low-polluting cars, they will more readily meet the target than if they produce high-polluting vehicles such as SUVs. The regulations thus provide an incentive for manufacturers to alter the mix of vehicles produced to reduce the emissions that will ultimately come when drivers purchase and use the vehicles. Canadian governments also regulate the sulphur content of gasoline. The regulations specify that oil refiners must produce gasoline containing on average no more than 30 mg/kg of sulphur (and never to exceed 80 mg/kg) as of January 2005.[5] Sulphur in gasoline, when combusted, produces sulphur dioxide, a contributor to smog and acid precipitation. The incentive effect here is this: abide by the regulation or you will be fined by the government.

[4] For the history of the development of CAFC guidelines see www.tc.gc.ca/eng/programs/ environment-fcp-history-630.htm, accessed September 26, 2010. Information on fuel efficiency of vehicles can be found at www.tc.gc.ca/eng/programs/environment-fcp-cafctargets-385.htm, accessed September 26, 2010.

[5] See Chapter 6 for a detailed discussion of the sulphur in gasoline regulations.

A more effective policy might be to design a system that takes advantage of firms' normal monetary incentives in such a way as to lead them to pollute less. For example, oil refiners could be taxed on the basis of the sulphur content of their gasoline produced. This may induce them to switch their production to lower-sulphur fuels so as to avoid the tax. They might increase the proportion of methanol derived from grains in their fuels. Methanol does not contain any sulphur. Gasoline prices are likely to rise, then providing an additional incentive to drivers to reduce their consumption of gasoline. The Canadian government decided not to tax sulphur, but to subsidize the production of ethanol at the farm level. This lowered the price of ethanol relative to petroleum, but had a number of negative consequences such as raising the cost of corn products worldwide and diverting corn from feeding people to producing vehicle fuels. Corn production is also very fertilizer and pesticide intensive, and can lead to undesirable environmental impacts. Section 5 looks at different ways government can design policies that are effective in meeting environmental and equity goals while minimizing adverse impacts to the economy. The essence of the economic incentives approach is to restructure the incentives facing firms and consumers in such a way that it mobilizes their own energy and ingenuity to find ways of reducing their impacts on the environment.

Incentives in the Pollution-Control Industry

The pollution-control industry develops waste recycling techniques, pollution-control equipment, and pollution-monitoring technology. It sometimes handles and treats waste products, and is often involved in managing waste-disposal sites. It also includes firms that develop new environmentally friendly products like low-sulphur gasoline, low-phosphate detergents, and recyclable paper products. A lively and progressive pollution-control industry is obviously needed if we are to come to grips effectively with all of our present and prospective environmental problems. Thus, one of the major things environmental economists must study is the incentives facing this industry—what causes it to grow or decline, how quickly or slowly it responds to new needs, and so on. In our example of air pollution from motor vehicles, the pollution-control industry could include manufacturers of zero-emission vehicles. These vehicles might run on fuel cells, on electricity, or use other technologies. Are policies needed to encourage these industries? One might argue that the existence of policies that provide incentives to reduce air emissions will be enough to stimulate the development of alternative fuels or engines. However, various governments have also subsidized the research and development costs for these manufacturers either through tax incentives or outright grants of funds. The rationale is that the development of the new technologies will have broad-reaching social benefits.

PRACTICAL ILLUSTRATION #2: GREENHOUSE GAS EMISSIONS AND CLIMATE CHANGE

Intergovernmental Panel on Climate Change: www.ipcc.ch

The carbon dioxide (CO_2) content of the earth's atmosphere has increased by over 38 percent since 1750.[6] Figure 1-1 shows the rising time trend of world CO_2 emissions since 1965. The key question is what effect these emissions have on the earth's climate now and into the future. The science of climate change is complex, with many uncertainties due

[6] See the Fourth Assessment Report of the Intergovernmental Panel on Climate Change, *Climate Change 2007: Synthesis Report*, for recent data on climate change and a discussion of the state of climate-change science and policy. Unless otherwise noted, all the numerical estimates presented in this paragraph are from this document. The report is available at www.ipcc.ch/pdf/assessment-report/ar4/syr/ar4_syr.pdf.

FIGURE 1-1
World Greenhouse Gas Emissions

Note: CO$_2$ emissions are from fossil fuel combustion plus cement processing and gas flaring.

Source: *Data from* World Resources Institute, *World Resources, Climate Analysis Indicators Tool,* http://cait.wri.org/.

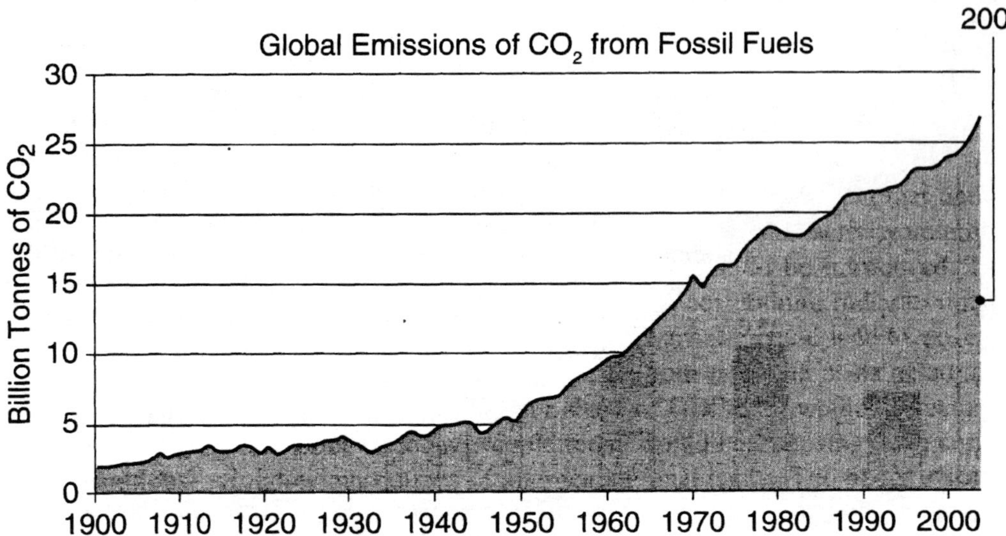

The time trend of CO$_2$ emissions for the past 100 years is positively sloped and has gotten steeper, with emissions increasing by five-fold since 1950.

U.S. EPA Climate Change Site: www.epa.gov/climatechange/

Environment Canada's Climate Change Site: www.climatechange.gc.ca

Natural Resources Canada's Climate Adaptation Site: http://adaptation.nrcan.gc.ca/

to the difficulty of measurement as well as interpretation of the data and attempts to determine cause and effect.[7] It is estimated that the average surface temperature of earth has risen approximately 0.6°C over the 20th century (with a confidence interval of $\pm$ 0.2°C).[8] Climate change models forecast a rise in the earth's temperature over the 21st century by anywhere from 1.5 to 6°C. Some models also predict an increase in climate variability and extreme weather events in the future due to the increase in emissions of greenhouse gases (GHGs)—carbon dioxide (CO$_2$) and other gases in the atmosphere. However, human and natural factors can affect models' results. Natural processes such as volcanic activity send bursts of gases and particulate matter into the atmosphere, causing changes in rainfall patterns and temporary cooling. Pollution, in the form of accumulated SO$_2$ in the lower atmosphere, reflects sunlight and works against the greenhouse phenomenon. Carbon dioxide is also absorbed by **carbon sinks** in the form of trees, wetlands, and oceans. Just exactly how much the sinks can absorb and under what conditions is an important area of study.

Climate change, global warming, or the *greenhouse effect* are the common names used to describe the potentially major changes in the world's climate. The principle of a greenhouse is that the enclosing glass allows the passage of incoming sunlight but traps a portion of the reflected infrared radiation, which warms the interior of the greenhouse above the outside temperature. Greenhouse gases in the earth's atmosphere play a similar role; they serve to raise the temperature of the earth's surface and make it habitable. With no greenhouse gases at all, the surface of the earth would be about 30°C cooler than it is today, making human life impossible. The main greenhouse gases (GHGs), their approximate proportionate contribution to global warming, and their major sources are shown in Figure 1-2.

If global climate changes result in global warming, the earth may become very different from its current state. The rate of heating is estimated to be at least 0.2°C per decade

[7] Many hundreds of books and articles have been written on the science and economics of global climate change. This section will just scratch the surface and hopefully stimulate more reading. New information is continually released that may help to resolve the uncertainties in climate-change predictions. See Chapter 20 for more detail on Canadian policy and the references at the end of the text.

[8] See Goddard Institute of Space Studies (NASA) at http://data.giss.nasa.gov/gistemp/graphs/ for data on world temperatures.

FIGURE 1-2 Global Anthropogenic Sources of GHG Emissions

Source: *Climate Change 2007: Synthesis Report. Contribution of Working Groups I, II, and III to the Fourth Assessment Report of the Intergovernmental Panel on Climate Change, Figure 2.1. IPCC, Geneva, Switzerland.*

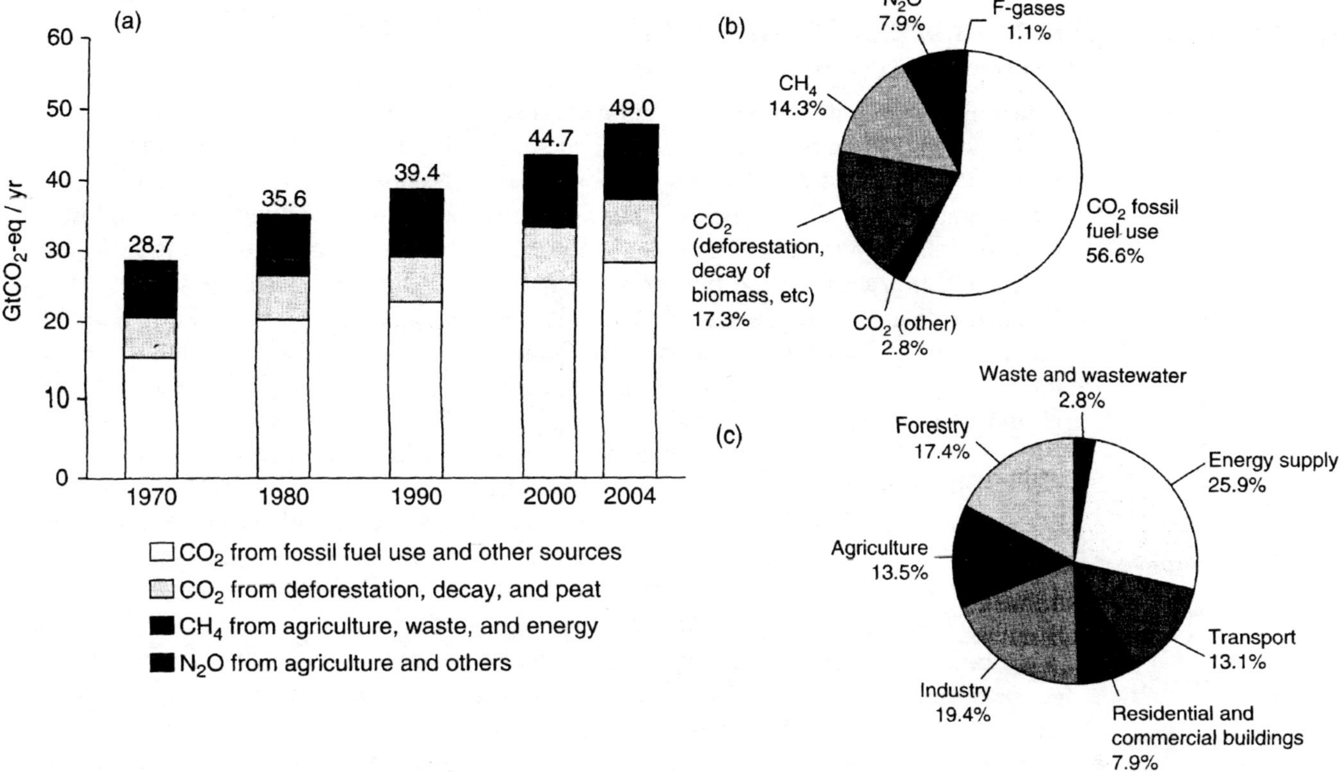

Anthropogenic sources are those created by human activity. The graph measures sources in gigatonnes (Gt) of the greenhouse gases in a common unit that takes into account their impact in the atmosphere (CO$_2$e for CO$_2$ equivalent). CO$_2$ is carbon dioxide, CH$_4$ is methane, NO$_2$ is nitrogen dioxide, and F-gases are fluorinated gases.

based on current levels of GHGs in the atmosphere.[9] This may not sound like a very rapid change, but historical studies have shown that in past episodes of warming and cooling, during which agricultural societies of the time suffered major dislocations, climate change occurred at a rate of only about 0.05°C per decade. The forecast rate of change for the 21st century is six times faster than the rates faced by humans in the past. If countries do nothing to offset the increase in greenhouse gas emissions, **adaptation** to climate change by future generations may be very costly, especially for some parts of the world. Adaptation refers to actions taken to offset or reduce the adverse impacts of climate change. For cooler countries in higher latitudes, with relatively little critical shoreline, adaptation costs may be fairly "modest." Countries in the opposite situation will have very high costs of adapting to higher temperatures and rising sea levels. Rising sea levels may inundate entire nations, such as some islands in the Caribbean and South Pacific, and require relocation of large populations that now live in low-lying coastal regions (e.g., those living along river deltas in Southeast Asia and the Nile). The Arctic polar ice caps are melting at a very high rate, threatening that fragile ecosystem and its inhabitants. Countries differ also in terms of agricultural adaptability—the ability to shift crops, varieties, cultivation methods, and

[9.] Fourth Assessment Report of the Intergovernmental Panel on Climate Change, *Climate Change 2007: Synthesis Report.*

so on—to maintain production in the face of climate changes and are likely to have very different perceptions about how they will be affected by global warming.

Responses to Climate Change: Scientific Uncertainties, the Precautionary Principle and Mitigation Strategies

Given the uncertainties in climate and natural science, there is an argument that until we "know for sure" that climate change is happening and is due to human activity no policies for reduction or **mitigation** of greenhouse-gas emissions should be introduced. There are several problems with this viewpoint. What if society does nothing today to mitigate GHG emissions, but there is a small chance that global warming could lead to extremely high adaptation costs in the future? Then, some years from now, the costs of adjusting to climate change could comprise a much larger share of GDP than would be realized if society initiates mitigation policies today. People today would be imposing huge costs on future generations—violating our notions of intergenerational equity. The **precautionary principle** says that society should weigh the trade-off between the cost of measures taken today versus benefits in terms of reduced future risk. Expected net benefits are calculated as the benefits minus the costs of each scenario weighted by the probability of the event occurring, taking into account that these benefits and costs will occur into the future. Chapters 6, 7, and 8 illustrate how these benefits and costs are measured and net benefits computed over time. If the probability that global warming raises average temperatures by 3°C in 50 years is low (e.g., .0005 or .005), society minimizes its costs by doing nothing today because net benefits are higher (a smaller negative number) with no current policies adopted. But if society estimates the probability at a 5- or 10-percent chance, action now to reduce GHG emissions becomes the preferred choice.

GHG mitigation policies could include taxes on carbon emissions, introducing standards to improve energy efficiency of vehicles, appliances, and buildings, and a host of other actions. By waiting to see what happens, society may incur much higher costs than if actions were taken today to put it on a more sustainable path that reduces carbon emissions. As well, if society does nothing and turns out to be wrong, climate change impacts could be devastating for countries that cannot easily adapt. The cost to the global economy would be enormous and inequitably felt across countries and regions. Another uncertainty that is difficult to quantify is the role of technological change in helping to mitigate global warming. It may be in society's interest to delay introducing specific mitigation policies in the present in the hope that technological improvements will allow it to reach a GHG target at much lower costs in the future. However, this does not necessarily suggest that no GHG policies should be introduced in the present. For example, a GHG tax at a very low rate could be introduced now with the rate rising over time. This tax will signal that it will be increasingly costly over time to release GHGs into the atmosphere. Putting a price on GHG emissions will help incent technological activity.

Recall how total emissions of vehicle pollutants were identified. A similar identity exists for GHGs and illustrates how they can be reduced.

Total GHGs = Population × GDP/population × Energy/GDP × GHGs/energy

The focus in the equation above is on energy because as Figure 1-2 illustrates, combustion of fossil fuels contributes the majority of GHGs to the atmosphere. One can read in for "energy" any other primary source of GHGs. The first term in the word equation is population. Other things remaining equal, larger populations will use more energy and therefore emit larger amounts of GHGs. The second term is GDP per capita, a measure of the domestic output of goods and services per capita. Increases in GDP are normally associated with economic growth. Neither of these first two factors can be considered likely candidates for reducing GHG emissions in the short run. Deliberate population control measures are a complex policy area that many countries do not want to pursue. Countries will be reluctant to reduce their rates of economic growth. In the long run, however, the interaction of these two factors will be important, as history seems to show that increases in income per capita are associated with lower population growth rates over time. This means that significant near-term GHG reductions will have to come from the last two terms in the expression. The third is what can be called **energy efficiency,** the amount of energy used per dollar (or per franc or rupee or peso) of output. The key here is to move toward technologies of production, distribution, and consumption that require relatively smaller quantities of energy. The last term is GHGs produced per unit of energy used. Since different energy forms have markedly different GHG outputs per unit, reductions in GHG can be achieved by switching to less GHG-intensive fuells.

Table 1-1 lists the major types of changes that could be made in different economic sectors to reduce GHG emissions. There is no single source that society could call on to get drastic reductions in CO_2 production. Instead, significant changes could be made in hundreds of different places—transportation, industry, households, and agriculture. These changes are both technical (as, for example, the switch to more energy-efficient equipment and low-CO_2 fuels) and behavioural (for example, changing driving habits and adopting less energy-intensive lifestyles). In Section 4, we develop economic models that show how regulation, taxes, markets, and other policies can be developed to mitigate GHGs

TABLE 1-1
Means of Reducing
Greenhouse Gases
 	
Source: *U.S. Office of Technology Assessment,* Changing by Degrees, Steps to Reduce Greenhouse Gases (*Washington, D.C. 1991).*
	Energy production
	   Reduce demand for electricity (see Households),
	   Switch to nonfossil fuels (solar, biomass, nuclear, hydroelectric),
	   Switch from high-carbon (coal) to low-carbon (gas) fossil fuels,
	   Reduce energy transmission losses,
	   Remove carbon from fuel and emissions.
	
	Households
	   Reduce demand for energy (less heating air conditioning, etc.),
	   Switch to less energy-intensive products,
	   Switch to more energy-efficient technologies (solar heaters, insulation, etc.),
	   Switch out of CFCs in car air conditioners.
	
	Industry
	   Increase energy efficiency of production processes,
	   Switch to low- or no-carbon fuels,
	   Increase energy efficiency in buildings, lighting, etc.,
	   Switch out of CFCs and other greenhouse gases.
	
	Transportation
	   Reduce kilometres driven and travel speeds,
	   Increase fuel efficiency of vehicles,
	   Switch to mass transit systems.
	
	Agriculture and food system
	   Reduce methane production from livestock production and rice paddies,
	   Improve energy efficiency in farming,
	   Reduce CFC use in refrigeration,
	   Reduce energy use in transportation,
	   Increase land uses that lead to greater carbon storage.
	
	Forestry
	   Reduce rates of deforestation,
	   Increase rates of reforestation.

and pollutants of air, water, and lands. Section 5 looks at what is being done in Canada to reduce emissions and improve environmental quality.

SUSTAINABILITY OF OUR ENVIRONMENT AND ECONOMY

Basic Issues

The previous examples of smog and motor vehicle pollution and climate change resulting from GHG emissions illustrate the enormous impact human activity has on the natural environment. Environmental economists argue that it is vital to link closely the economy with the natural environment. While the natural environment has always been treated as an essential input into production, few models looked explicitly at the interaction between ecological systems and the economy. The field of **ecological economics** examines these interactions more fully. An important objective of this field is to search for sustainable paths of economic development—actions that do not destroy ecological systems, but allow for increases in the well-being of people.[10] The essential idea is that a sustainable economy is one that has the ability to allow people's well-being to either rise over time or at least remain constant (i.e., not fall). To accomplish this, a number of economists argue that current generations cannot "use up" so much of the existing stocks of natural and environmental resources that future generations will be impoverished or non-existent. We must examine our economic activities with regard to the carrying capacity of our ecosystem.

All economies use natural and environmental resources to sustain life. Rising world population puts increasing pressure on our natural endowments all the time. Many fear that our current path of production and population growth is not sustainable. What can be done? One possible approach is to argue that each generation in a sustainable economy has the obligation to replace what it uses with investment in **social capital.** This is a very broad definition of "capital." It includes everything the economy can invest in—physical capital to produce goods and services, education, infrastructure, renewable and non-renewable natural resources, and, of course, the environment itself as a stock of capital. When we use up some of our existing capital, the only way the economy can be sustainable over time is to reinvest to keep the social capital stock at least constant. Pollution control and treatment is a means of keeping the environmental capital stock constant. So is recycling to some degree. Whether **sustainability** is achievable depends on the actions of people, industries, and governments. Some questions to contemplate: Will private markets keep the stock of social capital constant? Is government intervention necessary? If so, in what form?

Sustainability also depends on the degree of substitutability among natural capital (the environment and natural resources), produced capital, and labour. Technology and technological change is another vital element in the search for sustainable paths. Technology will influence the degree of substitution among factor inputs and affect the amount of inputs needed to produce a unit of output. Some technologies may promote sustainability, others not. Economists play important roles in helping to find answers to all these questions, by building models that explicitly incorporate the role of the natural environment and by examining these issues empirically. To recap,

> *a sustainable economy is one in which investment in social capital allows the economy to grow so that people are at least as well off in the future as they are in the present, while sustaining the health of ecological systems.*

[10.] See, for example, Peter Victor (2008), Herman Daly and Joshua Farley (2010), and Robert Costanza et al. (2011) in the selected references to this chapter.

Trade-offs and Sustainability

Economists illustrate the trade-offs between output of goods and services and environmental quality by using a **production possibility frontier (PPF).** A PPF is a way of diagrammatically depicting the choice faced by a group of people between two desirable outcomes—output of goods and services and environmental quality. The basic relationship is shown in Figure 1-3. Suppose we are exploring the trade-offs that arise from our use of fossil fuels: the goods and services they produce in our current fossil fuel intensive economy versus the degradation to our ecosystem and economy from climate change. The vertical axis has an index of the *aggregate economic output* of our *high-carbon economy,* the total market value of conventional economic goods sold in the economy in a year. The horizontal axis has an index of *environmental quality,* derived from data on different dimensions of the ambient environment; for example, what the economy would look like if, for example, we had fewer GHG emissions and airborne pollutants. The curved relationship shows the different combinations of these two outcomes—a carbon-intensive economy or one with higher levels of environmental quality and fewer GHG and air contaminant emissions—that are available to a country given its endowment of resources with which to work. The PPF is shown with a dashed line from an environmental quality below *e.* Below *e,* the economy cannot produce any additional goods and services because there are too few environmental resources to sustain production. E_{MAX} shows the maximum amount of environmental quality if there is no goods production at all (presumably meaning no human population).

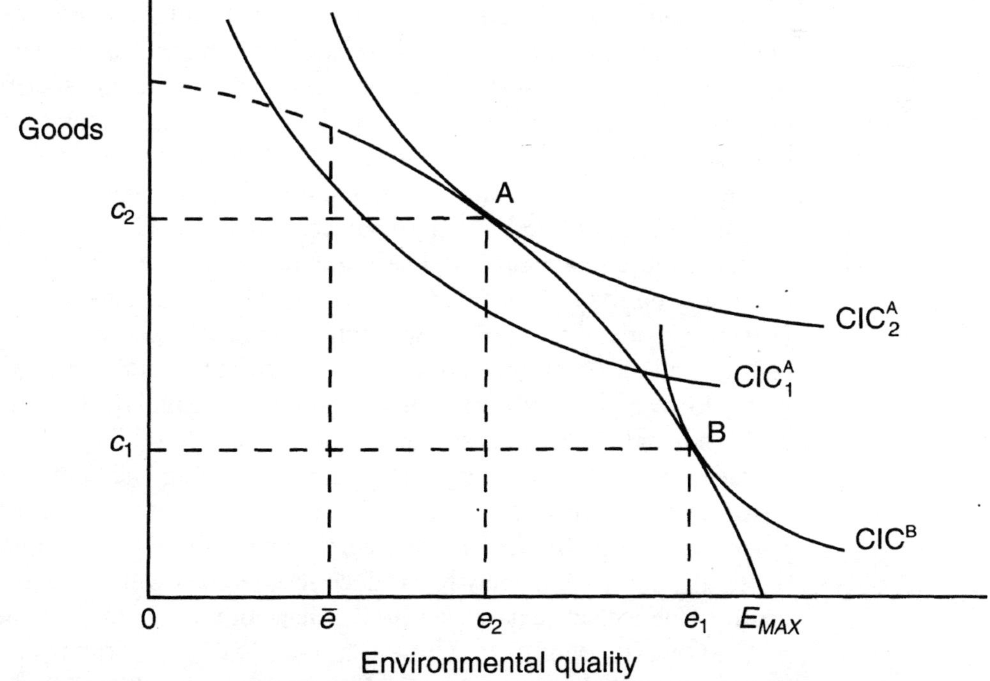

FIGURE 1-3

A Production Possibility Frontier (PPF) between a High-Carbon Economy and Environmental Quality

The PPF illustrates possible trade-offs between goods produced in a high-carbon economy and environmental quality. As society consumes more carbon-intensive goods, it gives up environmental quality. Below $\bar{e}$, no goods can be produced because environmental quality is too low to sustain production. Community indifference curves (CICs) indicate a country's choice of the mix of carbon-intensive goods and environmental quality. Country A chooses more goods/less environmental quality than country B.

The production possibility frontier is determined by the technical capacities in the economy together with the ecological facts—meteorology, hydrology, and so on—of the natural system in which the country is situated. It says, for example, that if the current level of economic output is c_1, we can obtain an increase to c_2 only at the cost of a decrease in environmental quality from e_1 to e_2. But while the PPF itself is a technical constraint, where a society chooses to locate itself on its PPF is a matter of *social choice*. And this depends on the relative values that people in that society place on conventional economic output and environmental quality. Economists illustrate social choices with a relationship called a social or **community indifference curve (CIC).** Community indifference curves are shown for country A on Figure 1-3. Each point on a CIC shows combinations of environmental quality and goods perceived by society to provide a given level of well-being. CICs that lie farther from the origin yield higher levels of well-being than those closer to the origin. Societies will seek the highest level of well-being that they can attain. This will be where the CIC is tangent to the PPF. For country A, this is CIC_2, tangent at point A, with e_2 environmental quality and c_2 goods. Another country might have a different set of social preferences that lead to choosing different bundles of environmental quality and goods; for example, at point B, with c_1 and e_1 being chosen. The choices made by society will affect the sustainability of the economy and environment.

The Environment and Growth: Sustainability over Time

Sustainability isn't just about choice in a given year, but what happens to the economy and environment over time. The PPF will not remain in the same place, as conditions such as production technology and environmental degradation change over time. We illustrate two possibilities. Figure 1-4 shows the possible trade-offs facing society in 50 years. Panel (a) presents a pessimistic scenario. Suppose we continue on our current path of consuming large amounts of carbon-intensive fossil fuels to produce energy for our economy and we thereby deplete our natural capital in the form of a degraded air quality and climate change that reduces agricultural output, displaces human settlement, and requires other forms of adaptation to climate change. These outcomes may be the result of having chosen to be at point A on the PPF in Figure 1-3 in preceding years. As a result, the PPF for the year 2050 lies inside of the PPF today. Society, no matter where it chooses to locate, now must consume either fewer goods or have lower environmental quality than is possible today. If we try to keep production of goods at c_2, environmental quality falls to e_3. Alternatively, if environmental quality is to stay at e_2, it is possible to produce and consume only c_3 goods.

Panel (b) is more optimistic. Suppose we develop and adopt new technologies to produce substantial amounts of energy from sources that neither release GHGs nor damage other components of our natural environment. Our PPF for the present now shifts out to reflect the ability of society to produce more goods with a higher level of environmental quality. Notice that we have skewed the shape of the PPF to show that at c_2—the same level of goods society chose in the base year—we have e_4 environmental quality rather than e_2, because a non-polluting energy source was developed. Alternatively, at e_2, production at c_4 is possible. These cases illustrate that the future is not independent of the choices we make today.

FIGURE 1-4
**Possible PPFs in 50
Years: Two Scenarios**

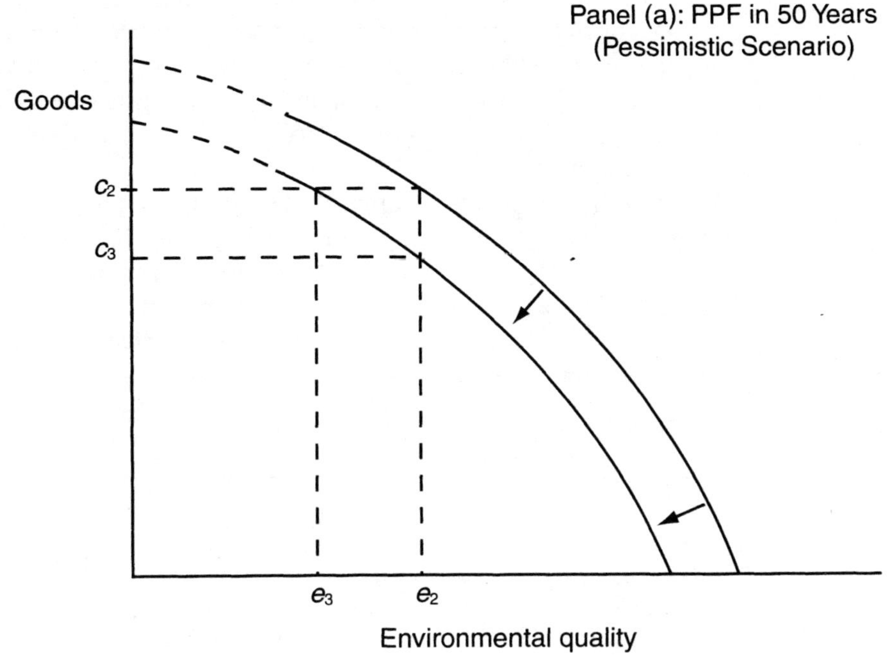

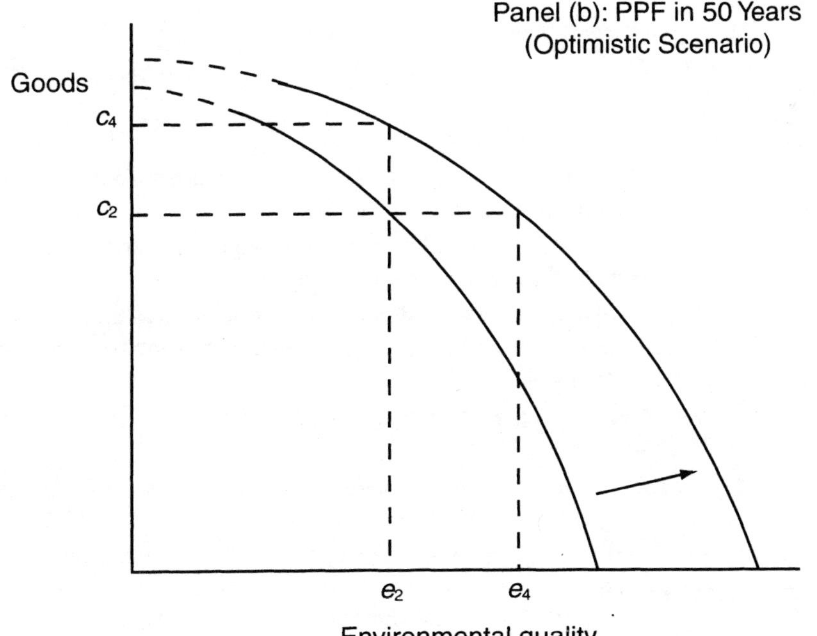

The PPF in panel (a) presents a pessimistic scenario, in which the PPF shifts inward due to environmental degradation. This means that the country can no longer consume at both c_2 and e_2; one must decline. Panel (b) is more optimistic. The PPF may shift out due to technological developments. Now consumption of goods and environmental quality can both rise over time.

Summary

The purpose of this chapter was to whet your appetite for the subject of environmental economics by indicating some of the main topics that the field encompasses, showing very briefly the approach that economists take in studying them. Our focus will be on microeconomic aspects of environmental economics—to see why externalities exist and persist and how to design and analyze economic policy instruments that can help improve the quality of our environment.

When we get involved in some of the conceptual and theoretical issues that underlie environmental economics, it is easy to lose sight of what we are trying to accomplish. We are trying to develop basic principles so that we can actually use them to address real-world problems such as air and water pollution. Although the principles may appear abstract and odd at first, remember the objective: to achieve a cleaner, healthier, and more beautiful natural environment that can be sustained over time.

Key Terms

Adaptation, *12*
Carbon sinks, *11*
Community indifference curve
 (CIC), *17*
Ecological economics, *15*
Economic efficiency, *3*
Efficiency, *2*
Energy efficiency, *14*
Equity, *3*

Externality/external
 effects, *6*
Incentive, *5*
Marginal benefits, *2*
Marginal costs, *2*
Mitigation, *13*
Opportunity costs, *2*
Precautionary principle, *13*
Private costs, *8*

Production possibility frontier
 (PPF), *16*
Property rights, *6*
Scarcity, *2*
Social capital, *15*
Socially efficient level of
 pollution, *6*
Sustainability, *15*
Trade-offs, *2*

Discussion Questions

1. "Annual testing of all motor vehicles on the road is not a cost-effective policy." Do you agree with this statement? Explain why or why not.

2. Why would a tax on gasoline provide a larger incentive to reduce air emissions from motor vehicles than an annual tax on owning a vehicle?

3. The Canadian CAFC standards apply to new vehicles as they come off the assembly line. Provide two reasons why this might have a perverse effect on total emissions from motor vehicles. Explain your arguments.

4. Does Canada need a voluntary CAFC standard when the United States has a mandatory one? Discuss.

5. What factors influence the trade-offs illustrated in the production possibility frontier? How can environmental policy affect these trade-offs?

6. Suppose there is a technological change that allows firms to produce goods and services with less energy and hence fewer GHG emissions. Show graphically and explain how this will alter the PPF and a society's potential choice of where to locate on the PPF.

7. If produced capital is not readily substitutable for environmental capital (natural resources, air and water quality), how will this affect the trade-offs between economic growth and the environment?

Unit 10 – Sweatshops and Child Labour

Working Conditions in Factories (Issue)

Gale Encyclopedia of U.S. Economic History | 2000 | 700+ words | Copyright

WORKING CONDITIONS IN FACTORIES *(ISSUE)*

During the late nineteenth century the U.S. economy underwent a spectacular increase in industrial growth. Abundant resources, an expanding labor force, government policy, and skilled entrepreneurs facilitated this shift to the large-scale production of manufactured goods. For many U.S. citizens industrialization resulted in an unprecedented prosperity but others did not benefit as greatly from the process. The expansion of manufacturing created a need for large numbers of factory workers. Although the average standard of living for workers increased steadily during the last decades of the nineteenth century, many workers struggled to make ends meet. At the turn of the century it took an annual income of at least $600 to live comfortably but the average worker made between $400 and $500 per year.

Factory workers had to face long hours, poor working conditions, and job instability. During economic recessions many workers lost their jobs or faced sharp pay cuts. New employees found the discipline and regulation of factory work to be very different from other types of work. Work was often monotonous because workers performed one task over and over. It was also strictly regulated. Working hours were long averaging at least ten hours a day and six days a week for most workers, even longer for others. For men and women from agricultural backgrounds these new conditions proved challenging because farm work tended to be more flexible and offered a variety of work tasks. Factory work was also different for skilled artisans, who had once hand-crafted goods on their own schedule.

Factory conditions were also poor and, in some cases, deplorable. Lack of effective government regulation led to unsafe and unhealthy work sites. In the late nineteenth century more industrial accidents occurred in the United States than in any other industrial country. Rarely did an employer offer payment if a worker was hurt or killed on the job. As industries consolidated at the turn of the century factories grew larger and more dangerous. By 1900 industrial accidents killed thirty-five thousand workers each year and maimed five hundred thousand others, and the numbers continued to rise. The general public became concerned with industrial accidents only when scores of workers were killed in a single widely reported incident, such as the many coal-mine explosions or the tragic Triangle Shirtwaist Company fire in 1911. In one year alone 195 workers in steel and iron mills were killed in Pittsburgh, Pennsylvania.

In order to save money many employers hired women and children to work in factories because these workers would work for lower wages than men. Some women were paid as little as six dollars per week, a sum much lower than a male would have received. Most female workers performed unskilled or semi-skilled machine work but some worked in industries that demanded heavy labor. Some women, for instance, worked on railroads, while others were employed as machinists.

Children also worked long hours for low wages. The number of children employed in factories rose steadily over the last three decades of the nineteenth century. By 1900 roughly 1.7 million children under the age of 16 worked in factories; less than half that many children had been employed 30 years before. Under pressure from the public many state legislatures passed child labor laws, which limited the hours children could work to ten hours per day, but employers often disregarded such laws. In southern cotton mills children who operated looms throughout the night had cold water thrown in their faces to keep them awake. Long working hours for children also meant that accidents were more likely to occur; like adult workers, many children were injured or killed on the job.

Worker responses to poor factory conditions and low wages were varied. Some employees intentionally decreased their production rate or broke their machines, while others quit their jobs and sought work in other factories. Other workers resorted to a more organized means of protest by joining labor unions although most industrial workers were not union members. Most workers, having few alternatives, simply endured the hardship of factory work.

In response to the problem of poor working conditions and the apparent indifference of industrial barons, membership in the American Federation of Labor (AFL), a union for skilled workers formed in 1886, grew rapidly from 256,000 members in 1897 to 1,676,000 in 1904. More radical and politically active trade unions often had even larger memberships, mostly because they were not as exclusionary as the AFL and because they welcomed unskilled labor, like those who worked in factories. One of the most radical, the Industrial Workers of the World (IWW), founded in 1905 and popularly known as the Wobblies, recruited primarily among the unskilled immigrants but also competed with the AFL to attract skilled laborers. Less radical than the Wobblies and more successful at recruiting supporters were the socialists, who gained political strength because of the growing numbers of immigrants and disenchanted unskilled laborers. The lack of real class conflict in the United States and the electoral reforms of the era undercut the socialists' efforts on a national level. Despite growing union activism the vast majority of workers remained unorganized throughout the first decade of the twentieth century.

Trying to prevent legislation to provide job security, guarantee a minimum wage, or ensure the safety of the workplace, most businessmen and conservatives argued that wages were set by the marketplace and that higher wages and worker protection would lead to higher prices for consumers. Government had long supported business using court injunctions and armed troops to put down strikes and break unions. In the 1890s, ruling that unions operated as "combinations in restraint of trade," the federal government used the Sherman Antitrust Act against unions more often than against businesses.

During the Progressive era several states passed legislation helpful to labor, such as laws establishing a minimum wage for women, maximum work hours, and workmen's compensation, and abolishing child labor and convict leasing. Groups such as the National Child Labor Committee, the Woman's Trade Union League, and the National Consumers League spearheaded the drives for many of these measures. Ironically, organized labor opposed minimum-wage laws for women because it preferred to win such measures through collective bargaining or strikes rather than through legislation. Business had to persuade labor to accept workmen's compensation plans, which unions opposed because the benefits were not very generous and many sorts of workers were excluded. Businessmen wanted the plans to protect themselves against the large payments that courts sometimes awarded in injury cases.

In 1904 a group of reformers established the National Child Labor Committee, an organization that dedicated to investigating the problem of child labor and lobbying state-by-state for legislation to end the abuse. It was, however, not effective because each state feared restrictive legislation could give other states a competitive advantage in recruiting industry. In 1907 a federal law against child labor, sponsored by Senator Alan Beveridge (1899–1911) of Ohio, went down to defeat and three years later in 1910 there were still an estimated two million children employed in factories. Only when the loopholes in state laws become apparent to reformers did they lobby for federal legislation, most of which did not come until the end of the 1920s.

In 1912 a Children's Bureau was established as an agency of the Department of Commerce and Labor. Its mandate was to examine "all matters pertaining to the welfare of children," which included child labor, and it was led by Julia C. Lathrop, the first woman to head a federal agency. Progress, however, was still slow. In 1916 senators Robert L. Owen and Edward Keating sponsored a bill that restricted child labor; the bill passed both houses of Congress with the strong support of President Woodrow Wilson (1913–1921). The law was based on a recommendation of the National Child Welfare Committee but it only prevented the interstate shipment of goods produced in factories by children under 14 and materials processed in mines by children under 16. It also limited children's workday to eight hours. In 1918 the Supreme Court declared this law unconstitutional because it was directed toward the regulation of working conditions not the control of interstate commerce. In 1919 Congress passed the Child Labor Act, which placed a tax on companies that used child labor, but the court again overturned the law. In 1924 there was an attempt to amend the Constitution to prohibit child labor but it never received approval from the required number of states.

Supply chain audits fail to detect abuses, says report

Research from the University of Sheffield argues audits are working for corporations but failing workers and the environment

Tansy Hoskins

Thursday 14 January 2016 16.42 GMT

The clothes you are wearing, the food you ate for dinner last night, and the component parts of your mobile phone - who made them, and how? Maybe they have a sticker or stamp that guarantees the environment wasn't harmed, that any animals were treated humanely, or that workers were treated well.

What if those claims aren't true? And what's more, what if the audits that produce those stamps make labour conditions and environmental standards worse by preventing governments from regulating and legislating? That is the claim in a new report (pdf) released today from the Sheffield Political Economy Research Institute, part of Sheffield University.

The report, based on interviews with business executives, NGOs, supplier firms and auditors, is blunt in its condemnation: "ultimately the audit regime is 'working' for corporations, but failing workers and the planet. Audits are ineffective tools for detecting, reporting, or correcting environmental and labour problems in supply chains. They reinforce existing business models and preserve the global status quo."

The report's authors cite the collapse of the Rana Plaza garment factory in Bangladesh in 2013 and the Guardian investigation into human slavery in the Thai shrimp industry in 2014. While both have been extensively documented, the authors point out that what has been less well reported is the fact that both took place within certified, audited supply chains. Paul Lister, who is responsible for Primark's ethical trading team, admitted that Primark had twice audited the Rana Plaza factory before it collapsed.

The reporting industry

Multinational corporations hire private auditors to inspect the factories in their supply chains. As a result, auditing has become an industry in itself, with leagues of assessors writing reports about voluntary codes.

The report argues that the voluntary nature of the auditing process means some corporations are prioritising the environment over labour concerns. It says businesses prioritise environmental issues over labour concerns because there is a more measurable and established business case for the environment, and environmental concerns translate more easily into business efficiency and financial gains.

Another major concern is that corporate control over the audit process means companies are able to dictate the extent of the audit. One auditor told the report's authors "we will audit as far down as the brand wants to go". This potentially misses subcontractor arrangements - often a huge and vulnerable section of supply chains.

The growth of corporate audit regimes has been interpreted by governments as a reason to step back from regulating the actions of corporations, the report argues, instead trusting corporations to self-monitor. By embracing and promoting audits, it says, corporations "have been able to deflect pressure" for stricter state and international regulation.

"Arguably it is the unsustainable business models of large corporations, which are reliant on cheap labour and environmental degradation, that drive abuses within supply chains," says one of the report's authors, Genevieve LeBaron. "Yet corporations, by working with a growing audit industry, are presenting themselves as the solution to the abuses."

The report argues that corporations get to look ethical and responsible while legitimising an economy that promotes consumption and environmental degradation.

The Rainforest Alliance, which allows products to carry its seal where it says "rigorous environmental, social and economic criteria" have been met, is mentioned in the report for its certification of tea estates which have been accused of illegal labour practices.

Edward Millard, acting director for Asia-Pacific in the Rainforest Alliance's field implementation group, says: "Any breach of local laws or non-compliance of the standards of the Sustainable Agriculture Network, which are the basis of Rainforest Alliance certification, are investigated immediately and appropriate action is taken, up to and including decertification of farms. Farms will need to correct any unacceptable conditions within an agreed upon time period; certification will be cancelled if a farm fails to meet these requirements." The Rainforest Alliance has now stripped one plantation of the seal.

If auditing is failing as a way to enforce standards, what measures could protect people and planet? LeBaron believes governments around the world must resume a more active role and put more boots on the ground to monitor and enforce labour and environmental standards. "Inspectorates need more funding and a stronger mandate, and workers need to be empowered to exert their rights to prevent abuses in the first place," she says.

chapter twelve

Sweatshops and Child Labour

"Child labour must be abolished!"

No one wants to see children exploited for their labour. Ever since the time of Charles Dickens, Western countries have passed laws that protect children from being abused and exploited. Now we see children in poor countries working under conditions that cause us pain. In our desire to help, consumers are boycotting products from countries that use child labour while the UN monitors the abuse of children in numerous countries. As much as we want to help these children, are we doing the right thing? Boycotting or restricting sneakers and toys that were manufactured using child labour may actually be making things worse for these children and their families by depriving them of wages and jobs they badly need.

In 1995, a 12-year-old Canadian named Craig Kielburger brought attention to the plight of children in Third World countries. His book *Free the Children* became a call to children in rich countries to help poor kids around the world who were being exploited and abused, especially those in the sweatshops making products consumed in Europe and North America. Since then, we've become used to seeing the hardship of children and families toiling away in subhuman conditions, eking out a living by performing the most menial and degrading work. One place that became the symbol of Third World poverty is a huge Manila garbage dump known as Smokey Mountain, where thousands of men, women, and children scavenge for scrap metal and recyclables.

Since Kielburger came onto the scene, children around the world in rich countries have rallied, usually through a storm of Web sites, in an attempt to help kids in poor countries. They have also had a political impact in their own countries. In Canada, the federal government established the Child Labour Challenge Fund and adopted legislation to prosecute Canadian citizens who engage in sexual exploitation of children in other countries. The Canadian government is also working with the UN Convention on the Rights of the Child and supports the work of the International Labour Organization (ILO) to develop a convention on the most extreme forms of child labour. And to make sure it is keeping on top of the situation, the federal government is also "monitoring" the abuse of children in forty countries. As it stands, the ILO estimates that there are 250 million working children, half between the ages of 5 and 14, who "work in dangerous, exploitive environments that hurt their health, their education and their normal development."[1] The cause of child labour has also been picked up by the anti-globalization movement in its Campaign for the Abolition of Sweatshops and Child Labor around the world.

But the movement has a greater ambition than just informing the public about child poverty and exploitation. It also wants legislation that restricts the import of products made by using not only child labour, but any labour practice deemed questionable. In the United States there is proposed legislation against the importation of textiles produced by child labour. Although there are no laws on the books in Canada, labour groups are trying to get major retailers such as Sears, Mark's Work Wearhouse, and Hudson's Bay Company to agree to a code of conduct that would prohibit them from importing goods manufactured using child labour.[2] And the trend to apply political pressure is gaining momentum. The ILO, Canadian labour groups, and anti-globalization forces routinely boycott products made by Nike, Adidas, and sports multinationals that operate in countries with labour practices they find offensive.

Consumers are also getting into the act by demanding products that don't exploit Third World labour. That's why some retail companies such as the Bay, sensitive to consumer pressure, are imposing restrictions on some products that use cheap foreign labour.[3] In sympathy with this trend is a movement called "fair trade." The assumption is that farmers in poor countries—and many working on those farms are children—rely on exported agricultural products such as coffee, and they should receive a fair price or "living wage" for their product regardless of the changes in market price. It is assumed that this fair trade policy will leave farmers with more money for health, education, and resources to better protect the environment. Companies such as Starbucks now routinely sell products that proudly display the fair trade logo.

It's hard to imagine that anyone would be in favour of policies that exploit children and force them into labour against their best interests. We all want to see children enjoy the benefits of childhood that most of us in the developed countries have come to take for granted. But are the policies advocated by many in the West in the best interest of children and their families in the developing world? There is plenty of moral outrage when one suggests that there are better alternatives to boycotts and import restrictions for countries that use child labour, but it's important to think through the implications of literally stopping the import of goods produced using cheap labour.

CHILD LABOUR IS NOTHING NEW

Given the recent publicity and media attention devoted to child labour, one shouldn't get the impression that it's a new and recently discovered phenomenon. Child labour has received considerable attention since the Industrial Revolution in Britain in the 1700s, when young children were used in factories in major urban centres.[4] But just as the Western nations have become wealthy since then, there are lessons to be learned about how countries work their way out of poverty. And one of those lessons is the benefit of open markets. This isn't to suggest that the poor and children around the world have to wait another 200 years before they get real help. But what is clear to economists is that trade, and plenty of it, is the most important strategy for increasing living standards around the world.

Another important question is why do the poor in developing countries have so many children when people in the West, who can afford more, have so few? The answer has to do with opportunity costs, as so many questions in economics do. In rich countries, as incomes increase, the cost of having children also goes up. They have to be raised and educated, which is time consuming, as any parent can attest. That's time that has to be taken away from earning money, and for those with high incomes, that process can be quite expensive in forgone income. That's why richer parents choose to spend more time on the job and less time parenting. Poorer parents get less reward from working and so spend more time parenting and have more kids. When wages and incomes are low, the opportunity costs drop and hence having that extra child is relatively cheap.[5] Besides, in poor countries where there are no pension plans, there is an incentive to have more children who could take care of you. People in wealthier countries depend on savings and pension plans to see them through in their old age. One sure way to decrease the rate of population growth in poor countries is to see that their overall level of income goes up. And that's where trade plays a major role.

MORE TRADE, PLEASE

Trade is good for every country, rich and poor. Most of the protestors around the world who try to disrupt every international economic conference base their protests on the thesis that globalization (read: greater free trade) is good only for big international companies and bad for poor countries. They're wrong on both counts. As we've already seen in Chapter 7 on the benefits of free trade, everyone benefits from more trade based on the economic principles of specialization and comparative advantage. If there is an iron law of economics, it's that more trade is better than less, and that applies to poor countries that have access to markets in developed economies. Take the example of the African Growth and Opportunity Act, a law passed in 2000 that opened U.S. markets for textiles from some of the poorest countries on earth. Within a year, South Africa's textile exports to the U.S. were up by 47 percent, Madagascar's by 120 percent, and both Malawi's and Nigeria's by 1,000 percent.[6]

IN PRAISE OF SWEATSHOPS

Nothing agitates and enrages some in the West as much as the sight of children working in sweatshops in poor countries so that we can wear fancy sneakers. Stories of child abuse are reported frequently, especially by groups that support the work of well-meaning kids such as Craig Kielburger. Are they right? Or are they doing more harm than good? Let's examine the issue a little more closely.

There's no question that workers in sweatshops aren't paid the same rates and don't work under the same conditions as workers in Canada and the U.S. But let's not forget that they are a quantum leap from what they were before. We find it difficult to believe that sewing shoes in China or Bangladesh for 60 cents an hour doesn't amount to exploitation. However, if we compare it to a farmer scraping by on half that amount to feed his family, we get a different picture of the factory worker. Companies in the Third World don't pay the wages we see in the West, but keep in mind the alternatives for these workers: scavenging on garbage heaps is the next best thing. There are also benefits for the environment as the poor come off marginally productive land to work in factories that pay higher wages. What may seem like hardships today may actually be laying the groundwork for a better life tomorrow, as in countries such as South Korea and Taiwan, which were once desperately poor.

Consequently, it's wrong to think that only the rich multinationals benefit. In essence the real winners are the workers in the Third World. Except for a few small Asian nations, the bulk of the world's Third World countries remain desperately poor because of tariff barriers that produce few jobs and keep their economies from becoming more efficient. In fact one could make the case that they became poorer as richer countries simply bought up their raw materials. For a number of reasons over the past two decades, such as lower tariff barriers, lower transportation costs, and improved telecommunications, producing goods in Third World countries has become more economically viable. This has allowed companies in the West to keep their prices down by producing in low-cost countries, the very conditions that benefit both them and us. These principles don't apply to every industry, only to those for which labour costs make up a significant part of the cost of production. For many companies it's still more economical to produce their goods in the West, but for many companies producing in low-wage countries makes more sense—for example, countries such as Bangladesh and Malaysia, which produce shirts, sneakers, and soccer balls. They get better-paying jobs, and we get low-cost goods. And as Chapter 13 (on paying off the debt of poor foreign countries) demonstrates, we know that simply giving aid is not the way to end poverty. In many ways, it simply entrenches dependence by these countries on "welfare" from the West.

Few of the anti-globalists protesting in the streets of Seattle, Genoa, Washington, D.C., or Quebec City have any appreciation of how poor the peasants and workers are in countries like Indonesia, where progress is measured in how much a person gets to eat. Since 1970, per capita intake has risen from less than 2,100 calories a day to 2,800 today. We are now also seeing similar improvements throughout the Pacific Rim. And still protesters would deny them these small benefits, thinking that boycotting their products will bring them more prosperity. Whatever benefits poor countries enjoy have not come from the good intentions of well-meaning people in the West, but indirectly from thousands of investors in the West and entrepreneurs in poor countries.[7]

Consider what would happen if those in the West who are outraged by the low wages paid in poor countries (where jobs are desperately needed) could increase salaries to a so-called "living wage" and impose labour standards, even child labour standards such as those in developed countries. Such an action would take away the only real advantage these countries have, which is cheap labour. The reality is that if sweatshops paid decent wages by Western standards, they would not exist. Deny them the ability to pay low wages, and you deny them the chance to develop their economies. Hard as it may seem to us, children in these countries benefit as well.

When the U.S. limited imports of textiles from Bangladesh to "protect" children from exploitation, the impact hurt the very group it was trying to protect. Children who were working in the factories were let go under U.S. pressure. Did they go back to school or to safer jobs? No. They found themselves right back on the streets and in more dangerous occupations. Even UNICEF, which has a reputation for protecting the interests of children in the Third World, admitted in its report, *What Works for Working Children*, that for children in the Bangladeshi garment industry, work was "less hazardous, more financially lucrative, and with more prospects for advancement than almost all other forms of employment open to children." The report also said that boycotts didn't distinguish between good and bad working conditions for children.[8]

HOW CAN WE HELP?

No one likes to see children working to support themselves and help their families. In the West we have strong feelings about the care and nurturing of children and want to see them healthy and well educated. But it wasn't always that way. In Canada, only when the country could afford it were laws passed about keeping children in school until they were 16 years of age. Poor countries don't have the income or the luxury to see that every child is in school, is well fed, and gets the proper medical attention. But we have to see the situation for what it is, not how we'd like it to be. Here's how the opinions of two reporters changed after visiting Asia:

"Like most Westerners, we arrived in the region outraged by sweatshops," they recalled fourteen years later. "In time, though, we came to accept the view supported by most Asians: that the campaign against sweatshops risks harming the very people it is intended to help. For beneath their grime, sweatshops are a clear sign of the industrial revolution that is beginning to reshape Asia." After describing the horrific conditions—workers denied bathroom breaks, exposed to dangerous chemicals, forced to work seven days a week—they conclude: "Asian workers would be aghast at the idea of American (and Canadian) consumers boycotting certain toys or clothing in protest."[9]

What about the criticism and worry that transferring investment to low-wage countries means a race to the bottom in labour standards in the West in order to remain competitive? If we end up paying low wages to workers abroad, won't that drive down wages at home, along with labour standards as firms move offshore? This argument doesn't hold up to analysis when one realizes that employers are concerned with more than just cheap labour. What really interests employers is the value of labour and not simply its price. Some companies will move routine tasks where the hourly rates are lower, but employers don't want cheap workers, they want productive ones. If the race-to-the-bottom argument were correct, you would expect **foreign direct investment** (FDI) to be pouring into low-wage countries. In fact, the U.S. is the largest recipient of FDI from around the world, and about 80 percent of U.S. FDI goes to other rich countries. In 1999 about 72 percent of FDI went to the U.S. and Europe, and only 7 percent to Asian countries.[10] Poor countries need to be helped by making it easier for companies such as Nike, Toys "Я" Us, and Gap to invest. The more capital these countries have, the higher their productivity rates and consequently overall economic well-being. Table 12.1 shows that countries with higher rates of physical

TABLE 12.1	Physical Capital Investment and Productivity (Annual Percentage Rate)	
Country/Region	**Output Per Worker**	**Physical Capital**
Indonesia	3.4	2.1
Korea	5.7	3.3
Malaysia	3.8	2.3
Philippines	1.2	1.2
Singapore	5.4	3.4
Thailand	5.0	2.7
Taiwan	5.8	3.1
East Asia	4.2	2.5
South Asia	2.3	1.1
Africa	0.3	0.8
Middle East	1.6	1.5
Latin America	1.5	0.9

Source: Adapted from *East Asia in Transition: Economic and Security Challenges*, ed. A.E. Safarian and Wendy Dobson (Toronto: University of Toronto, 2002), p. 7.

capital growth also have higher rates of productivity. Korea, with a high rate of physical capital investment, has a high rate of output per worker, in contrast to the Philippines, where the worker productivity rate is much lower. Also note that Africa has a dismal productivity rate along with low rates of physical capital investment.

Economists are in agreement that growth is the most important thing a nation can do for its poor. If we really want to help children and their families in poor countries, we should be encouraging more FDI in these countries, buying the goods they produce, and not restricting their products because they use low-wage labour.

It's easy for us in the West to think that passing laws that restrict or force exporting countries to impose higher labour standards solves the problem of poverty. If only wealth were created and distributed so effortlessly. Sweatshops don't cause low wages in poor countries and no amount of protesting will make it otherwise. To think so confuses cause and effect. The wages are low because these countries can't provide better jobs for their people, and we can't make the situation better by refusing to buy their products, regardless of how distasteful and deplorable the working conditions are. Through our good intentions we unintentionally make things worse for children in poor countries. If we want to really help, we should hold our nose and buy their products. To do otherwise condemns these children to a worse fate.

KEY TERM

Foreign direct investment

REVIEW QUESTIONS

1. Explain what would happen if we managed to force poor countries to adopt Western labour standards and wage rates comparable to Canada's? Who would this policy help and hurt?

2. How have countries such as Taiwan and South Korea, both extremely poor countries fifty years ago, managed to drastically improve their standards of living? What lessons can be learned for other poor countries?

DISCUSSION QUESTIONS

1. "Anti-sweatshop protestors may have good intentions, but their efforts are misguided." Comment.

2. What policies would you recommend for the Canadian government to help children in poor countries?

NOTES

1. Canada, Department of Foreign Affairs and International Trade, *News Release* 85 (3 April 1998).

2. See the Web site of the British Columbia Federation of Labour, **www.bcfed.com/Taking+Action/Child+Labour/index.htm**.

3. The anti-sweatshop movement got a great deal of public attention in the U.S. when it was discovered that Kathie Lee Gifford's clothing company employed Honduran sweatshop workers to produce a line of clothing for Wal-Mart. About 10 percent of the workers were between the ages of 13 and 15.

4. Their hardships were chronicled in classic novels by Charles Dickens such as *Oliver Twist*.

5. This insight comes from Nobel Prize–winning economist Gary Becker in his work on human capital.

6. Thomas Friedman, "Protesting for Whom?" *The New York Times*, 24 April 2001.

7. Paul Krugman, "In Praise of Cheap Labor: Bad Jobs at Bad Wages Are Better Than No Jobs at All," *Slate*, 21 March 1997, slate.msn.com/id/1918/.

8. Jo Boyden, Birgitta Ling, and William E. Myers, *What Works for Working Children* (Stockholm: UNICEF, 1998), quoted in Thomas R. DeGregori, "Child Labor or Child Prostitution?" in *Bountiful Harvest: Technology, Food Safety, and the Environment* (Washington, D.C.: Cato Institute, 2002).

9. Nicholas D. Kristof and Sheryl WuDunn, "Two Cheers for Sweatshops," *New York Times Magazine*, 24 September 2000, as quoted in Charles Wheelan, *Naked Economics: Undressing the Dismal Science* (New York: Norton, 2002), p. 202.

10. *Source*: Statistics Canada, *Canada's International Investment Position 1999*, Catalogue No. 67-202-XPB (Ottawa: Minister of Industry, 2000).

 **WEBLINKS**

web.mit.edu/krugman/www/berries.html   Protectionism and free trade.

www.swcollege.com/bef/policy_debates/sweatshops.html   Does the anti-sweatshop movement help or harm low-wage workers?

www.globalexchange.org/economy/coffee/background.html   Fair trade and coffee.

Module 5 - Good Behaviour

Unit 11 – Redistribution

6

SAVE MORE TOMORROW

In 2005 the personal savings rate for Americans was negative for the first time since 1932 and 1933—the Great Depression years. On average, American households spent more than they earned and borrowed more than they saved. Increased borrowing rates were fueled by substantial growth in home equity loans and in credit card debt. For many Americans, savings rates, especially retirement savings, are woefully low, if not zero. Consider, for example, the case of Tony Snow, the former White House press secretary, who resigned at age fifty-two in 2007 to return to the private sector. He said his motivation for leaving was financial. "I ran out of money," he told reporters. "We took out a loan when I came to the White House, and that loan is now gone. So I'm going to have to pay the bills." Before serving as press secretary, Snow worked a much more lucrative gig as a Fox News Channel anchor. But he arrived at the White House not having learned Retirement 101 lessons. "Snow conceded: 'As a matter of fact, I was even too dopey to get in on a 401(k).'"[1]

The fact that many people are not saving for retirement exacerbates the looming problems facing the Social Security system. As all politicians know but few are willing to say, we will eventually have to bite the bullet in order to make Social Security solvent, through some combination of tax increases or benefit cuts. Americans would be better able to deal with this problem if they were saving more on their own. And indeed, the government has often passed laws designed to encourage personal savings, typically by creating tax-favored savings accounts such as IRAs and 401(k)s.

Such programs are well intended, but many Americans who are eligible for such plans do not take full advantage of them.

What can be done to help? We will be offering two central suggestions. The first is automatic enrollment in savings plans; the second is the Save More Tomorrow program. To understand why these nudges would work, and why they are not part of the usual economics repertoire, we need to step back a bit.

The standard economic theory of saving for retirement is both elegant and simple. People are assumed to calculate how much they are going to earn over the rest of their lifetime, figure out how much they will need when they retire, and then save up just enough to enjoy a comfortable retirement without sacrificing too much while they are still working.

As a guideline for how to think sensibly about saving, this theory is excellent, but as an approach to how people actually behave, the theory runs into two serious problems. First, it assumes that people are capable of solving a complicated mathematical problem in order to figure out how much to save. Without good computer software, even a trained economist would find this problem daunting. The truth is that we know few economists (and no lawyers) who have made a serious attempt at doing it (even with software).*

The second problem with the theory is that it assumes that people have enough willpower to implement the relevant plan. Under the standard theory, flashy sports cars or nice vacations never distract people from their project of saving up for a condo in Florida. In short, the standard theory is about Econs, not Humans.

For most of their time on earth, Humans did not have to worry much about saving for retirement, because most people did not live long enough to have much of a retirement period. In most societies, those who did make it to old age were cared for by their children. In the twentieth century, the combination of rising life expectancies and geographical dispersion of families made it necessary for people to think about providing for their own retirement income rather than depending on their children to

*There are good software products available from many mutual fund companies as well as from such independent firms as Financial Engines and Morningstar, but many Humans find using these programs both difficult and boring.

do it. Both employers and governments began to take steps to help with this problem, with Bismarck's early social security program in Germany leading the way in 1889.[2]

Early pension plans tended to be defined-benefit plans. In such plans, participants are entitled to a benefit that depends on a specific formula, typically based on the participant's salary and the number of years the participant was a member of the plan. In a typical private plan, a worker is entitled to receive a benefit that is a proportion of the salary paid over the last few years of work, the proportion depending on years of service.

Most public social security systems, including that of the United States, are also defined-benefit plans. Your Social Security check depends on the amount you have paid in taxes and the number of years you have worked. The payouts are even adjusted for inflation, so you know exactly what you will be paid (unless Congress changes its mind, as it is entitled to do; the Constitution does not protect your right to Social Security benefits).

From the perspective of choice architecture, defined-benefit plans have one large virtue: they are forgiving to even the most mindless of Humans. With Social Security, the only decision a worker has to make is when to start receiving benefits. The only form to fill out is the one where you write down your Social Security number, and you have to fill it out if you want to get paid! In the private sector, defined-benefit plans are also easy and forgiving, as long as the worker keeps working for the same employer, and the employer stays in business. The decision about when to retire is not so easy, but it *is* only one decision; the same is true for the decision about when to start claiming Social Security benefits. We discuss that decision, and how the government might offer some useful nudges, at the end of this chapter.

While a defined-benefit world can be an easy one for someone who stays in one job her entire life, employees who change jobs frequently can end up with virtually no retirement benefits, because there is often a minimum employment period (such as five years) before any benefits are vested (that is, owned by the employee). Defined-benefit plans are also expensive for employers to administer. Many old firms are switching over to defined-contribution plans, and nearly all new firms offer only defined-contribution plans. Under a defined-contribution plan, employees, and sometimes employers, make specific contributions to a tax-sheltered account in the employee's name. The benefits received by employees in retirement depend on the decisions they make about how much to save and how to invest.

Defined-contribution plans, such as 401(k) plans in the United States, have many desirable features for modern workers. The plans are completely portable, so a worker is free to move from one job to another. The plans are also flexible, giving employees the opportunity to adjust their savings and investment decisions to reflect their own financial situation and tastes. However, defined-contribution plans are not very forgiving. Employees have to get around to joining, to figuring out how much to save, to managing their portfolio over a period of years, and then to deciding what to do with the proceeds when they finally retire. People can find the whole process frightening, and many seem to be making a mess of the task.

Are People Saving Enough?

Of course, a key question is whether people are saving enough. Are they? This turns out to be a complex and controversial question. For one thing, economists do not agree about how much saving is appropriate, because they do not agree on the right level of post-retirement income. Some economists argue that people should aim to have retirement income that is at least as high as the income enjoyed when working, because retirement years offer the opportunity for such time-intensive expensive activities as travel. Retired people also have to worry about growing health care costs. Others claim that retirees can use their greater time to live a more economical lifestyle: saving the money once spent on business clothes, taking the time to shop carefully and prepare meals at home, and taking advantage of senior discounts.

We do not take a strong position on this debate, but consider a few points. It seems clear that the costs of saving too little are greater than the costs of saving too much. There are many ways to cope with having saved too much—from retiring earlier than expected, to taking up golf, to traveling to Europe, to spoiling the grandchildren. Coping in the opposite direction is less pleasant. Second, we can say for sure that *some* people in our society are definitely saving too little—namely, those employees who are

not participating at all in their retirement plan, or are saving a low percentage of their income after having reached their forties (or older). These folks could clearly use a nudge.

For what it is worth, many employees say that they "should" be saving more. In one study, 68 percent of 401(k) participants said that their savings rate is "too low," 31 percent said that their savings rate is "about right," and only 1 percent said their savings rate is "too high." Economists tend to belittle such statements, and partly for good reason. It is easy to say that you "should" be doing many good things—dieting, exercising, spending more time with your children—and people's actions may tell us more than their words. After all, few of the participants who say they should be saving more make any changes in their behavior. But such statements are not meaningless or random. Many people announce an intention to eat less and exercise more next year, but few say they hope to smoke more next year or watch more sitcom reruns. We interpret the statement "I should be saving (or dieting, or exercising) more" to imply that people would be open to strategies that would help them achieve these goals. In other words, they are open to a nudge. They might even be grateful for one.

Enrollment Decisions: Nudging People to Join

The first step in participating in a defined contribution plan, such as a 401(k), is to enroll. Most workers should find joining the plan very attractive. Contributions are tax deductible, accumulations are tax deferred, and in many plans the employer matches at least part of the contributions of the employee. For example, a common plan feature is that the employer will match 50 percent of the employee's contributions up to some threshold, such as 6 percent of salary.

This match is virtually free money. Taking full advantage of the match should be a no-brainer for all but the most impatient or cash-strapped households. Nevertheless, enrollment rates in such plans are far from 100 percent. Roughly 30 percent of employees eligible to join a 401(k) plan fail to enroll.[3] Typically, younger, less-educated, and lower-income employees are less likely to join, but even high-paid workers sometimes fail to sign up, as the Tony Snow example illustrates.

To be sure, there are situations, say for young workers with other pressing financial needs, in which it could be sensible not to join even with an employer match. But in many cases, the failure to join is simply a blunder. One extreme example comes from the United Kingdom, where some defined-benefit plans do not require any employee contributions and are fully paid for by the employer. They do require employees to take action to join the plan. Data on twenty-five such plans reveal that scarcely half of the eligible employees (51 percent) signed up![4] This is equivalent to not bothering to cash your paycheck.

Some older American workers are also turning down "free money." To have this free money option, a worker must meet three qualifications: he needs to be more than 59½ years old, so that he faces no tax penalty when he withdraws funds from his retirement account; his firm has to offer a matching contribution (meaning that the firm contributes something if the employee does); and his employer has to allow employees to withdraw funds from their retirement accounts while still working. For such employees, joining the plan is a sure profit opportunity because they can join, then immediately withdraw their contributions without any penalty, yet keep the employer match. Nonetheless, a study finds that up to 40 percent of eligible workers either do not join the plan at all or do not save enough to get the full match.[5]

These extreme examples are just the clearest cases in which people's failure to join a plan is foolish beyond a doubt. In many other cases, workers take months or years to join the plan, and it is a reasonable assumption that most of these workers are just spacing out or procrastinating rather than making a reasoned decision that they have a better use for their money. How can we nudge these people to join more quickly?*

Making Savings Automatic

An obvious answer is to change the default rule. As things now stand, the default is nonenrollment; you have to do a little work to get into

*By the way, are you contributing the maximum to your retirement plan, or at least contributing enough to get the full match from your employer? Are your grown children doing so? If not, stop reading and get busy. You have more important things to do than read this book.

a retirement plan. When workers are first eligible to join (sometimes immediately upon employment), they usually receive a form to fill out. Employees who want to join must decide how much to put aside, and how to allocate their investments among the funds offered in the plan. Forms can be a headache, and many employees just put them aside.

An alternative is to adopt automatic enrollment. Here's how it works. When an employee first becomes eligible, she receives a form indicating that she will be enrolled in the plan (at a specified savings rate and asset allocation), unless she actively fills out a form asking to opt out. Automatic enrollment has proven to be an extremely effective way to increase enrollment in U.S. defined-contribution plans.[6]

In one plan studied in an early paper by Brigitte Madrian and Dennis Shea (2001), participation rates under the opt-in approach were barely 20 percent after three months of employment, gradually increasing to 65 percent after thirty-six months. But when automatic enrollment was adopted, enrollment of new employees jumped to 90 percent immediately and increased to more than 98 percent within thirty-six months. Automatic enrollment thus has two effects: participants join sooner, and more participants join eventually.

Does automatic enrollment merely overcome workers' inertia, helping them make the choice they would actually prefer? Or does automatic enrollment somehow seduce workers into saving when they would prefer to be spending? One telling bit of evidence is that under automatic enrollment, very few employees drop out of the plan once enrolled. In a study of four companies that adopted automatic enrollment, the fraction of 401(k) participants who dropped out of the plan in the first year was only 0.3 to 0.6 percentage points higher than it had been before automatic enrollment was introduced.[7] Although the low dropout rate is, of course, partly due to inertia, the fact that so few people drop out does suggest that workers are not suddenly discovering, to their dismay, that they are saving more than they had wanted.

Forced Choosing and More Simplicity

An alternative to automatic enrollment is simply to require every employee to make an active decision about whether to join the plan. If a worker is eligible when he is first hired, he might be required to check a "yes" or a "no" box for participation in order to get paid. With required choosing in place, employees have to state their preferences, and there is no default option. As compared with the usual opt-in approach (you are not enrolled unless you decide to fill out the forms), required choosing should increase participation rates. One company switched from an opt-in regime to active decisions and found that participation rates increased by about 25 percentage points.[8]

A related strategy is to simplify the enrollment process. One study tested this idea by analyzing a simplified enrollment form.[9] New employees were handed enrollment cards during orientation with a "yes" box for joining the plan at a 2 percent savings rate and a preselected asset allocation. Employees did not have to spend time choosing a savings rate and asset allocation; they could just check the "yes" box for participation. As a result, participation rates during the first four months of employment jumped from 9 percent to 34 percent. These simplified enrollment procedures are very much in the spirit of the "channel factors" we mentioned in Chapter 3. People really do want to join the plan, and if you dig a channel for them to slide down that removes the seemingly tiny barriers that are getting in their way, the results can be quite dramatic.

While automatic enrollment or "quick" enrollment makes the process of joining a retirement plan less daunting, expanding the number of funds available to participants can have the opposite effect. One study finds that the more options in the plan, the lower the participation rates.[10] This finding should not be surprising. With more options, the process becomes more confusing and difficult, and some people will refuse to choose at all.

Choosing Contribution Rates

Both automatic enrollment programs and forced choosing plans typically adopt a relatively low default savings rate of 2 or 3 percent, and a very conservative investment choice, such as a money market account. It turns out that many employees continue saving at the default rate of 2 percent. This rate is usually far too low to provide enough money for retirement. Many employees also remain in the default investment fund, and they lose a lot of money as a result. We will turn to investment strategies in

the next chapter. Here let's see how we can help nudge the people who are saving too little.

One indication that people need help in picking a savings rate and don't realize that they need the help is that most people spend very little time on this important financial decision. One survey found that 58 percent spent less than one hour determining both their contribution rate and investment decisions.[11] Most people spend more time than that picking a new tennis racket or television set. Apparently, many people are using some simple shortcuts. In many plans, participants are asked to state a desired savings rate as a percentage of pay. Many people simply pick a "round number," typically 5, 10, or 15 percent of income. Of course, there is no sensible reason why the correct percentage of your income to save would be an exact multiple of 5.

Another common rule of thumb is to contribute to a retirement account the minimum amount necessary to get the full employer match. If the employer matches employees' contributions up to 6 percent of pay, then many employees contribute 6 percent. If participants are behaving this way, then firms wanting to encourage employee savings might alter their matching formula to help workers. Changing the match formula from 50 percent on the first 6 percent of pay to 30 percent on the first 10 percent of pay would probably increase contribution rates. Those who use the match threshold as a rule of thumb would save more with a higher matching threshold. And by picking a round number as the threshold, the company would nudge those who use the "multiple of 5" heuristic.

Education

What else can employers do, if they want more employees to enroll in retirement plans, contribute an amount that will build a reasonable retirement nest egg, and allocate the funds among assets in an appropriately diversified way? Education is the obvious answer, and many employers have tried to educate their employees to make better decisions. Unfortunately, the evidence does not suggest that education is, in and of itself, an adequate solution.

One large employer, having offered its employees the chance to switch from a defined-benefit to a defined-contribution plan, provided a free financial education program.[12] The employer measured the effectiveness of this education by administering a before-and-after test of financial literacy. The quiz used a true/false format, so random answers would receive, on average, a score of 50 percent. Before the education, the average score of the employees was 54; after the education, the average score crept up to 55. Teaching is hard!

Employees often leave educational seminars excited about saving more but then fail to follow through on their plans. One study found that at the seminar everyone expressed an interest in saving more, but only 14 percent actually joined the savings plan. This was an improvement, but not a large one, over the 7 percent of comparable employees who did not attend a seminar and joined the savings plan.[13] Studies of the effects of attendance at a "benefit fair" also find only a small effect on participation in a tax-deferred savings account.[14]

Save More Tomorrow

Although automatic enrollment is effective at getting new and young workers to enroll sooner than they would have otherwise, participants tend to stick with the default contribution rate, which is typically quite low. To mitigate this problem, consider a program of automatic escalation of contributions, developed by Thaler and his frequent collaborator Shlomo Benartzi, called Save More Tomorrow.

Save More Tomorrow is a choice-architecture system that was constructed with close reference to five psychological principles that underlie human behavior:

- Many participants say that they think they should be saving more, and plan to save more, but never follow through.
- Self-control restrictions are easier to adopt if they take place some time in the future. (Many of us are planning to start diets soon, but not today.)
- Loss aversion: people hate to see their paychecks go down.
- Money illusion: losses are felt in nominal dollars (that is, not adjusted for inflation, so a dollar in 1995 is seen as worth the same as a dollar in 2005).
- Inertia plays a powerful role.

'Save More Tomorrow invites participants to commit themselves, in advance, to a series of contribution increases timed to coincide with pay raises. By synchronizing pay raises and savings increases, participants never see their take-home amounts go down, and they don't view their increased retirement contributions as losses. Once someone joins the program, the saving increases are automatic, using inertia to increase savings rather than prevent savings. When combined with automatic enrollment, this design can achieve both high participation rates and increased savings rates.

The first implementation of Save More Tomorrow occurred in 1998, at a midsized manufacturing firm. Employees were given the opportunity to meet one-on-one with a financial consultant. The consultant had a laptop with software designed to compute suggested savings rates based on relevant information provided by each employee (such as past savings and the retirement plan of a spouse). About 90 percent of the employees accepted the offer to meet with the financial consultant. Many were a bit surprised by what they heard. Because most employees were saving at very low rates, the adviser told almost every employee that he needed to save a lot more. Often the software suggested a savings rate equal to the maximum allowed in the plan, 15 percent of pay. But the consultant quickly realized that such suggestions were immediately rejected as infeasible, so he generally suggested increasing the savings rate by 5 percentage points of pay.

About 25 percent of the participants accepted this advice and immediately increased their savings rates by the recommended 5 percentage points. The rest said that they could not afford the cut in pay; these reluctant savers were offered the Save More Tomorrow program. Specifically, they were offered a plan in which their savings rates would go up by 3 percentage points every time they got a pay raise. (A typical pay raise was about 3.25 to 3.50 percent.) Of this group of employees who were unwilling to increase their savings rate immediately, 78 percent joined the program to increase their contribution with every pay raise.

The results provide a dramatic illustration of the potential power of choice architecture. Compare the behavior of three groups of employees. The first group consists of those who chose not to meet with the consultant. This group was saving about 6 percent of their income when the program started, and that percentage did not budge over the next three years. The second group contains the employees who accepted the advice to increase their savings rates by 5 percentage points. Their average savings rate jumped from just over 4 percent to just over 9 percent after the first raise occurred. This rate was then essentially constant over the next few years. The third group includes those who joined the Save More Tomorrow plan. That group started with the lowest savings rate of the three groups, around 3.5 percent of income. Under the program, however, their savings rates steadily rose, and three and a half years and four pay raises later, their savings rate had almost quadrupled, to 13.6 percent—considerably higher than the 9 percent savings rate for those who accepted the consultant's initial recommendation to raise savings by 5 percentage points.

Most of the people who enrolled in the Save More Tomorrow program stuck with it for the full four raises, whereupon the increases were halted because the employees had reached the maximum they were allowed to contribute in the plan. The few employees who did leave the program did not ask that their savings rates be dropped back to their earlier low levels. Instead, they just stopped increasing their contribution rates.

In the years since this pilot program, many retirement-plan administrators have adopted the Save More Tomorrow idea, including Vanguard, T. Rowe Price, TIAA-CREF, Fidelity, and Hewitt Associates. Save More Tomorrow is now available in thousands of employer plans. The Profit Sharing Council of America reports that as of 2007, 39 percent of large employers in the United States have adopted some type of automatic escalation plan. As the plan is implemented in various ways, we have been able to learn more about what makes the program work.

In the first implementation, as we have seen, participation was more than 80 percent, but this was in an environment in which each employee was approached individually by the financial consultant, and the consultant was able to fill out the relevant forms on the spot. In contrast, participation rates have been small in some cases in which employees have had to hunt for an obscure location on a financial-services Web page in order to sign up. Our main conclusion should not be surprising to anyone who has read this far into the book: participation rates jump when enrollment is easy. Holding a seminar to explain the plan helps; having the forms there to fill out helps even more. (Have we mentioned that channel factors matter?)

The most effective way to increase enrollment in a Save More Tomorrow plan is to combine it with automatic enrollment. The Safelite Group was the first to implement automatic enrollment in a Save More Tomorrow plan. The program was introduced to employees in June 2003. Ninety-three percent of participants took no action and thus were automatically enrolled in the program. In the year following the implementation of the program, only 6 percent actively opted out. Those who stayed in the program will have significantly more money available for retirement.

More recently, Vanguard has introduced thirteen automatic Save More Tomorrow enrollment plans.* These programs cover new hires only, and they are typically set with an initial deferral rate of about 3 percent of pay and an annual increment of 1 percent of pay. In the twelve months before the implementation of automatic enrollment, only 23 percent of employees opted into Save More Tomorrow. In the twelve months following automatic enrollment, 78 percent of the savers were participating in the program. The dramatic change in participation illustrates the power of inertia—and with respect to savings, the crucial role of choice architecture.

The Role of the Government

The initiatives discussed thus far have been entirely a private-sector phenomenon. Firms have tried automatic enrollment without any nudging from the government. The primary role government needed to play was getting out of the way by reducing the barriers to adoption of these programs. To an increasing extent, the federal government has done exactly that. Beginning in June 1998, Mark Iwry, then a Treasury Department official in charge of national pension policy, directed the Internal Revenue Service to issue a series of rulings (and official pronouncements) that defined, approved, and promoted the use of automatic enrollment in 401(k) and other retirement savings plans.

In the summer of 2006 Congress passed the Pension Protection Act, with enthusiastic backing on both sides of the aisle. The details are complex and boring, so we will put those in an endnote and simply point out that the law offers employers an incentive to match employee contribu-

*By 2007 about fifty more Vanguard clients were in the process of implementing the program on an opt-out basis.

tions, automatically enroll them in the plan, and automatically increase their contribution rates over time.[15] The incentive is that the employer is given a waiver from an annoying regulation. Although reasonable people can quibble with the specific provisions of the bill (which represent the usual sort of political compromises), we think that it is an excellent example of nudging. Employers are not required to change their plans, but if they do, they get a reward that actually saves the taxpayers money (because no one has to read or check the form that no longer has to be completed).

That is not to deny that government can badly blunder. Consider as a case in point the Social Security Administration. As we mentioned earlier, being a Social Security participant is a job even the most clueless of Humans can handle because there is one and only one decision to make: when to start claiming benefits. (The decision about when to start receiving benefits is independent of when to quit working. One can start collecting while still working and one can stop working and delay collecting.) Generally, a worker is eligible to start claiming benefits when she reaches age sixty-two. However, she can delay the start until age seventy, and the longer you wait to start receiving checks, the larger the checks get. Deciding when to start collecting the money is a tricky problem, even for an economist. Some of the factors that should go into your calculation include:

- How long you expect to live.
- The age, health, working history, and retirement expectations of your spouse.
- How much money you plan to make in the near future. (If you make money, then Social Security benefits are heavily taxed.)
- Impatience. The more eager you are to get the money (the higher your "discount rate" in economics parlance), the sooner you should start.

The Social Security Administration helpfully sends every American worker an annual statement that estimates how much she will collect if she retires at various ages. But for assistance in deciding when to start receiving benefits, participants are referred to the SSA Web page for help. We decided to have a look.

We discovered that the only tool available to help you is something called the Break-Even Age calculator.[16] This is the tool that is meant to help you decide whether to start collecting at age sixty-two or wait until, say, age sixty-six. One might think that this calculator would allow you to enter some information about the four factors mentioned above that should influence this choice. Instead, all the calculator does is tell you, given two possible start dates for receiving payments, how many years you have to live to "break even."* The calculator does not take interest, taxes, spouses, or anything else into account. The SSA might as well give every senior an abacus.†

If the SSA had a designated choice architect, she could surely do better. It would be possible to ask a series of questions to get at the important four factors. (Examples: Are you in good health? Do you plan to keep working? If so, how much will you make? At what age did your parents die? How old is your spouse? Is she working?) Then it would be possible to give some sensible advice—and possibly even a default option. (Hint to financial-service companies: build such a calculator and put it on your Web site.)

Saving for retirement is something that Humans find difficult. They have to solve a complicated mathematical problem to know how much to save, and then they have to exert a lot of willpower for a long time to execute this plan. This is an ideal domain for nudging. In an environment in which people have to make only one decision per lifetime, we should surely try harder to help them get it right.

---

*In other words, it answers the question, Will I have more money in total if I start taking lower payments now, or if I wait a few years until I can draw higher payments? A simple example illustrates that this calculation is one that even Humans can make by themselves. Suppose you can collect $1,000 a month at age sixty-two and $1,500 a month starting at age sixty-six. Four years (forty-eight months) of collecting $1,000 a month adds up to $48,000. How many months do you have to collect an extra $500 to make this up? Ninety-six. Duh.

†We discovered another odd thing about the SSA Web site. It does not operate twenty-four hours a day. Here are the hours:

Monday through Friday, all day (except 2:00–3:00 A.M.)

Saturday, 5:00 A.M.–11:00 P.M.

Sunday, 8:00 A.M.–10:00 P.M.

Holidays, 5:00 A.M.–11:00 P.M.

We had never heard of a Web site that works government hours (even extended ones)!

Unit 12 – Charitable Giving

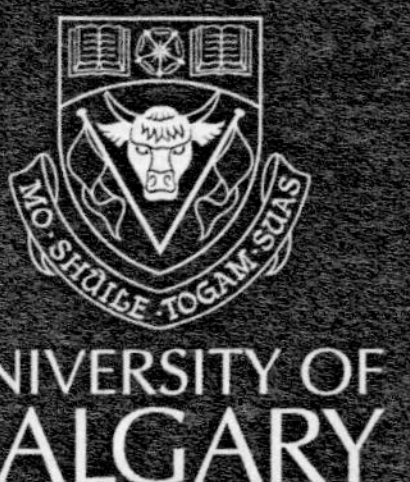

UNIVERSITY OF CALGARY

THE SCHOOL OF PUBLIC POLICY

SPP Research Papers

Volume 5 • Issue 34 • November 2012

CHANGING LANDSCAPES FOR CHARITIES IN CANADA: WHERE SHOULD WE GO?

A. Abigail Payne[†]

SUMMARY

Charitable giving in Canada has never been higher. Between 1992 and 2008, contributions to charitable organizations more than doubled, from $4 billion to more than $9 billion. Donations to charitable foundations grew at an even more remarkable rate: more than 250 per cent, over the same period.

But those striking numbers mask more puzzling, some might say more worrying, trends. While donations overall have grown, not all charity types have shared equally in the gains. Religious charities and health-related charities have seen the lowest amount of growth. Meanwhile, the country's larger charities and foundations have seen substantial increases in donations, but donation rates to smaller charities have been relatively flat. As for the donors, it's almost entirely high-income Canadians who seem to be giving significantly more, while the rate of giving among middle-income and lower income Canadians has hardly grown at all. In fact, the share of people claiming tax credits for donations in each income group is actually in decline, meaning fewer of us seem to be giving to registered charities, while the richest Canadians are primarily responsible for the rise in donations.

The reasons for these unusual trends are unclear — though there is some evidence that the more ethnically diverse our country has become, the less inclined we are to donate. And whether we should even be concerned about these uneven patterns — the wealthiest Canadians giving bigger cheques to the country's biggest charities and foundations — is also an open question.

But the uncertainty about what these trends mean, why they're happening, and whether they're even a problem, is not something we should take lightly. Changes may be coming soon to Canadian charity policy: Last year, a House of Commons committee began a sweeping study of charitable giving in Canada, and it is already evaluating dozens of suggestions for policy adjustments. But, while we can discern some patterns and trends in giving, the reality is that we actually still know very little about why Canadians give, and how we, as a society, want to change the way we give, if at all. And until we make the effort to learn considerably more, any policy changes aimed at altering the landscape for Canadian charities are at risk of being politically driven, rather than evidence-based, and they could very well end up creating more problems than they solve.

[†] The author wishes to acknowledge the helpful comments of the anonymous referees.

INTRODUCTION

Over the last few years, concerns have been raised about the state of charitable giving in Canada. These concerns range from: claims of declines in giving by subgroups of the population (e.g. younger adults) or across the board; the tax treatment of donations; and the oversight of charity operations. On December 15, 2011, The House of Commons standing committee on finance announced that it was undertaking a study of charitable giving in Canada in 2012. The committee has received over 55 submissions and held several days of meetings that covered presentations from many perspectives. The committee stated that the focus of the study would be:

> " … in respect of both individuals and corporations, current and proposed tax measures to encourage charitable giving. The examination will include the charitable tax credit amount and the possible extension of the capital gains exemption to donations of private company shares and real estate. The study will also focus on the feasibility and cost of changes to existing tax measures as well as the implementation of new tax incentives."

The submissions to the committee covered many ideas and suggestions. Some of the more popular points included:

- Creating a single tax credit, at least at the federal level. Current policy provides a federal credit of 15 per cent for the first $200 donated and 29 per cent for any amounts above $200.[1]

- Creating a "stretch" tax credit, which would increase the tax credit for giving if an individual gives more than she has previously given, but with a cap that would limit the extra credit so that it could be applied only to a maximum of $10,000 in additional donations.

- Eliminating the capital gains tax on donations of private (as opposed to publicly traded) company securities, placing it on equal footing as donations of publicly traded company securities.

- Eliminating the capital gains tax on real estate donations.

- Differentiating the level of tax credits available for donations based on the type of goods and/or services provided by the recipient charity and/or providing a greater tax credit for an initial dollar-level of donation, and a lower tax credit for every dollar beyond that threshold.

- Creating special tax incentives for donations of items such as food and basic necessities.

- Asking for more clarity in the information made public by registered charities and similar organizations (for example, the tax returns of non-profit organizations). Similarly: Promoting greater transparency and reducing regulatory abuse by charities to help promote public trust in charities.

- Promoting a regulatory environment that would allow charities greater flexibility in raising revenue to support their goods and services.

- Concerns regarding perceived declines in the donor pool and a shift in support to larger charities and foundations, hurting smaller and medium-sized charities.

---

[1] Note: Additional credits are available at the provincial level, providing donors with a higher tax credit overall. Federally, there is a cap on charitable donation tax credits equal to a maximum of 75 per cent of income.

A brief review of the submissions reveals that, while many of the submissions focused on encouraging individual giving through the enhancement of tax credits, most lacked an evidence-based analysis of charitable giving in Canada to support their positions. Moreover, there was little discussion about how a change in the tax treatment of private giving might impact direct government support of charity operations. This is a serious shortcoming. Policy prescriptions should be based on evidence-based research. Failure to do so increases the risk that policy decisions will become politicized and will be based on unsubstantiated beliefs.

What do we really know about charitable giving in Canada? What do we know about Canadian foundations and charity operations? It is easy to toss numbers around and make them sound meaningful. It appears that most advocates take it as given that giving in Canada has fallen. Is this true? Has giving changed in meaningful ways that could help us understand better how to direct our energies when it comes to charitable giving and charity operations? These are very big questions that will take more than one report to answer.

The focus of this report is to promote more critical analysis to help us understand the dynamics of giving and charity operations. This report explores the direction of changes in giving to charity and how these changes have impacted the charity landscape. Once we have a better understanding of the giving landscape in Canada, only then can we better evaluate whether and how to change it. Individuals give both money (including marketable goods) and time. This report focuses on the giving of money. Equally valuable, however would be a better understanding of the giving of time.

WHY USE THE TAX SYSTEM TO ENCOURAGE GIVING?

In general, when we think about tax incentives to promote giving, we use a model where individuals make economic decisions based on their preferences for charitable and other goods, given their income and wealth constraints. We can model these preferences in many ways. One commonly accepted model is where an individual cares about the overall provision of the charitable good and her donation towards that provision, something commonly referred to as the "warm glow" effect. If a donor's motives are purely altruistic — and not to feel a "warm glow" at all — then an increase in donations to her chosen cause by other donors, or greater government support for that cause, would result in a decline in her donation at a dollar-for-dollar rate (since she would believe the need served by her dollar would now be served, instead, by someone else's). If a donor is both altruistic and motivated for "warm glow" reasons, then an increase in donations to her chosen cause by other donors, or greater government support for that cause, would most likely result in a decline in her donation, but at a rate less than dollar for dollar (since the donor perceives a value in her donation beyond its utility).

For this reason, governments may support charitable giving through the awarding of grants and contracts to charities. Alternatively, the government can choose to forgo tax revenue, giving the donating individual a tax credit and/or deduction. The tax credit effectively lowers the price of giving. And so, by lowering the price of giving, individuals may give more. Bakija and Heim[2]

---

[2] Jon Bakija and Bradley Heim, "How Does Charitable Giving Respond to Incentives and Income? Dynamic Panel Estimates Accounting for Predictable Changes in Taxation," NBER Working Paper #14237 (2008).

summarize the research that studies how changing the price of giving affects giving. This effect is commonly referred to as the tax price elasticity of giving — meaning the level of responsiveness shown by individuals after a one per cent change in the price of giving (after the tax credit). More recent estimates suggest this elasticity is close to negative one (-1) meaning that a one per cent decrease in the price of giving should result in a one per cent increase in giving.

However, inducing a change in the price of giving may or may not be a societal benefit. Many of the changes in tax policies over the last 20 years have disproportionately benefitted wealthier taxpayers. If the types of charitable goods to which these taxpayers donate differs from the types of goods that are supported by the government, is this good or bad? Thus, in the next sections, let us examine patterns of giving and how they have changed over the last couple of decades.

PATTERNS IN REPORTED GIVING

Measuring charitable giving is challenging. There is no one source that captures fully how, and to what causes, Canadians give. On the data front, there are three main sources. The first source is to look at giving as reported on individual tax returns. Given that there are tax credits available for charitable giving, we might expect giving to be reported on tax returns. Tax credits, however, are only offered for gifts for which a tax receipt is issued. Giving money to a person on a street corner is not a donation for which a tax receipt is issued. Adding a donation to a grocery bill also does not count as tax-receipted giving. Buying a ticket to a fundraising event is typically not treated as a tax-receipted donation. Moreover, tax credits are non-refundable. Thus, if an individual has no tax liability, there is little incentive for reporting donations. Information from individual tax returns, thus, can only provide a partial picture. Given that tax-receipted giving represents a large portion of giving, however, data from tax returns can help us to discern patterns in giving and changes in those patterns over time.

A second source of information on giving is the periodic surveys conducted by Statistics Canada on individual giving and volunteering. These surveys are useful in that they ask individuals to report on different sorts of giving, including things such as giving to the person on the street corner, as well as the giving of time. A challenge with these surveys, as with any survey, is that they rely on the individual's recollection. Also, they are only conducted periodically, and while great efforts are made to capture a representative sample of Canadians, for several reasons it can be difficult to draw reliable conclusions about changes in individual giving habits over time and throughout someone's lifecycle.

A third source of information on giving is what charities report on their information returns. All registered charities are required to file returns with the Canada Revenue Agency (CRA). As charitable status can be revoked for failure to file a return, there is an incentive to file and to provide accurate information. The information return asks the charity to report funding from different revenue sources. This allows us to capture information about different types of giving, including those for which a tax receipt was issued, donations of non-cash items, and revenues from fundraising events. The charity information return should capture the donation that is given to a person on the street corner, provided that person is collecting money for a charity. It will not, however, capture the money given directly to a homeless person.

Let us look at all three data sources to discern trends in giving.

Individual tax return data: The number of donors has increased for some neighbourhoods and remained flat for other neighbourhoods. As the number of tax filers has increased over time, however, the share of tax filers reporting donations has fallen. Donations from higher income neighbourhoods have increased dramatically. Donations from lower income and middle-income neighbourhoods have remained flat or decreased.

Starting first with the individual tax return data, my analysis focused on urban and suburban areas in Canada. I obtained data for the period 1991 to 2010, at a local level, in areas that resemble small neighbourhoods: the area covered by the first three characters of the postal code (known as a forward sortation area, "FSA"), which typically covers 5,000 to 8,000 households. I classify each area as being in the bottom, middle, or top grouping as measured by average household income as reported in the 2006 census.[3] In Figure 1, I depict the number of tax filers reporting donations by these three classifications. For the lowest income and middle-income groups, the number of filers reporting charitable donations has remained relatively steady. For the higher income group, the number of filers has increased from more than 1.4 million in 1991 to approximately 1.9 million in 2010. There was a dip in 2008/09 (the period of the most recent recession), but donations appear to be bouncing back.

FIGURE 1   NUMBER OF TAX FILERS REPORTING DONATIONS, BY NEIGHBOURHOOD GROUPING

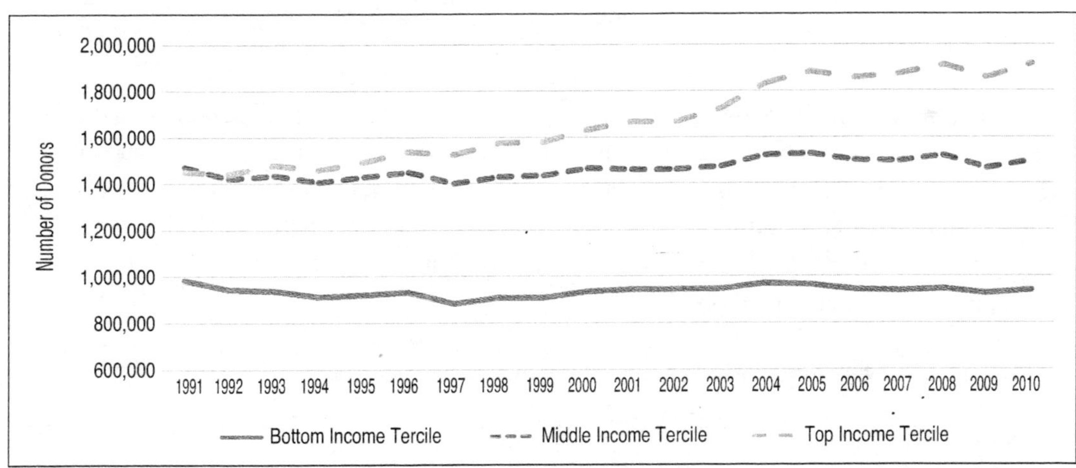

In Figure 2, I report the share of tax filers reporting charitable donations by income group. The share of filers reporting donations has declined across all groups. If the number of tax filers reporting charitable donations has increased overall, why are there claims that there has been a decline in giving by Canadians? There are two likely reasons. First, the number of tax filers has increased over the last two decades. For the neighbourhoods I studied, the number of tax filers increased from 12.4 million to 18.3 million. Thus, if we look at the share of tax filers that report charitable donations (Figure 2), we see that there has been a decline in this share because the rate of growth in tax filers is faster than the rate of growth in donors. Second, we

---

[3]   Between 1991 and 2010, neighbourhoods did change with respect to their socio-economic characteristics. I use the 2006 measure of average household income to reflect the most recent information available about each neighbourhood and to allocate each FSA to a single grouping. There are many ways the FSAs could be grouped (e.g. average income over the entire period or average income for the first part of the period). While not all variations were explored, when various different definitions were used to group neighbourhoods, the strongest growth in reported donations was still shown by higher income neighbourhoods.

have a tax system that generally provides greater tax benefits for couples who report their charitable donations on a single tax return. Over the last 20 years, there has been an increase in the use of tax software to complete personal tax returns. Most software programs identify the potential cost savings from combining and reporting donations on a single return. Thus, with these data, it is difficult to discern how much of the decline in the share of tax filers reporting donations is attributable to a wider use of tax software programs, which, ultimately, may be leading more couples to report their donations on one return.

FIGURE 2   SHARE OF TAX FILERS REPORTING TAX-RECEIPTED GIFTS, BY NEIGHBOURHOOD TYPE

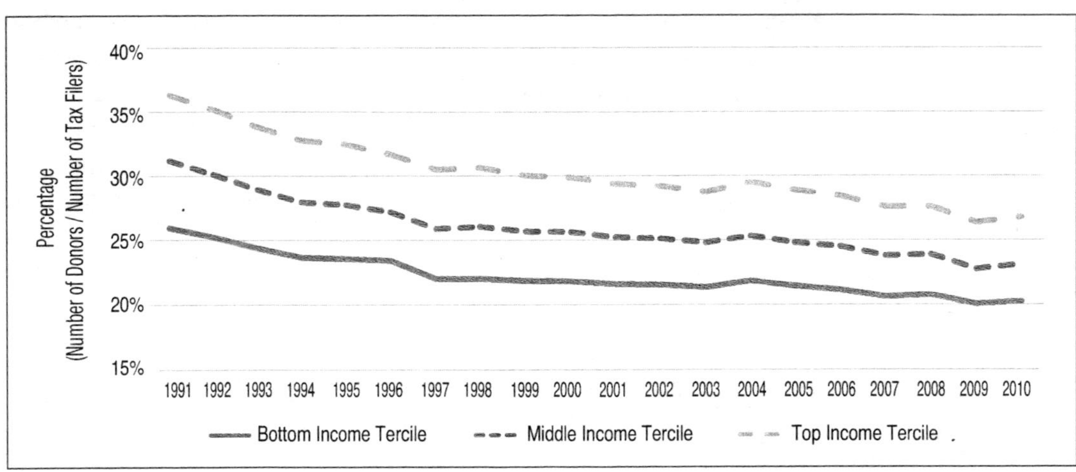

In Figures 3a and 3b, I report the total donations (adjusted for inflation) reported by the three neighbourhood groupings. Total giving is relatively flat for those in the lower income and middle-income neighbourhoods. If one adjusts for overall macro-level trends over the period, donations have been falling in the lower and middle-income neighbourhood groups. In both figures, however, there has been significant growth in giving reported by tax filers residing in higher income neighbourhoods.

FIGURE 3A   REPORTED TAX-RECEIPTED GIFTS, BY NEIGHBOURHOOD TYPE

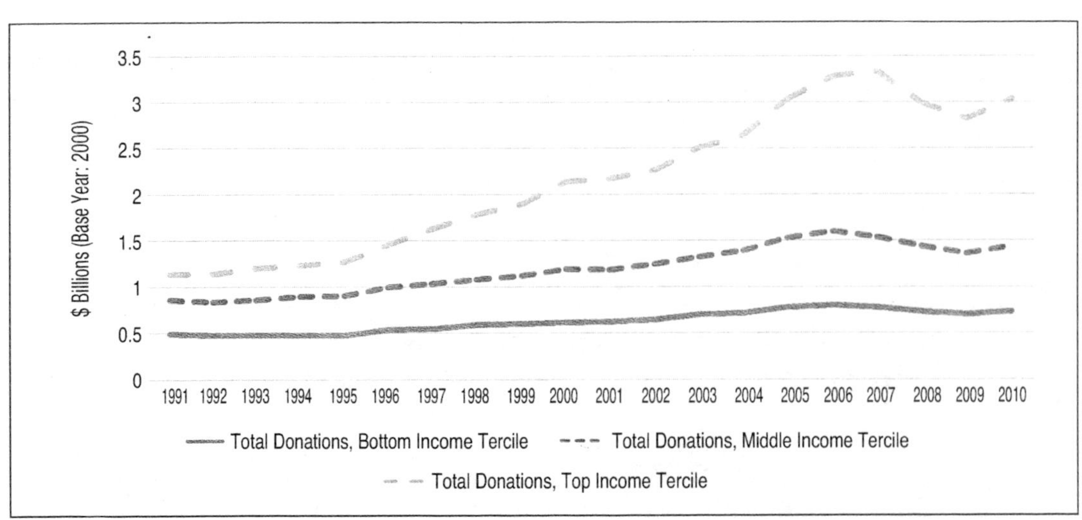

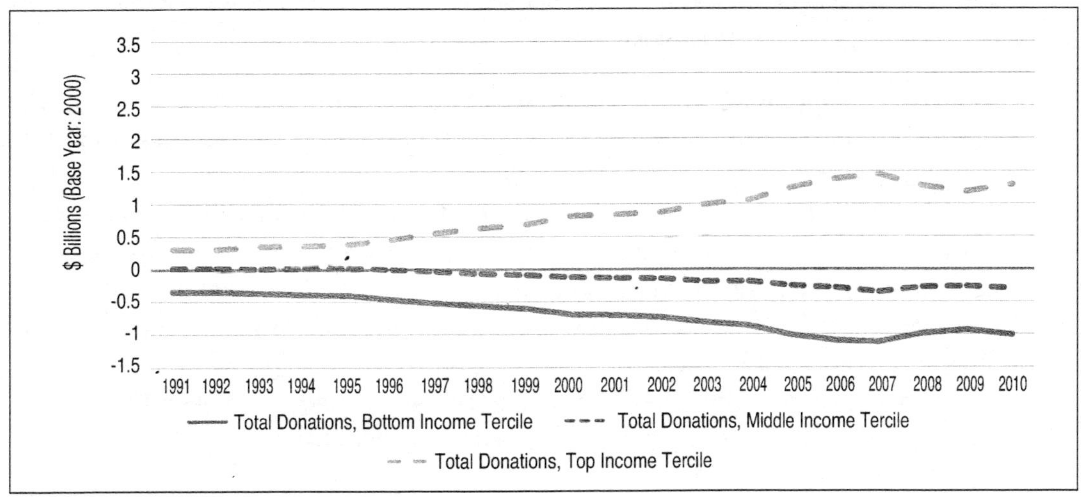

Judging solely from information from individual tax returns, it appears that growth in tax-receipted giving has been driven by individuals residing in wealthier neighbourhoods. This growth, however, has been tempered by slower growth in other neighbourhoods. In other words, while individuals residing in higher income neighbourhoods have been giving more, individuals residing in lower income neighbourhoods have been giving less. Understanding the dynamics of these changes would be greatly enhanced by using individual tax-return data that can be linked across years and across households.

Individual survey data on giving: Donation rates between 2004 and 2010 have remained flat

Recently, Statistics Canada announced the release of the initial results from the 2010 Canada Survey of Giving, Volunteering and Participating. Imagine Canada issued a report comparing the results from this survey with surveys conducted in 2004 and 2007. It found that the share of individuals that identify themselves as donors has remained relatively unchanged. Approximately 84 to 85 per cent of the respondents identify themselves as donors. It also found that the level of giving, after controlling for inflation, has remained relatively flat. Why is this different from the statistics found in individual tax returns? In part, it can be attributed to differences in what we might consider "donations": with tax return data, we are specifically considering donations for which a tax receipt has been issued and where the deduction has been claimed by the donor (or her spouse). In the Statistics Canada survey, what constitutes a donation is more broadly defined. It includes any amounts given to charities or nonprofits. At a minimum, it includes amounts that would not qualify for a tax credit.

In the tables issued by Statistics Canada, survey respondents who reported donations differ in their level of giving based on: age distribution (older people give more); income and educational background (people with higher levels of income and education give more); and geographic location.

Charity level data: The numbers of charities has increased in the last two decades. Overall giving to charities increased in the 1990s and 2000s; foundations grew substantially and big charities benefited from increases in direct government funding.

Turning next to data from charities, I have collected and cleaned data from the information returns filed by charities from the early 1990s to the present.[4] For the purposes of this report, I rely on the cleaned data and examine all charities and foundations that have completed an information return between 1992 and 2008. I exclude returns that cover an accounting period that is shorter than 10 months or longer than 14 months since it is important to study annual changes in revenues. I also exclude returns that are in the top 0.5 per cent of the distribution for revenues from private donations and government grants in each year of study. The reason for this exclusion is that it appears there are returns filed (or transformed into an electronic version) with absurdly high levels of revenues. These high levels of revenues may give a mistaken impression about the patterns in revenues experienced by most charities.

Charities are grouped based on their last known status with CRA: charitable organizations or foundations. In principle, charitable organizations are charities whose primary mission is to deliver goods and services, while foundations have a primary mission to raise funds and then distribute these funds to charitable organizations. The further classification of a foundation as a private or public foundation depends in part on the number of contributors to the foundation and the relationship between the foundation and its contributors. The difference between public and private foundations lies primarily in legal definitions that pertain to the relationship (arm's-length or not) between donors and the directors of the foundation. A public foundation is one with an arm's-length relationship between the directors and donors, and often involves many funders — for example, a community foundation. If a foundation receives the bulk of its donations from a few donors and/or maintains a non-arm's-length relationship with its donors, it is likely to be classified as a private foundation.

The number of charitable organizations increased...so did the number of foundations. Growth in giving to foundations, however, surpassed the growth in giving to charitable organizations.

The first set of figures examined in this section pertain to the growth in the number of charities in Canada and the distribution of these charities across broadly defined categories, which are based on the most recent category code that CRA has assigned to the charity. In Figures 4a and 4b, I depict the distribution of charities, by category, in 1992 and 2008, respectively. In 1992, there were approximately 58,000 charities and by 2008 the number had grown to approximately 73,000. At both the beginning and end of the measured period, those organizations classified as religious charities (churches, synagogues, mosques, etc.) represented

---

[4] To this day, returns from charities are filed manually with CRA. To create an electronic version, the returns must be scanned and/or input by hand. The data obtained from CRA, therefore, may suffer from a variety of data quality issues. The first issue pertains to the quality of the information provided by the charity. Many charities rely on volunteers to complete returns. From year to year, the person who completes the return may change. As the format of the information returns varies (there have been three significant changes in the forms since the early 1990s), the interpretation of the questions asked on the form may also vary. The second issue pertains to the quality of the transformation of the information return from a paper to an electronic version. As a result of these issues, it is important, as with any data set derived from administrative data, to explore the data and to try to resolve idiosyncrasies before using the data in analysis. I have spent the last several years developing methods that help make it feasible to use the information return as a more reliable source for research analysis.

the greatest number of charities, followed by those focused on welfare, education, and community-related work. While the share of charities falling within the religious category declined, the actual number of religious charities increased, from approximately 28,000 to 32,000. In contrast, the number of welfare-related charities increased from about 8,600 to nearly 13,000. The distribution across other categories remained fairly proportionate.

FIGURE 4A   1992 DISTRIBUTION OF CHARITABLE ORGANIZATIONS

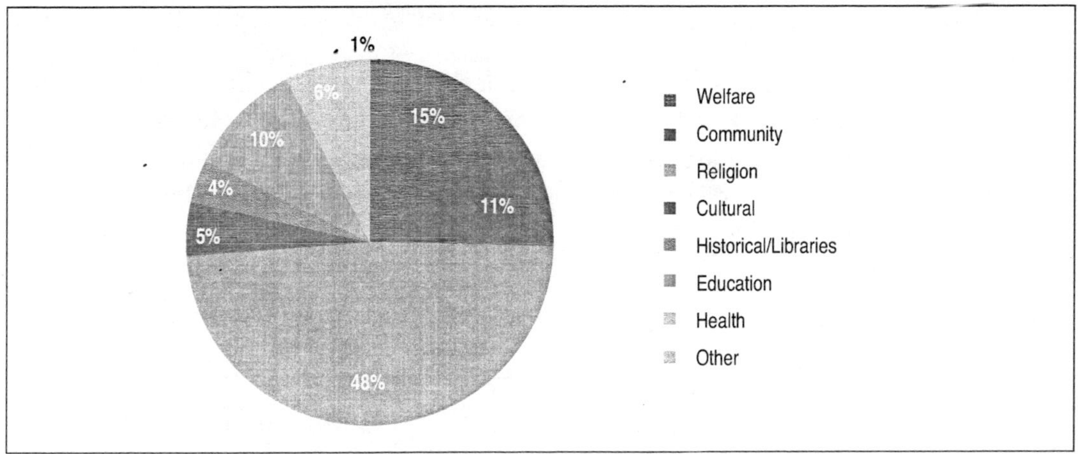

FIGURE 4B   2008 DISTRIBUTION OF CHARITABLE ORGANIZATIONS

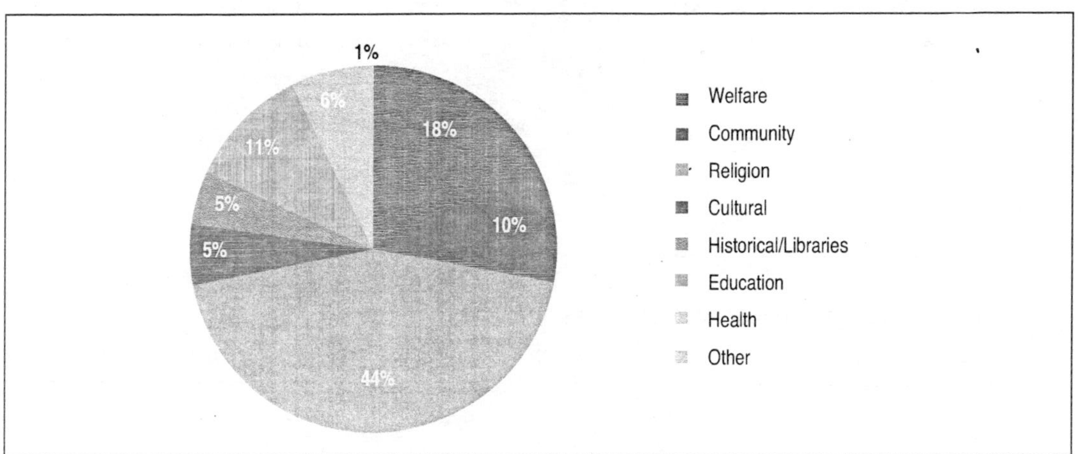

Another way to compare the distribution of charitable organizations is to compare total tax-receipted gifts and/or total revenues (excluding capital gains) reported by the charities. Overall, tax-receipted gifts grew by about 56 per cent between 1992 and 2008. Total revenues (excluding capital gains) grew by 154 per cent. In 1992, approximately 51 per cent of reported tax-receipted gifts were donated to religious charities, while between 10 and 12 per cent of tax-receipted gifts were donated to each of the groups of charities classified as welfare, education, health and "other" (with remaining groups, such as "community," "historic/libraries" and "cultural" each representing two per cent of donations, or less). By 2008, the share of tax-receipted gifts to religious charities declined to 48 per cent and the share of gifts to welfare- and education-related charities increased to 14 and 17 per cent, respectively.

By looking at total revenues, we can count funding not only from private sources but also direct funding from public sources. The share of total revenues collected by religious charities fell from nine per cent in 1992 to five per cent in 2008. There was little change in the share of revenues collected by welfare charities (which remained relatively flat, around nine per cent), community charities (relatively flat at just over two per cent), education charities (which stayed at approximately 36 per cent) and "other" charities (which continued to hover around three per cent). The share of total revenues that went to health-related charities increased from 37 to 43 per cent, while arts and cultural charities saw their share decline from 2.2 to 1.4 per cent.

In Figures 5a and 5b, I depict the distribution of foundations — public and private — in 1992 and 2008, respectively. Over this period, the number of foundations nearly doubled. In 1992, a high proportion of foundations were classified as welfare-related, education-related, and health-related. By 2008, there had been a shift in the distribution, with a substantial increase in the proportion of foundations classified as welfare-related.

FIGURE 5A   1992 DISTRIBUTION OF FOUNDATIONS

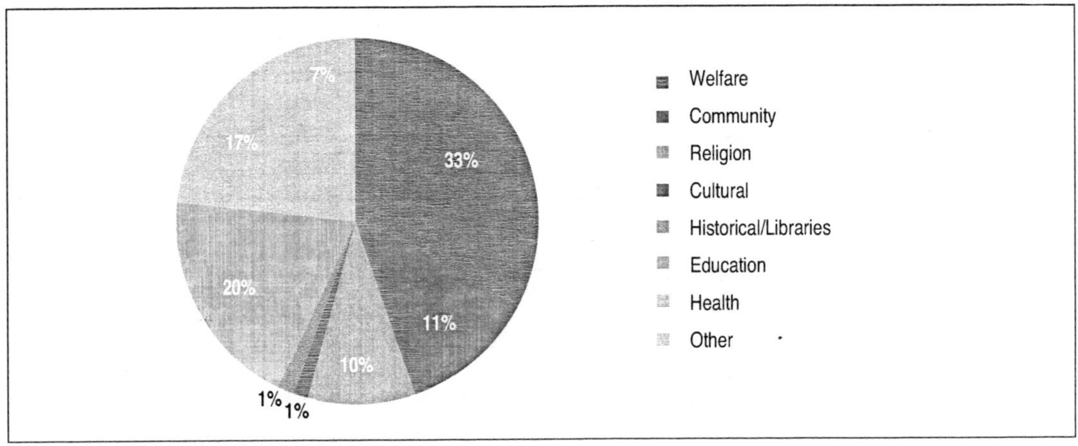

FIGURE 5B   2008 DISTRIBUTION OF FOUNDATIONS

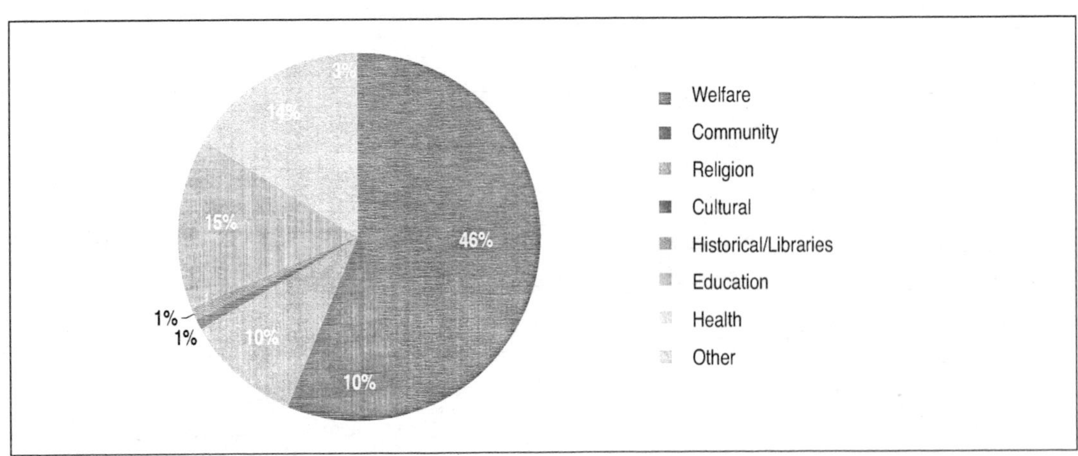

If the number of charities is increasing, how has that affected donations to charities? I depict in Figure 6 the total donations over the same period that charities collected from: tax-receipted donations; donations from other sources (except those from other charities or foundations); and revenues from fundraising activities for the three groups of charities. Overall, there was a growth in donations from approximately $4 billion in 1992 to more than $9 billion in 2008 — an overall increase of more than 130 per cent over a 16-year period. Contributions to charitable organizations increased around 117 per cent, whereas contributions to foundations increased more than 250 per cent. While these donation statistics show tremendous growth over a 16-year period, it is more difficult to measure that growth in a context that relates it to some measure of the changing need or importance of the goods and services these charities provide. For one thing, over this 16-year period, Canada's population increased by approximately five million. Moreover, the biggest donation growth was in contributions to foundations. In general, foundations disburse funds to charities, but they do so over time, meaning that not all of these contributions were actually used over the same 16-year period to support the goods and services delivered by charities.

FIGURE 6   TOTAL REPORTED DIRECT DONATIONS AND FUNDRAISING REVENUES, BY CHARITY TYPE

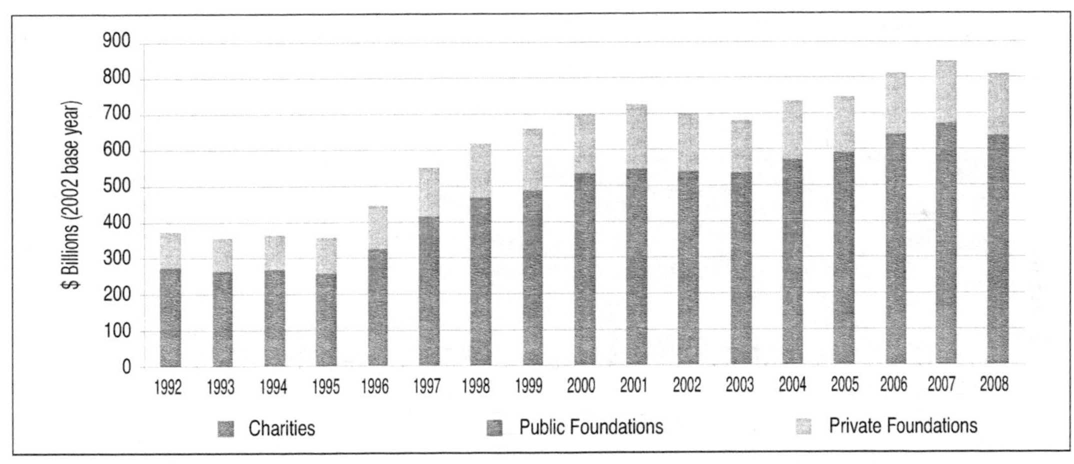

Medium-sized and large foundations benefited the most from private contributions. Contributions to small foundations were flat over the period.

Have all charities and foundations experienced similar growth in giving? To best answer this question, given the wide range in charity sizes, I narrowed the set of charities and foundations to those that existed prior to 1995 and continued to exist after 2005. In addition, I only looked at those charities for which we have at least 10 years of data. Thus, for the next set of figures, I exclude charities that have started up in the latter part of the sample period and those that have closed down during most of the period.

To best explore potential differences in the growth of public and private revenues across size, I grouped the charities based on the average of their total reported revenue (excluding capital gains) for the years 1992, 1993, and 1994. A small organization is one that had reported total revenues of less than $100,000 (including 60,853 charities, 3,935 public foundations and 3,811 private foundations). A medium-sized organization is one that had average revenues between $100,000 and $1 million (including 26,867 charities, 1,676 public foundations and 1,643 private foundations). A big organization is one that had average revenues of more than $1 million (including 5,863 charities, 516 public foundations and 494 private foundations).

Figures 7a and 7b depict the average of total private contributions to foundations (public foundations depicted in Figure 7a and private foundations in Figure 7b) in each of the three size groupings. What is striking about both charts is the difference in the growth rates for big foundations relative to the small and medium-sized foundations. Average revenues from private giving grew from approximately $1 million to almost $3 million over the period. Medium-sized foundations, saw contributions from private giving grow from an average of $150,000 to $450,000 — an increase of about the same rate. While the average revenues for the medium-sized foundations are about one-third less than those reported by big foundations at the end of the period, the growth rate provides some evidence that the public foundation sector is seeing a rise in the number of foundations with good revenues. In contrast, the average growth in revenues from the private foundation sector has been much flatter.

FIGURE 7A   AVERAGE REPORTED DONATIONS AND REVENUES FROM FUNDRAISING FOR PUBLIC FOUNDATIONS

FIGURE 7B   AVERAGE REPORTED DONATIONS AND REVENUES FROM FUNDRAISING FOR PRIVATE FOUNDATIONS

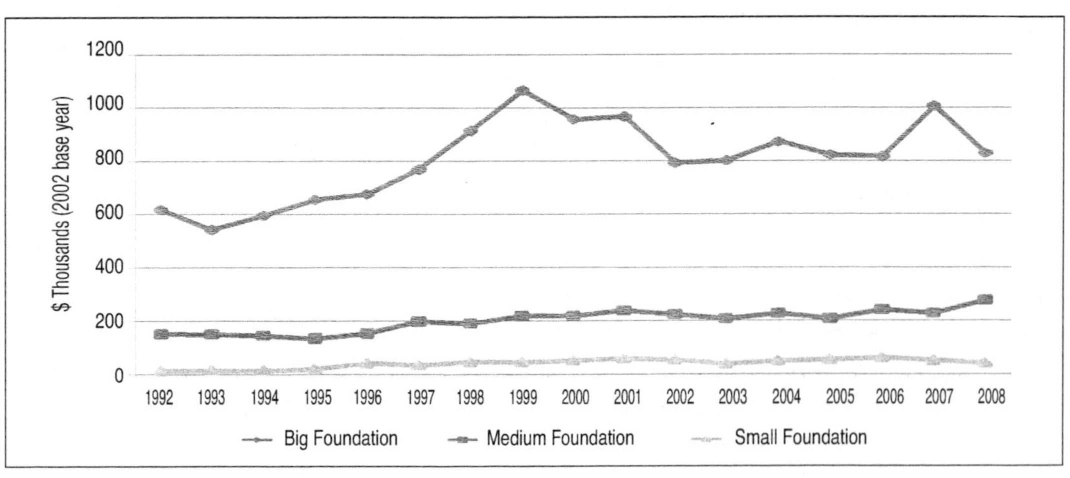

The next set of figures depicts changes in average private contributions to charitable organizations. The set also depicts average government funding to charitable organizations. While there has been much discussion about the merits of changing tax policy to promote greater charitable giving, a government offering a larger giveaway of tax credits will also decrease its revenue, inevitably making less public money available for direct government funding to charities.

Figure 8a depicts growth in government funding and private contributions for big charitable organizations. The average government grant far exceeds the average level of private revenues: At the beginning of the period, the average government grant was $5.8 million and the average level of private giving was $382,000. Because these figures depict average levels for the group of charities classified as big organizations, it masks differences across the charities in terms of their reliance on government and private funding. For the most part, both government funding and private giving increased over the period. Private giving increased most dramatically in the mid- to late-1990s and there is evidence of a slight dip at the end of the period. The growth in government grants to these charities increased more steadily. In Figure 8b, I depict the average private and public contributions to small and medium-sized charities. Both groups of charities have experienced, on average, greater growth in government grants than in private giving. The overall gap in private revenues grew between small and medium-sized charities, especially when we take into account that there are close to 61,000 small charities and 28,000 medium-sized charities that reported revenues for at least 10 years over the period.

FIGURE 8A AVERAGE FUNDING FROM PUBLIC (GOVERNMENT) AND PRIVATE (DONATIONS AND FUNDRAISING) SOURCES FOR CHARITIES WITH AVERAGE REVENUES > $1 MILLION PER YEAR

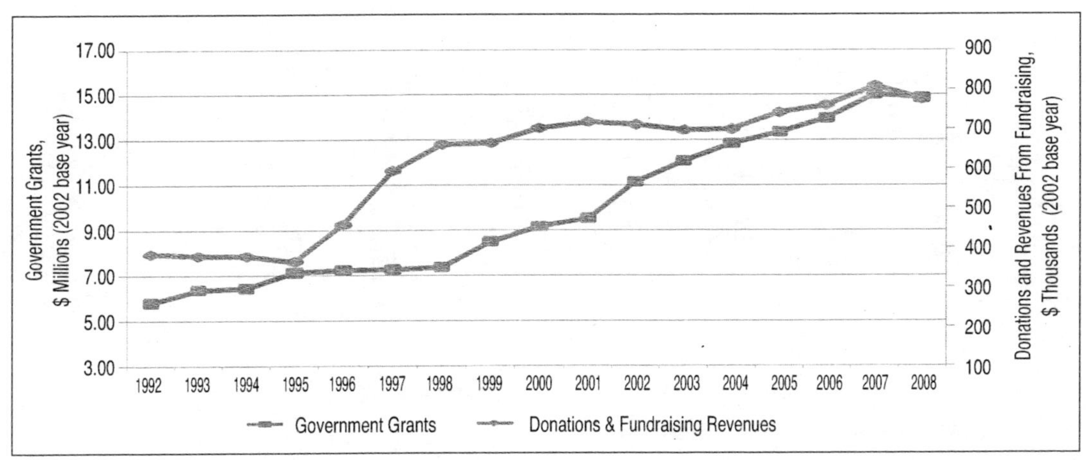

FIGURE 8B AVERAGE FUNDING FROM PUBLIC (GOVERNMENT) AND PRIVATE (DONATIONS AND FUNDRAISING) SOURCES FOR MEDIUM ($100K - $1MILLION) AND SMALL (<$100K) CHARITIES

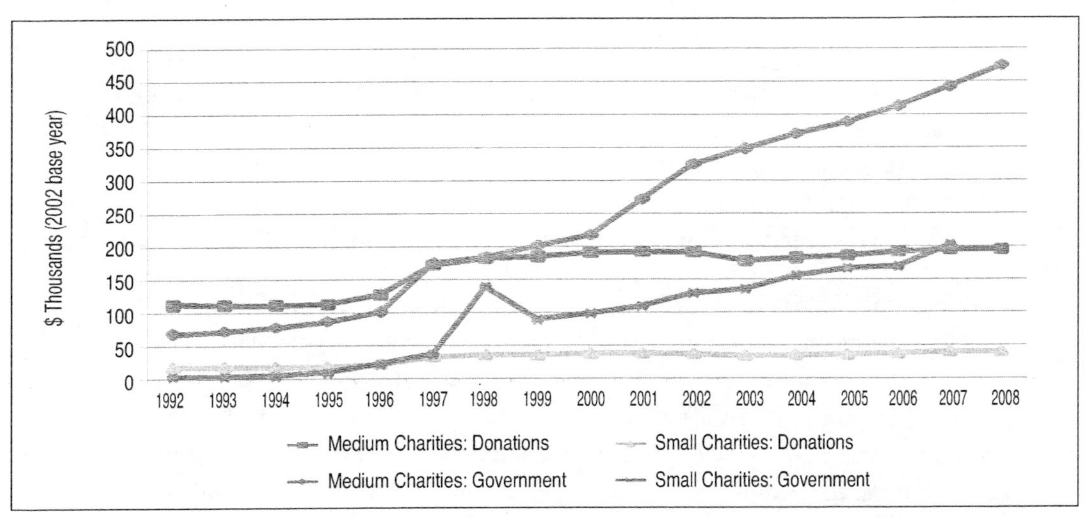

Another issue to consider when thinking about the growth in private giving to charitable organizations is whether the growth is similar across different charity types. In Figure 9, I depict the overall growth in private giving by charity type for the period 1996 to 2008. The greatest growth is seen in the charity grouping "other." Charities in the education group also experienced high growth in private giving. Surprisingly, charities in the health group and religious group experienced the lowest level of growth. One explanation for the relatively low growth in private donations to health-related charities could be that, if part of the growth in private donations to foundations is directed towards health-related areas, then this might reflect a shift from certain donors contributing to health charities directly, and instead concentrating their giving to health foundations. Given that there is a small proportion of foundations identified in the religious group, that same possible phenomenon could not be used to explain the lower growth in giving to religious organizations.

FIGURE 9   GROWTH IN DONATIONS AND REVENUE FROM FUNDRAISING (1996 - 2008)

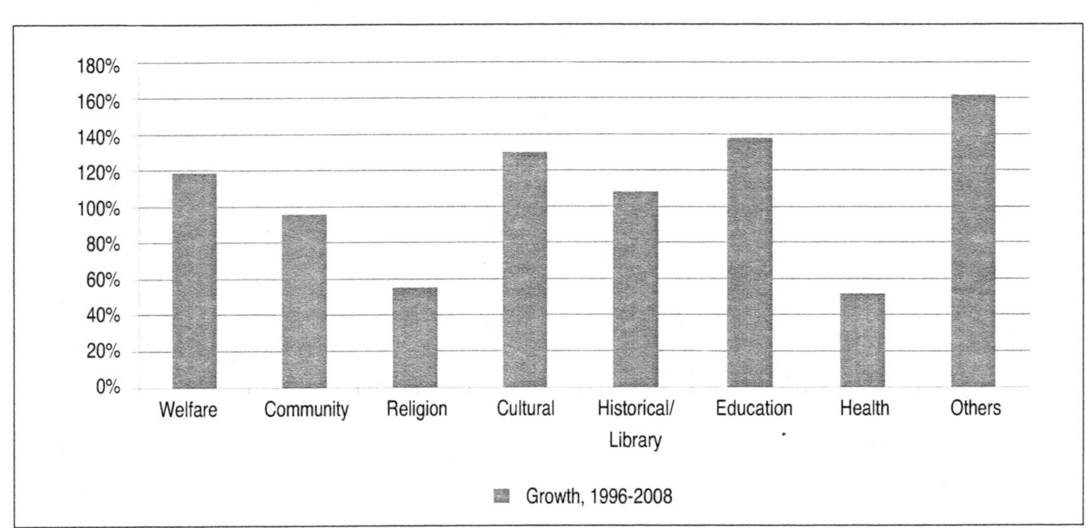

DISCUSSION

Based on the simple statistics depicted above, several stories begin to emerge. The first story is that growth in giving may largely be attributable to those in higher income brackets. This, in part, may be the result of changes in tax policy regarding the giving of such things as publicly traded securities and other donated items that are more likely to be held by higher income individuals. To truly understand whether this is one cause of increased giving by higher income individuals, however, would require a study involving using individual tax-return data.

A second story is that giving by individuals in lower income and middle-income neighbourhoods has, at best, remained flat, but has more likely declined. This decline, however, may be more attributable to an increase in the population than a change in individual giving behaviour. This raises the question of why overall giving has declined as our population has grown. And why do we observe a decline in giving if we study individual tax returns, but we don't observe a similar decline when we use the results from the Canadian Survey of Giving, Volunteering and Participating?

A third story is that the number of charities and foundations has grown substantially over the last two decades, but larger charitable organizations and foundations have enjoyed the greatest growth in giving and in direct government funding. Private and public support has been flatter for smaller charities and foundations.

Should these stories concern us? Possibly. I encourage further exploration of each story to understand in more depth the extent to which we are observing important changes in charitable giving and the potential impact of these changes on charity operations. This discussion below provides some direction for thinking about these stories, relying on current and past research on related topics.

What explains a decline in giving? What explains a lower growth in giving to smaller charities?

In the first story we saw that, while the number of donors has increased, the share of tax filers reporting donations has declined. In part, this decline is attributable to a growth in our population. Why would population growth decrease giving? There are several plausible explanations. One is that, as our population has increased, Canada has become a more diverse population. As the population becomes more diverse, the interest in supporting charitable goods and services becomes more diverse and so it becomes more difficult for charities to respond to these more diverse interests.

Andreoni, Payne, Smith, and Karp[5] explore the effect that changes in neighbourhood diversity has on charitable giving, using the grouped data from individual income tax returns in Canada. In urban areas across Canada and elsewhere, neighbourhood diversity is increasingly common. Diversity in communities is something that most Canadians would view as positive. From a public economics perspective, however, public-good provision has been observed in numerous studies to decrease with increases in diversity — this includes a decrease in spending on hospitals, roads, and schools.[6] If diversity results in fewer public goods, is the same true for charitable goods? Standard economic models suggest that the prediction of this effect is unclear. If charities benefit individuals outside of one's group, or provide services that are of concern to certain types of groups but not others, diversity may result in less giving by the members of the group that are not being serviced by the charity. On the other hand, if individuals group together based on characteristics such as ethnicity or religion, then organizations that cater to those groupings may enjoy an increase in giving. Andreoni, Payne, Smith, and Karp use a measure of diversity called a fragmentation index that combines the share of neighbourhood populations based on visible minority status or religious status. They find that, while the average adult contributes approximately $200 per year to charity, a 10 percentage-point increase for ethnic composition on the fragmentation index implies a decrease in giving of $27, a decline of 14 per cent. An increase in religious diversity in the neighbourhood also suggests a decline in giving, but the estimates from the analysis of religious diversity are estimated with less precision.

---

[5] James Andreoni, A. Abigail Payne et al., "Diversity and Donations: The Effect of Religious and Ethnic Diversity on Charitable Giving," NBER Working Paper #176118, in submission (November 2012).

[6] A. Alesina, R. Baqir, et al., "Redistributive Public Employment," *Journal of Urban Economics* 48(2) (2000): 219-241; A. Alesina, R. Baqir, et al., "Public Goods And Ethnic Divisions," *The Quarterly Journal of Economics* 114(4) (1999): 1243-1284; James M. Poterba, "Demographic Structure and the Political Economy of Public Education," *Journal of Public Policy Analysis and Management* 16(1) (1997): 48-66; C. Goldin and L. F. Katz, "Human Capital and Social Capital: The Rise of Secondary Schooling in America, 1910 to 1940," *Journal of Interdisciplinary History* 29(4) (1999): 683-723.

Do charities play a role in giving?

When we discuss charitable giving, we often assume that charities are passive in their collection of donations. Yet we know that most charities ask individuals to give. Some individuals are active in their giving and seek out information about charities. Other individuals, however, may be more passive, or may not know how to gather information about charities. And so, charities may need to fundraise in order to both ask individuals for contributions, and as a way to advertise or provide information about their goods and services. Fundraising, however, sometimes carries with it a negative connotation. Moreover, many charities may prefer to focus their efforts on the provision of goods and services, rather than raising revenues for their operations. Using data from the U.S. and from Canada, Andreoni and Payne[7] find that, typically, for every dollar spent by charities on fundraising and promotional activities, an average of five dollars is raised in private donations. These estimates correspond with other research on the impact of fundraising on private giving. In standard economic theory, charities are not behaving optimally; instead, these estimates suggest that charities may view fundraising as a necessary evil.

How does direct government funding of charities impact private giving?

In the past, the theory around how government funding impacts private giving has viewed charities as passive recipients of private donations. The extent of the impact that government grants can have on private giving depends on (a) how individuals value a charitable good and (b) the level of information the individual has on private giving. Individuals may care only about the provision of the charitable good, regardless of the source of funding. Under this assumption, an increase in government funding is predicted to decrease private giving, dollar for dollar. If, however individuals receive some private benefit (commonly called a "warm-glow effect") in knowing that part of the charitable good is coming from their donation, then traditional theory would lead us to expect that an increase in government funding would still decrease private giving, but a lower rate than dollar for dollar. In research using data from the U.S. and the U.K., Payne[8] and Khanna, Posnett and Todd[9] find that, when government funding increases, private donations decline, but at a rate that is less than dollar for dollar.

Alternatively, what if a donor has a difficult time assessing the value of a charitable good? Take for instance, a gift to support research in health, or other areas. Do most individuals know how to value a research project? In this instance, it may be that the government grant serves as a signal of quality. If so, then we would observe an increase in private giving when we observe increases in government grants. Payne[10] observes this effect when studying research funding to universities.

---

[7] James Andreoni and A. Abigail Payne, "Crowding-Out Charitable Contributions in Canada: New Knowledge from the North" (Mimeo, McMaster University, 2012); James Andreoni and A. Abigail Payne, "Is Crowding Out Due Entirely to Fundraising? Evidence From a Panel of Charities," *Journal of Public Economics* 95(5-6) (2011): 334-343.

[8] A. Abigail Payne, "Does the Government Crowd-Out Private Donations? New Evidence From a Sample of Non-Profit Firms," *Journal of Public Economics* 69(3) (1998): 323-345.

[9] Jyoti Khanna, John Posnett and Todd Sandler, "Charity Donations in the UK: New Evidence Based on Panel Data," *Journal of Public Economics* 56(2) (1995): 257-272.

[10] A. Abigail Payne, "Measuring the Effect of Federal Research Funding on Private Donations At Research Universities: Is Federal Research Funding More Than a Substitute for Private Donations?," *International Tax and Public Finance*, 8(5-6) (2001) 731-751.

But what if charities are not passive recipients of private donations? If charities must engage in efforts to fundraise and/or promote their charity, and view such fundraising as a necessary evil, to what extent do they decrease their fundraising efforts when they receive a government grant? Andreoni and Payne[11] observe this effect when studying American arts and social-welfare organizations. This decrease in fundraising results in declines in private giving. Using data from the U.S., Andreoni and Payne[12] find that the bulk of the decline in private giving that occurs when an American charity receives a government grant is attributable to a decline in fundraising.

Is this decline in giving also true for Canada? In preliminary work by Andreoni and Payne,[13] they find a similar effect. Overall, they find that a one-dollar increase in government funding reduces private giving by 80 to 98 cents. The bulk of this decline is attributable to a decline in revenue from fundraising activities. Funding from foundations and similar organizations also declines as government funding to the charity increases.

Can government policy counteract this crowding out effect from government funds? Possibly. One obvious response would be the use of matching grants. However, if an organization cannot raise the matching funds privately, then the government funding may be given to another organization that may or may not make the most effective use of the funding. Another option would be to find ways to encourage a grant-receiving charity to continue to fundraise and seek private giving. But this too has its challenges. While some fundraising is beneficial, as it helps to raise awareness about the charity and the goods and services it provides, it also can be wasteful and it detracts time and funding for the direct provision of the goods and services provided by the charity.

Is the significant growth in giving to foundations a good thing?

Based on data from 2008, of the 25 wealthiest charitable foundations in the world, none are Canadian. Foundations from the United States claim 18 of the spots. The United Kingdom comes in second with three foundations. The top three foundations in the world are the Bill & Melinda Gates Foundation (endowment of US$37.1 billion; founded in 1994), the Stichting INGKA Foundation in the Netherlands (endowment of US$36 billion; founded in 1982), and the Wellcome Trust in the United Kingdom (endowment of US$22.9 billion; founded in 1936).

By comparison, based on amounts reported on the information return to CRA in 2011, it appears there are only a couple of Canadian foundations with more than $1 billion in assets: The MasterCard Foundation ($2.3 billion) and the Lucie and André Chagnon Foundation ($1.3 billion). Of the nearly 5,000 Canadian foundations that have operated over the last 20 years, fewer than 15 per cent (750 foundations) have average annual levels of assets of more than $1 million. Of course, there are some notable charitable organizations (not foundations) with relatively high levels of assets. Most notably, several universities have substantial assets. For

---

[11] James Andreoni and A. Abigail Payne, "Is Crowding Out Due Entirely to Fundraising?," (2011); James Andreoni and A. Abigail Payne, "Do Government Grants to Private Charities Crowd Out Giving or Fundraising?," *The American Economic Review*, 93 (2003) 792–812.

[12] James Andreoni and A. Abigail Payne, "Is Crowding Out Due Entirely to Fundraising?" (2011).

[13] James Andreoni and A. Abigail Payne, "Crowding-Out Charitable Contributions in Canada: New Knowledge from the North" (2012).

example: University of Toronto ($4.6 billion); University of British Columbia ($4.4 billion); McGill University ($3.3 billion); University of Calgary ($2.9 billion); McMaster University ($1.9 billion); Queen's University ($1.7 billion); and University of Waterloo ($1.4 billion). But these assets are generally used by the recipient charitable organization, while foundations have the ability to spread their wealth across a number of charitable organizations.

For the most part, the growth in the wealth amassed by foundations over the last two decades should be welcomed. Whether the growth makes Canada more comparable to other developed countries, once we take into account population differences and other factors, is an open question. Most likely, Canada remains on the lower end of the spectrum. Why might supporting foundations be beneficial for charitable organizations? If foundations are adjuvant in distributing their funding, they can help stabilize charity funding during times of economic turmoil. Potentially, foundations can be more strategic and nimble with their funding than governments can, given that they are not encumbered by the added layer of politics. Moreover, the sole purpose of foundations is to support the charitable sector. Governments face pressures from many sources.

In preliminary research, Kryvoruchko[14] presents a model suggesting that foundation grants to charitable organizations may help provide a positive signal to individual donors about the quality of the charitable organizations. In her model, she assumes that finding information about charities, and the quality of the goods and services provided by these charities, may be difficult for the typical donor. Foundations, however, may engage in efforts to better understand the activities of the charities they fund. Using data on grants to charitable organizations from Canadian foundations, Kryvoruchko's initial findings suggest that, indeed, a charity that receives a grant from a foundation will also enjoy an increase in individual donations to the charity.

Is there a silver bullet to encourage giving? Would changing the tax system help?

Data on charities and individual giving suggest that, over the last two decades, the bulk of the growth in giving has come from individuals from higher income neighbourhoods, and has been directed to larger charities and foundations. This may be partly attributable to changes in federal tax policy, which has provided increased tax incentives for individuals donating publicly traded securities and other types of donations that are more likely to be held by higher income individuals. Whether there is a causal link, however, requires more research. But if this hypothesis is true, does it mean that if we create incentives for lower income individuals to donate more (e.g. through a "stretch" tax credit), they will respond accordingly?

The theoretical basis for thinking about how tax policy might affect giving is based on the notion that, if a tax credit is given for a donation, it effectively lowers the price of giving. If giving is treated like a standard good (e.g. a cup of coffee, a house, or any consumable item), a lowering of the price should result in greater demand for the good. For charities, this would

---

[14] Kryvoruchko, Iryna, "Does Foundation Giving Stimulate or Suppress Private Giving? Evidence from Canadian Charities" (Mimeo, McMaster University, 2012).

mean that lowering the price of giving should motivate individuals to give if they have not given previously or, if they have historically given, to give more. Bakija and Heim[15] summarize the research that studies how changes in the price of giving impacts giving (most of this research uses American data). In contrast, however, Rehavi[16] documents that in the U.S. there is an underreporting of donations on individual tax returns, which suggests that a change in the price of giving through the tax system does not impact all donors. For the most part, a reduction in the price of giving results in an increase in giving. This then raises the question of whether a reaction to a change in the price of giving is due to a permanent or a transitory shift in giving by the individual. A transitory shift is effectively one where a donor has already planned to give, but shifts their giving to favour tax policy incentives, and is mostly attributable to fluctuations in her income. A permanent shift is one where tax policy encourages an individual to smooth their giving out over time, and a change in policy encourages them to re-optimize their preferences about giving.[17]

In a recent working paper, Charles Clotfelter[18] discusses issues related to charitable giving and tax policy in the United States. One important insight he provides on the U.S. system that is equally true in Canada, is his consideration of whether our tax system should favour individuals of one income group over another. Unlike the U.S., our system of providing tax credits for donations, instead of a tax deduction, does indeed mean a more equitable treatment of donations across all taxpayers. But where we fall short from a tax-equity perspective is the more favourable treatment of non-cash donations such as gifts of publicly traded securities and land. If higher income individuals are more likely to hold these assets, then they receive a greater benefit from their donations than those that do not hold these types of assets.

But is a change in tax policy a costless endeavour? Presumably not. Assume the government chooses to introduce a policy that increases the tax credit given for a charitable contribution. A specific credit that is targeted at any cash donation would surely reduce tax revenue collected by the government. On the other hand, a credit that is targeted at an instrument such as a publicly traded security, may or may not represent lost revenue to the government. If an individual owner of a security was planning to sell it in any case, and instead decides to avoid the potential capital-gains tax by giving that security to a charity, rather than selling it on the market, then that would result in lost revenue for the government. If, however, the individual had no plans to sell the security, but is induced by tax incentives to give it to charity, then there would be no immediate foregone government revenue. Any foregone revenue would be tied to the ultimate sale of the security that would have happened at some undetermined point in the future.

[15] Jon Bakija and Bradley Heim, "How Does Charitable Giving Respond to Incentives and Income?" (2008).

[16] Marit Rehavi, "Partial Reporting: An Example from Charitable Giving" (Mimeo, University of British Columbia, 2010).

[17] Raj Chetty, "The Simple Economics of Salience and Taxation," NBER Working Paper #15246 (2009).

[18] Charles T. Clotfelter, "Charitable Giving and Tax Policy in the U.S." (Mimeo, Duke University, 2012).

For the sake of argument, assume that any new tax policy results in a loss of revenue to the government. Is this a good thing? On one hand, the donor who takes advantage of the tax policy is able to direct her donation to the charity and, ultimately, the type of good and service she is most concerned about. On the other hand, if the government sees a decline in revenues from the foregone taxes, this reduces its ability to directly support charities through government grants and contracts. If the government has better information about, or can better monitor, charity activities than private donors, then the shifting reliance by charities to private individuals for support may not be a good thing. Ultimately, we are seeking a balance between private and public support of charitable goods and services.

Clotfelter[19] compares the private and public expenditures on social goods as a percentage of GDP based on data from 2011 OECD Social Expenditures statistics for seven countries (Australia, Canada, France, Germany, Netherlands, the United Kingdom, and the United States). On a scale of highest to lowest public expenditures, Canada ranks fifth and looks very similar to the United States and Australia. With respect to private expenditures (i.e. those generated by charities and non-governmental units), Canada ranks third, just below the Netherlands and the United Kingdom, and well above the fourth-ranked country, Australia. Overall, however, Canada ranks sixth out of the seven countries. Thus, while we can boast that Canada has a relatively high level of givers if we analyze data from different sources, it seems that Canada still falls in the lower end of the distribution when it comes to overall levels of giving, despite the growth in our charities over the last decade.

It is likely that there is no silver bullet that will help charities. Our knowledge of charity operations and charitable giving remains relatively primitive. We have data, theories and many testable hypotheses. The government is an important player in supporting charitable goods and services. But there are other important players.

CONCLUSION

The purpose of this report was to highlight the changing landscape for giving over the last two decades to better understand charitable giving and charity operations, using the rich data sources that we have. While the landscape has changed, the policies we should implement to strengthen and improve the provision of charitable goods and services is less clear. Overall giving has increased, as has the number of registered charities and foundations. The sources for private giving, however, have shifted to Canadians with high incomes. Moreover, not all types of charities have benefited from this growth in giving.

At this stage, most, if not all, of the proposed changes to the treatment of donations and charities lack serious evidence-based analysis that should serve as a foundation for implementing change. Conjectures and unsubstantiated beliefs should not be the basis for making decisions. As we move forward in developing policies to help charities, some key guiding principles should include the consideration of:

- The balance between private and public support for charitable goods and services.

- The benefits of tax incentives for different groups of taxpayers.

---

[19] Charles T. Clotfelter, "Charitable Giving and Tax Policy in the U.S." (2012).

- The differences in the operations and needs of charities based on size and mission, and how charities may be differentially affected by changes in tax policies.

- The importance of striking the right balance between promoting the long-term sustainability of charities and addressing their short-term needs or fluctuations.

Overall, this report highlights the importance of engaging in more analysis on giving and on charity operations, prior to the adoption of new policies or the revocation of existing policies.

REFERENCES

Alesina, A., R. Baqir, et al. "Redistributive Public Employment." *Journal of Urban Economics* 48(2) (2000): 219-241.

Alesina, A., R. Baqir, et al. "Public Goods And Ethnic Divisions." *The Quarterly Journal of Economics* 114(4) (1999): 1243-1284.

Andreoni, James, and A. Abigail Payne. "Crowding-Out Charitable Contributions in Canada: New Knowledge from the North." Mimeo, McMaster University, 2012.

Andreoni, James, A. Abigail Payne et al. "Diversity and Donations: The Effect of Religious and Ethnic Diversity on Charitable Giving." NBER Working Paper #176118, in submission, November 2012.

Andreoni, James, and A. Abigail Payne. "Is Crowding Out Due Entirely To Fundraising? Evidence From a Panel of Charities." *Journal of Public Economics* 95(5-6) (2011): 334-343.

Andreoni, James, and A. Abigail Payne. "Do Government Grants to Private Charities Crowd Out Giving or Fundraising?" *The American Economic Review* 93 (2003): 792–812.

Bakija, Jon, and Bradley Heim. "How Does Charitable Giving Respond to Incentives and Income? Dynamic Panel Estimates Accounting for Predictable Changes in Taxation." NBER Working Paper #14237 (2008).

Chetty, Raj. "The Simple Economics of Salience and Taxation." NBER Working Paper #15246 (2009).

Clotfelter, Charles T. "Charitable Giving and Tax Policy in the U.S." Mimeo, Duke University, 2012.

Goldin, C., and L. F. Katz. "Human Capital and Social Capital: The Rise of Secondary Schooling in America, 1910 to 1940." *Journal of Interdisciplinary History* 29(4) (1999): 683-723.

Khanna, Jyoti, John Posnett, and Todd Sandler. "Charity Donations in the UK: New Evidence Based on Panel Data." *Journal of Public Economics* 56(2) (1995): 257-272.

Kryvoruchko, Iryna. "Does Foundation Giving Stimulate or Suppress Private Giving? Evidence from Canadian Charities." Mimeo, McMaster University, 2012.

Payne, A. Abigail, "Measuring the Effect of Federal Research Funding on Private Donations at Research Universities: Is Federal Research Funding More Than a Substitute for Private Donations?" *International Tax and Public Finance* 8(5-6) (2001): 731-751.

Payne, A. Abigail, "Does the Government Crowd-Out Private Donations? New Evidence From a Sample of Non-Profit Firms." *Journal of Public Economics* 69(3) (1998): 323-345.

Poterba, James M., "Demographic Structure and the Political Economy of Public Education." *Journal of Public Policy Analysis and Management* 16(1) (1997): 48-66.

Rehavi, Marit, "Partial Reporting: An Example from Charitable Giving." Mimeo, University of British Columbia, 2010.

About the Author

A. Abigail Payne is a Professor of Economics at McMaster University, where she is also Director of the Public Economics Data Analysis Laboratory ("PEDAL"). Her current research concerns understanding the motivations of private donors, the role of fundraising in private giving when a charity receives government funding and how policies and demographic changes affect charity operations.

Dr. Payne received her Ph.D. from Princeton University and she holds a J.D. from Cornell University and a B.A. from Denison University. She has published in the *American Economic Review, Journal of Public Economics, Journal of Law and Economics*, and several other journals.

ABOUT THIS PUBLICATION

The School of Public Policy Research Papers provide in-depth, evidence-based assessments and recommendations on a range of public policy issues. Research Papers are put through a stringent peer review process prior to being made available to academics, policy makers, the media and the public at large. Views expressed in The School of Public Policy Research Papers are the opinions of the author(s) and do not necessarily represent the view of *The School of Public Policy*.

OUR MANDATE

The University of Calgary is home to scholars in 16 faculties (offering more than 80 academic programs) and 36 Research Institutes and Centres including *The School of Public Policy*. Under the direction of Jack Mintz, Palmer Chair in Public Policy, and supported by more than 100 academics and researchers, the work of The School of Public Policy and its students contributes to a more meaningful and informed public debate on fiscal, social, energy, environmental and international issues to improve Canada's and Alberta's economic and social performance.

The School of Public Policy achieves its objectives through fostering ongoing partnerships with federal, provincial, state and municipal governments, industry associations, NGOs, and leading academic institutions internationally. Foreign Investment Advisory Committee of the World Bank, International Monetary Fund, Finance Canada, Department of Foreign Affairs and International Trade Canada, and Government of Alberta, are just some of the partners already engaged with the School's activities.

For those in government, *The School of Public Policy* helps to build capacity and assists in the training of public servants through degree and non-degree programs that are critical for an effective public service in Canada. For those outside of the public sector, its programs enhance the effectiveness of public policy, providing a better understanding of the objectives and limitations faced by governments in the application of legislation.

DISTRIBUTION

Our publications are available online at www.policyschool.ca.

DISCLAIMER

The opinions expressed in these publications are the authors' alone and therefore do not necessarily reflect the opinions of the supporters, staff, or boards of The School of Public Policy.

COPYRIGHT

Copyright © 2012 by The School of Public Policy.

All rights reserved. No part of this publication may be reproduced in any manner whatsoever without written permission except in the case of brief passages quoted in critical articles and reviews.

ISSN

1919-112x SPP Research Papers (Print)
1919-1138 SPP Research Papers (Online)

DATE OF ISSUE

November 2012

MEDIA INQUIRIES AND INFORMATION

For media inquiries, please contact Morten Paulsen at 403-453-0062.

Our web site, www.policyschool.ca, contains more information about The School's events, publications, and staff.

DEVELOPMENT

For information about contributing to The School of Public Policy, please contact Courtney Murphy by telephone at 403-210-7201 or by e-mail at cmurphy@ucalgary.ca.

RECENT PUBLICATIONS BY *THE SCHOOL OF PUBLIC POLICY*

A PROFOUND TAX REFORM: THE IMPACT OF SALES TAX HARMONIZATION ON PRINCE EDWARD ISLAND'S
COMPETITIVNESS
http://policyschool.ucalgary.ca/?q=content/profound-tax-reform-impact-sales-tax-harmonization-price-edward-islands-competitiveness
Duanjie Chen and Jack Mintz | November 2012

THE COMPREHENSIVE TRADE AGREEMENT WITH INDIA: WHAT'S IN IT FOR CANADA (OR INDIA FOR THAT
MATTER)?
http://policyschool.ucalgary.ca/?q=content/comprehensive-trade-agreement-india-whats-it-canada-or-india-matter
Eugene Beaulieu | November 2012

ENERGY LITERACY IN CANADA
http://policyschool.ucalgary.ca/?q=content/energy-literacy-canada.pdf
André Turcotte, Michal C. Moore, Jennifer Winter | October 2012

CAN WE AVOID A SICK FISCAL FUTURE? THE NON-SUSTAINABILITY OF HEALTH-CARE SPENDING WITH AN
AGING POPULATION
http://policyschool.ucalgary.ca/sites/default/files/research/emery-generational-balances-final.pdf
J.C. Herbert Emery, David Still and Tom Cottrell | October 2012

CAPTURING ECONOMIC RENTS FROM RESOURCES THROUGH ROYALTIES AND TAXES
http://policyschool.ucalgary.ca/sites/default/files/research/mintz-chen-economic-rents-final.pdf
Jack Mintz and Duanjie Chen | October 2012

THE GST AND FINANCIAL SERVICES: PAUSING FOR PERSPECTIVE
http://policyschool.ucalgary.ca/?q=content/gst-and-financial-services-pausing-perspective
Michael Firth and Kenneth McKenzie | September 2012

2012 ANNUAL GLOBAL TAX COMPETITIVENESS RANKING – A CANADIAN GOOD NEWS STORY
http://policyschool.ucalgary.ca/?q=content/2012-annual-global-tax-competitiveness-ranking-canadian-good-news-story
Duanjie Chen and Jack Mintz | September 2012

DANCING WITH THE DRAGON: CANADIAN INVESTMENT IN CHINA AND CHINESE INVESTMENT IN CANADA
http://policyschool.ucalgary.ca/?q=content/dancing-dragon-canadian-investment-china-and-chinese-investment-canada
Josephine Smart | September 2012

SUPPORT FOR BUSINESS R&D IN BUDGET 2012: TWO STEPS FORWARD AND ONE BACK
http://policyschool.ucalgary.ca/sites/default/files/research/j-lester-budget-2012-communique-final.pdf
John Lester | August 2012

SIZE, ROLE AND PERFORMANCE IN THE OIL AND GAS SECTOR
http://policyschool.ucalgary.ca/sites/default/files/research/mansell-oil-and-gas-july-18.pdf
R.L. Mansell, J. Winter, M. Krzepkowski, M.C. Moore | July 2012